Eggs in Cookery
Proceedings of the Oxford Symposium on Food and Cookery 2006

Photograph courtesy of Fuschia Dunlop.

Eggs in Cookery

Proceedings of the Oxford Symposium on Food and Cookery 2006

Edited by Richard Hosking

Prospect Books
2007

First published in Great Britain in 2007 by Prospect Books, Allaleigh House, Blackawton, Totnes, Devon, TQ9 7DL.

© 2007 as a collection Prospect Books
(but © 2007 in individual articles rests with the authors).

The authors assert their moral right to be identified as authors in accordance with the Copyright, Designs & Patents Act 1988. No part of this publication may be reproduced, stored in a retrieval system or transmitted in any form of by any means, electronic, mechanical, photocopying, recording or otherwise, without the prior permission of the copyright holders.

ISBN 978-1-903018-54-5

The photographs on the cover are courtesy of Fuschia Dunlop

Design and typesetting in Gill Sans and Adobe Garamond by Tom Jaine.
Printed and bound in Great Britain by The Cromwell Press, Trowbridge.

Contents

Foreword *Jane Levi*	9
Ovophilia in Renaissance Cuisine *Ken Albala*	11
The Egg: its Symbolism and Mythology *Joan P Alcock*	20
Cackleberries and Henfruit: a French Perspective *Fritz Blank*	30
On *Spaghetti alla Carbonara* and Related Dishes of Central and Southern Italy *Anthony F. Buccini*	36
Poached Eggs at the Revolution *Doug Duda*	48
Transforming Eggs in Chinese Culinary Culture *Fuchsia Dunlop*	54
Begué's Eggs *Rien Fertel*	60
The Language of the Egg *Anna Marie Fisker*	67
The *Patina* in Apicius *Sally Grainger*	76
Sustainable Is Beautiful: Pastured Egg Farming in Central New York *Naomi Guttman*	85
Saving the Lost, Sour Eggs: an Annotated Pictorial Documentation of an Almost Extinct German Egg Recipe *Ursula Heinzelmann*	92
Eggs and the Japanese *Naomichi Ishige*	100
The Egg Tree in America *Cathy K. Kaufman*	107

Eggs in Philippine Church Architecture and its Cuisine　114
Pia Lim-Castillo

The Deviled Egg: History and Present　125
Nancy R. McArthur

The History of Eggs in Irish Cuisine and Culture　137
Máirtín Mac Con Iomaire and Andrea Cully

Scrambled Class: Eggs and Refinement in Nineteenth-century America　150
Mark McWilliams

'Balut', the Fertilised Duck Eggs of the Philippines　160
Margaret Magat

Eggs, the English Breakfast and the Biography of a National Meal　171
Kaori O'Connor

Moorish Ovomania　181
Charles Perry

'The Ultimate in Cookery': the Soufflé's Rise Alongside Feminism in the 1960s　184
Phyllis Thompson Reid

Eggs in Art　202
Gillian Riley

Eggs in the Moon Shine With Cream. A Selection of Egg Recipes 1500–1800　209
William Rubel

The Encyclopaedic Egg　222
Barbara Santich

Turkey Eggs　229
Andrew F. Smith

Creating with Arctic Eggs　235
Zona Spray Starks with Anore Paniyauraq Jones

Egg Basket of the World　246
Dan Strehl

Let's Have an Egg　250
Hervé This

'Go to Work on an Egg' Is Not the Same for All Cultures *Michelle Toratani*	259
More than One Way to Crack an Urchin *Christa Weil*	264
Eggs in the Talmud *Susan Weingarten*	270
The Egg and Ice *Caroline & Robin Weir*	282
Salvador Dalí's Giant Egg *Carolin C. Young*	293
The Importance of Eggs in Rural Communities in Istria (Croatia) between the Wars *Tanja Kocković Zaborski*	312
About Eggs, Two Countries and a Cake, or, How the Lack of an Ingredient Can Tell us about Social Changes *Marcia Zoladz*	322
Eggs: the Sauces and the Sauced *Sami Zubaida*	333

Foreword

Often, before the papers appear and the Symposium is underway, there is a moment when we all wonder what on earth we will find to fill an entire weekend of discussion related to our chosen topic. Our theme for 2006, eggs, was no exception. Indeed, it raised a quite visceral response in many Symposiasts who proclaimed that they could not bear to consider the egg in detail. In the event, however, eggs provided a focal point for one of our most diverse and stimulating Symposia. Even the sceptics found themselves caught up in the excitement of learning about the myriad of uses, depictions, myths, and incidental details about these bewitching, essential objects. We learned that eggs are not merely edible symbols of reproduction and origin, but also of sustenance and continuity, and of death, punishment and rebirth.

Our plenary speakers provided important grounding for the weekend's exploration of eggs. Professor Marina Warner opened the proceedings with an illustrated talk, 'A Floating Island, a Nest of Myrrh, and a Paper Bag: Hatching Old Plots'. It ranged widely, starting with the Greek myth of Leda and her offspring (hatched from two eggs) and contrasting the idealisation of this myth and ideas of egg-laying in Italian Renaissance art with their depiction in the work of Hieronymus Bosch's triptych *The Garden of Earthly Delights*. Bee Wilson responded to this exciting talk by considering contemporary points of discussion on the cultural and social significance of eggs. Referring to many of the papers in this volume she reminded us that sometimes eggs are just eggs: not symbols, but highly practical things, ranging from physical building materials to the building blocks of cookery. To round out the scientific angles, Professor Hervé This' lecture, 'Let's Have an Egg,' was a whirlwind of whisking and micro-waving that systematically categorised the chemical possibilities of the egg. On Sunday, Professor Naomichi Ishige spoke on 'Eggs and the Japanese', a fascinating view of Japanese dietary change as characterised by egg consumption. The themes that our eminent speakers introduced are reflected, complemented and elaborated in the papers in this volume.

Thanks to Carolin Young, with the technical assistance of Charles Foster-Hall, the Symposium had its own gigantic symbolic egg dominating proceedings in the lecture theatre: a life-size maquette of a 10-foot egg, the first step in Carolin's project to create a real egg of the same size, originally proposed by Salvador Dalí in a letter to his dealer, Julien Levy. This egg began the weekend in mysterious two-part form, and thanks to the enthusiastic late-night efforts of a team of Symposiasts emerged triumphant as a complete egg on Sunday morning. Later it provided a splendid backdrop to a neo-Dada dumb show presented by Alicia Rios and Raymond Sokolov, wearing egg-inspired millinery, and demonstrating the use of three-foot egg-spoons in the manner recommended by Dalí. It is fervently hoped that Carolin will succeed in her *Guinness*

Book of Records-sanctioned attempt to construct the world's largest boiled egg, using the yolks and whites of the 154,000 hen's eggs she has calculated she will need.

In 2006 the Symposium relocated for the second time in its history, to St Catherine's College Oxford. The college proved to be an extremely happy and comfortable home, and we are looking forward to returning there next year and in years to come. We owe a debt of thanks to Catz's highly professional team of organisers, led by Caroline Carpenter, who made the whole experience so easy for us, and to the Steward, Bursar and their teams, all of whom could not have been more helpful, friendly and welcoming. We were sharing the college with the Noel Coward Society, who were perhaps rather surprised to find themselves subjected to the entirely egg-focussed menu designed for us by Anissa Helou and Caroline Conran! It was executed with such skill by chef Tim Kelsey and his team that I'm sure they joined us in praising its execution.

Sri Owen surpassed all previous fund-raising activities with the introduction of a grand raffle, which we hope will become an annual Symposium tradition. She persuaded people to part with an astonishing array of prizes, from dinners in Michelin-starred restaurants to prizes of the finest wine, food, books and cookery lessons. The donors are unfortunately too numerous to name here, but we give all of them immense thanks for their generosity, as well as to Sri for her inspiration and tireless hard work in support of the Symposium. The American Friends of the Oxford Symposium organised a special and highly educational tour of Hampton Court, at a time when its Tudor kitchen was in operation, and also increased their range of goods for sale, providing aprons, tea towels and handsome tote bags, raising a handsome donation for our charitable trust with both strands of activity. Thank you to Carolin Young, whose brainchild these initiatives were, and to Ray Sokolov, the Chair of the American Friends and to all of the committee who worked so hard to support them. Our range of goods for sale would not have been complete without an egg cup, and Caroline Conran designed a magnificent example for us in handsome pottery. And of course, our usual bring and buy sale was a great success thanks to the sterling work of Patsy Iddison and her team of volunteers.

As ever, the entire Symposium could not have happened at all without the hard work of our Organiser, Patsy Iddison, throughout the preceding year. She was supported on the spot by her husband Phil and numerous other willing Symposiast helpers, all of whom are owed an immense debt of thanks.

Please enjoy reading this collection of papers as much as we enjoyed our weekend spent with eggs.

Jane Levi,
London, July 2007.

Ovophilia in Renaissance Cuisine

Ken Albala

Sixteenth-century culinary literature ushered in what might be called the first Renaissance of egg cookery. While medieval cookbooks did feature eggs and they formed a significant part of the European diet at every level of society, it was in the sixteenth century that egg recipes truly proliferated. Eggs became binding liaisons in the vast majority of recipes, replacing breadcrumbs as the preferred thickener. Cookbook authors also experimented with novel ways to cook eggs from barely cooked *ova sorbilia*, to poached, fried, baked, roasted, even grilled eggs, not to mention numerous omelets, custards, zabaglione and egg garnishes. Furthermore, egg yolks were worked in some fashion into a surprising majority of Renaissance recipes as a universal flavor enhancer. As one of the most versatile of ingredients, eggs, more than any other food, became a showcase for Renaissance chefs hoping to impress their patrons with culinary innovations. The egg as big as twenty eggs is perhaps the best example of the culinary subtlety, intended to evoke marvel, but there were many more.

This sudden proliferation of eggs in Renaissance recipes may have had something to do with larger demographic and economic factors which ultimately led to a burgeoning trade in eggs supplying local and particularly urban markets. With a sudden spike in population coupled with rampant inflation, the average European household was increasingly pressured to find alternatives to meat which witnessed the sharpest rise in prices. Egg farming, as with dairy products in general, became increasingly profitable. The abundance of fresh eggs at the market in turn may have stimulated cooks in wealthier households to experiment with eggs even though versatility rather than cost would most likely have been the incentive.

The loosening of Lenten restrictions on dairy products, butter and eggs in particular, may have given further impetus to the development of egg cookery. In Catholic countries a range of new possibilities was opened for the so-called lean days, including every Friday. Not only fish and vegetable dishes but a series of omelets, flans and egg-enriched dishes suddenly became viable options. In Protestant countries, the gradual abandonment of these dietary restrictions altogether also made eggs an ideal ingredient for experimentation.

To begin, why were eggs used comparatively infrequently in late medieval cuisine? Apart from the low cost of meat and Lenten restrictions still in force, there also appears to have been an unwillingness to incorporate eggs into elaborate dishes. There was no apparent stigma against eggs, though of course those lower down the social scale would have eaten them regularly. In the dietary literature eggs were usually singled out as one of the most tempered, easily digested and nutritious foods. Among elite diners there must have been some other impetus for the relative neglect. It may have had something to do with the vogue for sweet and sour sauces redolent of spices. Eggs can get lost in such sauces. The gradual taste preference for smooth, creamy and perfumed flavors more readily lends itself to emulsions based on egg. That is when sharp piquant flavors lost favor to unctuous tastes and textures it may only be natural that eggs found a welcome place in cookery. Another gastronomic factor may have been the ubiquity of ground almonds and almond milk in medieval cuisine, which readily supplied creamy textures when called for, during Lent or outside of it. It may also have been a simple matter that the full range of egg-thickened sauces had not yet made their way into the culinary repertoire of cookbook authors – though this only accounts for sauces.

Whatever the cause, perhaps purely accidental, a survey of medieval recipes reveals that eggs while used are nowhere near the ubiquitous flavor enhancer they would come to be in Renaissance cuisine. Where eggs, or more precisely the yolks, were used most often was as gilding on roasts, color being one of the major preoccupations of medieval chefs. The Middle Ages also had its omelets, but again in nowhere near the proliferation as in later cookbooks. For example in the *Viandier*, among the 170 recipes in the Vatican manuscript there are only four dishes that feature eggs as the main ingredient, in this case as meatless pottages.[1] One is a *civé d'oeufs* which is eggs 'poached' in oil and then served in a broth of fried onions, wine, vinegar and verjuice which is then poured over the previous recipe for toast sops and mustard. A German *brouet* variation includes almond milk and spices, and a third variation is made bright green with parsley and sage and flavored with cheese.[2] Eggs are nowhere else featured as the main ingredient in the *Viandier*. This does not necessarily mean that they were not eaten. As with many early cookbooks, foods that were considered simple and commonplace required no recipes. It may be that like vegetables, they were prepared simply and so are largely absent from complex cookbooks. Nonetheless, this is itself revealing. No one was particularly excited about recording egg recipes, or indeed experimenting with them in complex cookery. This would not be the case in Renaissance cookbooks.

Furthermore, only one of the *Viandier*'s sauces uses egg yolks, mixed with milk and ginger – called a *Jance de lait de vache*.[3] Some of the other *Viandier* manuscripts contain an egg recipe here and there – a dish containing grated bread, bouillon and cheese with eggs strained in, or an herb and cheese pie held together with eggs, a flan with cream, eggs and sliced eels.[4] But in general eggs were not a major ingredient in any versions of this cookbook.

The *Ménagier de Paris* included a few more dishes in a section devoted to eggs, perhaps fitting for an urban professional household which would have depended more heavily on eggs, and as an advice book for a young bride it also makes sense that such basic procedures as egg cookery are covered. There is an omelet or *arboulastre* made of a wild variety of fresh greens and ginger. Also included are a handful of simpler recipes such as *oeufs perdus*, strangely eggs simply broken open and poured directly onto hot embers, wiped off and eaten. Another dish of the same name is merely yolks sweetened and fried and cut up into lozenge shapes. Decidedly inventive are yolks fried in melted sugar, and an odd *oeufs heaumés* (helmet eggs) which is an egg yolk cooked in half the shell set on a tile in the fire. We also find a recipe for eggs poached in oil in a sauce of fried onion, vinegar and water, similar the *Viandier*'s. Elsewhere the author also describes how to temper eggs with hot milk to use as a thickener.[5] All these are an indication that in more modest households eggs were a more important part of the diet, but this does not begin to approach the range and complexity of egg recipes in later centuries.

The same is true of English medieval cookbooks. The *Curye on Inglysch* offers a few simple egg recipes: *eyren in bruet* which is eggs poached in water with pepper, saffron, milk and cheese.[6] The *Forme of Cury* has a similar recipe which includes butter and verjuice. Both manuscripts also contain a *pochee* which is poached eggs in a thickened egg and milk sauce, an ancestor perhaps of hollandaise without the butter.[7] The recipe also appears to be directly related to the aforementioned broths in the *Viandier*, as is an *erbolat*, very similar to the omelet of greens.[8] These are the only three recipes featuring eggs as the main ingredient out of 205 in the *Forme of Cury*. Eggs are used occasionally in fritter batters, in stuffings or as thickeners, for example *mortrews* is boiled and chopped chicken and pork moistened with broth and egg yolks. Similarly the *charlet*, *cawdel* and a few other recipes are thickened with eggs. But on the whole, eggs are absent from the majority of recipes.

The two fifteenth-century Harleian manuscripts are similar, with a recipe for poached eggs[9] and a fascinating counterfeit egg (*eyroun in Lenten*) made with strained almond milk solids which are somehow put back into an empty shell and roasted.[10] As in the earlier cookery texts eggs are used in a handful of places, but there is no interest in them *per se*.

The fourteenth century cookbook whose author is known as Anonimo Veneziano features a stuffed egg recipe very much like a modern devilled egg though sweet, flavored with herbs and served hot. But that is the sole egg recipe out of 135.[11] As in the French and English cookbooks, they are only found in tarts or as a sauce thickener. The Catalan *Libre de Sent Soví* is much more interested in eggs, offering recipes for fried eggs with bacon, another with verjuice, in sauce (which is actually poached and placed on sops, very similar to the *Viandier*'s) as well as an *alidem ha hous* which denotes a sour sauce thickened with eggs, apparently of Arabic origin.[12] But once again, this is merely six recipes out of a total of 220.

As we cross the threshold into the early modern era, suddenly egg recipes proliferate. Signs of this change are apparent even in the cookbook of Martino of Como, written in the latter fifteenth century and published in Platina's *De honesta voluptate* of 1470. There are still some familiar medieval treatments such as the yellow broth with bread eggs and cheese and the herb omelet – here naturally called a *frittata*, but

13

also an entire chapter devoted to eggs that shows some remarkable innovations.[13] There are fried eggs, *ove sperdute* which are poached and topped with sugar, rosewater and spices – these can also be poached in milk or wine. There are stuffed eggs with a filling that contains raisins, aged cheese, herbs and spices served with a sauce of egg yolks and verjuice or *sapa* with ginger, cloves and cinnamon. Eggs on the grill is an entirely novel recipe. It involves first frying a thin *frittata* first folded into a square. This is then placed on the grill and fresh eggs are broken on top of it and cooked and the whole sprinkled with cinnamon and sugar. Equally new is eggs threaded onto a hot spit and roasted. Eggs are also cooked in little *patellettes*, which are probably like ramekins. They are roasted in hot ashes, soft-boiled in their shells, fried sunny-side up, which are called Florentine style, and hard-cooked on hot coals. One of his strangest inventions is frying the egg and then removing the yolk, mixing it with grated cheese, mint, parsley and raisins and more egg yolks. This mixture is then replaced in the hole, refried and topped with orange juice and ginger. Presumably it looks like a regular fried egg but with a surprise in the center. His last invention in this chapter wraps eggs in pasta dough like ravioli. The original form of this pasta was indeed turnip-shaped, *raffioli* as Martino calls it, and one can easily imagine a thin sheet of dough in the palm of the hand into which an egg is dropped and then sealed at the top like a purse. These can then be boiled or fried, though he prefers the latter. This sounds like a trick one might find in a trendy modern restaurant; breaking into each morsel lets it exudes its own sauce. In any case, Martino is clearly very interested in creating new egg dishes.

He also incorporates eggs into a large percentage of other recipes. They are usually offered as an option: 'If you wish to make your broth thick, add two or three egg yolks'[14] or, in the recipe for pie in a pot, 'if you like, add one or two beaten egg yolks.'[15] What this suggests is that Martino is taking recognizable recipes and adding eggs where they might not ordinarily be expected. Eggs go into stuffings and tarts, thicken sauces, bind sausage contents, hold dumplings together and even enrich a rice dish, though Martino comments that many won't like eggs in their rice, so leave it up to the taste of your patron.[16] Clearly he is looking for ways to incorporate eggs, even contrary to common taste preference. It is safe to say that practically anywhere Martino can fit them in, he calls for eggs. Interestingly, this text was written when the Lenten and lean days' prohibition was still in effect. At one point in a recipe for an eel tart he comments that if made at times when you can eat eggs, temper two eggs with verjuice and add to the other ingredients and it will be really good, and certainly not worse.[17] There can be no doubt that Martino was crazy about eggs. For Lent he even has an imitation egg dish far more detailed and precise than that found in the Harleian manuscript. It is made of almond milk, rice, starch and sugar fitted into molds surrounding a saffron-colored yolk, or in empty shells.[18]

In the sixteenth century the craze for eggs only intensified. In the 1540s there appeared a series of cookbooks in France, England and Italy all of which exhibit this new ovophilia. The *Livre fort excellent de Cuysine* offers a series of egg recipes, poached in butter, cooked in water but also a few fascinating presentation pieces. Eggs of many colors, although nothing so strange today, must have been startling at the time. They are boiled in water colored red with *racine de Garence* (which is *Rubia tinctoria*, a dyestuff) or with onion peels to make them yellow, or gold leaf to make them violet, though exactly how that works is unclear. Sounding even stranger is eggs cooked without fire. Here the eggs are nestled in a basket of lime (calcium carbonate) and the whole thing is dipped in water, which apparently cooks the eggs.[19]

The nearly contemporary *Proper newe Book of Cokerye*, was probably written around 1557–8 when the printers were active, also still distinguishes between meat and non-meat days, which makes sense during the reign of Mary. It does, however, include a salad with hard-boiled eggs for fish-days, so clearly that prohibition had been rescinded.[20] More inventive is the so-called 'dyshe full of Snow' which appears in most cookbooks of these decades. The author has muddled the directions a little, but essentially it is a whipped egg white and whipped cream concoction passed through a colander onto an apple stuck with rosemary branches which makes a little winter scene. The author also incorporates eggs into custards, various fritters, including *vautes* which are a thin omelet of veal kidneys, raisins and spices.[21] Even the tarts contain eggs, not only in the pastry, but the filling as well, whether made of beans, gooseberries, medlars, borage flowers and even strawberries are bound with egg yolks and bread crumbs. Like Martino, the author seems to be searching for ways to incorporate eggs: yolks go into apple sauce. *Egges in moneshyne* is perhaps the best-recognized dish in this cookbook, though the dish changes over time. Here it is merely whole egg yolks poached in melted sugar and rosewater – a conceit intended to resemble a bright moon in a limpid sky.[22]

In the contemporary Italian cookbook of Christoforo Messisbugo eggs are regularly featured in banquet menus both for flesh and fish days, interestingly served in the final course (before confections) with fruits, olives and pastries, served simply or sometimes just the yolks served *alla francese* (poached gently in butter) and sprinkled with sugar and cinnamon. In fact, there is scarcely a menu in which eggs are not featured on their own simply as 'fresh eggs' or 'eggs in various ways.' The recipes too are absolutely chock full of eggs and butter. Sweetened breads and pastries as well as savory dishes usually include eggs or yolks. To give an impression of the tastes and textures most appreciated in the Ferrarese court where Messisbugo worked, the *Pizze Sfogliate* is exemplary. It is made of the interior of bread soaked in water with flour, egg yolks, butter, rosewater and sugar. This dough is rolled into minutely thin sheets, basted with butter, rolled and sliced and then finally fried in butter and sprinkled with sugar.[23] One is almost hard pressed to find a recipe in this book that does not contain eggs in some fashion. They are worked into tarts both savory and sweet, pasta dough, fritters including an early *pâte choux*,[24] as well as fruit, vegetable and meat pies. Interestingly there are variant versions of most pastries made without butter or eggs, so it seems that at least during Lent restrictions were either still in force in Italy or these were variations offered for the sake of variety or austerity. A later section of recipes described as 'da magro' also excludes eggs.

Messisbugo also incorporates egg yolks into most of his soups and thicker *minestre* of rice, meat or vegetables as well as fricassees. A 'Hungarian' egg soup includes 40 eggs with verjuice, butter and sugar lightly cooked in a bain marie until thickened.[25] Eggs are similarly incorporated into sauces and there is also a *salsa di Torli d'uova* made with herbs, cooked egg yolks and vinegar.[26] Eggs are also served on their own, stuffed with raisins, pine nuts, herbs and spices[27] or in little rolled morsels of scrambled egg with spices, sugar and orange juice. Eggs are featured in *frittatas* served simply or stuffed with various ingredients such cheese, onions, fennel, prosciutto and even caviar. Eggs are served simply fried, on toast with or without cheese. In what appears to be a new recipe called *fritte a Scartozzo*, a thin layer of egg is fried, covered with grated cheese, pepper and a sprig of rosemary then folded over and served three to a plate, sprinkled with sugar.[28] Without belaboring the point, eggs are one of the most frequently used ingredients and find their way into the most elegant of banquet menus in sixteenth-century Italy.

One last cookbook should amply illustrate this sixteenth-century obsession with eggs, Bartolomeo Scappi's magisterial *Opera* printed in 1570. It may be the sheer size of the book that accounts for the wealth of egg recipes, but the willingness to include them in recipes and on their own is eminently characteristic of Renaissance gastronomy. Scappi has literally dozens of egg recipes. The variety of omelets, for example, includes one with ham, onions and cheese. Another is a made of stacked layers with sugar, cinnamon, nutmeg and fresh cheese, precooked garlic cloves and raisins splashed with orange juice. *Frittatas* are filled with veal or kid spleen, mixed with pork blood and spices, or with cured pork jowl, skin and cheese. Obviously lacking any aversion to organ meats, Scappi can be inventive and even slightly perverse – at least from our vantage point.[29]

Scappi also makes a clear distinction among his recipes which are merely for 'lean' days in which eggs and butter were allowed and which are for fasting days during Lent when oil replaces butter, almond milk stands in for dairy and eggs are also prohibited. Nonetheless the range of egg dishes suitable outside of Lent and for other lean days is impressive. There are *uova da bere* or what is called in the Latin writers *ova sorbilia* – drinkable eggs. These must be fresh, are pierced with a pin and then boiled for the length of a *credo* (about 30 seconds). It is cooked just until the egg will spin, or until it's too hot to hold in your hand. The top is broken off, it is sprinkled with salt and sugar, and then presumably drunk directly from the shell.[30]

Scappi also includes precise directions for every possible way to cook an egg, indicating that this is intended to be a complete guide to cooking from the basics to the most complex dishes imaginable.[31] There are details on how to poach an egg without breaking it that could stand in any modern cookbook. Another explains

Ovophilia in Renaissance Cuisine

French eggs, braised in butter in little earthenware ramekins, eggs fried in clarified butter – properly so the whites stay light and don't stick to the pan. There are also meticulously rolled over omelets (rather than *frittatas*) and fried eggs in a special pan with indentations (*padella fatta ad occhi di bove*) which is illustrated in the section on equipment. Scappi also suggests a technique I have seen nowhere else: soft-boiled eggs which are then floured and fried and covered in garlic sauce. Eggs are also stuffed in various ways, one with a hot almond and verjuice sauce. Rolled omelets are colored green with herb juice, or stuffed with marzipan, cut up, coated with an egg wash, battered and fried, called *cannoncini*. There are *frittate doppie* made with ten stacked flat omelets filled with cheese, herbs and raisins cooked in wine, as well as *frittatas*, made specifically with eggs that are not fresh, which become tough in cooking. These are filled with mint, marjoram, crushed *mostaccioli* cookies, pine nuts and truffles. Clearly eggs had been elevated among the most exquisite of dishes.

Another egg novelty is the *frittata* or *torta in acqua*: ten fresh eggs are beaten with some water and then poured into boiling in salted water, scooped out with a perforated spoon and drained. These too can be made green with spinach juice or fine herbs. Equally interesting is eggs cooked on a metal baker's peel with beeswax rather than butter or oil, and heated only from above (presumably in the oven) or they can be made on top of hot coals, or directly on the hot coals for picky people. There are also eggs called *barbagliate* which are slowly broken up and stirred over a gentle heat, a kind of soft scrambled eggs cooked with verjuice, orange juice, and sugar and rosewater at the end. Eggs are also made into thick soups as well as an herb-laden *vivarole* not unlike *straciatella* or egg-drop soup in which the eggs, bread and cheese are stirred into the boiling soup and cook in strands. Needless to say Scappi and Renaissance elite cooks in general experimented wildly with eggs in every possible guise, and this brief list only includes those recipes in which eggs are the major ingredient.

But even this is not the whole repertoire. In the book on dishes for the infirm another set of egg dishes appears. Again, soft-boiled or roasted eggs, poached in water, or in goat's milk or sweet white wine, all for some inexplicable reason considered appropriate for the sick, perhaps maybe as comfort food. How else can one explain eggs fried in capon or goose fat?[32] In any case, novel ways of cooking eggs and incorporating them into a wide variety of recipes was one of the hallmarks of Renaissance cookery.

Eggs would remain a major feature in elite cookbooks well into the seventeenth century, culminating in greater presentation pieces such as the 'great compound egg as big as twenty eggs' found in Robert May.[33] May incidentally offers no less than 64 egg recipes in their own chapter. Renaissance cuisine might also be said to have laid the foundations for the next great period of egg cookery, in French *haute cuisine*, when the soufflé, cakes and various egg-based sauces such as mayonnaise, hollandaise and béarnaise were invented. How eggs were demoted in modern cookery to breakfast food, and how the range of egg dishes narrowed in subsequent centuries remains a question that deserves further research, but it may be related to the overwhelming emphasis on and lower price of meat in the modern era, leaving eggs as a basic and far more humble ingredient.

Notes

1. Terence Scully, ed., *The Viandier of Taillevent* (Ottowa: University of Ottowa Press, 1988), p. 84.
2. Ibid., p. 85.
3. Ibid., p. 166.
4. Ibid., p. 194.
5. Jérome Pichon, ed., *Le Ménagier De Paris, Traité De Morale Et D'économie Domestique Composé Vers 1393, Par Un Bourgeois Parisien* (Paris: La Société Des Bibliophiles François. Tome Second, 1846), pp. 206–10.
6. Constance B. Hieatt and Sharon Butler, eds., *Curye on Inglysch* (London, New York, Toronto: Oxford University Press, 1985), p. 66.
7. Ibid., p. 118.
8. Ibid., p. 138.
9. Thomas Austin, ed., *Two Fifteenth Century Cookery-Books* (London, New York, Toronto: Oxford University Press, 2000), p. 24.
10. Ibid., p. 41.
11. Ludovico Frati, ed., *Libro di cucina del Secolo XIV* (Bologna: arnaldo Forni, 1986), p. 26.
12. Rudolf Grewe, *Libre de Sent Soví* (Barcelona: Editorial Barcino, 1979), pp. 184–187.
13. Maestro Martino, *Libro de arte coquinaria*, ed. Luigi Ballerini e Jeremy Parzen (Milano: guido Tommasi Editore, 2003), pp. 74–78. This book has also been translated into English as *The Art of Cooking* (Berkeley: University of California Press, 2005). Page numbers refer to the Italian edition.
14. Ibid., p. 6.
15. Ibid., p. 9.
16. Ibid., p. 26.
17. Ibid., p. 63.
18. Ibid., p. 101.
19. *Livre fort excellent de Cuysine* (2nd ed. Lyon: Olivier Arnoullet, 1555), fol. xxxixv.
20. *A Proper newe Book of Cokerye* (London: John Kynge and Thomas Marche, n.d.; c. 1557-8) Sometimes cited as c. 1545. Modern edition edited by Anne Ahmed: (Cambridge: Corpus Christi College, 2002), p. 36. This contains a useful facsimile of the original plus the editor's sometimes questionable transcription/interpretation. Another transcription was edited by Jane Hugget (Bristol: Stuart Press, 1995).
21. Ibid., pp. 54–6.
22. Ibid., p. 66.
23. Cristoforo di Messisbugo, *Banchetti* (Ferrara: Giovanni di Buglhat and Antonio Hucher, 1549). Facsimile of Second Edition: *Libro Novo nel Qual S'insegna A' far d'Ogni Sorte di Vivianda* (Bologna: Arnaldo Forni Editore, 2001), p 43v.
24. Ibid., p. 58.
25. Ibid., p. 81v.
26. Ibid., p. 87v.
27. Ibid., p. 109.
28. Ibid., pp. 110–112.

29. Bartolomeo Scappi, *Opera* (Venice: Domenico Tramezzino, 1570). Facsimile: (Bologna, Arnaldo Forni, 2002), pp. 83–86.
30. Ibid., p. 158v.
31. Ibid., pp. 158v–162v.
32. Ibid., p. 422v.
33. Robert May, *The Accomplisht Cook*, facsimile of 1685 edition (Totnes, Devon: Prospect Books, 2000), p. 433.

The Egg: its Symbolism and Mythology

Joan P. Alcock

Concept of the egg

Eggs, especially those laid by birds, both large and small, with their rounded, seemingly perfected form, the perfect package for food, have fascinated people throughout time becoming associated with symbolism and mythology. The egg has a perfect shape, strong without, fragile within, able to provide nourishment whether cooked or uncooked, yet able to give birth to a new generation. This new life within its dormant shape became symbolic of creation and resurrection summed up in the Latin proverb *'omne vivum ex ovo'* (all life comes from the egg). Folklore associates it with the goose that laid the golden egg; nursery rhymes with Humpty Dumpty[1] and fables with the story of the rats, the fox and the egg. Such mythology survived until the twentieth century when the author always obeyed her grandmother's instruction to break through the shell of her breakfast boiled egg to prevent a witch riding in the shell. This was, and still is, ritually observed. This is obviously linked to a belief told to the author by a Scottish friend that witches would collect any shells left whole and sail in them out to sea to sink ships. Other mythological beliefs include that those eggs that have no yolk are believed to be unlucky and that eggs given on the birth of a baby will bring good luck and prosperity to the child.

Classical and European mythology

In classical mythology the egg became part of tradition. One legend concerning the birth of Aphrodite is that she was born from an egg hatched by doves alongside the River Euphrates (Kerényi, 1951, 67). Leda, who was turned into a swan by Zeus to avoid her destruction by jealous Juno, laid two double-yolked eggs (Kerényi 1951, 107). From one, which was conceived by her earthly husband Tyndareus, came Castor and Clytemnestra; from the other, conceived by Zeus, came Pollux and Helen. The half-brothers, the Dioscuri or Gemini (twins), Castor and Pollux, one mortal and one immortal, became part of the Roman pantheon and were granted their own festival on 15 July and a temple in the Roman Forum. The constellation Gemini is said to represent the twins, with the brightest stars being Castor and Pollux. Zeus also sought out Nemesis who changed into a goose to avoid him but Zeus changed into a gander and the resultant egg produced Helen (Homer, *Odyssey* 9 299).

The Romans believed that eggs had aphrodisiac powers (Ovid, *Ars Amatoria* 2 12; Pliny, *Natural History* 29 48) and were symbolic of fertility. They were also symbolic that new life breaking forth from the egg indicated life after death. As such, and probably also to nourish the dead in the afterlife, they were placed in both Greek (Cumont 1922, 193) and Roman tombs, as for example at York and Colchester. A sarcophagus in the Museo delle Terme in Rome has the figure of a young boy on the lid; by his side are depicted a serpent (a chthonic symbol) and an egg. Nilsson (1907) commented that the egg 'an apparent inanimate and inert substance that carries within it a potent principle of life and that which has a special vital power, must perforce awake or enhance the vital powers to those whom it is offered'. Dionysus brought an egg to young people to announce their forthcoming death (Kerényi 1976, 369).

In the Finnish *Kalevala* (1.111–313), Ilmatar, goddess of the air longed for a son, so the East Wind made love to her until she conceived Vainamoinen, the child of the wind. She could not give birth and an eagle, flying overhead, swooped down and impregnated her. The result was six cosmic eggs, together with an egg made of iron. Rather than let Ilmatar have these the eagle collected them, sitting on them to protect them. Unfortunately she was also sitting on Ilmatar. When the goddess moved, the eggs rolled into the sea, the shells broke and a churning mass was created that divided into Heaven and Earth. One yolk became Paivatar, the sun, while the egg white became Kuu, the moon. Specks of eggshells created the stars, while the iron egg became a thundercloud. The impregnated child of the wind then emerged from the womb as an old man.

Recently I went to Timbuktu and joined a group of ten people, going through desert scrubland to Djemmé, a dry, hot, dusty town of mud brick houses, and containing the largest mud brick mosque in the world. On the top were ostrich eggs. Their purpose was said to be to ward off evil spirits and to bring good luck, thus illustrating the perpetuation of ancient traditions.

The medieval cosmic egg

The usual representation of the creation of the world in the medieval period depicts a universe arranged in a conventional geometric model, as indicted in Giovanni di Paolo's painting of the *Creation of the World with the expulsion of Adam and Eve* (Metropolitan Museum, New York; Lippincott 1990). The earth is surrounded by circles representing the universe (Randles 1999, 13). There is a variant to this in which the universe is depicted as egg-shaped. One theory links this to the mythical philosophical concept of the cosmic egg that is also linked to Neo-Platonic lore and the Orphic myth (Guthrie 1992, 74–107). This myth declares that 'the principle of the universe was born from an egg which was itself formed from the undifferentiated matter of primordial chaos' (Lippincott, K. 1992, 136).

There are two versions of this myth. One was promoted by the Roman author Varro in the first century BC. Heaven is like an eggshell and the earth is the yolk. Between these two is enclosed the moisture as a kind of humidity. This is the air in which there is warmth. The second was related to Greek mythology and was promoted by Clement of Alexandria in the fourth century AD (pseudo-Clement *Recognitionis* 10 17). According to Orphic fable, Chaos took the form of an egg in which was a confused matter of primeval elements. From this egg hatched an androgynous being, which made heaven out of fire and air and the world out of water and earth. Through the participation of this being all other things were born and generated out of the elements. Needless to say early Christian writers disputed this as being contrary to Holy Scripture.

The theory resurfaced for a short time in the twelfth century. Hildegard of Bingen's *Liber Scivias* is a series of mystical dream sequences written between 1141 and 1150 (Singer, 191, 1–55). One manuscript, the Wiesbaden Codex, prepared in 1179 just before her death, describes a structure of the world in the likeness of an egg surrounded by fire in which was the sun. Below it was a dark skin in which was 'a whitely radiant fire' (the moon). This egg-shaped universe torn by blasts of winds and raging fire is held in place only by means of a hierarchy of structure.

This concept of a cosmic egg has been associated with the eggs suspended in churches during the medieval and Renaissance period. Those that have survived are, however, ostrich eggs, which also hung and still hang in mosques, houses and shops in the Near East seemingly to ward off or be antidotal to the effects of the evil eye. In a detailed survey of the ostrich egg in European cultural history from the prehistoric period to the seventeenth century (Bock 2006), its use is noted in churches and mosques and as a feature valued for its aesthetic use, as for example in drinking vessels. In the medieval period the egg was used as a reliquary as in the case of that reported as early as 1148 hanging in the cathedral of Plock, Poland. When suspended in religious buildings, eggs were usually placed amongst lamps, which link them with an allegorical interpretation with lamps as stars which stand for the Pleiades.

Symbolism in painting

There are four Renaissance paintings in which an egg appears suspended above the head of the Virgin[2]. Of these the Piero della Francesca painting is the most controversial resulting in numerous articles in the *Art Bulletin* between 1952 and 1980. As well as an ostrich egg, the object has been described as a hen's egg and the egg of Leda, even as a pearl. Kenneth Clark (1951) saw it as symbolic of the Immaculate Conception with reference to a folklore notion that ostrich eggs fertilize themselves but the clue to its symbolic meaning may lie with a fresco over the tomb of Antonio dei Fissiraga in the church of San Francesca, Lodi, where the egg is seen suspended amongst stars (Bock 2003). This can be linked with a passage in the thirteenth century writings of Guilelmus Durantis[3], where he draws a parallel between the forgetfulness of an ostrich looking after its eggs and men forgetting God (Regusa, 1971, Fig 2.4). This refers to a passage in a late version of the Greek *Physiologus*.[4] A silver reliquary made between 1377 and 1380 by Francesco di Milano for Elizabeth, Queen of Hungary and kept in the church of St Siméon in Zadar shows the queen presenting a shrine to the church. An ostrich egg is suspended in the centre of an arch. This may be one of the objects referred to by Durantis (Petricioli, 1983, 20, fig 19).

Eggs as votive objects are seen in an early sixteenth century painting by Carpaccio; a row of votive offerings hanging in a church also includes human legs[5] but Durantis' comments imply that ostrich eggs are rare exotica and certainly the ones used in applied art were carefully recorded in inventories. Their inclusion amongst hanging lamps, symbols of stars, was intended to have the symbolic function of admonishment to recall men's thoughts to heed God's words and not forget Him. The custom was confined to Catholic churches. A domestic scene by Esaias Boursse, painted about 1663 (Bock 2006, 216) shows an egg suspended in a room although the fact that it is placed over a mother who sits with a child in a cradle besides her may be symbolic of the Madonna and child. It may, however, be intended for good luck and to avert evil.

In the paintings of two northern artists, Bruegel and Bosch, the egg is not related to the good but has dubious connotations. In Pieter Bruegel's painting the *Fall of the Rebel Angels* (1562) an egg with a curved spike on the end is about to crack open releasing further horrors. In *Dulle Griet* (1562) where the woman stalks through a world in which sin dominates, the egg symbolises gluttony. One contains five birds with their beaks open greedily seeking food. The *Land of Cockaigne* (1567), which is devoted to gluttony, has the image of an egg running up to be eaten with a spoon in it. In *Dulle Griet* the egg also refers to alchemy. A man supporting a boat on his head seems to be laying eggs, the contents of which he is removing with a spoon – gold coins which any alchemist wished to produce. These fall to the greedy crowd below. Three images in his painting *Flemish Proverbs* (1558) refer to eggs. According to Robert Hughes (1967, 92), these are: leave at least one egg in the nest (be discreet); if the eggs have not yet been laid, you cannot be sure of getting chickens (don't count your chickens before they have hatched); to take the hen's eggs and miss the goose's (to lose a big advantage in order to get a little one).

Eggs found in the paintings of Hieronymous Bosch seem also to be alluding to alchemy. In the *Temptation of St Anthony* (c. 1495) a tonsured demon is reciting a black mass. Two pseudo monks stand beside him. On the head of one is a funnel symbolising madness. On the head of the other is a nest holding an egg, symbol of alchemy and standing for the oval crucifix in which the philosophers' stone is concealed. The egg appears again on a platter and also scuttling along on bird's legs across the roof of the saint's cell. An egg with a knife in it alludes to the philosophers' fire or to the male sex. The eggs in *The Garden of Earthly Delights Triptych* (c. 1470) (Dixon 2003, 260–64) relate the symbolic language of alchemy to the vessel in which transmutation took place. Many images symbolise retorts, the largest of which is in the Hell panel where the hollow, egg-shaped body of a man-monster supports a table on which the vessel is placed. His hollow tree legs blaze like furnaces.

Eggs and Easter

The Christian church took the egg as a symbol of the Resurrection: new life emerging from the egg symbolised the emergence of Christ from the tomb. It could also be linked to the Trinity; the shell being the Father, the yolk the son and the white the Holy Spirit. Easter was also linked with the renewal of life in spring. The Saxon word 'oster' meaning 'to rise' was personified in Eostre, an Anglo-Saxon fertility goddess, whose pagan festival was grafted onto the Christian religious festival. Eostre was also associated with the Easter hare. According to legend she saved a bird with a broken wing by turning it into a hare, but a hare that still laid eggs, symbolic of springtime fertility.

Eggs were particularly welcome at Easter because they had been forbidden in the Western Church during Lent as they were classified with meat. In the Eastern Orthodox Church meat and dairy products were likewise forbidden and eggs were classified as 'dairy' being taken from the hen without shedding blood. Eggs had to be used by Ash Wednesday, hence the tradition of Shrove Tuesday (Pancake Day). Hens lay fewer eggs during this time of year. What were laid were hard-boiled, pickled or allowed to hatch to increase the flock ready for summer. One superstition, presumably circulated to prevent people breaking their fast too soon, claimed that if eggs laid on Good Friday were kept for a hundred years their yolks would turn to diamonds. Another stated that Good Friday eggs cooked on Easter Day would promote fertility and protect against sudden death. If the egg had two yolks this would indicate riches for the eater. It therefore became customary to have eggs blessed at Easter in the hope that eating them would ward off illness. The Roman ritual still contains a blessing.[6]

Egg shackling or egg tapping competitions were held in Dorset and Cornwall until fairly recently. This was akin to the game of conkers for the eggs were hit against each other. The winner was the last egg to retain its shape. Later, the eggs were placed in a sieve and rattled until they cracked. The winner was again the person whose egg retained most of its shape.

Pace eggs is a term derived from 'Pasch', the old English word for Easter and the Hebrew 'Pesach' (Passover). Pace egg plays took place in the north of England. The Midgley (West Yorkshire) pace egg play is a St George's mummers' play, which begins, and ends with a pace egg song (Tiddy, R. J. E. 1923). After the play the audience is given eggs. Pace egg processions in Lancashire included eggs carried by young men wearing animal skins; one once held at Burscough near Ormskirk included such characters as a Noble Youth, Lady Gay, Soldier Brave and Old Toss Pot (a drunken buffoon) (Home, 1961). An old Cheshire custom known to the author is that if children demanded eggs and none was given they chanted the somewhat malicious rhyme, 'If you won't give us an Easter egg, your hens shall all lay addled eggs and your cocks lay stones'. In Wales something similar was observed in the custom of demanding or clapping for eggs with wooden or slate clappers as well as hands (Owen 1959, 86).

Pace egg rolling was symbolic of the stone that was rolled from the tomb. In

The Egg: its Symbolism and Mythology

England it is still popular in northern areas. Huge crowds take part each year at Avenham Park, Preston, at Doncaster, Penshaw and Sunderland (Alexander 2002, 211). The winner used to be the one whose egg rolls furthest and whose shell is the least broken. At Barton on Humber, Yorkshire, they are rolled along a lane (Hole, 1941–42, 49). The custom was also known in Germany and was taken to the United States by settlers. An Egg Rolling took place in Washington on Capitol Hill until 1878 when the Turf Protection Law was passed. The wife of President Madison came to the rescue allowing the children to hold it on the White House Lawn. In 1981 pits were dug and filled with straw in which children had to search for eggs.

In Germany the custom of egg hunting was explained by the legend of the Easter hare laying the eggs and hiding them in its nest that the children had to find. Emigrating Germans took this custom to the United States; later it found its way to England where egg hunts in houses and gardens soon became popular. According to French legend when the bells did not toll from Maundy Thursday to Easter Day, they went to Rome to be blessed by the Pope. On their return they brought Easter eggs.

Pace eggs are often coloured. This is a very old tradition, one theory being that the Crusaders brought it from the Near East. In the Orthodox Church eggs coloured red symbolised Christ's blood, the shell was his three-day entombment. Hence the breaking of the shell indicated Resurrection and new life as well as the breaking of the bonds of sin and death. It was linked to a legend of Mary Magdalene giving a red egg, after Christ's Ascension, to the Roman Emperor with the words, 'Christ is risen'. An Orthodox custom is still to place red eggs on Easter breads and to mark the ends with a cross. A Ukrainian legend said that drops of blood fell from the Cross at the Crucifixion onto the eggs. The tears of Mary also fell on the eggs creating a marbled pattern. Mary gathered the eggs and went to Pontius Pilate to plead for her son's body. On the way she gave an egg to each child she met, but they fell from her hand and spread all over the world symbolising peace. A Polish legend says that the women took a basket of eggs to the tomb. When they removed the cloth they found that all the shells were coloured.

Coloured eggs, however, are not confined to Europe but are known elsewhere, for example in China and the tradition was noted in ancient Egypt and Rome. They are not however, popular in southern Europe and South America. Decorated eggs were known in England as early as in 1290 when the household accounts of Edward I record that 18 pence should be spent to decorate 450 eggs which were to be given to favoured members of the royal household (Hole 1961, 43).

Russian, Polish and Ukrainian eggs can be painted to any design, realistic or stylised.[7] Horses and deer are especially popular for they indicate strength and prosperity. A fish is related to Christ the fisher of souls. In former Yugoslavia the eggs are marked with the letters X V, for *Christos Vaskresse*. The Ukrainians use a method called *pysanky* (or *pisanka*) where a beeswax design is painted on the egg, which is then dipped successively into dye baths in a continual process. This provides an important defence against the evils of Satan. More prosaically in Lancashire, eggs are wrapped in onion-skins and boiled to get a golden mottled effect (Newall 1965).

In England the Reformation discontinued the giving of eggs where they were denounced as 'papal trappings' and the Enlightenment ensured that pagan irrational customs were not followed. Only in some parts did the old tradition survive. The revival of the custom of giving eggs, now with all symbolism lost, came in the nineteenth century when the first chocolate eggs were produced. The first were made in France where they were made in cardboard often decorated with velvet and satins. Cadbury provided 'French eating chocolate' in 1842 but chocolate manufactures improved on this. Fry's produced their first egg in 1873, Cadbury in 1875 (a dark chocolate egg filled with dragées), and Rowntree's in 1901. The earliest eggs were moulded as one but by the 1930s eggs were produced in two halves to enable a greater variety of chocolates or sweets to be included. After the Second World War eggs were put in cardboard boxes for more protection, an idea said to have been derived from the way in which electric light bulbs were packaged. In 2005 it was estimated that at least 80 million eggs were being sold, about 8 per cent of all chocolate sales. Cadbury produced a version of its popular creme egg in 1923, but the present variety was not sold until 1971. The ultimate form of the chocolate is the deep-fried creme egg, a variation of the battered deep-fried Mars bar, a delicacy well known in Scottish fish and chip shops.

A new use of the Easter egg is the virtual Easter egg used in computing where it is a hidden message, graphic, feature or sound effects placed in any computer programme or video game. It can also occur in a film or TV programme, a CD or a DVD. At first these were regarded as harmless but their dangers soon became apparent as, for example, a hidden code, and many companies now forbid them.

Fabergé eggs

The most exotic and symbolic eggs were made by the Russian jeweller Peter Carl Fabergé and his goldsmiths between 1885 and 1916 as presents for the Russian Imperial family (Snowman 1962; Snowman 1977; Forbes 1980). It was formerly believed that 57 eggs were made but research in Russian archives in the 1990s has now revealed that only 50 were produced (Welander 1997, 63). The first, in 1885, given by the Tsar Alexander III to the Tsarina, Maria Fyodorovna, was a white enamel egg which when opened revealed a gold yolk, which in turn revealed a gold hen. Inside this was a tiny crown with a ruby hanging inside. This not only replicated the Russian *matryoshka* nesting dolls but also was symbolic of the hope for a fruitful reign, which proved to be a tragic delusion.

The Tsar was delighted with the gift and the concept and commissioned Fabergé to provide a similar gift each year at Easter. This tradition was continued by his successor, Nicholas II. The first egg of his reign was the Coronation Egg (1897) that split open to reveal a replica of the imperial coach used in 1896 for the coronation of the Tsar and the Tsarina Alexandra Fedorovna in Moscow. This took 15 months to make. Its height was 3 inches (78.2 mm) and was inserted into a 5-inch-high egg. The 1900 egg, which was made to commemorate the completion of the Trans-Siberian Railway, was surrounded by a silver band with a map of the route, each station marked by a precious stone, but inside was a small exact platinum and gold replica of the engine and five coaches of the train. The last one was a travelling church and the train could be wound up to move. The 1903 Peter the Great egg symbolised the bicentennial of the founding of St Petersburg in 1703. When the egg was opened a gold model of the Peter the Great monument in the Neva rose up. The egg created to symbolise and commemorate the anniversary of the defeat of the French in 1812 opened to display a folding screen depicting signed miniatures of members of regiments of which the Tsarina was commander in Chief.

The outbreak of war in 1914 forced the Fabergé family to curb its output and by 1916 the firm had turned to war production and, somewhat ironically, its talents had been recruited to producing hand grenades. In 1916 the firm crafted a Military Steel Egg, which the Tsar presented to the Tsarina. The last egg to be presented to the Imperial family was in 1916. The Order of St George Egg depicted the cross of St George on a silver shell. When a button was pressed a portrait of the Tsar was revealed. Later two more eggs were made in 1917 but by then the royal family were under house arrest and their murder at Ekaterinburg ensured that the eggs were never delivered. The St George Egg had been presented to the Dowager Empress Elizabeth and by chance it escaped being found when the Bolsheviks ransacked her lodgings at Odessa. It left Russia with her when she escaped from Yalta on the British battleship, *H. M. S. Marlborough*, and was the only Fabergé egg to leave Russia with its original owner.

The first egg presented to the royal family had been symbolic of hope for a new regime. The last egg, the Order of St George Egg, was conceived equally in the promise of hope for a victorious Russian end to the First World War and a better economic future. Instead it symbolised the end of a dynasty.

Bibliography

Alexander, M., *A Companion to the Folklore, Myths and Customs of Britain*. Stroud: Sutton Publishing, 2002.

Bock, S., The 'Egg' of the 'Pala Montefeltro' by Piero dell Francesca and its symbolic meaning. http://archiv.ub.uni-heidelberg.de/volltextserver/volltexte/2003/3123/pdf/PieroEgg.pdf

Bock, S., *Ova Struthionis Die Straussbeneiobjekte in den Schatz-, Silber- und Kunstkammern Europas*. Friburg: Heidelberg, 2006.

Carroll, L., *Alice Though the Looking Glass*, 1872.

Clark, K., *Piero della Francesca*. London: Phaidon, 1951.

Cumont, F., *Afterlife in Roman Paganism*. New York: New Haven.
Dixon, L., *Bosch*. London: Phaidon, 2003.
Forbes, C., *Fabergé Eggs: Imperial Russian Fantasies*. New York: Abrams, 1980.
Guthrie, W. K. C., *Orpheus and Greek Religion: a study of the Orphic Movement*. London:Revised ed. Methuen,1935.
Hole, C., *English Custom and Usage*. London: Batsford, 1941–42.
Hole, C., *Easter and its Customs*. London: Richard Bell, 1961.
Home, B., 'The Tradition of the Easter Egg' in *Country Life*, March 30, 1961, 700.
Hughes, R., *The Complete Paintings of Bruegel*. London: Weidenfeld and Nicholson, 1951.
Jones, P., *The Siege of Colchester*, Stroud: Tempus Publications, 2003.
Kerényi, C., *The Gods of the Greeks*. London: Thames and Hudson, 1951.
Kerényi, C., *Dionysos. Architypal Image of Indestructible Life*. London: Routledge and Kegan Paul.
Lippincott, K., 'Giovanni di Paolo's Creation of the World and tradition of the *thema mundi* in late Medieval and Renaissance art', in *The Burlington Magazine*, 132, July 1990, 460–68.
Lippincott, K., 'Chaos and the Egg: new evidence from a fifteenth century Bolognese masterpiece', in *Il Luogo ed il Ruolo della citta di Bologna tra Europa Continentale et Mediterranea. Atti del Colloquio C. I. H. A., Bologna 1990*, Bologna 1992
Newall, F., 'Decorated Eggs' in *Folklore* 76, 1965, 266.
Nilsson, M., 'Das Ei im Totenkult der Alten' in *Archiv fur Religionswissenschaft*, 49, 530–46, 1907.
Opie, I. and P., *The Oxford Dictionary of Nursery Rhymes*, Oxford: Oxford University Press, 1962.
Pseudo-Clement, *Recognitionis; Homiliae. The Clementine Homilies*, translated by P. Petersen. Edinburgh: Edinburgh University Press 1870
Petricioli, I., *Der Schrein des Hl Siméon in Zadar*. Zagreb: Vereinigte Verleger, 1983.
Randles, W. G. L., *The Unmaking of the Medieval Christian Cosmos*. Aldershot: Ashgate, 1999.
Regusa, I., 'The Egg Reopened', in *Art Bulletin*, 53, 1971, 435–43.
Singer, C., 'The Scientific Views and Visions of Saint Hildegard (1098–1190)', in *Studies in the History and Method of Science*. Oxford: Oxford University Press, 1917.
Snowman, K., *The Art of Carl Fabergé*. London: Faber and Faber, 1962.
Snowman, K., *Fabergé 1840–1920. An International Loan Exhibition on the occasion of the Queen's Silver Jubilee, July–September 1977*. London: Debrett's Peerage in association with the Victoria and Albert Museum, 1977.
Tiddy, R. J. E., *The Mummers' Play*. Oxford: Clarendon Press, 1923.
Welander, E., *Carl Fabergé; Goldsmith to the Tsar*. Stockholm: National Museum, 1997.

Notes

1. Humpty Dumpty first appears in his egg illustration form as drawn by Sir John Tenniel in *Alice Through the Looking Glass* (Carroll 1872), but he has an older history, referred to in many European countries where the name is connected with drinks (especially ale and brandy), which make people tipsy, and riddles, which unnerve them (Opie 1962, 215). An English historical tradition refers to an incident during the siege of Colchester in July 1648, when a Royalist supporter named One-eyed Thompson was firing a gun at the Parliamentarians from the top of St Mary's at the Walls Church. When he was killed both he and his gun came crashing down hence the nursery rhyme reference as either Thompson or the gun was nicknamed Humpty Dumpty because both were of a large size (Jones 2003, 85–87).
2. Piero della Francesca. *Montefeltro Altarpiece*. Brera Gallery, Milan; Andrea Mantegna, *San Zeno altarpiece*. San Zeno, Verona; Giovanni Bellini, *Sacra Conversazione*, San Zaccaria, Venice; Bernardino Butinone. *Madonna and child with Saint John the Baptist and Saint Giustina*. Isola Bella, Palazzo Borromeo.

3. 'Some say that the Ostrich is a forgetful bird, which forgets its eggs and yet, when it sees a certain star is reminded and returns to them and warms them with its gaze. Eggs are therefore hung in churches to signify that man – forsaken by God on account of his sins – when he at last, illuminated by the light of God remembers, regrets his sins and returns to him, is warmed by his merciful gaze…They (the eggs) are thus suspended in churches so that each and everyone contemplates that man easily forgets God unless he is illuminated by a star, that is by the influence of the grace of the Holy Spirit, and remembers and returns to Him through good works'. (Guillelmi Duranti, *Rationale Divinorum officiorum*. Corpus Christianorum, Continuatio Mediaevalis, vol. 109, 49. Turnholt: Brepol Editores Pontificii, 1995.
4. 'The ostrich lays its eggs but does not warm them but sits and gazes at them with its eyes. The heat of the gaze warms them so that the young are born, but when they overlook them (the eggs) they are not born. For that reason eggs are suspended in churches as an example to us all. While we stand together in prayer we fix our eyes on God who has wiped out our sins'. Francesco Sbordone, ed., *Physiologus* (Mediolani: Soc. 'Dante Alighieri', 1936), 323.
5. Vittore Carpaccio, *Vision of Francesco Antonio Ottoboni, prior of San Antonio di Castello in Venice*, in Academia, Venice.
6. Prayer sanctioned by Pius V (1566–72) and modified later: 'We beseech thee, O Lord, to bestow thy benign blessing upon these eggs, to make them a wholesome food for thy faithful, who gratefully partake of them in honour of the Resurrection of Our Lord Jesus Christ'.
7. The Polish housekeeper of the priest living next door to the author, each year at Easter blew eggs and then painted them in the most exquisite designs. These eggs were given to children attending the Polish church in South East London. She also designed pictures of cocks made from polystyrene that adorned the church on Easter Sunday.

Cackleberries and Henfruit: a French Perspective

Fritz Blank

The first American edition of *The Encyclopedia of Food, Wine, & Cookery*, otherwise known as *Larousse Gastronomique*, by Prosper Montagne lists 10 'Basic Cooking Methods' plus 283 named recipes under the heading of 'Eggs'. This does not include a separate categorical listing of variously named omelets – both savory and sweet – nor does it reflect the multitude of recipes and dishes, which employ eggs as a major ingredient, such as Quiche, Soufflés, Cakes, Custards, Beverages, Ice Creams, etc. That eggs were considered a separate course for a formal noon or evening meal or buffet is testimony to the reverence and status that eggs played during the aristologic[1] reign held – if not invented – by the French. Recipes will be used to demonstrate the place eggs played in defining the evolution and history of *Le Haute Cuisine*.

Eggs have been described as one of the most difficult food items to cook properly. Indeed it is said, although highly disputed, that the 100 pleats in a chef's toque represent 100 ways of cooking eggs, which a chef must demonstrate in order to be confirmed as a Master Chef. The basic chemistry and physics of an egg are rather straightforward and yet it is this very simplicity that can be so daunting to anyone who has ever cooked an egg only to be disappointed with the results. Fortunately the mystique of egg cookery has been studied and clarified if not demystified by a team of scientists and expert cooks who are committed to foolproof cooked-egg technology. And so it is that the American Egg Board has provided as a public service a publication dedicated to the simple task of cooking an egg perfectly: *Eggcyclopedia Unabridged* is available from The American Egg Board, 1460 Renaissance Drive, Park Ridge, Illinois 60068, USA or online at 'http://www.aeb.org'

Five egg recipes of gastronomic distinction
Each of the following recipes will serve 4 persons. The following method for properly hard-cooking eggs may be used whenever any recipe calls for hard-cooked eggs.

Master cooking method for hard-cooking eggs
Hard-cooking or 'hard-boiling' eggs properly is not an easy task. Most home cooks – including my own mother, and even a lot of professional chefs – really do a bad job on eggs. By and large, overcooking is to blame and the results are all too familiar, viz. greenish-blue dry yolks with whites that are tough and rubbery, and an overall characteristic sulfureous odor leading to indigestion as well. No wonder so many Americans eschew hard-boiled eggs. [Sorry Mom !] The following instructions will produce hard-cooked eggs which are truly delicious to eat. They will smell and taste

like eggs, not dog farts. The whites will be tender, clean tasting, and the yolk will be attractively yellow, moist and unctuous.

1. Place the fresh whole 'extra large' chicken eggs in a single layer into an accommodating sauce pan and cover with cold water exactly one-inch above the tops of the eggs. 2. Place the pan over HIGH heat and bring quickly to a full rolling boil. 3. Immediately remove the pan from the heat and cover it with a lid. 4. Set a timer for 10 minutes.[2] Prepare an ice slurry bath using plenty of ice and just enough cold water to allow the ice to move freely. 5. After the eggs have steeped for 10 minutes,[2] remove them quickly from the hot water with a large slotted spoon or a 'spider,' and immediately plunge them into the ice bath. 6. Keep in ice water until ready to peel.

USDA 'Jumbo' = 12 minutes; USDA 'Extra Large' = 10 minutes; USDA 'Large' = 8 minutes; USDA 'Medium' = 7 minutes; USDA 'small' (aka 'pullet eggs') = 6 minutes

Helpful hints regarding hard-cooking eggs

If the number of hard-cooked eggs needed is 12, start with 13, and subtract one minute from the steeping time. So for example, when cooking USDA 'extra-large' eggs, set the timer for nine minutes rather than ten. When the timer goes off, quickly remove ONE egg and place it onto a carving board, and deftly cleave it in half, shell and all – Whack!! This will serve as a test to determine whether to remove and plunge the remaining 12 into the ice bath, and immediately stir them about, so that the ice bath shock is quick and complete. If the yolk of the test egg is still runny, allow the remaining 12 to steep in the hot water for another minute, before proceeding with the ice bath shock. Eat the hot test egg with a pinch of salt and some freshly ground black pepper – an epicurean pleasure reserved exclusively for cooks!

Egg recipe number one
Œufs à la Boulangère
(Eggs in the style of the baker's wife)

To serve 4 persons. For the Sauce: 16 hard-cooked eggs (8 for the sauce plus 2 each for 4 persons); 1½ cups chopped onions; ½ lb butter (that's the same as 1 cup); ¾ cup flour; 1 quart whole milk or half & half; 'bouquet garni' – made by placing 3 or 4 sprigs of fresh parsley, 4 whole black peppercorns, one bay leaf and one teaspoon of dried thyme in the middle of a 5-inch square of cheesecloth (may substitute a piece of cloth cut from an old clean linen dish towel): draw the corners of the cloth together and tie ends together with kitchen or butcher's twine, so that none of the spices are able to leak out; 2 teaspoons dried tarragon; ½ cup shredded Swiss or Jarlsberg or Gruyère cheese; 8 hard-cooked eggs chopped into ¾-inch chunks; ½ teaspoon salt; ½ teaspoon ground pepper; a pinch of grated or ground nutmeg. Preheat oven to 425° F. Cut or break the butter into 1-inch cubes and place into a 4-quart enameled pot aluminum ware can make egg and cream sauces turn a funny greenish-grey).

Place the pot over medium heat and as the butter is melting, add the onions. Cook over medium heat until they are soft and translucent. The cooked onions may be slightly golden, but not brown. Add the flour and stir mixture with a wooden spoon. Continue to stir and cook until a haze forms on the bottom of the pot. (This should take about 2–3 minutes.) IMMEDIATELY and quickly pour the milk and/or half & half into the pot – all at once, just dump it in. Add the bouquet garni, and dried tarragon. Stir the mixture with a whisk continuously until it begins to boil and thicken. The consistency should resemble thick tomato juice. Taste carefully and add the salt, pepper, and nutmeg. Taste again and pre-season with additional salt and pepper if necessary. Using two large slotted spoons, remove and discard the bouquet garni. Stir the chopped eggs into the sauce and set aside.

To assemble and complete *Œufs à la Boulangère*:

An oven-proof gratin dish; 8 whole hard-cooked eggs with the shells removed; about 1 quart of the sauce above; ¼ cup shredded Swiss, or Jarlsberg or Gruyère cheese. Trim the bottoms of 6 hard-cooked eggs so they are able to stand upright. Stand eggs into the gratin dish. Ladle the sauce over the eggs, and sprinkle the shredded cheese over the top. Place gratin dish into the preheated oven and cook for about 20 minutes – until bubbly hot and golden brown. Accompany *œufs à la boulangère* with toast-points for breakfast, brunch, and lunch, or serve for dinner as an hors d'œuvre.

Egg recipe number two
Pickled Eggs
(Pennsylvania Dutch Style)

Hard-cooked eggs in a vinegar pickle have been a standard method of food preservation by many cultures for many years. Particularly noticeable in Great Britain, jars full are found next to the cash register in most all pubs and taverns. These sour eggs are traditionally and enthusiastically gobbled-up by Englishmen while quaffing pints of various frothy brews. The Pennsylvania Germans ('Dutch') are famous for a pickled egg recipe which uses the liquid from cooked beets. This produces a ruby red and deliciously spicy product. At Deux Cheminées, we red-pickle small pullet eggs, which are then quartered and presented as a bright and tasty garnish for a variety of composed salads. Customers always enjoy this sometimes forgotten local treat. Two dozen peeled hard-cooked hens' eggs; 14.5 oz can of sliced beets (Del Monte® brand preferred); 2 cups white wine vinegar (Japanese rice wine or Champagne vinegar recommended); 1½ cups water; 2 three-inch sticks of cinnamon; 4 or 5 whole cloves; 3 bay leaves – preferably fresh; 1 tablespoon whole black peppercorns; 1 teaspoon salt (optional); 1 teaspoon sugar (optional); 4 or 5 raw onion rings. Place all the remaining ingredients into a large non-corrosive bowl or jar and mix well. TASTE and adjust seasonings. Carefully peel the hard-cooked eggs and place them into the brine. Refrigerate 24 hours or longer. (Eggs will keep up to three weeks.)

Egg recipe number three
Pickled Eggs
(English Pub Style)

8 peeled hard-cooked hens' eggs; 2 or more cups cider vinegar; 2 tablespoons whole black peppercorns; 2 tablespoons whole allspice berries; 1 two-inch piece of fresh ginger-root, crushed; 3 or 4 fresh bay leaves; 1 or 2 fresh or dried Thai bird-chillies (optional). In a saucepan simmer the vinegar and spices together for 5 minutes. Place the eggs in an accommodating glass jar, cover with the hot vinegar and spices. Refrigerate and serve with cold meats or cold poultry or game along with beer.

Egg recipe number four
Les Oeufs durs Jeannette
(An interesting and delicious recipe for hens eggs by Jacques Pépin)

'Eggs Jeannette' was the name given to this recipe by Chef Jacques Pépin in honor of his mother who apparently invented it. Always a favorite of the Pépin family, I too find it a wonderful addition to the repertoire of egg recipes which Americans too often relegate only to the breakfast table. Serve this dish as a first-course appetizer for dinner, or as a main course for lunch or a late supper, and imagine Madam Jeannette Pépin is sitting next to you. Thanks to Jacques for reminding us of the goodness and rightful place eggs deserve to have on our menus. Yield: plan on two eggs per serving and adjust the recipe accordingly. I find that preparing a few extra un-stuffed eggs ensures enough yolks to make the necessary amount of dressing.

For stuffing the eggs: 8 peeled hard-cooked eggs; 1 teaspoon chopped fresh garlic; 2 teaspoons freshly chopped 'Italian' flat leaf parsley; 2 or 3 tablespoons of milk; (season by titration with) salt and freshly ground or cracked black pepper; ¼ cup vegetable oil for frying.[3] *For the dressing:* 2 or 3 tablespoons of leftover egg stuffing; 4 tablespoons extra virgin olive oil; 1 tablespoon Dijon-style mustard; 1 or 2 tablespoons milk or cream; salt and freshly ground black pepper.

Procedure: hard-cook and peel the eggs according to directions and carefully split each in half lengthwise with a small sharp knife. Remove the yolks and place them into a small bowl along with the garlic, parsley, milk, salt and pepper. Using the back of a table-fork, smash the yolks and mix into a coarse paste. Spoon the stuffing back into the hollows of the egg whites. Be sure to reserve enough of the stuffing to make the dressing. Heat the vegetable oil in a well seasoned or non-stick skillet and place the eggs stuffed side down. Cook over medium heat until the eggs are 'beautifully browned' on the stuffed side. In the meanwhile, prepare the dressing by placing all the ingredients in a small bowl and whisking or forking until combined well. Remove and arrange the browned egg halves – stuffed side up – on a warm serving plate. Spoon or spread each egg with the dressing and serve lukewarm with crusty bread.

Cackleberries and Henfruit: a French Perspective

Egg recipe number five
Quiche Lorraine
(Savory Cheese & Custard Tart)

This recipe was given to me by the late Chef Louis Szathmáry and, when followed exactly, produces the very best (perhaps arguably 'the most authentic') rendition of *Quiche Lorraine* to be found. The 'secrets' of this recipe are:

#1. The nutmeg seasoning,
#2. The burned butter (as a seasoning),
#3. The addition of flour to the custard,
#4. The sieving of the custard,
#5. The pouring of the custard over the cheese,
#6. The baking of the *quiche* at two temperatures.

Pastry crust q.s. for two 9-inch tart pans or one 'half-bun' pan; ¼ cup butter, ¾ pound shredded cheese (use Swiss, Gruyère, Cheddar, Jarlsberg, or any combo.), 2 tablespoons grated Parmesan cheese, 5 tablespoons flour (for three separate procedures), a sprinkling of freshly grated nutmeg, 8 'large' eggs, 1 teaspoon salt, 4 cups half & half, 1 cup garnish (ham, sautéed mushrooms, smothered onions, crisp bacon, blanched asparagus tips, etc.). Roll out the dough and line the tart or bun pan(s). Prick the bottom all over with a fork. Preheat oven to 325°F. Cook the butter in a small sauce pot until it is dark brown and smells like toasted hazelnuts. Set aside and allow to cool. Line the tart shell(s) with aluminum foil and fill with rice. Bake for about 10 minutes, just to 'set' the dough. Remove rice and aluminum foil. Allow to cool completely. Toss and mix the cheeses, nutmeg, and one tablespoonful of the flour. Spread the mixture evenly over the pastry-lined pan(s). Beat the eggs with the salt and one tablespoonful of flour. Add and beat in the half & half and three more tablespoons of flour. (This is an important step.) Strain the custard mixture through a fine sieve (chinois for bouillon) into another bowl. Vigorously, whisk in the cooled 'burned' butter. It is important to thoroughly incorporate the butter into the custard mixture. Pour the custard over the cheese. Bake 10 minutes at 375°F. Lower the temperature to 325°F and bake an additional 15–20 minutes, until puffed and light brown on top. (Use the 'Clean Knife Test' to be sure the custard is done.) Serve warm, not hot, or at room temperature.

Bibliography

American Egg Board, *Eggcyclopedia Unabridged* (Park Ridge, Ill. American Egg Board 1999).

Barber, Richard, *Cooking and Recipes from Rome to the Renaissance* (London: Allen Lane – Penguin Books 1973).

Boulestin, Marcel and Adair, A. H., *120 Ways of Cooking Eggs* (London: William Heinemann, Ltd. 1932).

Brothwell, Don and Patricia, *Food In Antiquity. A Survey of the Diet of Early Peoples* (Baltimore and London: The Johns Hopkins Press 1969).

Customer Service Smart Inventions, *Eggstractor Eggstruction & Recipe Booklet* (n.p., n.d.).

Field, Michael, *The Michael Field Egg Cookbook*, ed. Joan Scobey (New York: Holt, Rinehart and Winston, 1981).

Filippini, Alexander, *One Hundred Ways of Cooking Eggs* (New York and Boston: H. M. Caldwell Company 1892).

Hirtzler, Victor, *The Hotel St. Francis Cook Book* (Chicago: The Hotel Monthly Press 1919).

Langstreth-Christensen, Lillian, *Gourmet's Old Vienna Cookbook* (New York: Gourmet Distributing Corp. 1959).

Marshall, Mel, *The Delectable Egg* (New York: Trident Press 1968).

Montagné, Prosper, *Larousse Gastronomique* (New York: Crown Publishers, Inc. 1961).

Nietlispach, Madam F., *Vegetable and Fruit Dishes, the healthy diet, rich in vitamins*, translated and adapted by M. F. Daniels (London: John Hamilton, Ltd.).

Paston-Williams, Sara, *The Art of Dining, A History of Cooking and Eating* (London: National Enterprises Ltd. 1993).

Ranhofer, Charles, *The Epicurean* (Chicago: The Hotel Monthly Press 1920).

Roux, Michel, *Eggs* (London: Quadrille Publishing Ltd. 2005)

Saint-Ange, Mme E., *Le Livre de Cuisine* (Paris: Librairie Larousse 1927).

Seran, Ann, *The Art of Egg Cookery* (Garden City NY: Doubleday & Company, Inc. 1949).

Southern Foodways Alliance, *Oral History Deviled Eggs* (Oxford, Mississippi: Southern Foodways Alliance 2003).

Visser, Margaret, *The Rituals of Dinner. The Origins, Evolution, Eccentricities, and Meaning of Table Manners* (Toronto, Canada: HarperCollins, 1991).

Wallace, Lily Haxworth, *Egg Cookery. A Complete Handbook of Tested Recipes for Breakfast, Luncheon, and Dinner* (New York: M. Barrows and Company 1945).

Notes

1. Aristology: the art and/or science of dining (*Oxford English Dictionary*).
2. Note well: the size of the eggs will determine the steeping time.
3. Jacques uses vegetable oil, but substituting bacon drippings adds a certain rustic fillip.

On *Spaghetti alla Carbonara* and Related Dishes of Central and Southern Italy

Anthony F. Buccini

1 Introduction[1]

There is a great deal of popular interest in the origins of famous dishes, who invented them and how and when and where they were invented, and among the famous dishes of Italy, few have been more of an object of speculation and debate than *spaghetti alla carbonara*, the combination of pasta with cured pork and eggs and cheese which is so closely associated with Rome. Though several theories have been advanced concerning the dish's origin, none of these pass beyond the anecdotal or considers the cultural context in which it appears. The goal of this paper is to examine carefully the origins of this dish in terms of the broader socio-economic and aesthetic contexts in which it arose; from this perspective, it can be seen that *spaghetti alla carbonara* is but one member of a family of closely related preparations originating in the Central and Southern Italian highlands.

2 Recipes for *Spaghetti alla Carbonara* and theories concerning its origins

Before attempting to consider the origins of *spaghetti alla carbonara* from our own perspective, it will be necessary to examine parameters of variation in the recipe itself, as well as the several theories of its creation that have been proposed.

2.1 *Parameters of Variation in the Recipe.* While it is not surprising that a very popular and presumably 'traditional' dish would appear in many variants, the degree of variation seen in recipes for *spaghetti alla carbonara* seems surprising in light of the simplicity of the basic idea. As mentioned above, it is a dressing for pasta that includes a cured pork product, beaten eggs, grated cheese and, in addition, ground black pepper, but most of the ubiquitous elements are subject to significant variation, including the form of the pasta, and there are, moreover, some other ingredients that some cooks feel the need to include. Our observations are drawn from a very broad survey of recipes for the dish in Italian and English language print and internet sources.[2]

• *Pasta.* The most common form of pasta used here is spaghetti. Non-Italian sources generally follow the Italian mainstream in this regard but outside of Italian kitchens sensibilities concerning appropriate combinations of sauce or condiment types and different shapes are more relaxed and occasionally wholly lacking. There is, however, a minority of Italian cooks who prescribe the use of *maccheroni* (tubular pasta) with the *alla carbonara* preparation, notably at the *Trattoria La Carbonara* in Rome; they use *penne*.

- *Pork.* *Pancetta*, cured pork belly, is probably the most commonly recommended form of pork in recipes, though many Italian writers and increasingly many English-language authors recommend one use *guanciale*, that is, cured pork jowl, if at all possible. Not surprisingly, English-language authors often recommend bacon as a substitute, which introduces a further and fairly assertive smoky flavour to the dish. It must, however, be noted that some Italian internet writers call for the use of *pancetta affumicata*, that is, smoked *pancetta*.
- *Cheese.* There are two hard grating cheeses that appear in recipes for *spaghetti alla carbonara*, namely, *pecorino*, the traditional sheep's milk cheese of Central and Southern Italy, and *parmigiano reggiano*, the famous cow's milk cheese from around Parma and Reggio Emilia. Many recipes, especially ones from Italy, call for just *pecorino* but a great many also call for just *parmigiano* and yet others call for a mixture of the two.
- *Eggs.* Of course, all recipes assume the use of chicken eggs here but variation between recipes does occur with regard to two points.

First, there is some noteworthy variation in the relative amount of egg included per person. Italian recipes generally call for either 2 eggs per 300 grams of pasta (to serve three people) or 3 eggs per 400 grams of pasta (to serve four people). Some call for a relatively smaller presence of egg – for example, the version in the translation of the so-called 'bible of Italian cooking', *The Silver Spoon* (2005: 300), includes but two eggs for four people and so too David (1977: 102) – but one also comes across recipes with a reinforcement of the egg element – Downie (2002: 98–9) uses three whole eggs for four persons plus the yolk of a fourth.[3]

Second, the treatment of the eggs in the preparation differs across recipes, though it seems generally, if not quite universally stated, that the result is intended always to be roughly this: that the eggs are to yield through gentle cooking a creamy sauce and not the curd-like texture of scrambled eggs. In essence, there are two approaches. The one demands that the beaten eggs be mixed together with the just drained and still hot pasta away from any direct source of heat, in the serving bowl for example, with the residual heat of the pasta and also that of the pork and its fat being intended to cook the eggs sufficiently to form a creamy sauce and no more; this approach seems to be increasingly popular over what seems to me to be an older approach. That older approach typically involves the joining of the drained pasta, beaten eggs and the pork and fat together in the pot used for boiling the pasta and stirring the mixture vigorously over low heat.

- *Black Pepper.* Perhaps the only ingredient of *alla carbonara* preparations which has engendered no controversy or debate is the black pepper: by universal agreement, the dish must contain this spice, freshly ground and in substantial measure.
- *Cooking fat.* The majority of recipes for the dish call for the use of a small amount of olive oil to be used in the pan in which the diced pork is then gently fried. Occasionally, butter is the recommended fat, as in, for example, *The Silver Spoon*

(2005: 300) and David (1977: 102). Others recommend the use of lard, which in my opinion was surely commonly used here in the past: Santolini's very traditionally oriented book on Roman cookery (1976b: 98–101) calls for either olive oil or lard in the recipes for both *carbonara* and *bucatini alla matriciana*, while Boni, in her book *La cucina romana*, calls only for lard in the pasta recipes that involve initial frying of cubed *guanciale*.[4]

The ingredients just discussed form the core elements of *spaghetti alla carbonara* and, it seems clear that to the sensibilities of Roman cooks, further additions to the dish are felt to be non-canonical, wrong and even offensive.[5] Nevertheless, there are three ingredients which are increasingly popular additions.

- *Cream.* The addition of cream to *carbonara* preparations is encountered very frequently in recipes written outside of Italy but one also encounters its inclusion in recipes on Italian cooking and chat sites.[6]

- *Garlic.* As with cream, garlic seems to be more often included in recipes for *carbonara* written outside of Italy; in the case of the United States, the inclusion of garlic here goes along with a widespread misconception about the use of garlic in Italian cookery and a relatively new-found and general love thereof. To some American palates, *carbonara* preparations are improved through a massive addition of garlic and recipes can be found in which two, three or even four whole cloves are included in minced form.[7] Inclusion of garlic by non-Roman Italian authors is not uncommon but then its use is virtually always limited to the flavouring of the oil in which the cured pork will be fried with one clove of garlic which is then discarded (see, for example, Piras & Medagliani 2000: 303 and *The Silver Spoon* 2005: 300).

- *White wine.* Some cooks include a touch of white wine in the recipe, added to the pan in which the pork has been fried.

2.2 *Theories of its origin.* As mentioned above, several theories have been advanced to account for the origin of the *carbonara* preparation, though to this writer's knowledge no detailed treatment of the subject has been made. The theories can be classified in two groups: a) those that take the name '*carbonara*' as the crucial starting point for the explanation; b) those that do not assign the name '*carbonara*' any special place in their account.

The basic meaning of the phrase *alla carbonara* is 'in the style of the charcoal burners' or "wood colliers".'[8] Briefly, the outstanding characteristics of the wood colliers' occupation were that they worked in the forests, especially in mountainous areas, and that they would spend extended periods of time in small groups away from any towns or villages. Their work consisted essentially of cutting wood, carefully building a large wood pile (in some dialects called a *carbonara*, standard *carbonaia*), monitoring vigilantly the slow burning of the pile which produces the charcoal, and finally dismantling the remnants of the pile and recovering the charcoal and then transporting it out of the forest for sale. The work thus involved an enormous amount of hard labour and difficult living conditions for most of the year, but also a fairly high level of skill.

On *Spaghetti alla Carbonara*

Curiosity about the history of *carbonara* has led people to imagine a number of possible connexions between it and the *carbonai*, the wood colliers. Perhaps the most widespread theory is that the connexion is direct: the dish was one invented and regularly consumed by wood colliers and it was introduced to Rome in the course of their visits selling charcoal to the urban population. A variant on this basic theory is that the dish was one popular with the *carbonai* but that its popularisation in Rome was a result of a family of charcoal burners moving to the city and opening a *trattoria*, where they naturally offered their beloved dish to an appreciative Roman clientele. This story has been linked specifically to the famous, old restaurant now on the Campo de' Fiori mentioned above, namely, *La Carbonara*, which first opened in 1912. Finally, a third theory that is regularly noted in preambles to *carbonara* recipes but then often given along with expressions of doubt regarding its plausibility is what one might term the poetic theory. The reasoning here is that the dish may or may not have had some actual link to the charcoal makers and sellers but the name was given to the dish on account of the very liberal use of black pepper as its finishing touch: the many black flecks of pepper allegedly evoked the coal dust on the clothes of a *carbonaio* and so, perhaps, the name for the dish was born.

Also taking the name *alla carbonara* as the starting point is another theory, which suggests not a connexion to the people in the charcoal making business but rather to the members of the political society named after the wood colliers, namely, the *Carbonari*. Like the Free Masons, that society, the *Carbonaria*, had its own arcane initiation rites and other ceremonies, secret symbols and a sort of secret code language as well. The political leanings of the group were liberal and patriotic and from 1815 to the 1830s it represented an important source of resistance to the foreign-based, conservative governments that ruled the various parts of Italy. Though there were *Carbonari* through much of Italy, they were most numerous and influential in the South – in the Bourbon Kingdom of the Two Sicilies – and in the Papal States of Central Italy. To my knowledge, any obvious or strong tie between the society itself and the actual pasta preparation is, however, lacking, despite at least one claim that links the dish to the society through an old restaurant where meetings were allegedly held.[9]

The main theory which does not hinge upon the actual name of the dish proposes that *spaghetti alla carbonara* is, in fact, a rather recent creation and more specifically one that dates back only to the last years of the Second World War. According to this view, the crucial factor in the dish's invention was the large presence of American servicemen in Rome after it was liberated from German hands in 1944. In effect, the claim is that there was a joining together of American taste for and supplies of bacon and powdered eggs with the local Roman love of *pasta asciutta*; Roman cooks came up with the recipe to make use of the American supplies and to satisfy the foreign troops, perhaps with some prodding from those troops who missed their familiar bacon and egg combination.

This theory of the American GIs' rôle in the creation of *spaghetti alla carbonara* is very widely cited in both cookbooks and on internet websites and has, in fact, gained the support of some very distinguished persons. Downie (2000: 96) indicates that Livio Jannattoni, a respected Roman journalist and author of an extensive book on the cookery of Rome and Lazio, subscribed to this view,[10] and Davidson advances this view in the entry on spaghetti in the *Penguin Companion to Food* (2002: 888): 'It has been suggested that this is a traditional dish of the *carbonari*, or charcoal burners, but that is implausible. A more credible explanation is that it was invented in 1944 as a result of the American occupation troops having their lavish rations of eggs and bacon prepared by local cooks. The name would then be from a Roman restaurant, the "Carbonara", which makes a specialty of the dish.'

It should be noted here that Davidson's version of the GI theory goes a step further than the vast majority of versions that one encounters in that he adds the important step of suggesting a way to account for the name of the dish, which this theory otherwise does not do on its own.

One last theory, found on a number of Italian based internet sites, must be added here, namely that *spaghetti alla carbonara* can be traced back to a Neapolitan dish and perhaps specifically to Ippolito Cavalcanti, who includes a recipe in his cookbook of 1839 that is said to resemble the modern Roman dish but is never actually cited by the web-page authors.[11] We shall return to Cavalcanti further on.

3 *Spaghetti alla Carbonara* in its culinary aesthetic context

The cuisine of the city of Rome is widely regarded as featuring a strong preference for the simple and the rustic. Romans are also known as being particularly fond of simple pasta dishes that are also quick to make. *Spaghetti alla carbonara*, as one of the most popular and typical Roman *primi piatti* reflects well the aesthetics of the cuisine: simple, quickly executed, and in the eyes of many decidedly rustic.[12] Indeed, for the many who subscribe to the theory that *carbonara* is in a direct sense linked to the *carbonai*, the charcoal burners, who spent the better part of each year living in the mountain forests and generally well removed from mainstream society, the rusticity of the dish is self-evident.

3.1 *A Family of Dishes*. In my opinion, it is precisely the 'rustic' character of this dish that is the key to understanding its history and place in the culinary landscape and, indeed, to appreciate its rusticity one cannot regard *carbonara* in isolation but instead one must view it as but one member of a family of aesthetically and historically related preparations. The core members of this family are four dishes which share not only status as traditional and popular Roman *primi* but also can be seen as variations on a basic theme. These dishes are:[13]

• *spaghetti alla gricia*: this dish is typically made with a 'sauce' of just diced *guanciale* or *pancetta* gently fried in either lard or olive oil along with hot dried chile pepper – *pepperoncino* – and, optionally, chopped onion; it is finished with grated

pecorino and ground black pepper.
- *bucatini alla matriciana*: commonly with the thicker and perforated *bucatini* rather than spaghetti, the cooked condiment for this dish is precisely the same as that of the *alla gricia* preparation with the exception that in this case tomatoes and, optionally, a touch of white wine are added. This dish is also finished with grated *pecorino* and black pepper.
- *spaghetti alla carbonara*: as discussed at length above, the condiment consists of the cured pork (*guanciale* or *pancetta*) cooked in lard or oil and egg beaten together with grated cheese, most often *pecorino*. And again, the dish is finished with more grated *pecorino* and black pepper.
- *spaghetti alla carrettiera*: a wide array of preparations for pasta share this name, including some from distant parts of Italy but in a Roman or Latian setting this name most often denotes spaghetti with a condiment made with a *soffritto* of *guanciale*, *pancetta* or *lardo*, garlic and olive oil, with *porcini* mushrooms and tuna preserved in oil; recipes seem to be divided roughly equally between those that contain also tomato and those that do not. Some people finish the dish with grated cheese.

As can be seen, these are in essence one basic dish with different secondary – though certainly prominent – ingredients featured in each version: as many have observed, *alla gricia* is *alla matriciana* minus the tomatoes, but then *alla carbonara* is in essence *alla matriciana* but with the beaten egg-cheese mixture taking the place of the tomatoes and *pepperoncino*. *Alla carrettiera* can be viewed in either of two ways: in the white version, it resembles *alla carbonara* but with mushrooms and tuna in place of the egg-cheese mixture, while in its red version, one could think of it as a variation on *alla matriciana* in which the mushrooms and tuna fill the slot left by the absent hot chile pepper.

Another noteworthy feature of this group of dishes is its use or non-use of two aromatic staples of the Italian kitchen, namely, onions and garlic. Onion seems to be a possible element in *alla gricia* and, not surprisingly then, also *alla matriciana*, but many traditionally minded cooks do not include it. The *alla carbonara* condiment seems clearly to include neither garlic nor onion, though the occasional use of onion is not surprising, given the relation of this dish to the *alla gricia* / *alla matriciana* pair; use of garlic in some versions of all three dishes looks to be an innovation to the recipes as they have gradually been adopted more broadly by those who have no attachment to the Central Italian tradition. Only in *alla carrettiera* does an aromatic, namely, garlic, seem to be obligatory.

In addition to the traditional ambivalence toward onion and garlic in this group of dishes, there is a complete absence of any herb, including the almost ubiquitous ingredient of Italian cooking, parsley. In point of fact fresh ingredients are – with two exceptions to be discussed below – not required here, making these four dishes which can be made wholly from the larder, with no need for short term access either to any shop or a vegetable garden. Of course, fresh tomatoes can be and are used in *alla matriciana* and *alla carrettiera*, but canned or bottled tomatoes are appropriate and in no way to be considered an unhappy substitute for fresh. In the case of the *porcini* mushrooms in *spaghetti alla carrettiera*, many recipes call for the fresh item, though others allow for use of the larder-friendly dried item. But we should call attention to the fact that fresh *porcini* mushrooms in Central Italy can be and regularly are picked by individuals in the forests where they grow, rather than bought in stores. The one remaining fresh item to be considered is the eggs for *carbonara* which are fairly perishable, as well as fragile, but these two problems are easily resolved for him who has an egg-laying chicken or two near at hand.

There are two conclusions to be drawn from the nature of the ingredients of these four dishes: 1) they are either items to be found in the larder or else relatively easily obtained, including by people living away from any towns and markets and in a forest; 2) they are, given the possibility of substituting dried for fresh mushrooms, almost completely free of any ties to the seasons. And one further unifying characteristic of this family of dishes is that each of them combines substantial portions of starch, fat and protein and thus can serve as a one-plate meal, as a *piatto unico*. Whether they originated amongst charcoal burners and other denizens of the forests or not, these four hearty dishes are certainly at home among hard-working mountain people.

3.2 *A Family of Names*. Just as the four dishes under consideration here display striking resemblances in their composition, so too are their names linked together semantically.

As already observed, the name of *spaghetti alla carbonara* evokes the charcoal burners of the region. One of the other names in the group, *alla carrettiera*, similarly evokes the men of a humble occupation, namely that of the wagon-driver. Though many wagon-drivers in Rome and the surrounding territory may well never have been involved in work that took them to the highland forests, it is worth noting that many wagon-drivers were so occupied, hauling wood, charcoal and other forest products to centres of population, and as a consequence, *carrettieri* were often in contact with other woodsmen, such as the *boscaioli* ('woodcutters') and *carbonai*, and were associated with them in the minds of city and town-dwellers.

Contrasting with these two names is that of *bucatini alla matriciana*; *alla matriciana* is Roman dialect and is undoubtedly the result of misparsing of the phrase *all'Amatriciana*, which is to say, in the style of Amatrice, a town of Rieti province in mountainous north-eastern Lazio, near the border of Abruzzo and Le Marche. Incidentally, Amatrice is famous for its pork products, especially its *mortadella*, and it also lies amidst areas where the *carbonai* did their work, up in the Apennine forests. Thus, though the *alla matriciana* name is of a geographical nature and stands out over against the two occupational names of *alla carbonara* and *alla carrettiera*, there is an obvious relationship between the three.

The fourth name, *alla gricia*, presents a more complicated situation. There are two frequently cited explanations of this name (e.g. Downie 2000: 84): 1) that it is, like the name *alla matriciana,* a geographical reference, specifically, in the style of the town of Grisciano, which lies in fact just a little bit to the north-east of Amatrice; 2) that the adjective is just the Roman dialect pronunciation of the word 'grey', Standard Italian *grigio,* Romanesco *gricio,* with the name of the dish being then 'spaghetti made the grey way', in reference to the alleged colour of the preparation. A third possibility should, however, also be considered, namely that the reference is to another humble occupation, that of the *gricio,* a Roman dialect word for a vendor of basic household goods, such as pasta, flour, bread, oil, soap, also known as an *orzarolo.*[14] An important but hitherto neglected fact can help to clarify the situation. Writing in the 1920s, Boni (1983: 46) doesn't use the name *alla gricia* for this recipe nor the more prosaic *spaghetti al guanciale* that one sees on occasion but rather the name *spaghetti alla marchiciana,* that is, 'in the style of Le Marche'. Given that the town of Grisciano lies practically on the border of Lazio and Le Marche, it seems reasonable to conclude that the recipe genuinely was associated with the area around that border zone and that the term *alla gricia* is a reinterpretation of an older (and perhaps excessively obscure) *alla grisciana,* in other words, that the name was probable adapted to fit the existing pattern of occupational names that included two of the dishes in the family, *alla carbonara* and *alla carrettiera.* In the case of *alla matriciana,* the reference to a larger and better known town presumably assured that no renaming would occur. Thus, while the occupational sense of *alla gricia* seems to be at odds with the mountain-forest associations of the other three names, it can be seen that *spaghetti al guanciale* once also bore names closely tied to the others, namely the attested *alla marchiciana* and the presumed *alla grisciana.*[15]

4 Origins of Spaghetti alla Carbonara reconsidered

We have demonstrated that in examining the origins of *spaghetti alla carbonara* one must consider the whole family of pasta dishes to which it belongs. We've also shown that this family of dishes has had in the minds of Romans strong connexions, real or imagined, with forested areas well outside of Rome and occupations associated with the forests. In light of this, it seems that the theory of the crucial rôle of American GIs in the invention and/or popularisation of the dish loses much force. Indeed, though the theory has had some distinguished supporters, it has little in the way of compelling evidence and seems rather to be motivated by two questionable assumptions.

Perhaps the primary motivation for the GI theory is that *spaghetti alla carbonara* is apparently not described or mentioned by name in any sources from before the Second World War; even in Boni's book on Roman cooking from the 1920s no such dish appears. Two factors strongly mitigate the weight of this argument. First, there is the matter of the nature and volume of descriptions of popular – and especially rustic – cookery which are preserved from the first part of the twentieth century and before. There is no question but that our knowledge in this regard is limited and full of holes. Second, there needs to be a distinction made between the invention of a dish and the invention of a particular name for a dish. We've seen that in the case of *spaghetti alla gricia* the current popular name, referring to an occupation, seems to have been preceded by the older prosaic name and ones referring to geographical points. Might it be the case that all three of the names of our family of dishes with occupational references owe those names to a fashion in renaming dishes that arose some time in the mid-twentieth century? If so, casual references to *pasta alla carbonara* or *gricia* or *carrettiera* cannot be expected to turn up in older sources. Anecdotal evidence offered by Downie (2000: 96–7) suggests that both of these claims are right: older native Romans he cites recall *carbonara* from before the Second World War though not under that name: lack of textual references to *carbonara* before the war don't prove the dish didn't exist.

A second reason that many people, including students of culinary history, have perhaps embraced the GI theory and found the connexion to the *carbonai* dubious or implausible is that the pork and egg combination of *carbonara* seems more akin to the bacon and egg pairing of the Anglo-Saxon world and quite far from what one usually thinks of as characteristic for Central and Southern Italian fare. Food writers are well aware of the concept of *cucina povera* and many dishes associated with it but there are different levels of poverty in the kitchen. What is most often discussed these days of poor recipes are ones that appeal to people today, dishes based on vegetables and olive oil and fish. But until the mid-twentieth century, many poor Italians, especially those living in the mountainous areas away from the coast, ate little fish and olive oil and for them pasta was reserved for special occasions. Polenta, corn bread and potatoes were the main staples, boosted in flavour and nutritional value with pork or pork fat, cheese and eggs.

From this perspective, the modern *spaghetti alla carbonara* seems like a rich and festive dish, even in its more austere traditional versions, which eschew such additions as butter and cream and, for that matter, the 'foreign' *parmigiana* that many use in place of the traditional local *pecorino*. But the dish is clearly just a variant of or close analogue to a dish that is and long has been enjoyed widely in Central and Southern Italy, namely, pasta *cacio e uova,* that is, pasta dressed with melted lard and mixed with a combination of beaten eggs and grated cheese. This dish appears regularly in Neapolitan cookbooks and is, in fact, the dish in Cavalcanti's Neapolitan cookbook of 1839 occasionally referred to in connexion with the origins of *carbonara*.[16] Interestingly, Downie (2000: 96) indicates that one of the names older Romans associate with *alla carbonara* from before the War is *cacio e uova*.

If *alla carbonara* is then just a new name for the old *cacio e uova*, a direct link between the dish and the *carbonai* may not have existed and, as in the case of the apparently renamed *spaghetti al guanciale,* the occupational name may be more poetic than socio-historical in nature. Further exploration of the nature of this link had, due to space restrictions, to be reserved for my presentation at the Symposium, where I discussed the evidence for the cuisine of poor Italians living in mountainous areas in times past and in particular the evidence for the lifestyle and diet of the *carbonai.*

On *Spaghetti alla Carbonara*

References.
Boni, Ada, *La cucina romana* (Roma: Newton & Compton, 1983).
Callen, Anna Teresa, *The Pastoral Land: food and memories of Abruzzo* (New York: Macmillan, 1998).
Cavalcanti, Ippolito, *Cucina teorico-pratica* (Naples, 1839).
Chiappini, Filippo, *Vocabolario romanesco* (Roma: Case Editrice 'Leonardo Da Vinci', 1945).
David, Elizabeth, *Italian Food* (Harmondsworth: Penguin, 1965).
Davidson, Alan, *The Penguin Companion to Food* (New York, London: Penguin, 2002).
Downie, David, *Cooking the Roman Way* (New York: HarperCollins, 2002).
Manuelli, Sarah, *Cucina romana* (Northampton, MA: Interlink, 2005).
Martini, Anna, *The Mondadori Regional Italian Cookbook* (Milan: Mondadori, 1983) [trans. of Italian original, *Vecchia e nuova cucina regionale italiana*].
Piras, Claudia, & Eugenio Medagliani (eds.), *Culinaria Italy: Pasta, pesto, passion* (Cologne: Könemann, 2000) [trans. of German original, *Culinaria Italia*].
Root, Waverley, *The Best of Italian Cooking* (New York: Grosset & Dunlap, 1974).
Rutigliano, Renato (ed.), *Favurite! Ricette di cucina napoletana* (Naples: Marotta, 1993).
Santolini, Antonella, *Napoli in bocca* (Palermo: Edikronos, 1976a).
——, *Roma in bocca* (Palermo: Edikronos, 1976b).
Schwartz, Arthur, *Naples at Table* (New York: HarperCollins, 1998).
The Silver Spoon (New York: Phaidon, 2005) [trans. & adaptation of Italian original, *Il cucchiaio d'argento*].

Notes
1. Many thanks are due to Amy Dahlstrom and Ernest Buccini Jr. for their help with various aspects of the preparation of this paper.
2. The printed sources will be cited as appropriate in the text below with bibliographical references given at the end of the paper. Internet sources have been for the most part used not as research resources for specific issues but rather to get a rough sense of what common opinion is among people interested in this particular dish. Internet searches were conducted using the Google search engine with key word combinations such as «spaghetti carbonara recipes», «spaghetti carbonara ricette», «carbonara guanciale», etc. In instances where a specific web page needs to be cited herebelow, appropriate documentation is provided.
3. It should be noted, however, that reduced amounts of egg in many recipes is paired with the addition of heavy cream to the dish, as in Callen's version in her Abruzzese cookbook with 3 eggs for six servings (1.5 lbs. of pasta) but (optionally) a half cup of cream (1998: 114–5). In the case of the *Silver Spoon* recipe (p 300), the relatively small amount of egg seems to be compensated with relatively generous quantities of other fatty elements, namely butter, pancetta and a mixture of the two grated cheeses. Martini's (1983:132–3) version is noteworthy for its comparatively heavy use of egg – 4 eggs for 350 grams of pasta – which is further supplemented with a touch of cream (2 tablespoons).
4. Note that Boni does not include a recipe for *spaghetti alla carbonara* in this book. There are, however, recipes for two other dishes – dishes which are in this writer's opinion to be viewed as direct relatives of the *carbonara* preparation – for which she indicates the use of lard, namely *spaghetti alla «matriciana»* and *spaghetti alla «marchiciana»* (1983: 45–6).
5. Downie (2002: 96–8) offers a brief and amusing account of the controversies surrounding the dish and the passions that they sometimes enflame. His own recipe (pp. 98–9) for the dish sticks to the core ingredients as indicated here, as do the recipes of other authors who are either natives of Rome or clearly students of the city's culinary traditions, e.g. Santolini (1976b: 100–1), Manuelli (2005: 16).
6. Callen's (1998: 114–5) recipe which calls optionally for cream has been mentioned above. An especially rich version can be seen in Root (1974: 54), where in addition to four eggs there are also

included 6 tablespoons of cream and both butter and oil.
7. Three cloves are suggested in the recipe that was apparently shown on the PBS show (2001 season) *America's Test Kitchen* in the United States; the recipe is also published on the related Cook's Illustrated website but it is available for viewing only by subscribers. A recipe which includes four cloves of garlic can be found at the following web-address: http://starchefs.com/chefs/MGiraldi/Minnies_Kitchen/html/recipe_01.shtml.

    The author, Minnie Giraldi, claims to have learned the recipe from Giuliano Bugialli but I find it hard to imagine that any version of *carbonara* suggested by Bugialli, a well-known traditionalist, would have included so much garlic, if any at all.

    Onion is relatively rarely encountered as an ingredient for *spaghetti alla carbonara* but it is worth noting that the recipe which appears in the regional section for Lazio on the Italian website cookaround.com – a section which includes many interesting, traditional recipes – is one in which a finely chopped onion is added in with the *guanciale* as a *soffritto*. The web-address (accessed on 7 May, 2006) is: http://www.cookaround.com/cucina/regionale/lazio/confro-1.php?id_ric=94.
8. The phrase is often incorrectly indicated in English language sources to mean 'in the style of the coal miners' rather than the correct 'wood colliers' or 'charcoal burners'.
9. I have encountered this theory on a few websites as part of the commentary accompanying recipes. The only version I have seen which offers some sort of detailed account for the application of the society's name to the dish is one cited on a website 'Carbonara Club' which was originally published in an Italian magazine. The owners of an old restaurant in a town in the province of Rovigo (between Ferrara and Padova) claim that in the early eighteenth century, Carbonari would regularly hold meetings there and consume the dish; in effect, the story is the basis for the restaurant's claim to be the place where the dish was invented. This story is related at the following web address: http://www.carbonaraclub.it/dintorni.htm.
10. At the time of this writing, I have not yet been able to see any of Jannattoni's writing on cooking, including his *La cucini romana e del Lazio*, a book of very considerable length on the topic.
11. One such website is Cibo360, which offers a brief review of the various theories on the origins of *carbonara* at the following address (last accessed 12 July 2006): http://www.cibo360.it/cucina/mondo/spaghetti_carbonara.htm.

    Cavalcanti is also mentioned as possible inventor of *carbonara* (along with other theories) in an Italian Wikipedia entry for the dish (last accessed, 12 July 2006): http:it.wikipedia.org/wiki/Pasta_alla_carbonara.

    The Swiss BettyBossi site also refers to the Cavalcanti recipe (without citing the recipe itself) in a run-down of the various theories (last accessed 13 July 2006): http://www.bettybossi.ch/de/schwerpunkt/iwb_spkt_reze_20050426170015_arc.asp.
12. Cf., e.g., Boni (1983: 13): 'Nella cucina romana si preferiscono le cose semplici e genuine: tutto quello che rappresenta la complicazione della cucina internazionale viene inesorabilmente bandito. Il romano ha una cordiale antipatia per le vivande troppo elaborate e, severo conservatore, non accoglie che con diffidenza ciò che si distacca dai suoi cibi consueti.'
13. Recipes for *alla gricia* appear in Downie (2000: 84) and Manuelli (2005: 73); Santolini (1976b: 84) and Boni (1983: 46) give virtually the same recipe but not under that name. Recipes for *alla matriciana* are also found in each of these books, as well most books on Italian cuisine. The *alla carrettiera* dish is not included in the aforementioned works but is known to many in Lazio; the recipes I've consulted have all been found on Italian language sites on the internet, e.g.: http://www.lericettedicucina.it/ricetta-scheda.php?idric=222; http://www.amando.it/ricette/paste-asciutte/spaghetti-carrettiera.html; http://digilander.libero.it/macromix/Ricette%20Word/Ricettario%20Cucina%20de'%20Roma.htm.
14. Chiappini (1945: 152–3, 220–1) explains that the term *gricio* 'grey' was applied to these grocers because the majority were (at some point) from the Valtellina, near the Grisons or *Grigioni*. According to him, they were in the Roman popular mind renowned for their avarice.

15. One could imagine that the reinterpretation of *alla grisciana* to *alla gricia* was, however, semantically motivated, either by the alleged avarice of the *orzaroli* (given the simplicity of the dish) or through some other association, based on the nature of the occupation and the foodstuffs the *grici* sold.
16. Cavalcanti (1839: 365): 'li [maccarune] può fa pure co caso e ova sbattute.' For more recent and detailed recipes, see Santolini 1976a: 95, Rutigliano (ed.) 1993: 63 and Schwartz 1998: 137 Rutigliano (p. 34) and Schwartz (p. 139) also include recipes for another related dish, *'o vermicielli 'a puveriello*, which combines lard, garlic, grated cheese and fried eggs.

Poached Eggs at the Revolution

Doug Duda

I did not know at the time that he is generally regarded as the father of the Spanish culinary revolution, and that without his *nueva cocina vasca* in the 1980s there would have been no Ferran Adrià in the 1990s. I only found out afterward that his little town of San Sebastian on the Basque coast has more Michelin stars per capita than Paris, and that the family tavern he transformed into a world-renowned restaurant has three of those coveted stars. But even today, I marvel that Juan Mari Arzak, cited as one of the 10 most influential chefs in the world, would choose to introduce himself by showing me his poached egg.

Elena Arzak Espina, his daughter, working partner and English voice, laughs and lets me in on a secret. 'We like to watch the reaction when people first see the egg.' They know that there is something about the sight of a typical breakfast egg that embodies the mundane, signifies ritual and habit, and deflates heightened customer expectation. For those who come to Arzak expecting exotic preparations and presentations, it borders on a letdown. But of course, this is not a typical poached egg, and Juan Mari and Elena know how this story ends. Almost everyone who tastes the *Flor de Huevo y Tartufo en Grasa de Oca con Txistorra Datiles* for the first time call it a shock, a surprise, a revelation. Many call it the best egg they have ever eaten in their lives.

That's what I thought the first time I tasted the dish, and although I thought of the subversion of expectation as one of the essential elements in the Spanish culinary revolution's credo, I marveled that Arzak had made the point with a poached egg rather than foams, liquefactions, or other more outré effects.

That first day in the kitchen with Juan Mari and Elena, there was a young man in chef's whites sitting at the table, watching all. He later introduced himself as the sous chef at Ferran Adrià's El Bulli, where they put the 'ooh' in outré. 'We are all friends, we all talk about what we do, and it is very open,' Elena explains, 'but we are not Adrià and he is not Arzak.' I began to think of the *Flor de Huevo* as a symbol of Arzak's aesthetic of surprise, and the intimate canvas on which he chooses to express it. If Adrià is the illusionist David Copperfield, making the city of Las Vegas disappear before your eyes, Arzak is a close-up magician, shaking hands with you just long enough to leave you wondering how he'd made off with your cotton shirt and exchanged it for silk.

I know from reading a number of similar accounts over the years that I am not the only one to be introduced to Arzak through his poached egg, that he likes to intrigue food writers by holding up the uncooked egg in its plastic wrap and telling them,

Poached Eggs at the Revolution

'it's simple, I just poach the egg in a bag,' as if a child could have thought of it, the same child that could have drawn any of Picasso's paintings. Without art, I ask Elena repeatedly where the idea came from, and as if picking flowers from a riotous garden, she gives me various answers. These answers have helped confirm for me that the *Flor de Huevo* is more than Arzak's favorite parlor trick, more than an edible Spanish Culinary Revolution for Dummies, and aptly regarded as his signature dish.

First, Elena tells me, ' you know, one of my father's favorite meals is breakfast, very typical eggs and chorizo, as we eat here in San Sebastian. The eggs we have fresh from the farm, the chorizo and the mushrooms, all very traditional.'

If you come to Arzak expecting an emu tortilla, your concept of the revolution he began needs fine-tuning. In 1976, the not-yet-famous Juan Mari Arzak met the very famous Paul Bocuse, spent 10 days visiting him back in Lyon, and returned to enjoin the San Sebastian culinary community to adopt *nouvelle cuisine*'s focus on lighter, fresher, less hidebound and more visual food. Throughout the 1980's, the *nueva cocina vasca* movement he spearheaded appeared to focus on lightness, creativity and visual appeal as Basque food was almost effortlessly faithful to the freshness principle, drawing on San Sebastian's natural riches as a seaport in the middle of farming, cattle and vineyard country. But the *Flor de Huevo* is about more than traditional sourcing. 'I am happy when people talk about tradition, because I know they are talking about authenticity, but in truth, we are not cooking traditionally,' says Elena. 'We are making familiar flavors more intense with modern techniques, and that is quite different.'

The taste of a farm-fresh poached egg is traditional, but the taste of the vinegar added to the water to accelerate coagulation is not traditional, distracts, and dilutes the intensity of the egg flavor. Hence, the idea of poaching in plastic film. 'It is hard to know where creativity comes from,' explains Elena as I ask again where the dish came from. 'Sometimes it comes from intent. Other times it comes from accident. We put the egg in film to eliminate the vinegar taste, to give a truer taste. Then we started adding duck fat and truffle oil in the bag, to magnify the richness.' I was reminded of a writer from *El Pais* who said Arzak's early *nueva cocina vasca* owed less to what he added to the traditional Basque cuisine than what he took away, like flour from sauces, so that the fresh seasonings were no longer obscured.

Elena then segued from intended effects to trial and error. 'Because plastic film breaks down in boiling water, we cooked it at a lower temperature, like *sous vide*, because we knew we would have more control over the texture. We experimented and finally decided we like it best cooking it at 100 degrees for 5 minutes, then letting it rest a minute before unwrapping it. When we unwrapped it, we saw the end we had tied up left marks in the cooked egg white. From that accident we have worked to consciously design the marks, so that they always come out the same.'

I recalled the egg yolk that decorated the top of the finished, unmolded, poached egg I'd first tasted, and how I'd asked Juan Mari if the egg was open at the top. 'No, we paint it,' he explained gleefully, delighted that I'd tumbled for the *trompe l'oeil*. The *Flor De Huevo* pays undeniable homage to the visual aspirations of *nouvelle cuisine*, but seems to me to go further. On the plate below the egg is a sweet and savory stripe of mousse composed of chorizo and dates, and a crunchy stripe of breadcrumbs and breakfast meats. At a right angle to these stripes is a spoonful of mushrooms. Familiar tastes are presented not simply in a novel way, but to encourage some tastes to be enjoyed in isolation, such as the mushroom, and others to be effortlessly combined, as when the opened egg melds with the intensified tastes of toast and meat. And the sunburst pattern of lines from the knotted plastic, once painted with yolk, present a literal picture of morning blazing, of a flower blooming. Many of Arzak's dishes work in this fashion, telling a story with dramatic characters and a clear sense of stage-setting. The *Flor de Huevo* is merely the epitome.

I have asked Elena if the idea of the egg was influenced by the idea of a cuisine in miniature, painting a little picture, inspired by *pintxos*, the tapas of Basque country. San Sebastian is famous for its *pintxos* bars, and Juan Mari can be seen in yellowed newspaper articles displayed in many of the bars, appearing with the local proprietor at one event or another, inevitably arm and arm. He also shows up in the introduction or credits in locally-produced *pintxos* cookbooks. None of this clicks with Elena. 'We like to go out to the *pintxos* bars, but this is not the same at all. This is more creative, more authored.'

The author is in the house these days at Restaurante Arzak. *Nueva cocina vasca* is, in concept, the adaptation and transformation of *nouvelle cuisine* that Juan Mari encouraged, but Elena describes their cuisine today as *cocina moderna vasca de autor*, 'which means the modern kitchen using Basque ingredients with the creativity of the author,' Elena explains. When I ask if this is an increased focus on the author or an increased acknowledgment of the modern tools, she laughs at my attempts to parse these movements and says, 'Do not focus on the difference between these two, eh? My father and I work together and what we do is evolve together. *Cocina moderna vasca de autor* is just an evolution.'

If *Flor de Huevo* is *nueva cocina vasca*, then the new egg dish Elena showed me a few months ago is clearly *cocina moderna vasca de autor*. An egg in its shell is cooked even more slowly, producing an even more delicate texture, and is then removed from the shell and spray-painted with two lacquers, a green one composed of parsley and truffle oil, and a black one based on squid ink. The *Graffiti de Huevo Elíptico* helped me understand the *Flor de Huevo*'s position in the evolution Elena described. The pastoral scene of the *Flor de Huevo* gives way to the more urban visual signature of graffiti, also an assertion of an author giving a fresh look to the mundane and elevating it to art. *Flor de Huevo* is still on the menu, still able to astound, but by comparison looks like an earlier canvas.

The last answer Elena gives about the origin of the *Flor de Huevo* is that it was simply created, it was not built on using slow poaching on another food, or on an

Poached Eggs at the Revolution

earlier egg dish, or even on the endless conversation among chefs that Arzak has instigated ever since 1975 that have marked him as a culinary statesman and invited such descriptions as 'father of the Spanish culinary revolution.' Just a few months before, Juan Mari had shown me around the new dining-room at the restaurant and discussed the Japanese visual influence, so I asked Elena hopefully if either the *Flor de Huevo* or the *Graffiti de Huevo* drew inspiration from *onsen tamago,* the slow-cooked hot-spring eggs of Japan. 'Ah, now that you mention it, we had a guest from Japan who asked that when we served him these eggs.' My last attempt: since so many chefs I spoke with knew the *Flor de Huevo* and many had tasted it, did Arzak notice other chefs experimenting with the ideas afterward? 'Yes, but that is something we encourage,' Elena says proudly.

The *Flor de Huevo* appears to symbolize the open dialogue and collaboration that characterizes the Spanish culinary revolution as a whole, and Juan Mari in particular. The dish not only lives on the plate, but in countless demonstrations and discussions he conducts with journalists, visiting chefs, and customers. Arzak has contributed to the conditions for a continuing revolution by making even some of his most successful secrets open secrets, so that influences can fly at a higher velocity, accelerating the creativity of all.

It is not an idyllic world. 'You understand that when we are together working we have loud conversations sometimes, that's just as we are,' Elena warns. In fact, I have many happy memories of father and daughter apparently not happy at all, arguing their positions to each other, but it had the feeling of family.

At the end of my first visit to Restaurante Arzak, Juan Mari gave me a copy of a book published at the millennium, called *Arzak and Adrià*. In the opening pages, before the recipes, there are two pages profiling each man. I recall the picture of Adrià, surrounded by acolytes in a modernistic setting, almost cold to the touch. And I remember Arzak's photo, yang to Adrià's yin, his arm around Elena, father of the revolution.

Flor de Huevo y Tartufo en Grasa de Oca con Txistorra de Datiles

For 4 people.

For the eggs:
 4 eggs
 20 grams duck fat
 10 grams truffle juice

For the egg yolk:
 3 egg yolks
 1 cc extra virgin olive oil

Poached Eggs at the Revolution

For the mousse of dates and chorizo:
  120 grams dates
  150 grams chorizo
  100 grams *agua* (100 ml water)
  1 gram ginger

For the tablespoon of mushrooms:
  30 grams *xixa-hori* (mushrooms)
  30 grams *hongos* (mushrooms)
  1 clove garlic
  Salt and chopped parsley

For the bread crumbs:
  60 grams minced chorizo
  60 grams minced bacon
  ½ clove garlic
  300 grams finely minced bread (crust removed)
  100 grams truffle juice
  100 grams water
  Salt and black pepper

For the grape vinaigrette:
  50 grams white grapes, seeded and cubed
  30 grams black grapes, seeded and cubed
  100 grams extra virgin olive oil
  30 grams rice vinegar
  Chopped parsley
  Salt, black pepper and powdered ginger

  Sprig of chervil
  Chopped chives

PREPARATION:

For the eggs:
  Spread out a sheet of plastic wrap and coat with a little oil.
  Deposit 1 egg on the plastic sheet with 6 drops of truffle juice and 3 drops of duck fat and a little salt. Pull the edges together and tie tightly. (May rest in fridge 1 day.)
  Cook in 100°C water for 5 minutes.
  Rest for one minute, then carefully unmold from the plastic wrap and set aside.

For the egg yolk:
  Mix the egg yolks carefully, add olive oil to emulsify, and season.

For the mousse:

Poached Eggs at the Revolution

Mix all ingredients in a blender, then pass through fine sieve.

Warm before serving.

For the tablespoon of mushrooms:

Mince the mushrooms finely and sauté together with chopped garlic and a few drops of extra virgin olive oil.

For the bread crumbs:

Toast the bread crumbs to a golden brown in a dry frying pan.

Add liquid ingredients and stir over a low fire until everything has reached the consistency of crumbs.

For the vinaigrette:

Take out the seeds of the grapes and dice them. Add olive oil, rice vinegar and seasonings.

PRESENTATION:

Place the warm egg in one corner of the plate. On top of the egg, paint the egg yolk mixture, then top with vinaigrette.

Below the egg, running from the bottom of the plate toward the egg, place two parallel lines, one each of bread crumbs and mousse.

Perpendicular to the lines, place the tablespoon and fill with the mushrooms.

Place a sprig of chervil to the right of the two lines, below the tablespoon.

Decorate egg with chopped chives.

References

Author's interviews with Juan Mari Arzak and Elena Arzak Espina, June, 2003 – July, 2006.

Photograph and recipe for *Flor de Huevo y Tartufo en Grasa de Oca con Txistorra de Datiles* (Truffled Egg Flower in Duck Fat With Mushrooms and Dates) provided by Juan Mari Arzak and Elena Arzak Espina, July, 2006.

Transforming Eggs in Chinese Culinary Culture

Fuchsia Dunlop

'Thousand-year-old eggs' – *pi dan* (皮蛋)

My first encounter with *pi dan* was one of the most appalling of all my Chinese food experiences. It was when I was on my way to China for the first time, and stopped off for a few days in Hong Kong. Some friends took me for dinner at the famous roast goose restaurant, Yung Kee, and we were given *pi dan* as an hors d'oeuvre, sliced in half and dressed in ginger and vinegar as a so-called appetiser. They looked, to me, revolting. The albumens of these duck eggs were a dirty brown, translucent jelly, their yolks were dark grey and oozy, and surrounded by a layer of mouldy-looking green. I tried one, and was repelled by its faintly sulphurous and ammoniac taste and forbidding appearance. To make matters worse, traces of the noxious, sticky yolk clung to my chopsticks, threatening to pollute the taste of all the other dishes I ate (I remember trying surreptitiously to wipe my chopsticks on a napkin).

These days, I love *pi dan*. Once you have recovered from the initial shock of their appearance, they have a rich, savoury, eggy taste which is quite addictive. One food-writer friend of mine compares their flavour to that of brown crab meat. I encourage my non-Chinese friends to eat *pi dan* by asking them to think of them as a Chinese version of European blue cheeses – a pretty disgusting idea, but delicious. And when you are used to them, they are positively beautiful, with their gentle layering of colours, described variously in Chinese as 'black-green', 'blue-green', 'grass-green', 'tea-coloured', 'ash-green' and 'earth-yellow'.

Pi dan are made by the action of strongly alkaline ingredients such as wood ash, lime, soda, lye (sodium hydroxide), or some combination of these, which break down the proteins within the egg. Harold McGee describes the process in *Food and Cooking*: to paraphrase, the alkaline material gradually raises the pH value of the egg from around 9 to 12 or more, which denatures the egg proteins, and breaks some of them down into simpler, highly flavourful components (including glutamates, which contribute to their rich *umami* taste). The proteins in the albumen gel, while the yolk proteins coagulate into a creamy mass. Side effects of this chemical process also give the albumen its brownish colour and lend a greenish tinge to the yolk, and release hydrogen sulphide, fatty acids and ammonia.[1]

Fine, flower-like patterns that seem to be etched beneath the surface of the albumen are a sign of quality in the best *pi dan*. They are made by crystals of the modified amino acids that are formed by the breakdown of the albumen proteins, and 'are thus an index of protein breakdown and flavour generation'.[2] Chicken eggs can be preserved in the same way as duck eggs, although I've never come across them in China (Sichuanese egg-preservers have told me that they are much inferior to duck eggs in terms of colour and flavour). Quail egg *pi dan*, which are now common, are said to be a relatively recent trend.

There are two basic methods for making *pi dan*. The older method ('raw-wrapping', 生包) is to coat the raw duck eggs in a paste made from salt and alkaline agents such as lime and wood ash, bound together by mud or a liquid such as tea or 'rice-soup'.[3] The covered eggs, usually then rolled in rice chaff, sawdust or dry ash to stop them sticking together, are dried, and stored until they have set and are ready to eat. A more recent method (immersion or soaking, 浸泡) is to steep the eggs in a strongly alkaline liquid, which is cleaner and more convenient, but produces a coarser taste. Most written sources suggest that the chemical transformation of the eggs takes one to three months, although some egg-preservers have told me they can mature them in seven to ten days, depending on the temperature. After they have matured, the eggs can be kept for up to a year.

One rather sinister aspect of traditional *pi dan* production is the addition of lead oxide, which produces a milder, soft-yolked egg. State regulations limit the use of this nasty additive (although enforcement is likely to be lax, and many *pi dan* seem to be made in small, fly-by-night workshops). Since the 1980s, China has produced 'low-lead' and 'lead-free' *pi dan*.[4]

In the past, making *pi dan* was a way of keeping egg supplies consistent, and ensuring that a glut of eggs in the high laying season wasn't wasted. A generation ago, they were commonly made at home. One friend of mine remembers mixing the ash left after burning rice straw with mud, lime, soda, salt and tea leaves, and using this paste to coat the eggs. These days, people generally buy them from specialist suppliers in the markets or, increasingly, from supermarkets. In a small, illegal *pi dan* workshop I visited recently on the outskirts of the Sichuanese capital, Chengdu, the duck eggs were rolled in reddish clay, to which were added salt, lime and soda. They were then rolled in rice husks, and fan-dried before being put into storage for seven to ten days before sale (quail eggs, they said, took only five days to congeal).

The names 'thousand-year-old egg', 'hundred-year-old egg' and 'century egg' are actually foreign inventions rather than direct translations from Chinese. In China, the eggs are commonly known as *pi dan*, which literally means 'skin-eggs', a reference to the paste that coats them. Other names, both contemporary and historical, include 'transformed eggs' (变蛋)', 'ox-leather duck eggs' (牛皮鸭子) and 'coloured eggs' (彩蛋) – the latter because of the layering of different colours that you see when you cut them into sections. The closest to the Western name for them is 'old eggs' (老蛋). Because of the flowery patterns found in the albumens of the most highly-prized *pi dan*, they are also known as 'pine-blossom eggs' (松花蛋).

It's not clear exactly when the *pi dan* method was invented. Most sources agree that the earliest clear written record of it is in an early Ming Dynasty text, dating back to 1504 (竹屿山房杂部). This text gives a recipe listing measurements for charcoal ash, lime and saltwater, which must be boiled together, allowed to cool slightly and then wrapped around the eggs. After some time, the source says, 'the yolks and albumens will coalesce'. Other sources from the later Ming ('养余月令', '物理小识') give broadly similar recipes, though they specify particular types of ash, including buckwheat ash and chestnut wood ash, or a mixture of different types of ash.⁵ Cypress ash is thought to be particularly effective in encouraging the development of 'pine-flower' patterns in the eggs.

The Qing Dynasty philosopher and scientist Fang Yizhi (方以智, 1611–1671) thought these different kinds of ash provoked different kinds of chemical reaction in the eggs, and suggested that the technology for making them had evolved out a much older method of salting duck eggs (see section below on salted duck eggs, *xian dan*). One of my sources for this paper, *Philological researches into eating* by Zhu Wei, examines this claim in some detail, and the author finds evidence that people in the region once known as Wu, and now part of southern Jiangsu and northern Zhejiang provinces, used an infusion made from the bark of a kind of tree (杭木) in making their salted eggs. The bark infusion was added to stain the eggs a festive red colour, and to help preserve them, but it was also slightly alkaline, so this practice, he suggests, may indeed have led to the invention of *pi dan*.⁶ Later texts give detailed recipes which are very similar to those used today, based on ash, lime and salt, with strongly brewed tea or 'rice-soup' used to bind them into a paste.

Colourful legends compensate for the lack of precise evidence of the origins of *pi dan*. One recounts the tale of an elderly teahouse owner who was in the habit of tipping his used tea leaves onto the ash heap outside his shop. The ducks that he kept liked to sleep on the ash heap, and lay their eggs there, and one day he discovered some eggs that had lain in it for a while. Opening them, he found that they had congealed, and that their shiny, dark flesh had an intriguing flavour. The man was a native of Jiangsu or Hunan Province, depending on the source of the tale. Another story tells of a farmer who had a lime pit behind his house during some construction work. Again, he kept ducks, and they laid their eggs into the lime pit, where they were transformed into *pi dan*.⁷

Two broad types of *pi dan* are distinguished by the textures of their yolks: 'soft-yolked' or 'sugar-hearted' (*tang xin* 溏心 or 糖心) eggs have half-congealed, syrupy yolks which some say are reminiscent of maltose, the sugar used in glazes for roast ducks and other Chinese recipes. They are easy to shell, relatively less alkaline and less salty, and 'contain a little lead'. 'Hard-yolked' (硬心) eggs have firmer yolks, are harder to shell and saltier, contain no lead, and have what is known in China as a light 'pungent and spicy flavour' (辛辣味).⁸ Sometimes other ingredients are added to the coating of the eggs: Chinese medicines which are thought to enhance their blood pressure-reducing effects, tea leaves, ginger, sugar or mixed spices. *Pi dan* are made all over China, but some areas are known for the excellence of their products, like Yiyang in Hunan Province, and Gaoyou (高邮) in Jiangsu, whose 'coloured eggs' were praised by the Qing Dynasty gourmet and cookery-writer Yuan Mei. According to Chinese medicine, untreated duck eggs are neutral, while *pi dan* are a cooling food. They are thought to be an effective treatment for high blood pressure and dysentery, to counter the effects of alcohol, to calm the liver and improve the eyesight. They are also thought to awaken the appetite, which is why they are often served as a first course. Because the chemical process 'cooks' the eggs, they can be eaten straight out of the shells, although they are best rinsed, cut open and left for a little while before serving, to disperse some of the harsher accents of hydrogen sulphide and ammonia in their fragrance.

The Cantonese usually serve *pi dan* with a dressing of vinegar and ginger; the acetic acid in the vinegar neutralises the alkaline tastes of the eggs. They also use the eggs in breakfast congees, often with slices of lean pork. In Sichuan, *pi dan* are usually served as an appetiser with chopped green peppers, soy sauce, and chilli oil; while the Taiwanese like to eat them with soft silken beancurd and a dressing of soy sauce and sesame oil. The Hunanese make an appetiser reminiscent of the Italian antipasto made with charred red peppers and anchovies: they blacken the peppers over a gas flame or a charcoal grill, skin them, and then serve them with segments of *pi dan*, garlic, soy sauce and vinegar. For Chinese banquets, whole *pi dan* can be set in an aspic terrine which is sliced before serving: the layers of different colours in the *pi dan* make this a radiantly beautiful appetiser.

Pi dan are also used in cooked dishes. In Hunan they are boiled with purple amaranth leaves and garlic, to make a soupy, savoury vegetable dish. In other parts of China they are made into stir-fries, and the Cantonese like to clothe them in sweet pastry and bake them for a teatime snack. Some chefs will steam pieces of *pi dan* and salted duck eggs (see below) in a light custard of regular chicken eggs: this is a delightful dish, intriguing in its various eggy tastes and textures (诸葛蛋).

Some other interesting Chinese eggs

Salted eggs – *xian dan* (咸蛋)

One of the ancient methods of egg preservation is salt-curing, which is described in Jia Sixie's great sixth-century agricultural treatise *qi min yao shu* ('Essential skills for the life of the common people') as a widespread practice in the Wu region (now part of southern Jiangsu and northern Zhejiang provinces).[9] Although the eggs of hens, geese and other birds can be salted, in practice only duck eggs are normally used. There are two methods of salting the eggs, which are similar in nature to those use in making *pi dan*. Sometimes the salt is mixed into a paste of mud or ash that is wrapped around the raw eggs; sometimes the eggs are steeped in brine, perhaps with the addition of spices such as Sichuan pepper and star anise, and a dash of clear grain spirits.

The salt draws the water out of bacteria and moulds and inhibits their growth, and causes the egg yolk to solidify (the albumen remains liquid).[10]

When the raw eggs are cracked open, the white spills out, a little cloudy, while the yolk, bright orange and waxy in texture, holds its shape. After cooking, it has a pleasantly grainy texture. The eggs have various culinary uses. Simply hard-boiled, they are often cut in half and served on the shell, their meat to be plucked out with chopsticks and enjoyed as an appetiser, perhaps with alcoholic drinks. Whole salted eggs are sold in breakfast cafes in Sichuan, to be eaten with rice gruel (稀饭) and other accompaniments such as fried peanuts and pickled vegetables; and in the south they are cooked in rice congee itself. They can also be added to soups: usually the whites are drizzled into the broth, where they form straggly pieces, and the yolks are cut into small pieces before being added to the pot. One everyday Cantonese soup is made in this manner with salted eggs, sliced pork and mustard greens (咸蛋芥菜汤).

The salted egg yolks are particularly rich and delicious, and are often used on their own (some Chinese food stores sell the egg yolks only, in vacuum packs). Because of their colour, they are a traditional substitute for crab coral, for example in a dish called 'sacrifice crab coral' (赛蟹粉). They are found along with chicken, dried shrimps and shiitake mushrooms in parcels of glutinous rice wrapped in lotus leaves, a favourite Cantonese dim sum snack. At the Mid-Autumn Festival, they are one of the classic stuffings for mooncakes because their shape echoes that of the round autumn moon (an extravagant mooncake may contain four whole egg yolks). My own favourite use of the yolks is in dishes whose names have the prefix 'golden sand' (金沙), like 'golden sand sweetcorn' (金沙玉米), in which the waxy salted duck egg yolks are steamed or boiled and then finely chopped. The sweetcorn kernels are stir-fried or deep-fried until they are fragrant, and set aside. The chopped egg yolks are then stir-fried in a little oil until they rise up in a yellow froth, and the sweetcorn is returned to the wok for a brief final stir-frying before serving. The kernels end up coated in a fragrant, *umami*-rich frizz of egg yolk – scrumptious. The same method can be applied to all kinds of other vegetables, or other ingredients such as prawns in their shells.

Salted duck eggs are eaten in at least some parts of China at the Dragon Boat Festival (端午节) on the fifth day of the fifth lunar month.

Pickled eggs – *zao dan* (糟蛋)
Here, duck, chicken or goose eggs are steeped in a boozy mixture of fermented cooked grains and salt, sometimes with the addition of vinegar. The process dissolves some or all of the eggshell, leaving the eggs partly coagulated in their membranes, and giving them a sweet, mellow flavour. The eggs can be eaten raw with a little grain spirits and sugar, or lightly steamed.[11]

Embryonic eggs – *dan xian* (蛋线)
The strings of half-formed eggs found inside freshly-killed hens are added to chicken

dishes. They have a mild taste and a curious texture, like egg yolk but a little firmer.

Tea eggs – *cha dan* (茶蛋)
Eggs (usually chicken eggs) are simmered in their shells until set, and then gently rolled in cold water to crack the shells all over without breaking the inner membranes. They are then simmered in a spiced broth stained dark brown by tea, until the tea-colour has penetrated the cracks in the shell and created a lovely pattern all over the white of the egg. These eggs are a common street snack, and are often sold on station platforms.

Spiced eggs – *lu ji dan* (卤鸡蛋)
Eggs, usually chicken eggs but also quail eggs, are boiled until set, and then simmered for some time in a broth flavoured with a rich variety of spices, including, perhaps, cassia bark, star anise, Sichuan pepper, dried ginger, male and female cloves and Chinese cardamom. They are eaten as a snack, like tea eggs.

'Iron eggs' – *tie dan* (铁蛋)
These I have encountered only in Taiwan. Chicken or quail eggs are simmered for many hours in a richly spiced broth until they have shrunk considerably in size, darkened in colour and become firm and chewy. They are sold in vacuum packs as a snack.

Short Bibliography
McGee, Harold, *McGee on Food and Cooking*, (Hodder & Stoughton, London, 2004).
任百尊 (主编), 中国食经, 上海文化出版社, 1999.
萧帆 (主编), 中国烹饪辞典, 中国商业出版社, 北京1992.
周国良, 肖天哨 (编), 松花蛋生产, 轻工业出版社, 北京1981.
朱伟 (编者), 考吃, 中国书名, 北京, 1997.
张伯福 (编者), 中华传统风味蛋制品, 中国商业出版社, 北京1988.

Notes
1. McGee (2004) p. 117.
2. McGee (2004) p. 117.
3. 米汤, the liquid left over when cooking rice.
4. 任百尊(1999), p. 254.
5. 任百尊(1999), p. 254; 朱伟 (1997), p. 196; 张伯福 (1988) p. 1.
6. 朱伟 (1997), p. 197.
7. See for example 朱伟 (1997), p. 199; 张伯福 (1988) p. 2.
8. 张伯福 (1988) p. 3.
9. 任百尊(1999), p. 254.
10. McGee (2004) p. 116.
11. 任百尊(1999), p. 255; 萧帆 (1992), p. 166.

Begué's Eggs

Rien Fertel

> Here, here!
> Now Momma, I'm your Big Butter and Egg Man.
> But I'm different honey.
> But I'm from way down in the South.
>
> Louis Armstrong from *Big Butter and Egg Man from the West*

In 1900, the Southern Pacific Railroad published a collection of recipes inviting tourists and travelers to dine at one of the more famed restaurants in New Orleans. *Mme. Begué and Her Recipes* (subtitled *Old Creole Cookery*) aspired to stir the appetites of anyone who read it promptly to buy a train ticket to the Crescent City. Turn-of-the-century New Orleans was a city reborn. The post-Civil War yellow fever epidemics and Reconstruction period had ended. The World Cotton Exposition of 1884 had enlivened the city with new architecture and an influx of visitors eager to dine on the famed local fare. New Orleans enjoyed a burgeoning metro population and new economic possibilities as home to the nation's second busiest port.

Begué's enjoyed an unmatched prominence among nineteenth-century New Orleans restaurants. The Vieux Carré location and antiquated faux-French interior romanticized the eatery. Proximity to the French Market, the city's version of Paris' Les Halles, ensured the use of the finest ingredients. And the always-genteel hosts Elizabeth and Hypolite Begué, politely referred to as Madame and Monsieur by guests, provided the charm and hospitality that affluent locals preferred and visitors lionized.

Begué's was famous for its second breakfast, what today we might call brunch, and is credited with making it the decadent meal we know today.[1] In fact, a late breakfast was all that one could eat at Begué's: one seating each day at 11 o'clock, reserved seats for thirty guests only. The feasts extended through midday, lasting three to four hours, and consisting of six courses and chicory coffee. Four- to six-egged omelets comprised the foundation of each breakfast, not the *chef-d'oeuvre*,[2] but rather the *chef-d'oeuf*. These omelets were stuffed with robust ingredients: Gulf oysters, slices of veal, fried potatoes.[3]

Madame Begué, née Elizabeth Kettenring, was born in Bavaria in 1831. Part of the second wave of German immigrants to settle in Louisiana, Fraulein Kettenring sought refuge with relatives in New Orleans. Beginning in 1721, ethnic Germans,

Begué's Eggs

preceding the French Canadians (or Acadians or Cajuns), became the first and one of the largest cultural groups to inhabit the Lower Mississippi Valley. Up until the Civil War, German immigrants poured into the port of New Orleans.[4]

Elizabeth's brother Philip Kettenring (by some accounts, her uncle) wielded a butcher's knife in the French Market that ran along Old Levee Street (now Decatur Street) between the French Quarter and the Mississippi River.[5] Originally an Indian trading post, the French Market, has been in continuous operation since 1791, making it the oldest city market in America. The French Market, a virtual United Nations of produce, meat, and seafood vendors, epitomized the mixture of cultures and languages in the nineteenth-century international port city of New Orleans.[6]

Elizabeth Kettenring arrived in the port of New Orleans in 1853 and soon encountered the man who was to become her first husband, Louis Dutrey. Dutrey (anglicized from the French Dutreuil) was born in the Gascon village of Trouley-Labarthe, in the Hautes-Pyrénées section of south-west France.[7] Gascon families enjoyed control of the French Market's butchery trade, providing meat to both local restaurants and households.[8] Within a decade, Dutrey and Kettenring were married and in business together, and in 1863 opened Dutrey's Coffee House at 207 Old Levee Street across from the French Market (now the corner of Decatur and Madison where the restaurant Tujague's currently resides). Louis presided over the front of the house, as host and bartender. Elizabeth was given the task of managing the kitchen. Not much is known about the early life of Elizabeth. Thus it is unknown how or where she gained her cooking expertise. J.S. Harmonson, who wrote the introduction to her second cookbook, *Mme. Begué's Recipes of Old New Orleans Creole Cookery*, described her as skilled in the 'art of German cooking,' upon her New World arrival.[9] The French Market undeniably was the most fertile ground for one with a passion for food. Presumably, Elizabeth spent her first ten years in New Orleans learning to cook the distinctly multicultural flavors and recipes that spice the local Creole cuisine.

Originally, Dutrey's customers consisted almost exclusively of French Market vendors and customers, especially Gascon butchers. Since the market opened for business well before dawn, the people needed nourishment before midday lunch. Coffee and food could be procured, mirroring the tradition of the 'second breakfast' found throughout Germany. Principally, *Brotzeit,* a Bavarian meal eaten an hour before noon and consisting of cold foods: bread or pretzels, sliced meats or sausage, and a beer.[10]

In September 1875, Louis Dutrey died. Hypolite Begué, another French butcher replaced him as host. Apparently, Elizabeth Kettenring-Dutrey's passions for French butchers lured her to the younger Monsieur Begué. After their union in 1881, their eatery was rechristened Begué's.[11]

When the 1884 World's Fair increased the nation's interest in the city, the fortunes of the new couple upsurged.[12] Begué's restaurant was 'discovered'. Taking advantage of this notoriety, Elizabeth and Hypolite developed the multi-course late breakfast.

Begué's Eggs

Customers reserved the restaurant's thirty exclusive seats weeks in advance and soon it became well known that one could not experience New Orleans without tasting the flavors of Begué's.[13]

Before long, Begué's became the Le Cirque of the nineteenth-century South. Every writer, actor, and well-heeled traveler passed through its doors on Decatur Street and joined butchers and farmers at the massive communal tables. Both poet and plebeian alike tried to out-rhyme all others who signed the massive guest book in which we read such nuggets as:

> Now comes a ghostly epicure.
> His breast filled with dismay,
> Ah me, he sighed, then loudly cried
> I never should have gone and died
> Until I met Begué.[14]

Elizabeth Begué's flavors and recipes were, like New Orleans, a mix of tastes and cultures: an abundance of the established local Creole cooking, a bit of German fattening, and the simpleness of the Gascon omelet. Gascony is a country of hills, valleys, and rivers; farms churn out food and drink in true rustic French fashion. In addition to the locally distilled Armagnac brandy, Gascony is famed for its poultry. The majority of foie gras, French fattened goose and duck livers, come from the farms of this south-west region. As France's poultry center, Gascon cuisine is naturally rich in the bounty of fresh eggs.[15]

Gascon egg dishes are usually prepared in the form of an omelet and served for any meal of the day. These south-west French omelets are not merely filled with ham, peppers, and cheese so ubiquitously found on American breakfast and brunch menus, but are rather stuffed with heartier meats: veal, foie gras, and seafood. The omelet is essential to French cooking and is considered by some epicures to be the national dish. As the French chef Stacpoole pronounced: 'All cookery rests on the egg. What is the masterpiece of French cookery, the dish that outlives all other dishes, the thing that is found on His Majesty's table no less than upon the table of the bourgeoisie – the thing that is as French as a Frenchman, and which expresses the spirit of our people as no other food could express it? The omelet.'[16] Typical omelets eaten in south-west France, sardonically named Priest's omelets for their not so spartan stuffings, include any odds and ends and leftovers into the folded egg.[17] Priest's omelets anticipate the egg dishes Madame Begué served and would be familiar to any New Orleanian raised on the city's famously versatile dishes: gumbo and the rice-mélange, jambalaya.

Madame Begué's menus highlighted an omelet dish every day of the week. The omelets fortified the daily second breakfasts, served mid-meal (sandwiched between meat or fish courses on either end, to be followed by fruit and coffee). In *Mme. Begué and Her Recipes* a week's menu is printed in full. The toast-bread omelet was served on Mondays.[18] Tuesday's customers ate the veal omelet prepared with mushrooms.[19] Ham omelets were served on Wednesdays, followed by the sublime sweetbread omelet on Thursdays. Friday visitors received an omelet of fried potatoes.[20] Saturday's guests ate fried oyster,[21] and on Sunday, veal omelets were served again. In fact, all of Begué's omelet recipes called for frying the central ingredient in lard and seasoned with simply salt and pepper. The use of frying lard (and not the more familiar to Louisiana cooking, French-derived butter or Mediterranean olive oil) in nearly every dish exhibited the only remnant of the chef's German heritage conserved in this New Orleans kitchen.

The importance of the omelet in Madame Begué's daily breakfasts may be further understood by examining the frequency with which turn-of-the-century New Orleanians consumed eggs. *The Picayune's Creole Cook Book* (1901), published one year after Begué's cookbook, became New Orleans' most popular kitchen manual. Reprinted from recipes in *The Picayune*, New Orleans' daily newspaper (now *The Times-Picayune*), the *Creole Cook Book* set out to train the influx of women who recently found themselves running their own households. Post-Civil War social conditions in New Orleans forced wives and mothers to manage kitchen duties that once fell to Black and Creole women. The introduction to the *Creole Cook Book* encourages 'ladies of the present day to do as their grandmothers did, acquaint themselves thoroughly with the art of cooking [and] the many excellent and matchless recipes of our New Orleans cuisine […] gather[ed] from the lips of the old Creole negro cooks and the grand old housekeepers who still survive, ere they, too, pass away, and Creole cookery […] will become a lost art.'[22]

The *Picayune's Creole Cook Book* also presents two suggested lists of three-meal daily menus, including one for households on a budget. The menu's recommendation for cooking eggs for breakfast (or for any meal in fact) is surprisingly rare. Eggs appear on the suggested weekly menu for breakfast just three times: scrambled eggs on Wednesdays, poached egg on toast for Thursdays, and *omelette à la Creole* on Saturdays. Spinach with hard-boiled eggs shows up for Wednesday's dinner.[23] The rarity of eggs in the New Orleans home-diet is startling considering the size of an ordinary breakfast during the early twentieth century. Compared with today's seemingly super-sized breakfast of a piece of fruit, a portion of meat, and a dish made from grain, the suggested menus contain upwards of eight to ten different plates of food.[24] Thus unsurprisingly, the Picayune's economical menu suggests the eating of eggs just twice: scrambled eggs for Wednesday's breakfast, and in Pain Perdu (New Orleans-style French Toast) on Friday.[25]

It seems then, that people in New Orleans did not eat eggs cooked from their own kitchens on a daily basis. Eggs were not the typical breakfast food that we consider them to be today. The preparation of eggs, cooked on the same iron skillets and griddles, remains unchanged over the past century. Chickens were commonly raised in city yards and homes, as *The Picayune's Creole Cook Book* contends 'hundreds of the

Creoles raise [their] own family supply of poultry and eggs.'[26] A 1906 census reveals the ratio of one chicken for every two people in urban areas.[27]

The answer to the rarity of the home eaten egg lies in economics. A United States government report gives the average retail price of selected foods. A dozen eggs cost twenty-one cents in the year 1900, at least a nickel more than the equivalent one pound prices of bacon, round steak, and pork chops, ten pounds of potatoes, a gallon of milk, or six pounds of flour. Only the prices of a pound of butter and five pounds of sugar exceeded the cost of a dozen eggs.[28] It was cheaper to furnish the daily diet with meat, vegetables, and cereals than it was the humble egg.

Until twentieth-century advances in breeding and farming techniques, the price of eggs was dictated by the laying-cycle of the chicken. Hens could produce an egg about every day and a half. These now-obsolete hens could produce only one hundred to one hundred and sixty eggs per year, subtracting three to four barren months for the molting period. Hypothetically, if an urban-dwelling family of six owned three chickens, which lay two eggs every three days, only three total omelets (made from four eggs each) could be made each week. New Orleans families breakfasted on often yolk-less meals because eggs were a luxury item.[29]

Fittingly, eggs and omelets became the prodigal centerpiece of the celebrated meal at Begué's restaurant. And soon, other Vieux Carré restaurants were serving their own egg dishes, and became renowned for their own afternoon-erasing second breakfasts. Established in 1840, Antoine's carries the honor of being the oldest family-operated restaurant in the United States. Jules Alciatore, son of the late owner Antoine, became proprietor in 1887, adding French-style omelets and now world famous dishes such as Oysters Rockefeller and Eggs Sardou to the menu.[30] The legacy of the three-hour second breakfast survives at Brennan's restaurant, which since 1946 has served its famed late-morning feast. The restaurant is famous for its elaborate omelets stuffed with escargot, shrimp, and crab.[31]

Madame Begué died one century ago, as I write this, in October of 1906. Her husband Hypolite remarried, and the restaurant remained open for another generation. Elizabeth Begué's fame was noted in several national publications; *The New York Times* carried an obituary,[32] while travel essayist Felix J. Koch writing for *The Boston Cooking School Magazine* offered an emotional canonizing. 'Madame Begué is dead.' Koch pines, 'No more Epicurean breakfasts in the Quartier Latin for the *bon-vivants* of the nation.'[33]

Like any other culinary trend, the popularity of New Orleans and Creole cooking ebbs and flows. The first wave occurred in the last quarter of the nineteenth century, when the Lucullan feasts served at restaurants such as Begué's and Antoine's attracted gourmands near and far. The second wave happened exactly a century later, during New Orleans' second World's Fair. Although largely an economic and political failure, the 1984 World's Fair and Exposition proved the catalyst to propel New Orleans and Creole cooking back into the culinary spotlight. South Louisiana Cuisine (including Cajun fare) became the vogue food of the 1980's. Chef Paul Prudhomme served blackened redfish, among other nouvelle Creole and Cajun delicacies, by the thousands to diners in New Orleans and New York. Emeril Lagasse, whose personality and catchphrases harmonized with the spicy food he was cooking, became the biggest star of television's Food Network. Madame Begué started this procession of famous New Orleans chefs. Today, New Orleans needs to be 'rediscovered,' its foods and culinary history treasured more than ever. We cannot wait another hundred years.

Bibliography

Anderson, Jean and Hedy Würz, *The New German Cookbook* (New York: Harper Collins, 1993).
Block, Petra, *The Evolution of the Cuisine in New Orleans* (München: Ludwig-Maximilians-Universität, 1996).
Deutsch, Hermann B., Brennan's *New Orleans Cookbook* (Gretna, Louisiana: Pelican Publishing Company, 2004).
Folse, Chef John D., *The Encyclopedia of Cajun & Creole Cuisine* (Gonzales, Louisiana: Chef John Folse & Company Publishing, 2004).
Guste Jr., Roy F., *Antoine's Restaurant Cookbook* (New Orleans: Carbery-Guste, 1979).
Harmonson, J.S., *Mme. Begué's Recipes of Old New Orleans Creole Cookery* (Dominic C. Bush and Donald M. Myers, 1937; reprinted ninth ed., Baton Rouge: Land and Land Printers Inc., 1992).
Hill, Kate, *A Culinary Journey in Gascony* (Berkeley: Ten Speed Press, 2004).
Historical Statistics of the United States: Colonial Times to 1970 (Washington D.C.: Department of Commerce, Bureau of the Census, Part 1, Bicentennial Ed., 1975).
Kendall, John Smith, *History of New Orleans* (Chicago: Lewis Publishing Company, 1922).
Koch, Felix J., 'The Passing of Madame Begue's' (*The Boston Cooking School Magazine*, Vol. XI no. 5, December, 1906).
Mayo, H.M., *Mme. Begué and Her Recipes: Old Creole Cookery* (Chicago: Poole Bros., 1900) reprinted by Antique American Cookbooks, 1984.
Nau, John F., *The German People of New Orleans*, 1850-1900 (Leiden: E.J. Brill, 1958). New Orleans Bee (September 24, 1875, p. 1, c. 5).
Smith, Page and Charles Daniel, *The Chicken Book* (Athens: University of Georgia Press, 2000).
The New York Times, 'Mme. Begue Dead.' (October 21, 1906, p. 9).
The Picayune's Creole Cook Book (New Orleans: The Picayune, 1901) reprinted by Antique American Cookbooks, 1984.
The Times-Picayune (April 5, 1917, p. 11, c. 4).
Wolfert, Paula, *The Cooking of Southwest France* (Hoboken: John Wiley & Sons, Inc., 2005).

Notes

1. The term 'brunch' is English, having first appeared in *Punch* magazine in 1896. Folse p. 166.
2. That would be **Liver à la Begué** – 'Secure a fine bit of calf liver, fresh and of good color. Skin well. Have quantity of lard in frying pan, well heated. Slice liver in thick slices. Place in lard and let cook slowly after seasoning with pepper and salt. Let lard cover liver. Simmer on slow fire, and when cooked drain off grease and serve on hot plate.' Mayo p. 54.
3. Mayo pp. 10–15.
4. German immigration peaked in the 1850's. In the decade between 1848 and 1858 over 225,000 thousand ethnic Germans made their entry through New Orleans. Nearly 60,000 remained in the city. Nearly half of those soon died from the yellow fever epidemic. Nau pp. 7, 69.

Begué's Eggs

5. Harmonson p. 10.
6. Block pp. 37–39.
7. *New Orleans Bee* (1875) p.1.
8. Block p. 41.
9. Harmonson p. 10.
10. Anderson and Würz p. 27.
11. *The Times-Picayune* (1917) p. 11.
12. Kendall p. 457.
13. In *Saratoga Trunk* (1945), Ingrid Bergman, upon her character's arrival in New Orleans, exclaims, 'First to the French Market […] then Mme. Begué's for breakfast.' With Gary Cooper, she dines on omelet soufflé, among other dishes.
14. Signed H.M.M. Mayo p. 23.
15. Hill pp. 180–181.
16. Smith & Daniel p. 363.
17. In her treatise *The Cooking of Southwest France*, Paula Wolfert gives a recipe for a more extravagant Priest's Omelet made from veal kidney, foie gras, cèpes (porcinis), and truffles p. 280.
18. **Toast bread omelet** – 'Cut two cupfuls of stale bread in dice and fry in hot lard. When crisp spread over all four well beaten eggs seasoned with salt, pepper and a spoonful of chopped parsley. When of a nice brown remove from the pan and serve hot.' p. 55.
19. **Veal omelet** – 'Take a nice piece of tender veal, cut in small squares and fry. Add a few mushrooms. When done set on the side. Beat six eggs seasoned with salt, pepper and a spoonful of chopped parsley. Throw in this the fried veal, but not the lard, and stir well. Have your pan ready with very hot lard and pour in the omelet. Let it come to a nice brown, turn on a plate and slip back in the pan. When both sides are done serve at once.' p. 57.
20. **Potato omelet** – 'Pare and slice three large potatoes; fry in hot lard. When almost done add an onion chopped fine and let fry with the potatoes. Have ready five well-beaten eggs; season with salt and pepper, and spread over the whole. When done on one side put a plate over the frying pan and turn the omelet. Then slip it in the pan again and let the other side brown also. This must be sent warm to the table.' p. 54.
21. **Oyster omelet** – 'Drain two dozen oysters. Have ready some hot lard and throw them in. Let fry until they begin to curl, then spread over them four well beaten eggs seasoned with salt and pepper and stir all together until done. Serve hot.' p. 54.
22. *The Picayune's Creole Cook Book* p. 6.
23. *The Picayune's Creole Cook Book* p. 431.
24. Menu for Wednesday's Breakfast includes: Prunes or iced figs (in season), wheatena (a cereal served hot) with milk, broiled tenderloin of trout with *sauce à la Tartare*, potato chips, olives, broiled ham, scrambled eggs, French toast with butter, *café au lait*, and of course the *Daily Picayune*. p. 431.
25. *The Picayune's Creole Cook Book* p. 438.
26. *The Picayune's Creole Cook Book* p. 439.
27. Smith & Daniel p. 233.
28. *Historical Statistics of the United States* p. 213.
29. Modern chickens can lay twice the eggs of nineteenth century hens. Smith & Daniel pp. 248, 279.
30. **Eggs Sardou**, named for a visit by the French playwright Victorien Sardou (author of the play *La Tosca*) comprises poached eggs, artichoke hearts, anchovy, ham, and truffle topped with Hollandaise Sauce. Guste p. 88.
31. Or their original, the **Eggs Hussarde**, which stacks poached eggs, ham, and tomato onto Holland rusks (English muffins) and smothered with Hollandaise and Marchand de Vin sauce (a brown gravy perfused with red wine), mushrooms, ham, onion, and garlic. Deutsch pp. 43–51.
32. *The New York Times* (1906) p. 9.
33. Koch pp. 226–227.

The Language of the Egg

Anna Marie Fisker

'A rose is a rose is a rose', wrote Gertrude Stein in her text 'An Elucidation' from 1923. In his essay from 1978 *'A Rose is a Nose is a Rose'*, Roland Barthes went one step further on a voyage through the linguistic eccentricities of the painter Arcimboldo. Barthes examined Arcimboldo's 'Composite Heads' with the meticulousness of a dermatologist or allergist. Both of them are enchanting. Like Gertrude Stein, Barthes and architect Arne Jacobsen are the ideal partners for my essay 'The Language of the Egg'. But let us proceed, and from the technical playfulness of Martin Gardner draw inspiration to continue the series of analogies with 'an egg is an egg is an egg' (Gardner, 1997:57).[1] These three citations suggest a reading of the three topics, or the three languages that I have worked with regarding the egg: The language of architecture, *modelling*; the language of gastronomy, *food*; and the language of linguistics, *semiotics*.

Gardner says: 'The egg is a small physical thing with a beautiful geometrical surface. It is a microcosm that obeys all the laws of the universe. And at the same time it is something far more complex and mysterious than a white pebble. It is a strange lidless box that holds the secret of life itself' (Gardner, 1997:57). Then let us delve into that or those secret(s) and ask the question: Which came first, the hen or the egg? Well, if you read to the end of this article, you will find that I conclude the egg to be more beautiful than the hen. But that is an entirely different matter; let us not forestall the narrative.

The American streamline designer Raymond Loewy was once asked, which form he perceived to be the most flawless. And he answered – The egg! – That is one form that is going to be difficult to surpass. It is brilliantly thought of by the chicken that has here created strength in a light shell, aerodynamic and easily popped out of even the most tightly pursed up chicken rump. Let us examine the inherent qualities of the egg, and at the same time situate it in dialogue with the physical world, with architecture, and attempt to approach another 'Egg'. For Danish architect Arne Jacobsen copied the form in one of his designs for the Royal Hotel in Copenhagen.

After World War II, there was an increasing interest in 'organic forms' in architecture. This development should probably be perceived as a reaction to and a continuation of modernism's strict mode of expression. As early as in the 1940s, the USA witnessed beginning attempts to incorporate organic and biomorphic forms, first and foremost within design, but later also in architecture. Danish architect, Arne Jacobsen, was one who succeeded in creating a beautiful synthesis between the strictly geometrical and the organic in architecture and design. This synthesis is particularly distinguishable in The Royal Hotel from 1958. The latest construction principles of the time were employed in the construction of the building. It has strong international references and possesses a unique character of its own. At the time, the sharply cut outer form stood forth as a gigantic, homogenous glass volume in central Copenhagen. The building consists of two large cubes, of which the upper has been erected vertically on a horizontal cube of similar size. There is a rare unity between building and design. Both aspects are characterised by the particularly sophisticated variant of modernism, of which Denmark and Scandinavia were exponents.

Behind the straight lines of the glass facade, Arne Jacobsen let all his talents unfold in what was to be the period's most consistent example of total design, comprising everything from furniture and textiles to cutlery and ash trays (Sommer, 1995:134). The geometry of the building itself is preserved in the interior – in the layout of the rooms – and, consequently, a new dimension is added to the rooms due to Arne Jacobsen's conscious utilisation of his furniture as an architectonic tool. With the organically sweeping lines of the furniture, a contrast is created to the clearly defined grid of the rooms. Jacobsen contrasts the geometry with soft lines and creates a harmonious total experience. There is a rhythm and lightness to the sweeping furniture, which is expressed brilliantly as a free – yet tight – expressive form. It poses an interesting challenge to the regular, cubic space of the hotel (Sommer, 1995:134). The chair has simply been named the 'Egg', underlining its biomorphic origin, and it appears like free standing sculptures in the geometrical space.

If any piece of furniture could speak, the 'Egg' would be it. I would like to claim that it does speak to us through its symbolism, which the beholder more or less recognises. This is a decisive reason why the chair, even today, must be perceived as a rhetorical architectonic classic. Let us pay closer attention to such rhetorical 'cases'. In a certain way, the painter Arcimboldo is also a rhetorician. Barthes finds that with his heads, Arcimboldo throws an entire collection of rhetorical images into the conversation. One might say that Arcimboldo's canvas is a veritable laboratory for figurative expression, for tropes.[2]

What are these tropes? A cucumber symbolises a nose: that is a *metaphor*. Many ears of corn refer to a field – that is where the corn grows: that is a *metonymy*. Ears of corn become a sophisticated suit: that is an *allegory*. To draw fruits, peaches, pears, cherries, strawberries, the ear of a corn cob and thereby call attention to summer: that is an *allusion*.[3] I will pursue such tropes in relation to the egg. Regardless of whether they are in the form of metaphors, metonymies, allegories or allusions, the egg has a central meaning in one of Sherwood Anderson's finest stories. It is called 'The Egg' and appears in his book *The Triumph of the Egg*. The story is narrated by a boy, probably a representation of the author himself as a young boy. His parents, formerly the owners of a miserable chicken farm, had bought a restaurant in Picklesville not far from Bidwell, Ohio. His father fancies himself as a showman. One rainy night the only customer in the restaurant is a young man named Joe Kane, who is waiting for

The Language of the Egg

the late train. The father decides to entertain him by performing his favourite egg trick (Gardner, 1997:55).

> 'I will heat this egg in this pan of vinegar', he said to his customer. 'Then I will put it through the neck of a bottle without breaking the shell. When the egg is inside the bottle it will resume its normal shape and the shell will become hard again. Then I will give the bottle with the egg in it to you. You can take it about with you wherever you go. People will want to know how you got the egg in the bottle. Don't tell them. Keep them guessing. That is the way to have fun with this trick' (Anderson, 1921:61).

When the father grins and winks, Joe decides that he is crazy, but harmless. The vinegar softens the shell of the egg, but the father forgets an essential part of the trick. He neglects to heat the bottle (Gardner, 1997:56).

> For a long time he struggled, trying to get the egg to go through the neck of the bottle.... He worked and worked and a spirit of desperate determination took possession of him. When he thought that at last the trick was about to be consummated, the delayed train came in at the station and Joe Kane started to go nonchalantly out at the door. Father made a last desperate effort to conquer the egg and make it do the thing that would establish his reputation as one who knew how to entertain guests who came into his restaurant. He worried the egg. He attempted to be somewhat rough with it. He swore and the sweat stood out on his forehead. The egg broke under his hand. When the contents spurted over his clothes, Joe Kane, who had stopped at the door, turned and laughed.
> (Anderson, 1921:61)

Roaring with anger the father grabs another egg and hurls it at Joe, barely missing him. Then he closes the restaurant for the night and tramps upstairs, where his wife and son have been awakened by the noise (Gardner, 1997:56).

> Father came upstairs to mother and me with an egg in his hand. I do not know what he intended to do. I imagine he had some idea of destroying it, of destroying all eggs, and that he intended to let mother and me see him begin. When, however, he got into the presence of mother something happened to him. He laid the egg gently on the table and dropped on his knees by the bed as I have already explained. He later decided to close the restaurant for the night and to come upstairs and get into bed. When he did so he blew out the light and after much muttered conversation both he and mother went to sleep. I suppose I went to sleep also, but my sleep was troubled.
> (Anderson, 1921:62)

The Language of the Egg

Good stories have a tendency to turn into allegories. What does the egg in Sherwood Anderson's story represent? Gardner thinks it is nature, the Orphic Egg, the vast world that is independent of our minds, under no obligation to conform to our desires (Gardner, 1997:57). For Gardner, it is important to understand the mathematical laws and to control them to an incredible degree, as modern science and technology testify. If you fail to understand its laws, he states, forget them or ignore them, nature can be as malevolent as the white egg in Anderson's tragedy. So the question will come, which is more important, the chicken or the egg? Anderson's narrator concludes his account of human failure.

> I awoke at dawn and for a long time looked at the egg that lay on the table. I wondered why eggs had to be and why from the egg came the hen who again laid the egg. The question got into my blood. It has stayed there, I imagine, because I am the son of my father. At any rate, the problem remains unsolved in my mind. And that, I conclude, is but another evidence of the complete and final triumph of the egg – at least as far as my family is concerned.
> (Anderson, 1921:63)

Biologically speaking, the egg is a reproductive unit, produced by the female, which eventually evolves into a new individual. The egg allows for the necessary continuation of life and thus builds a bridge between generations. In connection with birds, the development of an egg occurs over the span of approximately one day and night. When the egg cell, which primarily consists of a ball of yolk, has been fertilised, it slides down the uterine tube where the egg white and shell are developed. The egg white functions as protection for the foetus, but it also has an important nutritional function as a supplement to the protein and water contained in the yolk. Between the egg white and the shell are the two parchment-like membranes; when the membranes are formed, they are quite loose, but at a later stage the white expands, wherefore the membranes are tightened. The innermost layer of the white is stretched between the ends of the shell, and contributes to maintaining the yolk in the centre. The shell consists of calcite, a form of fibre-reinforced calcium carbonate, which is attached to the underlying membrane. The shell is perforated by thousands of small pores that allow oxygen, carbon dioxide and water to pass through. Consequential to its form, the egg is able to withstand compression. During its development, this barrier continually protects the egg from its surroundings.

If one was to be overly exacting about the form of Jacobsen's 'Egg', it is not quite identical to that of an egg. The top is too pointy, and, of course, a part of the shell has been cut off, otherwise, though, it is fairly egg-like. And yet, the biological analogy is quite plain. Both because the chair has, literally, been named after its biological counterpart, but also because of the concrete outer form, which immediately leads the associations towards an understanding of its symbolism. I will try to explain why the

The Language of the Egg

chair, even today, 50 years after its genesis, still holds a general appeal. As an architect, Jacobsen has been able to create a work, which, due to its inherent qualities, is able to communicate with its surroundings through a language that reaches beyond its own time and is transmitted through time. The symbolic function of the 'Egg' is enhanced by its beautiful form. The 'Egg' can be perceived as a symbol of a primordial embryo from which the world later arose.[4] The Orphic Egg, the Cosmic Egg, is usually represented as an egg surrounded by a coiled serpent. The egg symbolises the belief in the Greek Orphic religion that the universe originated from within a silver egg. The first emanation from this egg, described in an ancient hymn, was Phanesdionysus, light personified: 'ineffable, hidden, brilliant scion, whose motion is whirring, you scattered the dark mist that lay before your eyes and, flapping your wings, you whirled about, and through this world you brought pure light'.[5] In his chair, Arne Jacobsen creates space through the breakage of the shell. The space of the chair, however, is of an ambiguous nature. It simultaneously forms a clearly defined space around the individual, and it opens up towards the surroundings and exists in interplay with them. Man is still in control of its inner universe, though, as the personal privacy sphere is kept more or less private due to the turning mechanism of the chair.

The Egg was specifically intended for use in the large lobby of the hotel, which is highly trafficked by arriving and waiting guests and where the high back of the chair would thus serve to 'shield' its user. It was one of the intentions with the Egg that the high shell should shield the user from the surroundings, just as several chairs together created their own room in the larger room. As the chair is mounted on a swivel foot, with a gentle push with his/her foot, the user could orient him/herself towards, or shield him/herself away from anywhere in the room. Consequently, the chair gains the signification of a cavern. It functions as a part of a common room, but with encoded boundaries – encoded a post-structuralist linguistic code for pausing. To encode means both to hide and not to hide. The message is hidden, but only insofar as the eye is unable to perceive the meaning of the aggregate details.[6] In order to further scrutinise the *meaning* of the 'Egg', a quick summary of the relation between the concept of the sign to form is called for. The *sign* is the point of departure in semiotics. According to Saussure's conception, the sign is a dual unit consisting of a *sensuous* and a *material significant*, but the terms *signifier* and *signifié*, or *signified*, the conceptual content evoked by the signifier, are also applicable. Is it possible to link this conception of the sign to form and the understanding of form, in this case implying the Egg? If so it is necessary to enhance architectonic language also to comprise the *conceptual content* evoked by the form. The sign appears in various types of messages, either denotatively or connotatively. *Denotation* and *connotation* characterise respectively a *literal* and a *symbolic* level in the messages transmitted through the sign.[7] As modellers, as architects and designers, our work is traditionally concerned solely with the literal. In the 'Egg', however, Jacobsen attempts to communicate with the user, and so he follows the semiotic conceptual content where the messages are an attempt to influence the way in which signs can enter into other signs as *significant* and *signifié*, respectively. It is a kind of dynamic mechanism, which can explain how signs combine into new and enhanced meanings. The precondition for carrying out the aforementioned 'grasp' is that the form is not only perceived as a mute, material, physical shape, but that it *communicates its own existence*, or, in other words, that it *means* to a group of receivers. In his analysis of architecture as a sign, which transmits meaning, the Italian philosopher and literary scholar Umberto Eco posits *function* as a focal point. According to Eco, the denoted message of architecture is its *immediate applicability*, whereas the connoted message has to do with the range of *symbolic meanings* that can be tied to this applicability. It is the codes that determine the reading of architecture as signifying form. The interpretation of a building, a modernist residential building or a chair, hinges on the applied codes, in construction as well as reading.

Jacobsen's 'Egg' further elaborates on the myth (the story) of the egg whereby it gets a more profound meaning. Barthes states that it is the story that supplies the form of the myth with analogies, rather than the analogy being formed out of a logical structural coherence. The meaning of terms and concepts is unequivocally determined by the cultural context, what Barthes labels the story. Therefore, an analogy cannot be said to represent a firm connection to reality, as reality has been surpassed by the story.[8] Sherwood Anderson is not the only author to have dealt with the story of the egg.[9] In her short poem from 1911–1912 'Tender Buttons', Gertrude Stein, a friend of Sherwood Anderson's, seeks a new poetic symbolic language, free of habitual thinking and artistic conventionality. Here, the egg moves beyond reality and becomes a cunning shawl, a cunning shawl to be steady.

> *Eggs*
> Kind height, kind in the right stomach with a little sudden mill.
> Cunning shawl, cunning shawl to be steady.
> In white in white handkerchiefs with little dots in a white belt all shadows
> are singular they are singular and procured and relieved.
> No that is not the cows shame and a precocious sound, it is a bite.
> Cut up alone the paved way which is harm. Harm is old boat and a likely dash.
>
> (Stein, 2004:80)

When I perceive the 'Egg' as form, I have perceived shaping as the process, where a shaper shapes and develops an object, a chair, with a view to satisfy the users. This is not a piece of art, but an object with a purpose. Such a design process can be classified as dogmatic, because it describes or prescribes how to proceed. In the production of the 'Egg', the biological process has been turned 180 degrees. In the industrial manufacturing process, the shell is cast first. Today, it is produced in polyurethane,

The Language of the Egg

which, as in the shell of the biological egg, creates a protective wall around the encased individual. The idea would have seemed appealing to Freud, for in the Egg we return to the womb where we can hide, seek warmth and be snug. The hardened shell is covered in a moulded foam material of varying thickness. The foam material accommodates the rounded human body by the same principle as an egg white. On the contact surfaces, where body meets chair, the chair is upholstered with a fabric or leather membrane. As a gesture to the human body, the membrane of the cushion of the chair eases off when seated, and one experiences a fantastic comfort. It was due to the most recent technical and production advances that Arne Jacobsen was able to realise his ideas. The finished version of the shell consists of moulded foam-plastics, styropor. This new material enabled the production of hitherto unseen forms in furniture artwork, and these possibilities for renewal were exploited in the Egg (Sommer, 1995:135).

The initial phases of the chair's design were carried out at a sculptor's, who modelled the form and subsequently made a plaster cast. A process like this one often helps materialise the concept/model and the product becomes an *artefact*.[10] The communication of a design occurs within a context that contributes to infusing the artefacts with meaning. When it comes to simple artefacts with a long history, this is usually unproblematic. We recognise a chair, a cup and a pot when we see them. When conventions regarding the appearance of a design – its *archetype* – are broken, which Jacobsen most certainly did, it is no longer obvious that it is, in fact, a chair, nor how it should be used. If the artefact is removed from its *context*, it is no longer self-explanatory. The context can thus replace a theoretical explanation for the artefact. Similarly, Stein situates the egg in a new context, supplying it with new content/*signifié*. When Stein writes of the egg that 'No that is not the cows shame and a precocious sound, it is a bite. Cut up alone the paved way which is harm. Harm is old boat and a likely dash', then it is a new *signifié* (Stein, 2004:81).

We ask whether the analogy exists? Yes, indeed. But I believe that a Gardneresque view is required to understand its bizarre mathematics. According to Barthes, the math of *analogy* is when one recalls that etymologically *analogy* means *proportion*. And meaning is dependent upon the level with which one identifies. Let me be more specific. If, as Barthes, one was to behold a painting by Arcimboldo from close range, nothing but fruits and vegetables would be visible. Should one take a few steps back, though, nothing less than a princely looking man appears. It is the combination of distance and proximity that establishes the meaning. Is this the great secret of semiotics? According to Barthes, understanding is gained from a variation of articulation (Barthes, 1987:28). Meaning arises from a combination of meaningless elements, which he calls *phonemes*. Stein said that she felt language: 'It does not make any difference to me what language I hear, I don't hear a language, I hear tones of voice and rhythms, but with my eyes I see words and sentences.'[11] In 'Tender Buttons' the poem of the egg is tied to the cow. It is as in Arcimboldo's painting. All we see at first

The Language of the Egg

is a heap of vegetables and corn. And it is only when we distance ourselves, when we are removed from the painting, by changing the level of perception, that we receive another message, i.e. a head.

I thus attempt to alter my level of perception of the egg. Beyond the initial message, the chosen subject, is where I place the hyper-farsighted apparatus that Barthes employs, which at once gives me the opportunity, like a cryptographer, to perceive the full meaning, the 'true' meaning. It is by and large the same exercise as when I (now) force you to perceive the meaning of the 'language' of the egg. Barthes labels Arcimboldo the 'Triumphant Ruler of the Metaphor'. Everything in Arcimboldo's work is a metaphor. Nothing is ever signified, since all the characteristic features, strokes, forms, turns that comprise a head already *have* a meaning. (Barthes, 1987:28). And this *meaning* draws attention to another meaning; in fact it is almost diverted back at itself. It indicates the etymological meaning of the word 'metaphor'.

Can we then force the egg to become anything other than its natural self? For his entire life, Arne Jacobsen was fascinated by the challenge that faced the designer grappling with technical and constructional possibilities, and he forced the egg to become a chair, thus enhancing its meaning. I have elected to broaden the scope of my investigation from *literal form* to *symbolic form*, and I have tried to elucidate new and enhanced meanings. What characterised Barthes' writings was, as mentioned, an analysis of *signification*, i.e. the active production of signification rather than *meaning*, in other words the semantics of language. Barthes states that food is a *communication system*, a collection of notions, or a *system of customs and behaviours in concrete situations* (Barthes, 1987:28). In the depths of this field, a *signification structure* can be sensed. And, because of Arne Jacobsen's 'Egg', it also applies to architecture.[12]

The egg definitely came before the chicken. And, oh yes: the egg. *Naturally* the egg came first, as chickens have not always existed. At some point, a bird, which was not a chicken, laid an egg wherein lay the chicken mutation, and the little mutant could form the genesis of a brand new species. The chickens, the morning egg and the eternal discussion could commence. An egg is an egg is an egg!

Notes

1. For a period of 30 years (1956–1986), Martin Gardner has written regularly for the journal *Scientific American*.
2. *Trope*. Greek for 'figure of speech' or rhetorical figure. It is a word used figuratively. The function of the trope is to alienate and please. The corresponding word in Latin is *figura*. Most rhetoricians do not differentiate between trope and figure. Examples of tropes and figures are: metaphor, metonymy, irony, allegory (Lütken, Fibiger and Mølgaard, 2001:523).
3. *Metaphor*. A figurative expression where the object itself is replaced by an image. *Metonymy*. A rhetorical trope or figure – the opposite of a metaphor. The metaphor hinges on similarity, *similaritas*, between two objects or words, whereas the metonymy hinges on proximity, *contiguitas* (Lütken, Fibiger and Mølgaard, 2001:523). *Allegory*. A rhetorical trope or figure (Latin: *inversio*), in which you say one thing, and mean another. Allegory can be apprehended as an expanded metaphor (Lütken,

Fibiger and Mølgaard, 2001:523). *Allusion*. Reference, insinuation.
4. In Hindu, Egyptian, Chinese and Greek symbolism, the cosmic egg – the origin of the universe – suddenly cracks. Until this point, it had been one whole containing all existing and potentially existing within the confined space of the shell.
5. http:altreligion.about.com/library/glossary/symbols/bldefsorphicegg.htm 10.7.2006.
6. *Post-structuralism*. Umbrella term for a long range of theories and thinkers who all take their point of departure in the structuralist notion of a linguistic code that precedes speech or use. Roland Barthes states that the code cannot be broken only circumvented. Post-structuralism is not a term by which the thinkers it implies would describe themselves (Lütken, Fibiger and Mølgaard, 2001:517).
7. *Connotation*. The concept is taken from structural semantics and it implies an identification of the sub-textual overtones of the linguistic utterance, which appear in the specific (often poetical) text in which it appears. The term differs from *denotation* in the sense that the latter designates the lexical base meaning of a given term and appears most commonly in the unequivocally uniform language of science.
8. Conceptual realism, on the other hand, contends that in some capacity or other there is a *determination*. The fact, according to Barthes, that the *myth* is motivated is testament hereof.
9. In 1921, the same year that Sherwood Anderson wrote *The Triumph of the Egg*, Sylvia Beach introduced Gertrude Stein to the author Sherwood Anderson, who was to become a lifelong friend of hers (Stendahl, 1994:86).
10. *Artefact*. Man-made, rather than natural object. *Archetypes*. C.C. Jung's term for the most common symbols of the collective unconscious. The archetypes are human ur-images that are found in most religions, myths, dreams and fairy tales (Lütken, Fibiger and Mølgaard, 2001: 479).
11. An examination of the works of Gertrude Stein confirms that her focus is constantly drifting away from structure and conventional composition. Her language begins to take on a new opacity. One might argue that Stein invents another version of modernism by circumventing the image and by exploring the exact self-sufficiency of language (Fisker, 2003).
12. Depth level is, according to structuralism, when there are two levels in a given text; a surface level, the actual text, and a depth level that comprises an underlying structure of meaning, which has evoked and controls the surface (Lütken, Fibiger and Mølgaard, 2001: 489). *Meaning*. The contents or the meaning of a sign or a text. A basic concept of structuralism and semiotics. When the traffic light is green, it means drive. When a silhouette of a female figure has been placed on a door, it indicates a ladies' room. Meaning emerges as signs and texts are determined both by their structure and by their use. Structurally, the sign must be different from other signs (a green traffic light being different from a red one). Regarding usage, conventions must exist, which specify how to use a sign (it has been decided that green means drive, and the use of words is often based upon unconscious custom). Meaning in language and other sign-systems is often referred to as semantics (Lütken, Fibiger and Mølgaard, 2001: 481).

References

Anderson, Sherwood (1921), *The Triumph of the Egg*, B.W. Huebsch, Inc.
Barthes, Roland (1987), 'A rose is a nose is a nose', *FMR* magazine, no. 24, Jan, 1987, London.
Fisker, Anna Marie (2003), 'Mad og Arkitektur', Aalborg : Institut 19 Arkitektur & Design, 2003, *AAU Forlag*, ISSN 1399–3291.
Gardner, Martin (1997), *The Last Recreations*, New York.
Lütken, Johannes, Fibiger, Gerd and Mølgaard, Niels (2001), *Litteraturens tilgange*, Gads Forlag, Copenhagen.
Sommer, Anne-Lise (1995), *Arkitektur & design*, Politikens Forlag, Copenhagen.
Stein, Gertrude (2004), *Ømme dupper*, Borgens Forlag, Copenhagen.

The *Patina* in Apicius

Sally Grainger

Eggs played an important role in the meals of the financially secure Roman. The adage 'from soup to nuts' is mirrored in Latin with 'from eggs to nuts,' suggesting that they traditionally began the meal. These may have been simply boiled and served with salad and possibly a dressing, or they were combined with other ingredients in the dish known as a *patina*. The recipe collection that we now believe was effectively called *Apicius* rather than written by anyone called Apicius has numerous *patina* recipes and it is the nature of these dishes that I wish to bring to your attention. I have often, with tongue in cheek, described *patinae* as quiches without the pastry. We will see that this is not so far from the truth as we can trace a direct link, through ingredients and cooking method, between Roman *patinae* and the '*tortes*' of early medieval cuisine.

In its simplest manifestation the term *patina* refers to a round shallow vessel made of terracotta used to cook and serve food. The Greek influence on Roman food terminology is extensive and is apparent here as the terms *patina/patella* stem from the rare Greek *patanÁ/batanÁ*, meaning 'general dish' or 'vessel'. *Patella* is a diminutive form and almost certainly the same kind of vessel though when the term is used it often appears to have a greater depth and frequently refers to metal, particularly bronze, rather than ceramic, though not necessarily all the time.[1] As the term refers to a distinct vessel with corresponding archaeological remains as well as a specific cooked egg dish, there can often be confusion as to which is intended. As a rule we have rendered any reference to the vessel as 'dish' in our translation and where the cooked egg dish is meant we have left the term in italics in the translation. I must briefly look at the vessel before tackling the eggs.

The vessels vary in diameter and can be flat with low straight sides, or slope deeply inwards towards a small base. Archaeological finds suggest that these had a curved wall with a relatively small base, allowing the dish to be pushed down into a bed of embers but making them unstable on a flat surface. Some of these vessels are found among the imported African red slip fabrics and their typical shape corresponds with form 191.3 in Hayes 1972 and in the local African form 469 in Riley 1979.[2] The shape is a standard, late-Hellenistic form that was made and exported throughout the Greco-Roman world from the second century BC through to the second century AD. They are common in the archaeology and support the literary evidence that suggest continuity between Greek and Roman use.

The fabric is a rough coarse unslipped orange clay with natural or added lime, quartz and mica, giving the vessel a granular texture. This additional material in

The *Patina* in Apicius

the clay allows the vessel to take the thermal shock of contact with the fire without breaking.[3] Flat-based vessels function on a trivet but the curved-base *patina* is actually buried in the embers of a mature fire: this fire has plenty of semi-carbonised wood resembling charcoal which generates radiant heat but without the immediate heat of flame which is necessarily too intense and precise for a ceramic vessel. The heat is gentle and controllable and this is particularly important when we consider that eggs are the primary ingredient. These vessel can also function with a matching lid.

In Book 4.2.33, a *patina* is cooked according to the instruction *in thermospodio pones, ac subtus supra thermospodium habeat* (put in the hot embers, let it have hot embers above and below).[4] The Form 191 in Hayes has a 'flat recessed band on the inside at the junction of the rim and wall to receive a lid'.[5] Lids occur in a similar fabric designed to fit these vessels in equal numbers and are Form 192 in Hayes. They have a low domed shape with a plain rim and a large inverted foot which acts as a lifting knob. The inside of this inverted foot is the ideal surface to place hot ashes, as is the rim. Some lids from local African ware even have a pronounced turned-up edge to the lid, preventing the ash from falling into the dish as it is lifted off.[6] A recipe at 5.3.2 of *Apicius* has a dish called *pisam farsilem* (stuffed peas) which we translate as 'peas mould'. It is a form of *patina* in all but name as eggs are used to set mushy peas interlayered with various kinds of meat and vegetables. It seems to be made in a deeper vessel with straight sides, and the finished dish should be turned out. To cook it, it is either put in the oven or over a slow fire so that it sets *ad se deorsum* (from the top down). This term has been misunderstood by previous editors: in his French translation, André reversed the meaning and suggested that the 'peas mould' would cook from the bottom up; and the entire phrase was left out from their English translation by Flower and Rosenbaum. It is now clear that embers were placed on the lid so that the 'peas mould' would cook downwards as well as through the heat rising from the fire beneath. In this case the vessel was placed on a trivet over a fire rather than in the embers. This cooking technique of adding coals to the lid of a vessel and thus creating top heat or in effect oven heat was fundamental to the development of complex cookery in the medieval period. We find the process used with the 'Dutch oven' where fire is placed on the lid of a cauldron which stands in the fire place and it was also employed to set and give colour to the '*tortes*' that closely resemble *patinae*, and seem to be a stage in the development of the quiche.

> White *torte*. Then make the dough or rather crust in a pan (*patellam*), suitably thin, and cook very slowly, applying heat from below and above and be sure it is browned on top from the heat. (Platina VIII.44.)

The recipe for *miliacum* (VIII.31) has a direct link to *patinae*: it does not use a pastry shell and is made with many eggs and cheese with barley meal. A *patellam* is used to make the dish and 'it is cooked suitably with coals placed below and above' using an *operculum* lid with coals on the top. The terminology has changed somewhat from *Apicius* however. It seems that a ceramic vessel is now termed a *testu* from its basic meaning of a clay tile. Its original Roman meaning was as a portable clay domed oven that functioned in precisely the same way as these medieval vessels i.e. fire was placed on the rim as it was placed on the lid. The standard term for a metal vessel that holds these *tortes* is now a *patellam* and this seems to correspond with the common but not consistent use of this term to mean metal dishes in *Apicius*.

These *torte* could also be placed in the oven and cooked as we would cook a quiche, and it seems that it was also possible to cook Roman *patinae* this way. In the recipe for 'peas mould' above, oven cooking is an option. However it seems that cooking in 'embers' is not only efficient and successful but an effective means of using up the latent heat found in the residue from heating ovens and large stock pots. These embers need to be utilised as they are effectively a fire hazard when they first become available. Not surprisingly, timing is an important part of the process. The dish needs to be ready to bake just as the embers are ready to be taken out of the oven. The egg needs to set but cannot over-cook and the finished dish needs to be held and cooled slightly so that diners can handle the pieces at table.

Let us turn to the egg *patina* in *Apicius*. The vast majority of these *patinae* recipes contain eggs as a setting agent.[7] The dish may contain a mixture of various kinds of fish, meat or vegetables (or combinations of all three) flavoured with a sauce and then bound with eggs and allowed to set or cooked over a charcoal fire. Sometimes the dish was deliberately not stirred, and the finished *patina* resembled a savoury custard. A recipe called *tiropatinam* 'cheese patina' is none other than an egg custard flavoured with honey and though the instructions are sparse the need for top heat is essential to set this custard effectively.[8] The intention was I believe to set the egg in the gentlest of fires so that it didn't curdle or boil and over-cook. The texture could be quite smooth and clear and might be as good if you had cooked a cream caramel in a bain-marie. My experiments so far have allowed me to demonstrate that such a texture is possible though it is a very delicate and skilful procedure. The embers underneath are manipulated continuously to prevent the egg from overcooking at individual places in the vessel and the embers above are just sufficient to allow the custard to set and take on colour. On other occasions it is clear that the egg mixture had to be stirred continuously as we would do for an omelette or scrambled egg and the finished *patina* would have a far less appealing appearance. The herbs and spices commonly used render the egg a sludgy grey/brown in colour and the grainy texture when loosely formed may only be eaten with a spoon. However the ratio of egg to liquid is quite high in many of the recipes and this can result in a firmer mixture which can 'set' as an omelette would and as a result be cut into wedges and even eaten with the fingers when either warm or cold. We can see that the medieval *torte* with its pastry shell enabled the contents to be held safely and hygienically by the diner though it is clear that the early versions of the '*tortes*' were made with a flour and water dough known as a 'coffin' that was not necessarily meant to be eaten.

The following recipe, which has very precise quantities, reveals that the volume of liquid to egg is such that a firm texture is possible.

> 4.2.4. **Another soft *patina***: take alexanders, trim, wash, cook, refresh and wring them out. Take 4 brains, remove the sinews and cook them. Put in a mortar 6 scruples of pepper, pour on *liquamen* and pound; next add the brains and pound again; add the alexanders and pound all together. Next break 8 eggs (into the mix), add a *cyathus* of *liquamen*, a *cyathus* of wine, and a *cyathus* of *passum*. Blend thoroughly with the pounded mixture. Grease a dish (*patinam*), (pour in the mixture), place in the hot embers; then afterwards when it is cooked sprinkle with pepper and serve.

A *cyathus* is the equivalent of 1½ fl oz or 45 ml of fluid and thus the ratio of total fluid to egg is something like 135 ml. There are a great many different kinds of *patina* in *Apicius*: some appear so simple, in fact no more than a Spanish omelette in form, that without the more expensive spices one might imagine all types of Romans eating them, while some are very complex, with numerous ingredients and a layered structure. The elaborate *patina Apiciana* at 4.2.14 is constructed from a rich sauce of meat and fish bound with egg just after it comes off the heat so that it begins to set in the pan, ladled onto layers of thin bread in a deep sided vessel called a *patellam aeneam*. It is then turned out onto a dish and served either in layers (my theory) or alternatively in wedges. Although the bread is called *lagana*, there is no more than a homonymous connection to *lasagna*. This dish is bread-based, not a proto-pasta. As if in confirmation, the finished dish does not need to be cooked again.

Other simple *patinae* involve green leaves such as nettles, beet or any wild pot herb, lightly cooked and squeezed dry, arranged in a greased vessel which is already in the fire and then a little flavoured sauce and eggs are poured over. A lid and coals complete the process and the resulting thick frittata would not be out of place in any tapas or snack bar across Europe. In recognising the ancient common ancestry of the *patina* and the *torte*, Platina complained of the reversal of all things ancient: 'the pampered tastes of our contemporaries want meat (*tortes*) from birds and whatever fowl they wish, not from vegetables. They are revolted by beet, gourd, turnip, parsnip and borage: their native fare.'

There is little reference to *patinae* in ancient literature. We hear little of *patinae* being specifically included in high-status menus. The vast majority of recorded menus include food items such as roast boar or a particular fish, but named compound dishes are lacking. However, a menu recorded in Macrobius lists amongst many things oyster *patina*, fish *patina* and sow's udder *patina*.[9] The date for this feast is *c.* 50 BC, suggesting that these dishes were early components of Roman cuisine and almost certainly part of the Greek tradition that preceded it. This Greek tradition is shown in such recipes as *patella thirrotaricham*,[10]

> **4.2.17. Salt fish and cheese *patella* using any salt fish you like:** cook (the salt fish) in oil and remove the bones. (Take) cooked brains, the flesh of the fish, (cooked) chicken-livers, hard-boiled eggs, soft cheese washed in warm water. Heat up all these things in a dish. Pound pepper, lovage, oregano, rue berries, wine, *mulsum* and oil. The dish is placed on a gentle heat so that it cooks. Thicken with raw eggs, arrange (on a serving dish), sprinkle with finely ground cumin and serve.

In the Latin the eggs are used to thicken the dish as a secondary stage and it is not clear whether the mixture is meant to set sufficiently to turn out and be cut or that it would resemble a lumpy scrambled egg. The latter seems unlikely and this ambiguity in the Latin is particularly common in *Apicius*. This would certainly resemble a quiche without the pastry and when it was cold it would be possible to turn it out and cut it into wedges that the diner could handle.

This recipe is probably rather more complex than the similarly named *tyrotarichus* eaten by Cicero.[11] Cicero makes it clear that this dish was an ordinary, unpretentious meal (the use of salt fish does indicate everyday food) and is in contrast to the luxury dinners he had lately begun to consume. It was probably a much simpler mixture of fish and cheese in a sauce that is set with egg.

We also hear of a giant dish and egg *patina* ordered to be made by Vitellius at a cost of 100,000 *sestertii*. According to Suetonius, this *patina* was called the 'Shield of Minerva,' and contained 'liver of pike; brains of pheasants and peacock; tongues of flamingos and the 'blood' of lamprey' (blood *garum*) no doubt all bound with egg.[12] A mixture such as this seems entirely unappealing to us and we suspect it was equally so to the guest who had to eat it! This kind of food is essentially about showing off; the items are rare and exclusive and have very little to do with taste.

Complex compound *patinae* with many different ingredients were commonplace. The following is stuffed full of all manner of ingredients but we do not think that all the listed items were intended. We think only a selection of the ingredients was expected: the cook would choose from the list what his master would like and what was available and so we have rendered the meaning of the Latin *singula* by the word 'some'.

> Take a dish and arrange some of the following in it: hearts of mallow and beet and mature leek, celery, young greens and boiled greens, chicken meat cooked in a sauce, boiled brains, *lucanicae*, hard-boiled eggs cut in half. Put in pork sausages stuffed with a Terentine mix, cooked and sliced; chicken livers, flaked fried hake, sea-anemones, oyster flesh, fresh cheese. Arrange these in alternate

The *Patina* in Apicius

layers with pine nuts and sprinkle on whole pepper. Pour on the following sauce: pepper, lovage, celery seed, *silphium* ... (4.2.13. *Patina* with milk)

Eggs are used to set the whole as we should expect and there is a possibility that it is then turned out. Previous commentators might look at such a recipe and imagine it justly represents the stuffed to bursting image that Roman food has acquired and equate it with Vitellius' 'Shield of Minerva'. Often commentators look at elaborate recipes and see vast numbers of ingredients as words on a page which seem just 'too many' but they cannot see the dish. They cannot visualise the food being cooked or served and so have a rather one-sided image of its nature. As a chef I 'read' all recipes as visual representations and when it is possible to do this one gets a rounded and full image of the food and it is always more than the sum of its parts. A selection of the ingredients bound as a quiche and baked firm is in fact rather good.

One would not expect that understanding the simple *patinae* recipes in *Apicius* would help us to understand and define the very nature of *Apicius,* but it is fact the case. The most important question we had to ask as we worked on the text of *Apicius* was this: had the recipe collection been compiled in the Late Empire from numerous other books including an original *Apicius* text, by a single compiler? This was Brandt's theory and according to him this compiling mind was rather inadequate and appeared to make a selection from many other books and took recipes out of their original order and put them in a new order while failing to remember to miss them out when they later appeared again as he copied. This phenomenon of misplaced recipes as well as Brandt's belief that the Latin in *Apicius* was 'late' rather than 'vulgar' formed the basis of his theory of a late compilation.

Because *Apicius* is clearly written in Vulgar Latin, Brandt assumed that it therefore must also be late in date, because only at the end of the Roman empire did serious writers employ such language. However, it is clear from inscriptions and other evidence that 'vulgar Latin' coexisted with the polished style of a Cicero or a Livy, and other features of *Apicius* indicate it is not the work of such an author, but an artisanal product – the work of slave-cooks – and some of it could be the product of any period from the first century BC onwards

I thought Brandt's theory was flawed and sought to evaluate it by looking first at his theory about misplaced recipes. His argument is particularly relevant in respect of the precise nature of *patinae*. The arguments are complex but worth exploring and while it may seem that these big issues of the nature of *Apicius* and its format have no bearing on the question of eggs the reverse is not the case: the nature of these eggs dishes can have a fundamental effect on the big picture of what and who is responsible for *Apicius*

At 4.2.6 a recipe for asparagus *patina* does not cook the vegetable but simply pounds the coarser ends and infuses them in wine before throwing away the green matter and mixing the liquid with a sauce and eggs and allowing it to set into a custard. This is a very successful dish, I might add. In the next recipe in order at 4.2.7 we find 'This is how you make a *patina* from wild herbs, black briony, mustard greens, or cooking cucumber or spring greens'. The implication is that all these vegetables should be treated in the same way i.e pounded without cooking the vegetable. Brandt took it for granted that this was wrong. The vegetables listed surely needed to be cooked first he thought and he found evidence later in Book 4 that other vegetables in *patinae* were cooked and this suggested to him that a recipe had been moved from its original place. At 4.2.19 a recipe for a *patella* of horse-parsley (a form of greens) is cooked in the first instance and then seasoned. It finishes with 'You can make this dish with any herb you like'. Brandt decided that the greens listed in 4.2.7 such as mustard greens should have been cooked in the same way as those in 4.2.19 and so must have originally been placed before 4.2.19. His compiler must have moved it, he supposed.

However it is not that simple: the *patella* recipe at 4.2.19 involves cooking the greens and adding a sauce thickened with starch instead of using the eggs which is the standard setting-agent for these *patinae/patellae*. This occasionally happens and it appears to reflect the fact that any food cooked in a *patina* vessel would have been given that name, even without the eggs. The recipe 4.2.7 is for an egg *patina*, and its instruction *ita facies* (do it like this) is actually part of the previous *patina* recipe at 4.2.6 as there is no rubric initial to separate them and is therefore closely associated with 4.2.6 in the manuscript tradition (the numbering is maintained in order not to confuse the various recipes with other editions). I have experimented with these recipes and have found that vegetables such as asparagus stalks can be pounded with wine, without heat, to extract their flavour, while leaving all the material behind: the resulting 'custard' is smooth, but still flavoured with the vegetable. There is no reason why such a treatment should not be undertaken with the vegetables in 4.2.7, and in fact the resultant green custard is very appetising. The greens used may have been not quite fresh and so more useful in this manner of cooking than leaving them in. We therefore conclude that these recipes are not 'out of place', but rather follow in a reasonably logical sequence, as defined by the cook who gave them that order. The imaginary compiler of Brandt had not taken these recipes from another book at all: and in fact he vanishes away when we applied similar analysis to the other recipes that he found to be 'out of place'. The cooks were responsible for the recipes and where they fall in the text and it is not possible to identify any other literary source for the recipes.[13]

The simple *patina* and its cooking method can also reveal to us information about the later history of the text known as *Apicius*. I believe a scribe or editor after the end of the Roman period attempted to edit the text in some small ways and he did so particularly in *patinae* recipes. We can see that he was confused and added material to the text that can be detected and reveal his hand.

At 4.2.5 a recipe for a simple asparagus *patina* contains the instruction to pound pepper with *liquamen*, adding wine, *passum* and oil, then to heat it and to 'grease a dish, in it mix 6 eggs with the *oenogarum*'; the *patina* dish is then put in the hot ashes. At this point we are told to 'put in the sauce written above'; but this has obviously already gone in, with the eggs; the ingredients listed are those of a standard *oenogarum*. The fact that the superfluous line comes *after* the instruction to put the dish in the hot ashes is also an indication that someone has misunderstood the preceding instructions.[14] Perhaps a scribe or compiler, who does not realise that the *oenogarum* is the 'the sauce written above', has attempted to correct what he saw as a confusing or incomplete recipe. It is likely that the phrase 'put in the sauce written above' has been lifted directly from recipe 9 in this section, where, in context, it makes perfect sense.

And finally looking at *patina* in wider literature: food in Plautus is fraught with problems and has many layers of meaning, we must allow, and to attempt to build up a picture of culinary practice from the passages that describe food is difficult. However there is one particularly interesting passage which deserves discussion simply because it is a *patina* that is being described. We are now equipped with a detailed description of *patinae* as they later appeared in culinary literature and in *Apicius* and we can therefore ascertain whether all Plautan food is entirely imaginary as some commentators suggest: a parody reflecting no actual practice and how much of it is simply overblown descriptions of real food.

> I don't season a dinner like other cooks, who serve up seasoned meadows in their *patinae*, who make the dinner guests cattle and pile on the greens and then go on and season those greens with other greens; they chuck on coriander, fennel, garlic, black cabbage, they put on sorrel, brassica, beet and orache, and they drench the lot with a pound of *laserpicium* and miscreant mustard is pounded up, stuff which makes the eyes of those who pound it run with tears before they have finished grinding it. When these fellows cook a dinner and season it, they don't season it with seasonings but with screech-owls which eat out the insides of the guests while they still live![15]

Analysis of this passage in the past has been over-concerned with the ingredients, from the point of view of vegetarian-versus-meat, vegetables-versus-herbs, and also with the origin of the listed items: which of them might be Greek, which Roman and consequently whose food is being parodied Greece or Rome? We think this passage can and should be taken far more literally. What we have is a *patina*: a composite dish of many ingredients set with egg with too many seasonings. The passage suggests that the seasonings are strong and cruel in the mouth but of course they are not: there is a list of mild green pot herbs and the *silphium* and mustard are common ingredients in the later recipes and not necessarily out of place in any dish, there are just too many of them in this particular one. It is just the kind of *patina* that we find in *Apicius* but not surprisingly, given that it is Plautus, it has even more seasonings than the cooks later used. The objects of the parody are Greek cooks and their masters who want dishes seasoned with too many things, and the resulting dish is a confused mess in every sense. Given the date that Plautus was writing, *c.* 200 BC, Roman food as a cuisine was in its infancy, unformed and to some extent as yet 'uncorrupted' by the 'sophisticated Greeks'. One has to ask: whose cuisine is being parodied here, if it is not the cooking style and traditions of the Greeks?

Notes

1. Athenaeus 169e–f; *patanÁ* became *patina*, deriving from the same root as 'pan' in English. For its possible connection with paella: see also Barbara Santich, 'Testo, Tegamo, Tiella, Tian: The Mediterranean Camp Oven', in *The Cooking Pot: Proceedings of the Oxford Symposium on Food and Cookery* 1998, p. 139. *Apicius* 4.2.14–15 where the titles to both recipes use *patina* even though the vessel is named as a *patella aenea* that also has some depth.
2. J. W. Hayes, *Late Roman Pottery* (British School at Rome, 1972). A. Riley, 'The Coarse Pottery', in J. A. Lloyd (ed.) *Excavations at Sidi Khrebish, Benghazi (Berenice)* (Tripoli, 1979), vol. 2, 91–467.
3. This fabric is also fired at a relatively low temperature (estimated at 900°F rather than 1000°F+). This is indicated by its soft, easily-scratched surface. This soft fabric is less inclined to break in a fire as the clay particles are not fixed, as in harder fabrics, and are able to move as they are heated.
4. Previous commentators have believed that the *thermospodium* was a separate piece of equipment of some sort such as a hearth box, or a distinct kind of cooking oven. See A.L. Cubberley *et al.,* 'Testa and *clibani:* The Baking Covers of Classical Italy', in *Papers of the British School at Rome* 61 (1988), 98–119; A. Cubberley, 'Bread-baking in Ancient Italy: *clibanus* and *sub testu* in the Roman World', in *Food in Antiquity*, ed. J. Wilkins, D. Harvey, M. Dobson (Exeter, 1995), 55–68; J. Frayn, 'Home baking in Roman Italy', *Antiquity* 52 (1978), 57–157. *In thermospodio* is used interchangeably with *cineri calido,* 'hot embers,' in recipe 4.2.9; they are simply synonyms.
5. Hayes, op. cit. p. 205.
6. Lid with turned-up edge: D766 in Riley, 'The Coarse Pottery', 1979; Many of these vessels and lids are discoloured grey or black on the outer surfaces and this is defined as damage caused by inadequate firing in the kiln. Replica vessels used to cook various *patinae* turn grey/black after being used, in a distinctive manner that may indicate that the genuine vessels have been used in hot embers.
7. There are a number of recipes where eggs are not used but the finished dish still has the name *patina* 4.2.37;34;32;30;29;25;24;23;22;21;19;11; 12 out of 37 *patinae* do not use, or omit, egg.
8. 7.11.7.
9. Macrobius 3.13.12. The feast was in honour of the inauguration of Lentulus as the priest of Mars; Caesar, as *rex sacrorum,* was among the guests.
10. From *tyro,* 'cheese', and *tarichos,* 'salt fish'.
11. Cicero, *Ad fam.* 9.16.9.
12. Pliny *HN.* 35. 165; Suetonius, *Vitellius* 13.
13. Brandt, *Untersuchungen* p. 36. There are a number of other recipes that Brandt assumed had been moved for similar culinary reasons though they are not defined as *patinae* and are therefore outside the scope of this paper.
14. It would be sensible to put the dish in the ashes first to warm it up before adding the mixture so that the contrast in temperature did not break the vessel, as occurs in recipe 9 above.
15. Plautus, *Pseudolus* 810–21.

Sustainable Is Beautiful: Pastured Egg Farming in Central New York

Naomi Guttman

It might seem that an egg which has succeeded in being fresh has done all that can be reasonably expected of it.

Henry James

The Mohawk Valley region of New York State, where I live, is largely agricultural, with small farms dotting the sides of its rolling hills. In the past 25 years, many farms have been abandoned, but there seems to be a renaissance of interest in farming among a new generation of farmers. There seems to be a growing movement of sustainable small farms throughout the region, organic vegetable farms and grass-fed animal farms, and several of these farms raise chickens and eggs. One of these is Windhaven Farm in Sauquoit, New York, 10 miles south of Utica. Formerly a family maple farm, Windhaven was bought by new owners nine years ago and converted to a grass farm for pastured poultry, eggs, cattle, pigs, and sheep. Along with the meat and eggs, the farm produced sheep's milk yogurt and cheese.

Last May, this 94-acre farm was sold again to Andrea and Ethan Tancredi, a young couple with three children who had been raising meat and eggs in Pennsylvania on rented property but were eager to own their own farm. The farm is half open pasture and half woods, which the Tancredis plan to let the pigs forage in as soon as they put up more electric fencing. Both Ethan and Andrea have moved around the country a lot, and both are college educated. Andrea has a BA in psychology and Ethan received a Master's in Classics, but, she says, they both always wanted to farm: 'It was our dream,' Andrea tells me as we stand in her milking parlor listening to the rain come down on the corrugated tin roof like a team of horses.

Earlier that morning Andrea Tancredi had phoned me to postpone our meeting by several hours. It had been a wet night, and several of her cows had broken through the electric fencing in order to sit under some trees in the distance; her sheep had followed. The problem was rounding up the sheep again, which she had to do by herself, since her kids were still finishing the school year back in Pennsylvania and her husband was there with them, tying up loose ends and taking care of the move.

Completely clad in olive-green rain gear, Andrea looks like the picture-perfect farmer, or a fisherman. Her broad face is tanned, her hair is pinned up behind her head, and she looks happy and at ease. She has a friendly smile, with a gap between her two upper front teeth. It is a hot afternoon in late June, with many rain showers, and vertical flags of mist hang over the hills. The weather service has announced flash flood warnings, and my two and a half hour tour and interview is punctuated by heavy rains. The countryside around is lush and beautiful, with rolling hills, silos, and maple stands. It would be perfectly bucolic except for the several clusters of newly built suburban-style homes springing up along the roads.

I've come here particularly to investigate the small-egg farm in this region because I am curious about the local Slow Food movement and the ways in which it fits into the larger economy. Even though I have subscribed to a local CSA, shop at an independent health food store as much as possible, and have for several years bought pastured meats in bulk from another grass farm, I still feel there is a lot to learn about small farmers, how they get their product to the market, and the compromises that must be made in order to keep their businesses afloat. When we speak, Andrea refers not to consumers, but to 'customers,' and in spite of the hardships and mishaps of farming, she is enthusiastic about showing me the farm and discussing all aspects of the business and greater policy issues.

The American consumer, or customer, is awash with information – and misinformation – about eggs. While annual egg consumption in the U.S. dropped from 402 per capita in 1945 to 233.5 in 1991, this decrease in eggs eaten per capita corresponds to the rise in industrial egg production. In the 1940s most eggs came from small farms, but today 98 per cent of U.S. eggs come from huge battery-cage egg factories where chickens lay eggs in appalling conditions. As Marion Nestle observes in her book *What to Eat,* battery production 'confines tens of thousands of chickens in cages piled one on top of another in batteries infamous for accumulated feces, feathers, and the overpowering smell of ammonia from the hens' wastes.'[1] In addition to these practices, many websites and books document the use of cruel practices such as de-beaking and forced molting among the large egg-producers in the U.S.

While some consumer groups have been trying to educate the public about the cruel fate of chickens in this system, most U.S. consumers either remain unaware of how eggs are produced or don't care, so long as eggs are abundant and cheap, which they are. Unlike the EU, which has committed to phasing out battery hen production by 2012 and has a series of agreed-upon labels that will be clearly understood by both producers and consumers, the U.S. has no such plan to phase out caged-hen egg production and the terms used by the industry to differentiate and add value to their products are unregulated.

So called 'designer eggs,' which include everything from guarantees that hens are humanely treated to boasts of high Omega-3 fats, have taken a small share of the market. Yet according to an organization critical of the egg industry called United Poultry Concerns, the labels used to advertise poultry and eggs are 'not all they're cracked up to be.'[2]

Whereas we may think 'free range' indicates we're eating eggs raised from hens who live outside on a grassy pasture, able to sustain themselves, the USDA's only criterion for the free range label is that the birds have access to the outdoors. This means only that a door be left open, and while the USDA does have guidelines for free-range poultry that is to be used for meat, no standards exist for egg-producing hens, and no guidelines are posted as to the size of area of this access, the amount of time allowed outdoors, the number of birds, or the amount of space per bird.[3] However, some advocates feel that free-range is more honest than cage-free, which is also unregulated. Cage-free hens are often crowded together in large sheds or barns and have barely more room than they would in a cage. Another cagey label used by the egg industry has been Animal Care Certified, a label made up by the egg industry, which recently had to change its label to 'United Egg Producers Certified' under pressure from Humane Societies who registered complaints with The Better Business Bureau. The BCC determined that Animal Care Certified was misleading consumers who would assume that the animals were being well-treated when in fact they were still in battery cages. 'Certified Organic' indicates that the birds were fed an organic diet, received no antibiotics, and had some access to the outdoors. 'Certified Humane: Raised and Handled' does not indicate what the birds are given to eat, but does guarantee that the birds were treated better than some. However, this agency is not government regulated and consumers must take on faith that the Humane Society is able to properly monitor the egg-farms that produce eggs with this label.

In contrast to the muddle of terms above, pastured eggs, while they have no regulatory body, and are not necessarily organic, are probably the best guarantee of humane treatment: in pastured egg production, hens live in portable range houses that are moved regularly around the pasture which is then enclosed with electric fencing. Because the hens have room to move and can peck into the grass, there is no reason to de-beak them, a common practice in conventional egg farming to prevent hens from pecking at one another. In addition, moving the hens frequently prevents the build up of ammonia from their waste and allows them to get 20–30 per cent of their nutrition from grasses, insects, and slugs. According to the Compassionate Consumer website, 'the most humane choices are fertile eggs and pastured eggs. Fertile eggs, while also unregulated, do require that a rooster be allowed to roam with the hens.… Pastured eggs mean that the hens are living outside in the grass.'[4]

One organization recommends that the best way to ascertain the treatment of the hens that produce the eggs you eat is to go to the farm. And this is precisely the ethos of the small farmers with whom I met during the course of my research. As Andrea puts it, 'we are customer-inspected.' Nancy Grove, who runs Old Path Farm, the CSA farm where I get my vegetables during the season, affirms this when she says that Community-Supported Agriculture has another side: Agriculture-Supported Community, and that the give and take between customer, or community, is what the Slow Food or Sustainable Agriculture movement looks to for its own sustenance.

While the rain stops for an hour or so, Andrea and I walk around her farm. Three hundred chickens live in the range houses, which look like Iroquois long houses, but are made of metal tubes and blue tenting. Each house has space for a hundred chickens to roost and lay eggs, with 6–10 layers per nest, and contains waterers, perches, and a long metal trough for feeding that has been moved outdoors for the summer. In the winter she and her husband will insulate the houses with hay around the edges, but she assures me that hens winter well outdoors and don't need heaters as long as they are dry and able to perch. They are fed twice a day, a mixture of corn meal with vitamin and mineral supplements. The flock the Tancredis inherited is made up of Red Stars with a couple of Black Stars, Leghorns, and Anaconas thrown in here and there. Eventually, they plan to breed and raise Delawares, which are dual-purpose, meat and egg hens. Andrea likes Delawares because they are a heritage breed, which she values for its hardiness and for tradition. Whereas Leghorns are bred as layers for their productivity, the Delaware and other heritage breeds are sturdier. 'They have different personalities, too,' she says. 'Leghorns are really nervous, flighty.' Like Jean Brodie, Andrea has an affectionate relationship with what she terms her 'girls.' Her hens are bought ready-to-lay at 20 weeks, or raised from chicks, and each lives for two years of good production – three laying seasons – before she is butchered for meat.

While eggs only contribute a fraction to the farm's gross income, about 15 per cent she estimates, in Andrea's view they are essential to the farm's economy, because, she says, they provide innumerable benefits to the farm's environment by distributing their droppings, scattering grass seed, and aerating the soil with their pecking. As omnivores, the chickens eat insects and other small creatures. Thus the chickens 'pay for themselves' and she wouldn't want to part with them. I ask her if she has affectionate reasons for keeping birds. She smiles. As a psychology major Andrea focused on animal behavior and negotiation, and believes she draws on her training in these areas every day as a farmer. 'Yes, I love the birds. They all have their quirks.' She points to an albino Anacona with a crooked beak whom they refer to as 'Crooked Beak.' And indeed, the small, pale creature has a bent whitish beak. 'She's peculiar, but she's tough and has a great personality.' This bird does not produce, but is more of a pet, or farm character that makes herself at home outside the flock.

Along with their sheep's yogurt and cheese, the Tancredis sell the eggs through several local health food stores, a creamery, and a bagel store. When I ask how many eggs she sells, she says she's not sure. Her hens produce six to seven eggs a week in the summer, four to five in winter. 'I sell every egg I've got and if it's cracked, I feed it to the pigs.' During the last school year, she also sold quite a number of eggs to Ruben Haag, chef for Hamilton College's food service provider, Bon Appetit. Last October, in a deal with the Humane Society of the United States, Bon Appetit, which has headquarters in Palo Alto, California, pledged to start selling only eggs from uncaged birds in all its venues. Haag was thereby given the green light to buy eggs that carry the Certified Humane label, but he is interested in promoting local agriculture and, wanting to help out the previous owner of Windhaven, agreed last semester to buy her eggs. He hopes that Bon Appetit will give him the green light to continue the relationship, but he's still waiting.

Andrea also likes to sell directly to the consumer. If she were to sell to large grocery stores, they would demand a lower price, which in turn would mean she would have to increase production. And that would mean increasing her production on all fronts. 'It would mean we couldn't have the chickens on pasture – if there were more of them, they'd be putting a lot more nitrogen and doing a lot more scratching on the ground, and there's only so much the soil will take.' 'We're not looking for monoculture,' she says. 'On a farm like ours, everybody has their job, and the chickens' job is to fertilize and aerate the soil.' In order to remain diversified, Andrea feels they need to remain small: expanding egg production would mean expanding all over for the sake of balance. And they are not ready to do that.

When I ask Andrea who she feels is her competition, she says she has a cooperative rather than competitive relationship with other grass-fed producers. For example, when she was having problems with a predator and needed eggs, Wendy Gornick of Sweetgrass farms supplied Windhaven with eggs so that Andrea could continue to supply her customers. When she was farming in Pennsylvania, a local farmer who had some land saw that she and other grass-raised chicken farmers could get $3.00 a dozen for organic eggs, and set up his own local production. It took a while for Andrea to educate her customers to see that his eggs were not like hers. His chickens were indoors with little space; he fed them cheap grain, and his scale of production was much bigger. Eventually she got most of her customers back. Andrea believes this is evidence that 'every town could probably support several grass farm producers.'

Andrea doesn't grade the eggs, figuring that consumers enjoy getting a variety of sizes and colors of egg in their boxes. At the moment, Andrea buys her grain from a local provider who does not grow organic. 'It's a toss up,' Andrea says, 'whether to get organic feed that's lots more expensive and from another place or to feed them locally grown grain.' She will look into finding a local organic grain producer eventually, but knows that this will increase the price of her eggs by 50 per cent. At their previous farm, they fed certified organic grains to their hens, but didn't bother to go through certification for the eggs themselves. 'What certification gives you is credibility with people who don't know you. We are customer-inspected.'

Clearly, the Windhaven flock is treated much better than an industrial flock, but Andrea also notes differences between her eggs and commercially produced eggs. Her eggs look and taste better: the yolks are orange and are firmer and the eggs have a better texture. Andrea believes that her pastured eggs also have more nutrients than conventional eggs and recommends I read Jo Robinson's *Pasture Perfect,* which I do. Robinson cites one pastured egg farmer's study that indicated her eggs had '40 per cent more vitamin A and 400 per cent more omega-3 fatty acids' as well as 34 per cent lower cholesterol.[5]

Pastured Egg Farming in Central New York

In my conversations with Andrea and with Nancy Grove of Old Path Farm, sustainability rather than scale is key. We discuss what kinds of interventions one is willing to use to have sustainable rather than, necessarily, 'organic' farms: Is it better to leave a light on for the chickens to extend their day during the winter and thus boost their productivity, or are you going to keep everything hard line? 'The light is just one intervention among many one could have, e.g. antibiotics or arsenic in the food' says Andrea. Though both Nancy and Andrea would like to be 100 per cent organic, they are not necessarily eager to become certified. 'This is why there's resistance to the organic label – there needs to be wiggle room. e.g. 'Access to pasture' – what does that really mean? Does it mean that that product is better, that the animal was better treated than mine?' Andrea asks.

Nancy Grove's egg operation is much smaller than Windhaven's. Currently she has 30 laying hens and collects around 20 eggs a day. Some of the hens are older, so they are not laying as frequently as the young ones. Though Old Path does sell eggs to some of their neighbors, because they are a vegetable farm and a CSA, most of their eggs go into what Grove calls 'the barter larder' for trading for various foods and as gifts to the volunteers who come to help them tend the crops. Grove's brother, who runs a local restaurant called The Bagel Grove, uses her eggs in the winter months when there is no market and thus more eggs than they can handle. They hope one day to be able to supply the entire Bagel Grove need for eggs, which is about twenty-dozen a week. While their current winter housing facility can only accommodate the hens that they have, Grove does foresee more egg production at her farm, making it a more substantial part of the business. She hopes to increase the flock to up to two hundred birds. Like the Tancredis, Grove sees many benefits to having the hens on the farm, both as part of their barter system, of giving back to the community, and as a way to maintain the soil: 'We enjoy having some livestock here because it brings a different life to the farm's agro-ecosystem. With the portable poultry fence, we have great flexibility as to where the chickens range. Currently they are feasting on several beds in the garden where we have completed the vegetable harvest. The hens eat the plant residues and dig up the soil as they search for bugs. They love slugs, which are a threat to several of our vegetable crops. They also deposit their manure on the garden and thus offer a hands-free form of fertilization that will benefit our growing next year. Additionally, as we move them around the farm homestead, they keep the grass down and thus limit our need for mowing.'[6]

Ten years ago the U.S. Secretary of Agriculture issued this memorandum on USDA sustainable agriculture policy: 'USDA is committed to working toward the economic, environmental, and social sustainability of diverse food, fiber, agriculture, forest, and range systems. USDA will balance goals of improved production and profitability, stewardship of the natural resource base and ecological systems, and enhancement of the vitality of rural communities. USDA will integrate these goals into its policies and programs, particularly through interagency collaboration, partnerships and outreach.'

Pastured Egg Farming in Central New York

While most Americans remain ignorant of the role farming plays in their lives and the power of big agriculture to shape what and how they eat, small steps are being taken. McDonalds and Burger King have both been pressuring their egg suppliers to change to more humane modes of production. While these businesses have yet to go 'cage-free,' decisions such as these raise the profile of sustainable and humane practices. Across the country college students and food services are looking for more humane egg and meat suppliers. We can only hope that it's only a matter of time before we embrace the sustainable egg in larger numbers: 'It's tastier, healthier, more environmentally sound, and less cruel. With fresher, tastier eggs, perhaps we will be willing', as Jo Robinson writes, 'to pay more for [our] food and eat less of it.'[7]

Bibliography

Grove, Nancy, e-mail correspondence, July 8th, 2006.
Nestle, Marion, *What to Eat* (North Point Press: Boston, 2006).
Robinson, Jo, *Pasture Perfect: The Far-Reaching Benefits of Choosing Meat, Eggs, and Dairy Products from Grass-Fed Animals* (Vashon Island Press: Vashon, Washington, 2004).

Notes

1. Nestle, 260.
2. www.upc-online.org.
3. Ibid.
4. www.compassionatesconsumer.org.
5. Robinson, 54.
6. Grove.
7. Robinson.

Saving the Lost, Sour Eggs: an Annotated Pictorial Documentation of an Almost Extinct German Egg Recipe

Ursula Heinzelmann

Saving the Lost, Sour Eggs

Saure Eier
Mehlschwitze, nicht zu dick
40g Fett – Butter
40g Mehl andünsten
½ l Flüssigkeit nach + nach dazugeben. Etwas kochen lassen. Mit - 1 Eßl. Essig + 1 Eßl. Zucker abschmecken. Kl. Flamme Eier hineinschlagen, wenn das Weiße etwas fest wird umdrehen u. noch eine kurze Zeit, nicht zu lange da das Gelbe sonst zu fest wird.

That is what my mother wrote down when recently I urged her repeatedly to give me a copy of her recipe for sour eggs, one of my very favourite childhood dishes. Here is a literal translation:

Sour eggs
Roux, not too thick
40g fat – butter
40g flour sweat
½ l. liquid add gradually. Let cook a little. Season with about 1 tbs vinegar and 1 tbs sugar. Low heat drop eggs in, when the white starts to thicken turn and a little longer, not too long because otherwise the yolk gets too hard.

My mother never had a written recipe for this dish – she just cooked it. Also, she is not used to writing recipes. She starts with an instruction, then it seems as if she looks up a recipe to explain this instruction – hence the systematic listing of the first ingredients, but also the addition of the word 'butter' to the indicated fat as a personal comment and the word 'liquid' where at the stove she never uses anything other than water. After that she gets into the flow and writes down what she thinks she does at the stove. We will see that she forgets to mention salt and underestimates the amount of vinegar needed.

Sour eggs, or sweet-sour eggs, as they are also sometimes called, are the opposite of restaurant-style cooking. They belong to the domestic kitchen table, are children's food and with their bland colour and comforting mushiness almost a nursery dish. The recipe is not included in any of the contemporary standard cookery books. However, a quick field research in the kindergarten my mother works at as well as on the Internet, showed that it is still known – but an interesting point became clear: sour eggs are almost always mentioned in connection with grandmothers. Either Oma – Granny – makes them, or somebody else – mostly grandchildren – tries to make them as granny did, perhaps in the search for a lost world.

There is clearly a strong nostalgic element here. If we look a bit closer at these humble eggs, we find that they belong to a very different world, which existed long before our culinary obsession with everything Mediterranean and the triumph of *nouvelle cuisine*. Only now and very slowly is roasted flour making a hesitant comeback after all the butter that we used to bind sauces during the last 30 years. A roux is one of the most basic elements of classic French cuisine, but it does require some experience. You have to juggle with the temperature, which should be low each time you add some more liquid and then higher as you bring the sauce to the boil again. It is one of those cooking methods you need to be shown once, which then with your own experience becomes what the Hungarian scientist and philosopher Michael Polanyi called 'tacit knowing'. The American philosopher Lisa Heldke discusses this idea especially in connection with cooking and uses the terms 'bodily knowledge' and 'thoughtful practice'.[1]

You can see very well how my mother almost instinctively lifts the pan off the hot plate at certain moments and how she trusts the lumps to transform into a smooth homogenous sauce. She has always used butter for cooking, but never fussed around with stock for this recipe. My aunt, her sister, some time ago started using potato water, but my mother thinks this interferes with the taste she is looking for in the final dish.

Sweet and sour in a savoury dish – salt is just as important in this recipe as vinegar and sugar, in fact so much that my mother takes it for granted – is a very ancient taste combination. As Laura Mason has explained in the *Oxford Companion to Food*, it is traditional and still very common in Scandinavia and (Northern) Central Europe, although even there since the 1950s it has gradually been superseded by Mediterranean flavours – or rather the tomato/olive oil/basil/balsamico combination most people regard as archetypically Italian. There are several observations to be made in this context. First, as Mason also writes, there is a strong tradition for *agrodolce* all around the Mediterranean, mostly combinations of sharp tasting fruits or vinegar and raisins, which may go back to the honey and vinegar sauce of Apicius fame – which in fact is indicated for soft-boiled eggs, 'in ovis apalis'[2] – and beyond that. But this aspect of culinary Italy is almost never included in the modern export version, just as most people north of the Alps think that Italians only ever use balsamic vinegar when they want acidity. It was partly for that reason that during the 1980s and '90s a real fashion for 'good' vinegar took place not only in Germany. It started with the introduction of French raspberry vinegar and culminated in the Doktorenhof, an entire wine-estate in the Pfalz dedicated to the production of 'Aperitif-Essig'. Traditional vinegar which tastes much sharper and in the north is mostly made from potato spirit, was thereby degraded to a 'cheap product'.[3]

But the humble eggs want a humble vinegar. Vinegar production, closely linked to the mustard, sauerkraut and pickle industries used to be important all over Germany; Kühne, originally a Berlin company whose vinegar my mother still uses, was founded in 1722. However, it is an interesting thought that balsamic vinegar, especially in its less concentrated commercial version connects with the old Northern predilection for sugar and acidity.

Saving the Lost, Sour Eggs

It should come as no surprise that sour eggs succumbed to the culinary Mediterreanisation in West Germany, but throve in the East. They were regarded as a typical Monday canteen dish – not much preparation, filling and cheap. However, looked at closer, there is a fundamental difference between that dish and the one my mother makes. Whereas for the hungry socialist workers hard-boiled eggs were placed on a mountain of roughly puréed potatoes and covered with sauce, she poaches the eggs in the sauce and the yolks must stay soft so that they mix with the sauce and potatoes when eaten.

On one hand this makes the dish easier to prepare as it saves several separate pans and steps. On the other hand though, poaching eggs is considered to be among the higher culinary skills. Again, as with the roux, experience and confidence is needed. Not least the unfussy, pragmatic Edouard de Pomiane dedicates a whole page to the method.[4] It is interesting to note that he – in common with all other modern cookery books I know of – points out that the water in which the eggs are poached, must not be salted, but a little vinegar added. Salt would dissolve a certain part of the egg white and result in threads and a less perfect shape, whereas vinegar is thought to help the coagulation process. In former times cooks were mostly convinced of the opposite. Harold McGee, the American cooking scientist, debunks it all though; he thinks that the freshness of the eggs is most important, as the white becomes thinner with time, and that the poaching liquid must be under boiling point, so that a thin coagulated coating can form unhindered. In German poached eggs are called *verlorene Eier*, lost eggs. This refers to the so-called *Windeier*, wind eggs, when a bird occasionally lays an egg without shell, generally mostly because of a calcium deficiency.

Let us look at some poached egg recipes through the centuries to get an idea of the historical background of my childhood favourite. Scanning the Internet for the present brings up: the nostalgic granny connection in blogs;[5] the GDDR Monday canteen version as an alternative to equally quickly prepared *Spirelli* noodles with tomato sauce;[6] a contemporary theatre bistro in Brandenburg offering them on a menu next to spinach with scrambled eggs and meatballs;[7] a sour eggs recipe on the website of the Sorbian town of Schleife/Slepo;[8] then on a website dedicated to genealogy, a Canadian with German family roots has published two cookery books which his Silesian grandmother (!) started in 1914 in Liegnitz: her recipe is almost identical to that of my mother.[9]

My mother's might be a toned-down nursery version, because most recipes start with bacon and onions in small cubes and roast the flour longer to achieve a brownish colour. Bay leaf, allspice, pepper and, mustard are used as seasonings, sometimes dill and even capers. The eggs are either boiled in their shells or poached separately. Sometimes they are called *Eier in (saurer) Specksauce*, eggs in (sour) bacon sauce. A slim East German publication from Leipzig of 1959 about eggs in general explains in great detail how to poach eggs, then comments somewhat disparagingly that they are mostly 'only' known as sour eggs and proceeds to give several pages of supposedly more 'elegant' recipes.[10] The 1963 edition caves in and includes the sour egg recipe,[11] but in 1982 there is no mention of it at all. In 1980 though Scharfenberg includes it (again with a brown bacon sauce) in his somewhat nostalgic collection of traditional German regional recipes – published in West Germany and Switzerland – which may be interpreted as the step from living dish to documented tradition.[12] The *Lexikon der Küche*, a standard reference book for professional chefs gives 288 traditional *garnitures* for poached eggs.[13] But although these include one named after the famous Berlin painter and architect Karl Friedrich Schinkel as well as an *à l'allemande* and an *à la polonaise* version, there is nothing which would even roughly resemble our sour eggs.

The highly successful Time-Life series of the 1980s does not mention sour eggs in any recognisable version either, but includes the French classic *Oeufs en Meurette* and a Tuscan version[14] – in both the eggs are poached in wine which is then used to make the sauce.

Going back in time however, we find them – once again with bacon – in both Mary Hahn's and Henriette Davidis' books, a standard recipe for bourgeois households from the middle of the nineteenth century.[15] Before that time we have to look for the heading 'lost eggs'. Maria Schellhammer was from Braunschweig but published her substantial cookery book in 1723 in Berlin under the name of *Brandenburgisches Kochbuch*. She serves poached eggs (indicating salted water!) in two versions: either warm and seasoned with mace,[16] or cold with a sauce made from cress grated with good wine vinegar, strained and seasoned with ginger, pepper, cinnamon, sugar and salt.[17] Over a century earlier Franz de Rontzier, longstanding personal chef of the dukes of Braunschweig-Lüneburg, published his *Kunstbuch von mancherley Essen*. Book and man have always stood somewhat in the shadow of Marx Rumpolt and his best-selling *Ein new Kochbuch*, published 17 years earlier, in 1581 when he was *Mundkoch* to the Elector of Mainz.

It is always interesting to compare recipes from those two publications. Rumpolt, who was Hungarian by birth, shows much more Romanesque influence and grandeur, although Rontzier in Wolfenbüttel resided over a kitchen that had to serve a duke who was well into baroque splendour and magnificence, especially after marrying a Danish princess. Rontzier mentions neither salt nor vinegar for poaching his *verlorne Eyer*, but six different ways to serve them,[18] of which the fifth might somewhat resemble our dish in taste: gooseberries with small raisins, sugar, a little butter and wine are made into a sauce. Rumpolt does not explain at all the method of poaching eggs, he just asks for them in two different recipes.[19] In one he warms them up in a sauce made of egg yolk, pea stock, vinegar and a little butter, alternatively sprinkled with ginger or fresh chopped herbs, in the other he warms them in a little pea stock and butter to which sour mustard dressed with vinegar is added before serving.

The combination of egg yolk and vinegar finally brings us to Pliny the Elder who presented his contemporary Apicius as a glutton and spendthrift. Indeed, the rich

Saving the Lost, Sour Eggs

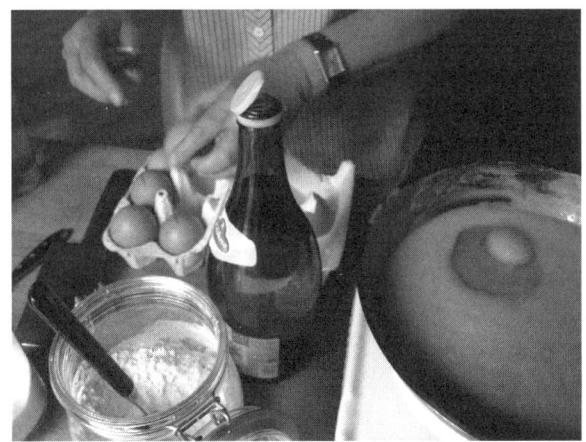

Apicius serves 'in ovis apalis', presumably soft-boiled eggs, with a sauce made from pepper, lovage, soaked pine nuts, honey, vinegar and liquamen, the salty fish sauce. Pliny on the other hand is more interested in their medicinal side: he says to stop diarrhoea use the yolks of eggs boiled in vinegar until hard then grilled with ground pepper.[20]

My mother has never thought of sour eggs as a medicine, but without any doubt the dish for me will always speak of her love and care. It requires a lot more culinary skill and experience than she is aware of – and I certainly hope that those eggs will never be *verloren*!

My thanks go to Nilesh Patel, London based architect and film maker whose beautiful film *A Love Supreme* (2001) shows his mother making samosas. It is a wonderful way to document a dish and the pictures I was able to show at the Symposium and in this paper are but a poor attempt to do something in that direction.

Bibliography

Anonym [Maria Sophia Schellhammerin], *Das Brandenburgische Kochbuch oder: Die wohl-unterwiesene Köchinn* (Berlin: Rüdiger, 1723, repr Rostock: Hinstorff, 1984).

Apicius, Marcus Gaius, *De re coquinaria Über die Kochkunst*, transl. and ed. Robert Maier (Stuttgart: Reclam, 1991).

Capatti, Alberto and Massimo Montanari, *La cucina italiana, Storia di una cultura* (Roma-Bari: Laterza, 1999).

Casdorff, Heinz, ed., *Das Buch der sauren Arbeit: Essig-Kühne* (Hamburg: Broschek, 1938).

Clauss, Stephan, *Essig, Der Guide für Kenner und Feinschmecker* (München: Heyne, 1996).

Curtin, Deane W. and Lisa M. Heldke, eds., *Cooking, Eating, Thinking, Transformative Philosophies of Food* (Bloomington and Indianapolis: Indiana University Press, 1992).

Davidis, Henriette, *Praktisches Kochbuch für die gewöhnliche und feinere Küche* (Bielefeld und Leipzig: Velhagen & Klasing, 1845).

Eier Milch Rezepte für herzhafte und süße Gerichte (Leipzig: Verlag für die Frau, oJ [1963]).

Eier roh gekocht gebraten gebacken (Leipzig: Verlag für die Frau, oJ [1959]).
Eier und Käse (3. Aufl. – Amsterdam: Time-Life Books, 1982).
Hahn, Mary, *Praktisches Kochbuch für die bürgerliche Küche* (16. verb. und erw. Aufl. – Berlin-Steglitz: Mary Hahn's Kochbuch-Verlag, oJ [nach 1934]).
Hering, Richard, *Lexikon der Küche* (20. neubearb Auflage – Gießen: Fachbuchverlag Dr. Pfanneberg, 1990).
Milch, Quark, Eier Gesunde Ernährung (Leipzig: Verlag für die Frau, oJ [1982]).
Plinius Secundus, Gaius, *Natural History*, in 10 volumes, trans. W.H.S. Jones (Cambridge, Mass: Harvard University Press & London: Heinemann, 1963) .
Pomiane, Edouard de, *Cooking with Pomiane*, trans. and ed. Peggie Benton (London: The Cookery Book Club, 1969).
Rontzier, Franz de, *Kunstbuch von mancherley Essen*, ed. Manfred Lemmer (Wolfenbüttel, 1598, repr. Leipzig, 1979).
Rumpolt, Marx, *Ein new Kochbuch* (Frankfurt am Main: Feyerabend, 1581, repr. Hildesheim, New York: Olms, 1976).
Scharfenberg, Horst, *Aus Deutschlands Küchen* (Bern und Stuttgart: Hallwag, 1994. Aufl.).

Notes
1. Curtin and Heldke, p. 218–20.
2. Apicius, p. 119.
3. Clauss, p. 10.
4. Pomiane, p. 36.
5. Saure Eier – Oma's Rezept, Whitby, 9.1.2005 (www.wer-weiss-was.de/theme96/article2651195.html, 20.06.2006); Saure Eier mit Kartoffeln (www.kinderrezepte.de, 20.06.2006); Süß-Saure Eier (www.frag-mutti.de, 20.06.2006).
6. DDR, Rezepte, Speisen, Gerichte – Kochrezepte der ehem. Deutschen Demokratischen Republik, der DDR: Süss-Saure Eier mit Quetschkartoffeln (www.kirchenweb.at, 20.06.2006); Typische Gerichte der Uckermark – Quetschkartoffeln und süss-saure Eier (www.uckermark-erleben.de, 20.06.2006).
7. Märkische Allgemeine Zeitung (Brandenburg/Havel) 05.01.2006: Regionale Nachrichten (www.maerkischeallgemeine.de, 20.06.2006).
8. Homepage Gemeinde Schleife/Slepo (www.schleife-slepo.de, 20.06.2006).
9. Unsere deutschen Wurzeln – Our German Roots – Schlesien und Siebenbürgen (www.freepages.genealogy.rootsweb.com/~bgwiehle, 20.06.2006).
10. *Eier* 1959, p. 10–12.
11. *Eier Milch* 1963, p. 10.
12. Scharfenberg, p. 216.
13. Hering, p. 145–58.
14. *Eier und Käse*, p. 91/2.
15. Hahn, p. 234.
16. Schellhammer, p. 440.
17. Schellhammer, p. 450.
18. Rontzier, p. 532.
19. Rumpolt, p. CXLVI.
20. Pliny, book 29, 49.

Eggs and the Japanese

Naomichi Ishige

Symbolism of Eggs

Japanese myths show the idea of the Cosmic Egg, which is a metaphor for a primordial form of the universe. *Kojiki Nihonshoki*, which is also known as *Nihongi*, is one of the oldest Japanese history books and was written in the early eighth century. The following is the beginning: 'Of old, Heaven and Earth were not yet separated, and the In [Yin] and Yo [Yang] not yet divided. They formed a chaotic mass like an egg which was of obscurely defined limits and contained germs. The purer and clearer part was thinly drawn out, and formed Heaven, while the heavier and grosser element settled down and became Earth. The finer element easily became a united body, but the consolidation of the heavy and gross element was accomplished with difficulty. Heaven was therefore formed first, and Earth was established subsequently. Thereafter divine beings were produced between them'.[1] This is the first written material in Japan in which the term 'egg' appears.

Although in the West birds' eggs are often treated as symbols of life and resurrection, it is not as common in Japan. However, fish ovaries, which are full of fish eggs, are regarded as symbols of fertility and family prosperity. The Japanese are famous for eating fish in large quantities. However, they also relish fish eggs. In some varieties of fish, eggs are more expensive than the rest of the fish. Fresh fish eggs are often seasoned with soy sauce and Japanese saké and boiled. They are also cured in salt or dried as preserved food. They are enjoyed as a costly delicacy like caviar.

For instance, herring's eggs, brit, are called *kazunoko*. They are soused in bonito soup stock, soy sauce, and Japanese saké and eaten fresh. *Kazunoko* is seen as lucky food for family prosperity and particularly used for wedding ceremonies and New Year's Day, which is the most important annual event for Japanese. Herring is caught in the north part of the Japanese islands. It has been circulated as dried food or salt cured food all over Japan since the Edo Period (1603–1867). It is an expensive food now due to the decrease of herring catches in Japan. However, since it is an essential part of New Year's Day, salted brit is imported from Canada, the United States, and Russia.

Other cases of eggs in Japan

Although ant eggs are eaten as a delicacy in China, there was no custom of eating insect eggs in Japan within the scope of written history. Reptile and amphibian eggs are also not treated as food. *Trionychidae sinensis japonica*, which is a soft-shelled turtle, is an exception. Its ovaries are cooked with meat, though its post-spawning eggs are not gathered for food. There are regions in south-east Asia where people eat marine turtle eggs. One kind of marine turtle lays eggs on Japanese sandy coasts; its eggs are comparatively large and easy to gather. However, people do not eat them. Traditionally, marine turtles have been viewed as a symbol of good fortune. If marine turtles accidentally became tangled in fishermen's nets or if fishermen found marine turtles coming ashore for spawning, they used to give them Japanese saké and set them free. This custom is based on a tradition that marine turtles like drinking.[2]

It is assumed that people ate wild bird eggs in the Stone Age in Japan because people relied on hunting and gathering for food. However, no archaeological evidence for this has been found. In addition, there is no written material that records people using wild bird eggs as food. Interestingly, eating chicken eggs was taboo in Japan. Thus, it is possible that eating wild bird eggs was also viewed as taboo.

Traditionally, chicken and ducks have been bred in the rice paddy areas of northern South China and south-east Asia. Thus, people had access to duck eggs. Rice paddy farming was introduced from China to Japan around 500 BC. Since then, Japan has become an agricultural society focused on rice cultivation. Although chickens were introduced to Japan with rice farming, the breeding of ducks was not brought. Eating chicken eggs became taboo in the seventeenth century, thus consuming duck eggs must have started from the end of the sixteenth century. At that time, ducks began being raised for their eggs in some places in south-west Japan. Thus, before this period, eating eggs meant eating chicken eggs in Japan.

The taboo of eating meat

I shall mention the prohibition of eating meat in Japan now, as the custom is closely related to avoiding eating eggs. Buddhism was introduced to Japan in the sixth century and rapidly developed with the protection of the Imperial family in the seventh century. It became the official religion in Japan. Emperor Tenmu established the first prohibition of eating meat in Japan in 675. The period prohibited the eating of cattle, horses, dogs, monkeys, and chickens from the 1st of April to the 30th of September in the lunar calendar. The five kinds of animals that were banned from being eaten by the prohibition were chosen based on the description of Buddhist scriptures: 'Dogs give a bark in the night. Chickens announce the dawn. Cattle help cultivating. Horses serve the march. Monkeys belong to the same kind of humankind. Therefore, people must not eat those animals.' This gives evidence that people ate chickens at that time. Such orders that prohibited eating meat were issued occasionally until the twelfth century. Consequently, not only the five kinds of animals but also eating any mammal meat became prohibited. However, the law did not apply to eggs.

Around the tenth century, the clergy, aristocracy, and inhabitants of the city began to feel a sense of guilt for eating mammal meat due to the expansion of Buddhism teaching. Later, the concept of reincarnation penetrated rural areas, and people believed that they would be reborn after death and that the new life would not always be humankind but might be another creature. In accordance with this belief, people became superstitious that people who ate meat might return as animals in their next life. In other cases, people were afraid of eating relatives that had been reborn if they consumed animal meat. The taboo of eating meat advanced based on these ideas.

Game such as wild ducks and pheasants were not the subject of the prohibition, but ordinary people rarely had a chance to obtain game meat by hunting. Hence, the Japanese avoided eating meat for several centuries and eating eggs fell out of practice. Unlike Buddhist monks and nuns who were strictly required to be vegetarians, ordinary Buddhists were allowed to have fish and shellfish. This is why the Japanese learned to cook fish in a variety of ways and why this practice developed well in Japan.[3]

Eating eggs was also avoided by another Japanese religion. Shinto is a Japanese indigenous religion, and it treats chickens as special birds. Chickens are respected as divine messengers. As such, they are often bred near shrines. Moreover, some shrines banned Shinto believers from eating chicken meat and eggs.

The expansion of the taboo of eating eggs

To my knowledge, there are only four references that indicate eating eggs in Japan from the sixth century, the period in which written materials began to appear, to the end of the sixteenth century.

One indicates that in the second half of the tenth century, aristocracy participated in cherry blossom viewing and brought boiled eggs and salt to the party. This description is found in *Kojidan* (The Collection of Old Tales), which is a book published in the beginning of the thirteenth century. In this case, eating eggs was not criticized.

In contrast, eating eggs in the other three descriptions is denounced based on Buddhism. For instance, *Nippon Ryoi Ki (Nihon Reikai)* (The Spiritual World of Japan Strange Tales of Buddhism), written in the beginning of the ninth century by Keikai, a Buddhist monk, contains a story of a man who does not believe Buddhism and always eats boiled eggs. One day, the man kept running around barley fields crying loudly, 'Hot! Hot!' Villagers helped him and asked what he was doing. They knew that the ground was just barley fields, but learned that he saw it as fields covered by charcoal fire and blazing mountains. He could not escape from fire but continued to run. His legs were actually burnt, and he died soon after. The book tells that this is a realised example of a Buddhist sutra in which a person who eats fried or boiled eggs is thought to go to a hell which is filled with hot ash, after death.

In another description, there is a picture *Jigoku Zoushi* (A Picture of Hell), which was drawn at the end of the twelfth century. The picture shows a hell called 'Chicken Hell' in which there is a huge cock in a hellfire that inflicts great pain on sinners. A person who likes fighting and is cruel to animals and birds is believed to be sent to 'Chicken Hell' after death.

The idea that people would be sent to hell if they ate chicken or chicken eggs gradually expanded to ordinary people through sermons by Buddhist monks. As a result, most Japanese began to avoid eating eggs. A menu containing dishes with chicken meat or eggs was non-existent from the sixth century to the sixteenth century. Nevertheless, people customarily bred chickens. Farmers kept them, usually as a cock and hen pair, and left them free on the ground. Farmers neither penned them nor raised a large number of them. Thus, professional feeding of chickens was not realised. Chickens were kept not for their meat or eggs but as pets that announced the dawn or for cockfighting.

The impact of Southern Barbarians

Now, we shall see what changes occurred after the Japanese met the Europeans. A Portuguese merchant ship, which was filled with Chinese junk, drifted down to a small island in the southern part of Japan in 1543. This is the first official recorded contact between the Japanese and Europeans. In 1549, Saint Francis Xavier came to Japan and devoted himself to diffusing Christianity throughout the country. Later, missionaries of the Society of Jesus visited Japan and energetically propagated their teaching in the latter half of the sixteenth century. Portuguese and Spanish merchants also came for trade. They sailed from the south; so, European people who came from the Iberian Peninsula were called *Nanban-jin* which means 'Southern Barbarians'.

The Japanese who became Christians because of the propaganda were liberated from Buddhist and Shinto taboo, and they began eating meat with missionaries. In addition to Christians, ordinary people also began eating beef in areas around Nagasaki and Hirado harbours of Kyushu, which were the anchorage sites of Portuguese and Spanish ships. As a result, the price of beef rose at Nagasaki, and the breeding of pigs for meat was restored in areas around the harbours. During this movement, Chinese ships began to make port calls at the two harbours, and Chinese colonies were established there.

Eating beef, chicken, and chicken eggs came into fashion in the western part of Japan from the end of the sixteenth century to the beginning of the seventeenth century due to the influence of Europeans and the Chinese. We can find plenty of various recipes today that were introduced from the Iberian Peninsula and China at that time. One of them, *kasutera*, is a kind of sponge cake using eggs, and it is still popular today. The word *kasutera* was derived from *bolo de Castella*, itself referring to the kingdom of Castille.

A Portuguese missionary Luis Frois, who stayed in Japan 1562 to 1592, recorded his fruits of preaching in 1593: 'The Japanese eagerly want to have our food recently. They are specifically interested in eggs and beef, though the foods were really hated in the past.'[4]

Buddhist monks, who held a hostile view of Christianity, attacked the new custom of eating meat and eggs. The monks identified eating meat as one of the subjects that was used for slandering missionaries and circulated vicious rumours about their habits;

for example, that Christians ate human flesh or killed children and drank their blood.

The Tokugawa government was afraid of Christianity and the possibility that Europeans would colonise Japan using their religious influence. Thus, the government issued a government ordinance in 1612 stating that the propagation of Christianity was strictly prohibited and missionaries and those who did not convert to Buddhism would be deported from the country. At the same time, the slaughter of cattle and horses for food was also prohibited. Later, the government broke off any relation with other countries except Dutch and Chinese ships for trade, only allowing these two countries to make port calls at Nagasaki harbour. All foreigners were banned from landing in Japan and all Japanese were banned from making voyages abroad. Known as Sakoku, Japan closed itself off from the outside world for two centuries.

The use of eggs in the Edo period (1603–1867)

Although eating meat was prohibited again with the implementation of Sakoku, control of eating chicken was less strict. People, however, still felt guilty having chicken since they had to kill it for eating. This is the description in *Ryouri Kondate Hyou Syu* (A Menu Book) published in 1674: 'If you cook chicken, you should prepare another dish as well. There might be a case that replacement is required because many people do not like chicken.' In contrast, chicken eggs expanded as food without a sense of guilt, and people came to breed chickens for their eggs in the seventeenth century. Ducks were also kept for their eggs in some regions.

The first recorded recipe of eggs in Japan is found in *Ryori Monogatari* (The Cooking Story) in 1643 in which there were four ways to cook eggs. *Banpou Ryouri Himitsu Bako* (How to Make a Hundred Secret Recipes), published in 1785, is a specialised book of egg recipes that describes 103 ways to cook eggs. The book was probably the first cookery book specialising in egg recipes in the world. The author's background is unknown since the person used a *nom de plume*, but appears to use highly sophisticated skills, judging from the contents. Hence, the book is written for a professional more than for ordinary people, and most of the recipes can be reproduced today, though a few are impossible. For instance, the recipe that tells how to make a boiled egg that reverses the yolk and the white, which cannot be realised.

Boiled eggs were a favourite with people in the Edo period. There were even peddlars of boiled eggs in big cities. Eggs were expensive at that time, so the price of a boiled egg in the 1850s was equal to a bowl of noodles, which was a popular snack for ordinary people. Eggs were believed to be effective in increasing energy, so they were sold in brothels as well. In addition, although Japanese eggnog, which is made of eggs, sugar, and warmed saké, is famous as a cure for colds, having Japanese eggnog is also understood as a metaphor for a sexual act. *Kousyoku Ichidai Otoko* (The Man Who Spent His Life Love-Making) is a novel written by Saikaku Ihara and published in 1682 in which a hero repeats love affairs throughout his life like Don Juan. At the end of the novel, the hero sets sail with his amorous friends for a voyage of discovery to a legendary land where only amorous women live and men happily die during sexual acts. His ship is carrying a full cargo of eggs.

Moreover, eating eggs in Japan is characterised by a preference for raw eggs. The simplest way to eat them is to put a raw egg and soy sauce on warm rice and mix them. Raw eggs are also used as a source for Sukiyaki; cooked meat and vegetables are put into a beaten raw egg and then eaten.

The development of consumption of chicken eggs in the modern period

The feudal system created by the Tokugawa government was overthrown in 1868. Government was centralised, and Japan started on the path of a modern nation state. The national goals of Japan at that time were twofold: 1) the realisation of the industrial revolution in Japan through the introduction of the modern industrialisation of Europe and the United States and 2) establishing a modern military force based on a draft system. In order to achieve these purposes, it was necessary to raise robust labourers and soldiers. Intellectuals who were well informed about European and American circumstances considered the lack of meat and milk in the Japanese menu the reason why Japanese had a poor physique and were short on physical strength. Consequently, the prohibition of eating meat was removed, and the government encouraged consuming meat and milk.

Eggs were also encouraged as it was thought that their inclusion in the diet might also lead to improved physique and strength. Western and Chinese cooking books containing egg recipes and books on chicken farming began to be actively published. Eggs were viewed as energising and were brought to the sick as gifts in the hope that they would enable the invalid regain their strength. This custom lasted until the 1950s. Today, this practice has disappeared because the price of eggs is very cheap.

Artificial incubation spread in the late nineteenth century, and poultry farmers raising immense numbers of chickens appeared. In addition, a way to identify chick sex was found, and chicken sexing became an established Japanese specialty. As a result, it became possible to select and buy only female chicks, which would develop into productive chickens for poultry farms. In the 1920s, it was no longer necessary to import eggs from China because Japan was able to produce enough domestic eggs for the population. In 1931, the government designated chickens and their eggs as important exports.

Today, chicken is the cheapest meat in Japan. Twenty eggs can be bought for the price of a single bowl of noodles. Chicken eggs are always kept in the home because they are the cheapest nutritious food. In 2002, the Japanese Ministry of Agriculture, Forestry and Fisheries examined egg consumption per person per year in 12 countries. According to this research, Japan consumes the largest number of eggs (19.8 kg), followed closely by the Netherlands (15.36 kg), which consumes the second largest number of eggs, and the UK ranked as eighth (11.6 kg).[5] Japan consumes the largest number of eggs in the world.

Notes

1. [ ] is added by the author of this article. Nihon Shoki, Nihongi: *Chronicles of Japan from the Earliest Times to A.D. 697*, trans. W.G. Aston (London: Kegan Paul, Trench, Trubner and Co., 1896).
2. Some areas that were separated from the body of Japan developed their own cultures, such as Okinawa. Although people in these regions eat marine turtles, whether they eat marine turtle eggs has not been determined.
3. The taboo of eating meat did not penetrate the Ainu, the indigenous people of the northern island of Japan, nor the people of Okinawa, the southern island of Japan. Ainu society depended on hunting and gathering. Thus, bears and deer were important food sources for people. Okinawa was once an independent kingdom from Japan and largely influenced by Chinese Confucian culture. People in Okinawa bred and ate pigs and goats due to their interaction with China.
4. Frois, Luis, *Nihonshi* (Japanese History), vol. 5, trans. Takeichi Matsuda and Momota Kawasaki (Tokyo: Chuou Kouron Sya, 1981), p. 325.
5. Ministry of Agriculture, Forestry and Fisheries, General Food Policy Bureau, *Food Balance Sheet 2006* (Tokyo: Association of Agriculture and Forestry Japan, 2006), p. 249.

The Egg Tree in America

Cathy K. Kaufman

In 1977, the *Los Angeles Times* promoted community Easter holiday activities, including an egg decorating contest in which the embellished eggs would be placed on an egg tree. In case anyone was baffled by the unusual display, the newspaper helpfully added that an egg tree is 'like a Christmas tree, only hung with decorated eggs instead of Christmas ornaments.'[1]

Virtually all Americans are familiar with the ubiquitous Christmas tree. From television coverage of the annual lighting of the mammoth tree at Rockefeller Center to merchants' displays in snooty boutiques or mass-market megastores, the decorated evergreen (real or fake, and sometimes rendered in colors not found in nature) is a Christmas icon. Much less popular is the egg tree, the paschal season's arboreal offering.[2] While occasionally fashioned from evergreens, they are most commonly made from saplings or cut branches of deciduous trees, the branches festooned with colored and decorated eggs. They can be tabletop decorations, freestanding displays, or made from exterior trees and shrubs. Their charm lies in the contrast between the gaily-colored eggs and early spring's naked branches, with the life-affirming egg portending the start of the new growing season. Occasionally, branches from fruit trees are cut and forced into premature bloom as an obvious metaphor for rebirth. Any iteration of egg tree would seem an ideal symbol for the start of spring and for Christian celebrations of Easter, yet egg trees are a dismal failure when compared to Christmas trees, found only in a few public fora and very scattered homes.

The origins of the custom in America are murky. Most accounts ascribe it to German, especially the awkwardly named Pennsylvania Dutch, immigrants, although some credit Swedes (who perhaps learned of the custom during their seventeenth-century invasion of Moravia) for introducing the decorated trees to Americans or claim (erroneously) that the custom is homegrown.[3] The earliest published reference to egg trees in America appears to be in 1876, and was identified by folklorist Alfred L. Shoemaker as coming from the *Reading Eagle*, a newspaper centered in Pennsylvania Dutch country. According to the *Reading Eagle*, one

> R.D. Lingle, druggist, at Tenth and Chestnut, has in his parlor, for the pleasure of his little daughters, a new kind of tree, which was placed there on Easter Eve, and has been called an 'Easter Egg Tree.' It is probably the only one of its kind put up in this city, and is apparently a new idea. Spruce boughs are hung with egg shells beautifully ornamented with paint, gilt, and colored paper. Besides these are paper ornaments, representing bouquets, goddesses of liberty, 'Cross

anchor and heart' combined, hanging baskets, banners, flags, etc., all tastefully arranged. Excepting the eggs, the tree presents very much the appearance of a Christmas tree.[4]

The following year, the *Lebanon* [Pennsylvania] *Daily Times* reported on an egg tree as 'quite a novelty,' and ten years later, the *Norristown* [Pennsylvania] *Register* similarly found newsworthy the erection of an egg tree in the parlor of a former city councilman.[5] Children's literature described jolly parties where young guests were surprised with egg trees; the implication of all the tales is that the clever hosts, inspired by the more well-established Christmas custom, independently struck upon the decorated Easter tree.[6]

Notwithstanding the rather breathless tone of these press reports attesting to the novelty of egg trees, the custom hardly was invented in the 1870s and '80s: indeed, as Shoemaker points out, the Easter tree was neither common through Pennsylvania Dutch country nor was it lacking in precedents. Shoemaker documents an oral history of 'Egg Bushes,' in which elderly residents recall decorating bushes in the yard with uncolored eggs. Most attested that the custom went back to their parents and grandparents' time, likely pushing back the custom to the early nineteenth century or beyond. The key point for Shoemaker, however, is that the custom of egg trees and egg bushes in America was not universally observed by the nineteenth-century Pennsylvania Dutch. This spotty observance by German-Americans paralleled observations that egg trees were regional specialties in Germany, being most common in north-east Germany.[7] Even as staunch a defender of German folk customs as Sarah Josepha Hale seemed unfamiliar with egg trees. Her 1868 treatise, *Manners, or, Happy Homes and Good Society All the Year Round*, never mentions Easter trees, although she vociferously advocates the adoption by all of the charming German custom of the Christmas tree.

From Shoemaker's vantage point in 1960, it appeared as if the Easter egg tree was finally going to take its deserved place next to the Christmas tree as an icon of American pop culture. Shoemaker himself had played a pivotal role in spreading the gospel of the egg tree. Shoemaker learned of one Mrs Elmer L. Palsgrove, who, starting in 1930, every year created an egg tree in her home with upwards of 1,000 colored eggs decorating the branches. As curator of the Berks County Historical Museum in Reading, Pennsylvania, Shoemaker invited Mrs Palsgrove to relocate her egg tree to the museum.

The egg tree was seen by Katherine Milhous, an illustrator of children's books with a passion for things Pennsylvania Dutch, who fashioned a story based on the Palsgrove display.[8] Writing in 1960, Shoemaker opined that:

One of the most remarkable things that happened in the past decade has been the nationwide acceptance, almost overnight, of the custom of decorating a

The Egg Tree in America

The Easter Egg Tree created by Mrs Elmer Palsgrove in 1949 for the Berks County Historical Association.

tree with colored eggs at Easter – all brought about by the appearance in 1950 of 'The Egg Tree,' a children's book by Katherine Milhous, a Philadelphia author.[9]

Winner of the Caldecott Medal for the year's most distinguished picture book, *The Egg Tree* became the darling of primary school teachers looking for arts and crafts projects suitable for their young students.[10] Museums and libraries catering to children displayed seasonal egg trees much like Christmas trees, with officials quickly proclaiming the start of a new tradition and promising to store blown and decorated eggs from one year to the next.[11] With eggs added each year, the trees rapidly grew more elaborate: a tree displayed at a library in Chicago started with 300 eggs in 1953, grew to 700 in 1954, and bore more than 1000 decorated eggs in 1955. There would have been many more, but for the fact that mice had nibbled away at some 500 shells in storage: quickly, the good librarians of Chicago devised a mouse-proof system to alleviate this concern.[12] Egg trees were also considered cheery brighteners for hospitals and fundraisers.[13] New York City's Metropolitan Museum of Art began displaying egg trees no later than 1949, the year before Milhous's book was published; the museum invited Milhous to contribute to its display in 1950, and with the help of some friends, she delivered 600 hand-decorated eggs to the museum.[14] Although Shoemaker could not have known it, Easter egg trees' popularity was cresting in 1950s and '60s America, and the tradition would fade within a generation. At some time during the early 1980s, the Metropolitan Museum of Art stopped its display;

although some archivists and librarians at the Met remembered the egg trees and even had decorated a few in years past, none knew why the tradition was halted.

Shoemaker had learned of the egg trees and Mrs Palsgrove no later than 1936, from Cornelius Weygandt's *The Blue Hills: Rounds and Discoveries in the Country Places of Pennsylvania*. Weygandt described egg trees as '[t]he most curious manifestation of the egg cult that I have come upon in all Dutchland ... It is one of the customs that those who resort to it are loath to admit' and that no one discussed in company.[15] According to Weygandt, egg trees were made by barren wives as a talisman to ensure fertility. Legend told of many successful pregnancies in the year following the decorating of an egg tree. By the 1930s, however, Weygandt reports that few women erected them for their magical powers and they had, instead, become a children's amusement for the comfortable and economically self-sustaining Pennsylvania Dutch.

Although the earliest written evidence of egg trees comes from Pennsylvania Dutch country, there are occasional references to hanging eggs or creating egg trees outside of this geographic context, well before folklorists began popularizing Pennsylvania Dutch customs. In 1881, *Harper's Illustrated Weekly* reminisced about the old custom of blowing out eggs, filling them with sugarplums, tying ribbons about them, and then hanging them up 'where it would be seen the first thing in the morning, just like the Christmas stocking.'[16] In 1895, the society pages of the *New York Times* described a charity ball hosted by Louis C. Tiffany. Among the evening's entertainments was an Easter egg tree, dazzling with different colored eggs (although there is no suggestion that they were made of glass).[17] As the twentieth century dawned, egg trees continued to provide Easter season entertainments, although never on the same scale as the Christmas tree, notwithstanding the Easter trees' mimicking of decorations and small toys and presents hung amid the branches.[18]

Not all egg trees were linked to Easter and the celebration of Holy Week. In Europe, egg trees might appear at May Day festivals, at Royal Oak Day festivals in England (Royal Oak Day or Oak-apple Day falls on 29 May, the birthday of Charles II, the day he entered London at the Restoration), at summer solstice celebrations, and Whitsunday. Occasionally eggs decorated Christmas trees or branches at harvest festivals.[19] Heavy use of eggs for spring and summer holidays was spurred by the onslaught of egg-laying season for hens and other fowl before the advent of year-round, industrially-induced laying. In a world attuned to agrarian rhythms, the use of eggs as harbingers of the growing season appears to trace back to the late-winter folk festival of 'Carrying out Death,' a Lenten holiday. According to Venetia Nevill, different Germanic and Central European groups had closely related customs. Eggshells decorated effigies of Death that were marched out of town, consumed in a bonfire, or drowned in a river. Other communities pelted witchy figures with eggshells in the belief that this would vanquish evil. Still others associated the eggshells with fertility, placing them on fruit trees to shake off winter dormancy and encourage bountiful harvests.[20]

The Egg Tree in America

The association of eggs, trees, and witchcraft reached American shores in two different forms. The egg tree could be an amusing diversion for the well-to-do, as evidenced by an 1891 article in the upscale *Harper's Bazaar*. It gave detailed instructions for creating a 'fortune tree' to enhance a charity fair scheduled for the post-Easter season. *Harper's* recommended coloring 400–500 emptied eggshells (required by pooling the resources used by prominent households to supply the Easter table), decorating each shell with a different comic face, and providing a hat for each egghead, into which a written fortune could be tucked. Suggested characters for the eggheads included a 'Turk' and 'darky' made by boiling shells with coffee grounds, Indians, nuns, May queens, and a somber paterfamilias looking shocked at the cost of the fair, a '"Paddy" with his pipe and sprig of shamrock, …milkmaids in sun bonnets, crying babies in lace caps, soldiers and sailors', Buffalo Bills, Lady Teazles, and plenty of variations on the crowd-pleasing Santa Claus. The eggs could be sold or distributed by 'a coquettish young girl …dressed as a witch to take care of the tree, in a gown of scarlet and gold, buckled shoes, and a tall, pointed black hat covered with cabalistic figure.'[21] All good frivolity for those leading already-charmed lives.

Egg trees figured in the lives of the rural poor as a deeply meaningful charm. Appalachian and Ozark Mountain residents displayed egg trees and bushes in the early twentieth century to keep witches away, although the tradition was waning. One of the most poignant descriptions of the egg tree, and one that harks back to the Pennsylvania Dutch tradition of a fertility sacrifice, is found in James Still's 1940 novel, *River of Earth*. Still settled in the 1930s as a young writer in Cumberland County, Kentucky, in a log cabin built in 1837 by immigrants from the Black Forest. The cabin was his home for the rest of his life and provided a perch to observe the struggles of the Appalachian poor. In *River of Earth*, Alpha Middleton Baldridge, the wife of a coal miner whose tenuous employment at various mines in Appalachian Kentucky requires the family to lead a peripatetic existence between company towns and subsistence farming, loses her third child, a toddler, to malnutrition. Some months later, Alpha and her eldest child are stringing eggshells, meticulously broken at both ends and blown out to preserve the shape, on a dead willow tree. The narrator, Alpha's seven-year-old son, reports:

> 'I allus did want me an egg tree,' Mother said. 'I hear tell it's healthy to have one growing in the yard. And I figure it'll be brightening to the house. A sight o' folks will be coming to the funeralizing. My dommers ought to lay nigh enough to kiver the last branch before the time. Eggshells hain't a grain o' good except to prettify with.'[22]

Shortly thereafter, Alpha's husband, Brack, demands that the family move, with promises of better work and housing. In one of the rare fights between the couple, Alpha argues that she hates to leave the egg tree. Brack lashes back that it was 'fresh news,' 'foolishness,' and that he hadn't seen another egg tree 'since before I was married and was traipsing around Buckhorn Creek.' In the end, Alpha dutifully follows Brack, abandoning her egg tree. Brack, however, does not disappoint, and steals out in the middle of the night to retrieve the egg tree and transport it to the new house, albeit battered and losing eggs over journey. Alpha gives birth to a healthy baby the following year.

River of Earth, of course, was not a suitable vehicle for popularizing egg trees: the depressing story lacks the holiday spirit of the Milhous's pleasing children's tale. The custom of decorating trees failed to catch the American imagination to the same degree the decorating the Christmas tree is a national passion. Perhaps the added step of blowing out eggs before dying them seems too tedious, and Americans of all persuasions, including the Pennsylvania Dutch, are often content with an Easter basket of colored eggs. To the extent that contemporary versions of the tree exist, they are reminiscent of the original analogies to happy Christmas trees, with small presents and candies forming part of the tree's paraphernalia. Websites offer kits for making Easter egg trees or sell plastic or ceramic eggs to bedeck plastic or ceramic branches as tabletop ornaments. A few municipalities continue to display egg trees at Easter: a popular event is the Garden City, New York, annual Easter parade of antique cars that terminate in a park with an egg tree. Few churches have embraced Easter egg trees, in contrast to the decorated evergreens found both inside and out of churches at Christmas. One exception is the Church of Larger Fellowship which promotes creation of 'Unitarian Universalist' egg trees to highlight values important to the group, such as Nature, world religions, and flaming chalices.[23] The recommended verses to accompany the egg tree revel in the miraculous regeneration found in the egg.

Notes

1. Mindy Kaye, 'Special of the Week', *Los Angeles Times*, April 5, 1977, H12.
2. The only private egg trees I have ever seen are displayed in areas of the Hudson River Valley that had significant German immigration in the early eighteenth century; this area was called the Palatinate and German immigrants relocated from New York's Palatinate to create Pennsylvania Dutch country in the mid-eighteenth century.
3. Anita Gold, 'Antiques', *Chicago Tribune*, April 22, 1973, W8; *New York Times*, April 16, 1981, C9; *New York Times*, March 28, 1959, 20.
4. Quoted in Alfred L. Shoemaker, *Eastertide in Pennsylvania: A Folk Cultural Study*, Kutztown, PA: Pennsylvania Folklife Society, 1960, 63.
5. Op. cit.
6. *The Youth's Companion*, April 14, 1892, p. 191.
7. *Lothrop's Annual* (1895), cited in Shoemaker, 64.
8. Katherine Milhous, 'The Egg Tree and How it Grew', *The Horn Book Magazine*, 27:218–27, July–August 1951.
9. Shoemaker, *Eastertide*, 63.

10. Pearl Frankenfield, 'Egg Trees Everywhere', *Library Journal*, 78:480–3, March 15, 1953; *Chicago Daily Tribune*, April 4, 1954, SW2.
11. *Chicago Daily Tribune*, April 18, 1954, SW2.
12. *Chicago Daily Tribune*, April 10, 1955, S4.
13. *Chicago Daily Tribune*, March 12, 1951, B11, and April 15, 1968, A17
14. *New York Times*, April 14, 1949, 31; *New York Times*, April 6, 1950, 40.
15. Cornelius Weygandt, *The Blue Hills: Rounds and Discoveries in the Country Places of Pennsylvania*, New York: Henry Holt, 1936, 361.
16. *Harper's Illustrated Weekly*, April 30, 1881, 286.
17. *New York Times*, April 18, 1895, 16.
18. *New York Times*, March 2, 1904, 9; 'An Easter Tree,' *The Youth's Companion*, March 14, 1918, 134.
19. Venetia Nevill, *An Egg at Easter: A Folklore Study*. London: Routledge, Kegan & Paul, 1971, 310–13.
20. Nevill, 315–18.
21. 'A Fortune-Tree,' *Harper's Bazaar*, April 11, 1891, 24: 295.
22. James Still, *River of Earth* (1940), foreword by Dean Cradle, University of Kentucky Press, 1978, 173.
23. http://www.uua.org/clf/connections/2001spring/eggtree.html.

Eggs in Philippine Church Architecture and its Cuisine

Pia Lim-Castillo

Introduction

The Philippines is the only country in South East Asia that was colonized for three centuries by one country. When Ferdinand Magellan of Spain discovered the Philippines in 1521, he arrived in Cebu bearing a gift of the Infant Jesus to Rajah Humabon and his wife. Magellan was killed by Lapu-Lapu, the leader of Mactan Island. King Philip II of Spain did not give up and in 1565, another fleet arrived in the Philippines under the stewardship of Miguel Lopez de Legazpi. He came with members of the Augustinian order. In the following years, more clergy followed such as the Franciscans in 1577, the Jesuits in 1581, the Dominicans in 1587 and the Augustinian Recollects in 1600. These friars inculcated in the Filipinos their religion. Catholicism became and is still the predominant religion in the country. In 1594, each order was assigned a specific region or group of islands.

The Augustinians started their mission evangelizing the Filipinos when they arrived with Legazpi's expedition in 1565. To this Order goes the credit for having built the greatest number of churches in the Philippines (Jose, 1992, p. 20). The Augustinians acquired extensive territories in Bulacan, Pampanga, Batangas, Panay, Cebu and the Ilocos. The second-most favored Order was the Franciscans who arrived in 1577. They were granted the Bai Lake towns now called Laguna, Quezon, Bicol and Morong, Rizal. The Jesuits came in 1581. The Jesuits were given Cavite, Bohol, Leyte, Samar and other areas in the Visayas and Mindanao. The Dominicans, who came in 1587, were given the Chinese community in Manila as well as Cagayan and Isabela. The Recollects were assigned Bataan, Zambales, Pangasinan and other areas of the Jesuits after their expulsion from the Philippines in 1768 (Coseteng, p. 7). The secular clergy came to the Philippines as early as 1565 but were always too few. They occupied positions in cathedrals but also held a few scattered parishes.

The development of Spanish religious architecture in the Philippines drew its form and inspiration from Spanish-American (Mexico) sources. The relationship between the two Spanish colonies through the galleon trade and the exchange of religious personnel allowed the flow of artistic influence from Spanish America to the Philippines. The rich and extensive development of Mexican colonial architecture in the sixteenth century inspired the friars to create in the Orient an architecture worthy of the Faith. The flowering of Mexican baroque in the seventeenth and eighteenth centuries gave a strong impetus to Philippine religious architecture (Coseteng, p. 4) or what can be termed as peripheral baroque. This architecture took into account the tropical climate, the frequent earthquakes, typhoons and fires. It was an architecture that

Eggs in Philippine Church Architecture and its Cuisine

recognized technical and material limitations and local and foreign artistic influences from the Chinese and Muslims.

A kind of architecture was forced to develop in the Philippines in an attempt to follow the baroque style, in vogue in Europe during the seventeenth and eighteenth centuries. The friars relied on their memory of similar structures seen in Spain and Mexico when they designed the churches (Villalon, p. 266).

Most of the churches in the Philippines were built under the supervision of friars of different religious orders who were not architects but they tried to replicate what existed in Europe and Mexico. The remoteness of the Philippines from Spain and the uncertainty of fortune in the new colony discouraged competent and well-known architects of Spain from visiting the Philippines. In time, there emerged a master-builder class of competent Filipinos and Chinese-Filipino *mestizos* who took over the supervision and construction of religious buildings which were formerly the preserve of the friars (Coseteng, p. 3).

The psychological impact of a grand edifice upon a people used to seeing and living only in small houses of lighter and non-permanent materials was to make the Filipinos feel the superiority of ecclesiastical architecture. At the same time, the building objectified a builder's capabilities and memorialized his power and pride. The bigger and more splendid they were, the more proud they must have felt about the structures. These grand edifices were seen as affirmations of dominion – statements of power and authority. While it is true that Spanish talent may have conceptualized the structures, the immense labor that went into the realization of the buildings was Filipino (Hornedo, pp. 26–27).

The method of construction was determined by the climate, and the sociological and cultural circumstances of the country. Professional architects were nowhere to be found. The friars were responsible for the plans whose realization depended on the skill of the *maestros* or master-builders and masons. The parish priest drew up the plans and got them approved. The townspeople helped build the church by providing labor and materials while the priests paid for the services of the masons and carpenters and for the cost of the construction materials. Personal labor was scheduled throughout the year except during the planting and harvesting seasons. For sure, there were isolated cases of conscripted labor but they were more of an exception than the rule (Galende, p. 12–13). The menfolk hauled logs from the forest, while women and children carried eggs and sand to the construction site (Jose, 1992, p. 30).

The structure of a stone church was simple. The materials used were mainly adobe or porous stone in Luzon, bricks and stone in Ilocos and coral stone in Cebu and Panay. The ground plan consisted of a rectangular structure following the Latin cross form. The proportions were generally large. The roofs were originally covered with cogon grass but were later fitted with clay tiles and eventually, galvanized iron sheets. A few had stone vaults. The walls were very thick and were supported by massive buttresses to protect the structure against earthquakes. Churches in the coastal areas regularly faced the sea. Central towns had their churches oriented to the east. Special attention was focused on the façade of the church, the main altar with its *retablo* (the panel behind the altar enclosing revered saints) and the pulpit (Galende, p. 15).

Construction was slow, taking several decades to finish. Sometimes, churches would be burned midstream or destroyed by natural calamities such as earthquakes. Oftentimes, a new church would rise fifty years later on its old foundation. But the religious were so single-minded in their compulsion to build bigger and stronger churches in stone, brick and mortar that it was not unusual for curates to spend all their money on their churches. The different orders rivaled each other striving to outdo each other. Thus, the friar's success as a missionary came to be measured not by the number of souls under his administration or the amount of tributes he collected, but by his church, the elegance of his residence, and the height of his belfry and the number of bells in it (Coseteng, p. 10).

By the turn of the seventeenth century, the friars began to compete with each other in the construction of stone edifices like those in Spain and the Americas. Earthquakes toppled some of their first structures until the people learned to build 'earthquake-proof' buildings. Churches were not built so high and they thickened the walls and propped them with outsized buttresses. Lighter materials were used for upper walls such as brick and mortar over interwoven branches (Jose, 1992, p. 34).

The most interesting churches showcasing different styles of architecture and construction are the following. These have been enumerated according to the dates when they were built. The dates differ depending on one's source as some churches may have been built several times after being demolished by natural calamities. In most cases, the new church was constructed over the old foundations. Other times, there would be changes in the supervising clergy and with that came design changes as well. In most cases, these were the Jesuit-built churches that were turned over to the Recollects around 1780 when the Jesuits were expelled from the Philippines.

- The Church of San Agustin in Intramuros, Manila is the oldest church in the Philippines made of adobe stone built by the Augustinians between 1571 and 1601. This is a UNESCO World Heritage Site.
- The Church of the Holy Rosary in Binondo Manila was built by the Dominicans in 1596 outside the walled city of Manila where the Chinese enclave lived.
- The Church of San Geronimo in Morong, Rizal was built by the Franciscans in 1615. It is one of the most splendid baroque facades in the country. It was built of cut stone. It is one of the few churches with an octagonal bell tower crowning the church.
- The Church of Our Lady of Remedies in Malate, Manila was originally built by the Augustinians in 1677 but was damaged beyond repair in 1863. In 1894 it was restored and embellished to its present shape and façade. It blends Moorish and baroque elements with octagonal end buttresses which turn into belfries.

Eggs in Philippine Church Architecture and its Cuisine

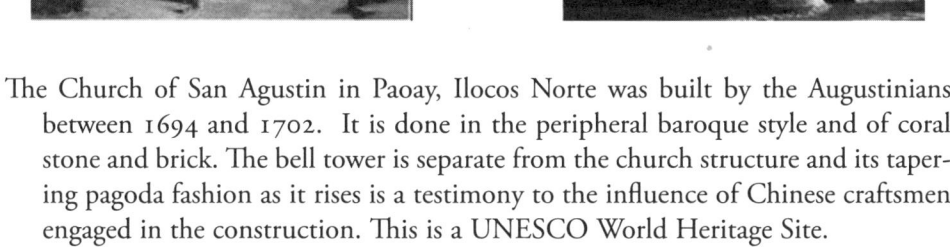

Above: San Agustin Church Manila

Below: Paoay Church Ilocos Norte

Above: Tumauini Church, Cagayan

Center: Miagao Church, Iloilo

Below: Sta. Maria Church, Ilocos Sur

The Church of San Agustin in Paoay, Ilocos Norte was built by the Augustinians between 1694 and 1702. It is done in the peripheral baroque style and of coral stone and brick. The bell tower is separate from the church structure and its tapering pagoda fashion as it rises is a testimony to the influence of Chinese craftsmen engaged in the construction. This is a UNESCO World Heritage Site.

The Church of the Immaculate Conception in Guiuan, Samar was built by the Jesuits in 1700 and later additions were made by the Recollects. This is an excellent example of 'fortress baroque' making use of coral stone and seashells.

The Church of the Immaculate Conception of Mary in Baclayon, Bohol was built by the Jesuits in 1727. It was built of finely cut coral stone and fronts the sea.

The Church of our Lady of the Gate in Daraga, Albay was built by the Franciscans in 1772 and was built perched on a hill to protect it from the cycles of destruction wrought by Mayon Volcano. The construction material used for this church was cut lava rocks from the volcano.

The Church of St. Mathew the Apostle in Tumauini, Cagayan was built by the Dominicans between 1783 and 1788. Tumauini is unique because of its intensive and exclusive use of bricks for wall-finishings and decoration. Brick was used because there was a lack of good stone for construction in the area. Cagayan clay took to firing at high temperatures which produced excellent bricks that could be used not only for structural purposes but also for exterior facing. It allowed a different approach to construction and a more fluid architectural style. The style of brick construction is evident in several churches built in the Cagayan area during the eighteenth century.

The Church of St. Ildefonsus in Tanay, Rizal was built by the Franciscans in 1783. Its façade is made of grey adobe which was plentiful in the area.

The Church of Santo Tomas of Villanueva in Miag-Ao, Iloilo was built by the Augustinians. It is made with yellow sandstone and was completed in 1797. Sandstone was plentiful in Iloilo. The towers serve as lookouts for pirate raids and the church was built on a hill with a dominant view of the sea below. Like the church in Paoay, the style is also peripheral baroque. This is a UNESCO World Heritage Site.

The Church of Our Lady of the Assumption in Sta. Maria, Ilocos Sur was built in 1810 by the Augustinians. It is made from bricks and is different from the other churches because it is a departure from the flat, pedimented, triangularly topped Philippine church facades. The rounded forms at both corners of the plain façade show a different affinity to the curvilinear shapes of European baroque. This is a UNESCO World Heritage Site.

The Church of Our Lady of Light in Loon, Bohol was built by the Jesuits in 1815. This was started by the Jesuits but was turned over to the Augustinian Recollects after their expulsion. This church is the crowning glory of Recollect ecclesiastical architecture in Bohol.

The Church of San Vicente in Sabtang, Batanes was built by the Dominicans in 1844. This is the northernmost church in the Philippines and was made of stone and mortar to weather the extreme winds and rains in the area.

The Church of Our Lady of Mount Carmel in Barasoain, Bulacan was built by the Augustinians in 1859 following the same style as the Sta. Maria church in Ilocos Sur.

The Church of St. Catherine of Alexandria in Carcar, Cebu built by the Augustinians between 1860–1875. Done in Greco-Roman style, it has Moorish influences in its minaret domes housing the bell towers.

The church of Santa Ana in Molo, Iloilo was built by a Chinese-*mestizo* secular named Fr. Locsin in 1863 and is done in Gothic Renaissance style using coral stones. The plan is fundamentally Renaissance, evident in the arcade of Corinthian columns in the interior, the use of semi-circular arches, and the disposition of space. The church's height, however, and its narrow width points to affinity with the Gothic. This is further emphasized by the decorative elements, of spires and lancets.

The Basilica of St. Martin of Tours in Taal, Batangas was built on top of a hill by the Augustinians to avoid the eruptions of Taal Volcano. It was finished in 1878. It is the widest church built during the Spanish occupation.

Santo Domingo Church in Manila was built by the Dominicans in 1868. This was the first facade in the neo-gothic style of church in the Philippines. It is the work of the first qualified Philippine architect, Felix Rojas. Its façade is a literal imitation of York Minster in England. It didn't survive the second World War as it was bombed by the Japanese in 1941.

The church of St. Isidore the Worker in Lazi, Siquijor was built by the Augustinian Recollects in 1884. The walls are made using the rubble construction technique where the stones and corals are lumped one on top of the other and bonded by lime mortar. The facade of the church and most of the convent walls and columns are made using cut stone construction. In this method, coral stones are cut into shapes and joined using some interlocking device.

The Church of Our Lady of Mount Carmel or the San Sebastian Church in Manila was one of the later churches built in the gothic style and is the second all-steel structure in the world then, next only to the Eiffel Tower in Paris. The prefabricated metal was manufactured in Belgium by Belgian engineers and the parts sent to Manila via steamships. The church was blessed in 1891 (Guerrero, p. 26).

Some of these churches have several similarities as successful plans were copied by the same Order in different locations or it may also have been possible that an Order's earlier design is copied by another order several years later.

These are just a few examples of the beautiful colonial churches in the Philippines. From the northernmost tip of Luzon to Mindanao, a necklace of seventeenth to nineteenth century churches used to sparkle at the heads of town plazas situated along the Philippine coastline. This is our heritage as all these churches were built by Filipinos. The local artisans were a varied mixture of people. When building a church, the Indios, a reference to the natives at the time, contributed much of the needed labor force. The Filipinos were good builders of wood and bamboo, but they were unskilled in building with stone. Hence, Chinese laborers were hired when such a specific skill was required. Muslims were also recruited to render labor. In several churches in the south, this resulted in minaret-like belltowers with onion-shaped roofs, trefoil arches, and geometric patterns. One good example is the Carcar church in Cebu. Muslim influence also prevailed in the central north, as the Malate church in Manila illustrates. The gathering of artisans with different ethnic backgrounds plus the fact that Filipinos have a strong Malay heritage, eventually led to the infusion of non-Western motifs into the architecture, further creating a distinct style. The facade of the Miag-ao church in Iloilo is an extreme example of how a Western idea was transformed to suit the taste of the local artisans.

Sadly, these vestiges of the Filipino heritage are slowly disappearing due to the destructive forces of nature and total disregard for proper restoration. Some thought that exposing the structural component by peeling off the protective stucco plastering was the correct and voguish thing to do only to realize later on that the removal of the protective plaster caused further deterioration (Villalon, pp. 272–303). With the assistance of UNESCO by including four of the above churches in their world

Eggs in Philippine Church Architecture and its Cuisine

Details of coconut trees and other tropical fruits in Miag-ao Church Façade and Minaret style bell tower of the church in Carcar Cebu

heritage sites, proper care has been given in their restoration but the main burden of caring for our legacy remains with the Filipinos.

Eggs as an ingredient in church building

The introduction of stone masonry can be attributed to at least two persons, who both arrived in Manila in 1580. The Jesuit Antonio Sedeño taught the natives and the Chinese to cut stone, use lime, and make tiles, while Fray Domingo de Salazar searched the banks of the Pasig River for convenient sources of building material.

A wall of masonry could be made of rubblework, cut porous stone (adobe or coral stone) or brick. Bricks were made of clay formed in wooden molds and baked in kilns. Brick was the basic building component throughout the Cagayan Valley, Ilocos and Pangasinan as well as in parts of the Bicol Region. In the Cagayan Valley, the bricks were so durable that many of the walls did not need protective coating. However, bricks used in the Ilocos region were not as sturdy as those in Cagayan so they were protected with layers of *palitada*, a plaster finish to prevent the bricks from the destructive forces of rain and wind. *Palitada* comes from the Spanish word *paleta* or trowel. Where the *palitada* was worn away, the brick quickly decomposed. In Manila, most of the stone churches were made of volcanic tuff or adobe which were quarried in the nearby provinces. In the Visayas region, limestone was used and the colors varied depending on the elements of its composition. It ranged from red–orange in Miag-ao to the grey of Oton. A whitish coral stone from fossil coral reefs and accretions of shells and other marine life was also used. Both materials could be cut finely with blocks meticulously hewn to fit into each other (Jose, 2003, p. 18).

In some constructions, sections of brick were regularly inserted into the adobe face. Layers of brick alternated with stone such as the churches found in Pakil, Laguna and Lucban and Tayabas, Quezon. Whether this was meant for aesthetic reasons such as those found in classic Roman architecture or for strength is not certain.

In order to protect these walls, a mortar or *argamaza* was used to bind the building material. This consisted of sand (as salt free as possible), lime (cal) and water. Unlike today's concrete, the organic ingredients of *palitada* facilitated the evaporation of moisture, so that the walls could breathe and perspire (Jose, 2003, p. 29). To make the *palitada* more durable, egg white, molasses and plants were added to the *argamasa*. Certain plant leaves were chopped and soaked in water before being added to the mixture to make the *palitada* waterproof. Recipes for the *palitada* varied from region to region. Some used plant juices and tree sap, molasses, carabao's milk, goat's blood and lastly eggs.

There is historical evidence in different church archives to show that egg whites were used for church constructions then. Records show that the dome of the Manila Cathedral was sealed in 1780 with a layer of lime, powdered brick, duck eggs and bamboo sap. Fr. Mariano Gomes of Cavite, listed duck eggs for the mortar in his expense list for 1824; his predecessor in 1808 also used duck eggs. It was also recorded that two hundred duck eggs were used for the *palitada* of the cistern of the convent in Imus Cavite in 1828 (Jose, 2003, pp. 37–38).

Filipinos were not the only ones who used eggs in mortar. In the seventh century AD, monuments at Mamallapuram, India made use of eggs in the stucco (Jose, 2003, p. 29). The use of eggs as a binding agent is credible, particularly the egg whites or albumen. Albumen is a water soluble protein found in egg white, milk and blood. Albumen is a strong, coagulating protein that is used in adhesives and varnishes. Albumen is listed among the organic additives used for the preparation of stucco marble.

Food by-products of the use of eggs in construction

Were duck eggs used or chicken eggs? Records show that most of the requirements were for duck eggs which were probably the only available eggs at that time. Unlike egg tempera painting where the yolks are used, only egg whites were used in the *palitada* mix. Taking into account all the churches built then, the number of eggs used ran into the millions.

The Filipinos developed a taste for sweets. A meal is never complete if not ended with something sweet. Historically, the fondness for sweets or desserts was partly developed during the Spanish occupation as they brought and introduced some of their favorite desserts. During pre-Hispanic times, the dessert or *panghimagas* of the Filipinos were just fruits served fresh, like banana, coconut, watermelon, mango, guava, melon and other tropical fruits. When the Spaniards came the dessert array was enhanced with the addition of *leche flan* (milk custard or crème brûlée), *yema* (egg yolk sweets), *mazapan* (marzipan), *canonigo* (meringue with sauce), *brazo de mercedes* and *torta del rey* (the King's cake). Many of these have been indigenized through time by the use of available ingredients; like *leche flan*, substituted cow's with carabao's milk, and *turrón* with cashew or peanuts instead of Spanish almonds. Filipino biscuits were traditionally made with rice or arrowroot flour as wheat was not grown in the country. However, with the coming of the Spaniards, they brought in wheat as well as techniques of bread and biscuit making. Biscuits like *hojaldres, rosquillos, enseimada* and *galletas* are all of Spanish origin (Fernandez, p. 54). These were the first products that came out of the local bakeries or *panaderias* when churches were being constructed. Thus our pastries (known to be Filipino by current popularity) still have Spanish names.

The extensive use of egg white and egg shells brought about the ingenuity of the Filipino women who saw all these egg yolks being thrown in the river. Recipes were created to make use of the egg yolks like *pan de San Nicolas, yema, tocino del cielo, leche flan*, pastries and *tortas*. Although most of these snack and dessert foods also have Catholic origins, these foods have survived to this very day as comfort food for Filipinos. This was true of the Church of Molo in Iloilo where Panaderia de Molo started. The first biscuits of Panaderia de Molo were made purely with egg yolks and lard. These were the *galletas, rosquillos* and *hojaldres*. The *enseimada* of Malolos, similar to a brioche, which is made of egg yolks and lard must have been a bread that was prepared way back when the Barasoain Church was being built. In Cebu, a well-known snack and loved by so many Cebuanos is a cake called *torta* which is made with pure egg yolks using lard as the shortening and leavened with *tuba* (coconut sap wine).

The traditional Spanish sweets such as *tocino del cielo, leche flan* and *yema* were taught to the Filipinos.

Tocino del cielo means 'heavenly fat'. Origins of this dessert came from Spain when sherry makers used egg whites to clarify their sherry. Egg yolks were then donated to the convents where nuns created this dish. The name could have described the texture or appearance like a slice of fat but a flavor as sublime as the sky.

Yema is the Spanish word for yolk. In the Philippines, *yema* is a confection that is made with egg yolks, condensed milk, lime zest and sugar. They are intensely rich and coated in caramelized sugar.

Leche Flan was also taught to the Filipinos by the Spaniards with *flan* being their national dessert. However, the *flan's* roots could be traced way back to the Ancient Roman period. The word *flan* was derived from the Spanish word *flado* meaning custard. There is no striking difference between the Spanish *flan* and our *leche flan* except that way back during the church construction period, duck egg yolks were probably used which would make for a much thicker *flan*.

Pan de San Nicolas is a cookie similar to shortbread. Where arrowroot is found, the *San Nicolas* cookie can never be too far behind. The ingredients are arrowroot flour, sugar, and egg yolks. Some versions include anise, lime rind and coconut milk. The cookies are made to celebrate the feast of San Nicolas, the patron saint of bakers. Its characteristic leaf shape is created by rolling the dough then pressing it into wooden molds carved with the saint's likeness.

Galletas are thin cookies of Spanish origin as well. Most bakeries still make it to this very day. Other products are *hojaldres* which are similar to the French *palmiers* but particularly at Panaderia de Molo, they use lard as the shortening as this gives it the flakiness that only saturated fat can give.

Rosquillos is a biscuit that originated in Cebu. The word is derived from the Spanish word *'rosca'* meaning ringlet. It has a crunchy texture and the ingredients are flour, egg, sugar, shortening and baking powder.

Most of these snacks survive to this day in local bakeries particularly in the provincial areas. Although most of these recipes have evolved ever since egg whites were no longer used in church construction, several bakeries still make them the traditional way. In addition to their product line are egg white based pastries such as meringues and angel food cake.

Twentieth-century shift from the use of eggs in *palitada* to cement and its effect in the production of delicacies

The use of egg whites lasted until concrete was introduced in the last decades of the nineteenth century. Since then, it has become the material of choice. Facades of concrete were built for some churches around the early twentieth century. After that, the neo-gothic style became the vogue towards the second quarter of the twentieth century. Many convents and schools were turned into private schools. During the Japanese occupation, a number of these were used as garrisons by the enemy troops (Javellana, pp. 10–11).

With the introduction of cement in architecture, the use of egg whites as mortar for construction became a thing of the past. Recipes have had their share of evolution as well with meringues and desserts as commonplace in bakeries where egg yolk snacks are still being baked to this day.

In most cases, recipes of biscuits and desserts changed to making use of whole eggs rather than pure egg yolks as the market for egg-white-based foods such as meringues was not enough to continue pure egg yolk products. Thus, the quality became less rich in flavor and cholesterol. Economics also played a part in the changes. It became less costly to use whole eggs for the different bakery products than to create two different products such as a biscuit and a meringue. Eventually, the taste for the traditional flavors and textures wore off. Health-wise, people started to shy away from lard and egg yolk products because of its high and bad cholesterol. It was not only the use of eggs as the emulsifying agent that changed. Most run of the mill bakeries still make the traditional products but even the shortening has changed to cheaper options such as vegetable lard or margarine and chemical essences as opposed to natural flavors. As most of these bakery items are snacks traditionally enjoyed by Filipinos, keeping the price competitive and within reach of the masses became the main reason for the recipe changes.

Like the churches suffering from improper restoration techniques and endangering these last vestiges of colonial history, even the food items learned from the Spaniards are evolving or slowly disappearing. Luckily, one can still find remnants of these great foods that have spanned several generations. Bakeries such as Panaderia de Molo continue to do the biscuits the traditional way and following the same formulations way back in the 1800's. Other items such as *yema, leche flan,* and *enseimada* can still be bought from entrepreneurs making them for an elite market who can afford to pay for what have become expensive products. But for how long these traditional products will last, only time, economics and market forces can tell.

References

Coseteng, Alicia M. L., *Spanish Churches in the Philippines* (Quezon City: UNESCO, 1972).

Fernandez, Doreen G., *Palayok: Philippine Food Through Time, On Site, In the Pot* (Makati: Bookmark, Inc., 2000).

Galende, Pedro G. OSA., *Angels in Stone, Architecture of Augustinian Churches in the Philippines* (Manila: G.A. Formoso Publishing, 1987).

Galende, Pedro G. OSA and Regalado Trota Jose, *San Agustin Art and History 1571–2000* (Manila: San Agustin Museum, 2000).

Galende, Pedro G. OSA and Rene B. Javellana, *Great Churches of the Philippines* (Makati: Bookmark, Inc., 1993).

Guerrero, Amadis Ma., *Great Churches of Old Manila* (Manila: Philippine Daily Inquirer, June 19, 2006).

Hornedo, Florentino H., *On the Trail of Dominican Engineers, Artists and Saints in the Cagayan Valley and Batanes* (Manila: UST Publishing House, 2002).

Javellana, Rene B., *Wood and Stone for God's Greater Glory-Jesuit Art and Architecture in the Philippines* (Quezon City, Ateneo de Manila University Press, 1991).

Jose, Regalado Trota, *Simbahan: Church Art in Colonial Philippines 1565–1898* (Makati: Ayala Museum, 1991).

Jose, Regalado Trota, *Visita Iglesia Bohol* (Manila: National Commission for Culture and the Arts, 2001).

Jose, Regalado Trota, *Zero In 2003* (Makati: Ayala Foundation, Inc., 2003).

Villalon, Augusto F., *Lugar: Essays on Philippine Heritage and Architecture* (Makati: Bookmark, Inc., 2001).

The Deviled Egg: History and Present

Nancy R. McArthur

Two feet in diameter, the round platter of deviled eggs balanced precariously in the hands of its 70-year-old African American maker as she carried them across the church hall. Founded by freed slaves, this church was celebrating 170 years of worship as the first black church in Newark, New Jersey. The celebration required deviled eggs, many dozens of them, to feed the hundreds gathered to remember their past. The halves of hens' eggs were filled with a fluffy yellow yolk mixture, textured with fork tines and sprinkled with crimson paprika.

A few months beforehand, 70 people gathered around the heavy laden kitchen table of an Alabama farmhouse. It was Decoration Day, reunion day for the Scotch-Irish Nance family, but originally a commemoration begun by Confederate war widows. This day, Alabama families came together as they always had with fried chicken, potato salad and most importantly, deviled eggs. Pickle relish and other secret ingredients of the maker made these a singular indulgence, and the rush toward the front of the line said the obvious, only the strongest and fastest would have deviled eggs that day.

During the same week, the Washington, DC reception crowd glittered, smartly dressed, with both the powerful and the wannabes. Rail-thin blondes reached out manicured hands to pick up tiny deviled eggs, quail eggs of course. No paprika here. Caviar nestled atop the finely piped yolk mixture on the silver tray of the waiter.

The deviled egg or stuffed egg evokes nostalgia and comfort food sensations in its current day aficionados. Imagery reigns in its presentation. Frequently topped by paprika, its deep red heart and brimming yellow center fill virginally white, tender egg cases evoking the contrast of good and evil. Suggesting fertility and bounty, the filled egg does not disappoint on the tongue with its creamy rich interior delighting the mouth with fillings tangy, savory or sweet yet tempered by the egg white's gentle flavor. A chameleon dish, stuffed eggs, now colloquially known as deviled eggs, are expected at informal picnics and yet appear in more elegant forms as an appetizer or brunch entrée in elegant surroundings.

This paper will address the preparation, history and current forms of the deviled egg. Its scope will include egg preparations which leave the white intact but use additional ingredients to refill the white for serving. Most frequently, the yolk is the base of these fillings.

The Deviled Egg

Deviled, devilled, dressed or stuffed?
Many names have been given to the stuffed egg during the past seven centuries with most terms still in use today. From the middle of the eighteenth century, deviled was used to describe spicy foods, and by the late nineteenth century, the name deviled eggs was applied to any spicy egg preparation, stuffed or not. In its 1912 recipe for deviled eggs, one cookbook notes, 'Deviled dishes are those that are highly seasoned with condiments. They are not considered wholesome as a regular diet, but may be partaken of, on occasion, with advantage as well as pleasure.'[1]

In 1995, *The Food Lover's Companion* described the verb devil as 'to combine a food with various hot or spicy seasonings such as red pepper, mustard or Tabasco sauce, thereby creating a "deviled" dish.'[2] In current American parlance, deviled eggs is the term applied to virtually all cold preparations of stuffed eggs without regard to their spiciness, and the term 'dressed' is used in certain regions. Even stuffed whites filled as dessert offerings fit the colloquial definition of deviled eggs despite the cheesecake, ambrosia or devil's food fillings offered in a recent cookbook.[3]

Core preparation methods
Preparing deviled eggs or stuffed eggs requires perfectly peeled, *hard-cooked* eggs as the core ingredient. Keys to the egg preparation are the age of the eggs and the boiling and peeling processes. The eggs that are at least five days-old ensure that air between the shell and membrane is sufficient to enable easy peeling. Should one wish to achieve perfection, the eggs may lie on their sides for 12 hours or more before cooking in order to center the yolks within the whites. Gentle stirring during the boiling process may also achieve this effect.

Cooking recommendations range widely among cooks. Some suggest bringing the water to a simmer then allowing the eggs to cook gently for 10 minutes or more. Others recommend turning the water off once it achieves a robust boil permitting the eggs to cook in the ever diminishing heat for up to 17 minutes. The author recommends gently boiling, not simmering, large eggs for 10 minutes. Salt in the water ensures that any cracks will not leak significant amounts of egg white. Once boiled, remove the eggs immediately to an ice-bath, and as soon as possible thereafter, remove the shells under running water.

Next, split each egg in half, either lengthwise or crosswise. Crosswise splitting is favored for presentation by some chefs including Julia Child[4] with the suggestion that small slices off the ends permit the halves to stand upright. Once the yolks are removed to a separate bowl, they are sieved or mashed then combined with the ingredients that refill the white. Cooks have mixed views about the use of the food processor, but it produces smooth consistency of the yolk mixture without introducing rubbery texture if used with mayonnaise based fillings. Additions such as relish or chopped meats necessitate hand mixing. Once refilled, the egg halves may simply be garnished and served as a cold appetizer or side dish. Alternatively, they may become a core ingredient for another dish which may include sauces, coatings, and additional cooking. The composition of the fillings as well ongoing preparation required by some dishes will be focus areas of this paper going forward.

Evolution of the dish

From their beginnings in the Spanish medieval kitchen, stuffed eggs traveled with cooks to Italy, France, Belgium, England and their colonies. Fillings and sauces of the eggs reflect the taste preferences, available ingredients and health considerations of their times. Their appearance in a nation's cookery reflects not only abundant supplies of eggs from domesticated fowl but also an evolved level of cuisine prepared by cooks with time and skill.

While Marcus Apicius describes a Roman first course of peeled, quartered eggs topped with a piquant dressing,[5] stuffed eggs make their first appearance in a thirteenth-century Andalusian cookbook by an anonymous author.[6] In this recipe, the yolks are pounded together with cilantro, onion juice, pepper and coriander then beaten with *murri*, oil and salt. Once filled, the whites are fastened together with a small stick and sprinkled with pepper.

From these origins, stuffed egg preparations next appear in Italian cookery possibly the result of the Spanish Borgia and their pervasive influence in the states that now constitute Italy. Written in 1462, Platina's *De Honesta Voluptate* features fillings which include parsley, marjoram, mint and additional egg whites along with raisins and cheese.[7] A heated sauce of yolks, spices (ginger, cloves, and cinnamon) and raisins moistened with verjuice accompanies the dish. Platina, whose name was Bartolomeo Sacchi, created the book using recipes of Martino d'Rossi, cook to a Roman Cardinal during the papacy of Calixtus III, the first Borgia pope. Worth noting is that Platina's protector, Francesco Gonzaga of Mantua, enabled Platina to study Greek in Florence at the court of Cosimo de' Medici; these activities placed him in the cultural incubators of the Italian Renaissance. Other fourteenth- and fifteenth-century cookery books provide recipes for preparing stuffed eggs with very similar fillings such as the Venetian *Libro di Cucina/Libro per Cuoco* which suggests using the fattest, sweetest cheese to blend with the herbs and spices and the *hard-cooked* yolks.[8] After the filled whites are fried, they are powdered with sugar and served hot.

Recipes for stuffed eggs likely traveled to France along with many other Italian practices upon the marriage of Catherine de' Medici to the future King Henri II in 1533. Along with ballet, music, and fashions, cookery was an area which Italian influence transformed during her 56-year reign as Queen, Regent and Queen Mother. The place of eggs in the diet varied in the French religious calendar from the time of Charlemagne when eggs were forbidden during Lent but permitted on fish days. When not permitted for consumption, the eggs were stored until Easter or placed under a hen for hatching. The great abundance of eggs available in spring and at

The Deviled Egg

Easter produced many traditions among them the egg-intensive recipes for stuffed eggs noted here.

The role of eggs during flesh days, fish days and Lent is reflected in *The French Cook*,[9] La Varenne's work first published in Paris in 1651 and in London in 1653. In this work, the recipe 'Eggs farced' calls for the halving the hard-cooked eggs, either crosswise or lengthwise, then mixing and cooking the yolks with sorrel, butter and other herbs. The yolk mixture is served with the whites after they are sautéed in butter. Earlier in the seventeenth century, along with the recipes for stuffed egg halves, 'May Eggs' are detailed in the Belgian *Ouverture de Cuisine* which calls for not only removing eggs from the pan while the yolks are still uncooked but also removing the yolks through a pea-sized hole in each shell.[10] Salt, pepper and parsley are combined with the yolks and replaced into the shells refilling the cooked egg white. White bread plugs the holes, and the eggs are returned to the boil until cooked throughout. After peeling the eggs, they are cut in half and topped with a sauce of butter and sorrel juice.

Interestingly, August Escoffier's recipe for 'Deviled Eggs' departs completely from the stuffed egg form.[11] He calls for breaking the eggs into a frying pan of sizzling butter and after turning the eggs with yolks intact, slides them onto a plate. After adding vinegar to the browned pan butter, this sauce is reduced and poured over the eggs.

Of the French chefs, Henri Paul Pellaprat offers the greatest range of stuffed egg recipes including more modern forms of the medieval dishes. The May Egg's tradition is represented in two dishes, Eggs Elizabeth[12] and Egg Surprise.[13] For both dishes, a hard boiled egg is not sliced open, but instead, its yolk is removed through a small hole in the end of the egg. Eggs Elizabeth provides for refilling the center with a yolk mixture that includes artichoke bottoms, butter and Béchamel sauce, covering the filled egg with Mornay sauce and cheese; and browning all on a croûton. Egg Surprise replaces the yolk with foie gras, minced meat or mushrooms then calls for deep frying the eggs after they are coated with batter. In the section 'Les Oeufs Farcis' of his *Modern French Culinary Art*, Chef Pellaprat provides recipes for Eggs Aurore and Eggs Chimay as hot dishes.[14] While each recipe features stuffed egg halves, Aurore's yolks are combined with butter, salt and pepper as well as tomato and Béchamel sauce before reheating. Eggs Chimay add mushrooms to the Aurore mixture and brown the dish topped with Mornay sauce, cheese and crumbs. A range of cold stuffed egg dishes is also provided by Pellaprat.[15]

Also of French vintage in the twentieth century, Jacques Pepin offers his favorite egg recipe from childhood, 'Eggs Jeannette,' named for his mother. The yolk filling includes chopped garlic, parsley, milk, salt and pepper. After filling the whites, they are sautéed face down in butter and oil then served lukewarm with a dressing of leftover egg stuffing, oil, Dijon mustard, water, salt and pepper.[16]

The earliest British mention of stuffed eggs, *A Book of Cookrye*, was published in 1591 and offers A Pudding in Egges.[17] The whites of hard-cooked eggs are filled with the chopped mixture of cooked beets, cooked yolks, grated bread, and spices. Mutton broth blended with verjuice, dates, butter, salt and sugar then thickened with yolks tops the dish.

In 1891, *Cassell's Vegetarian Cookery*[18] provides 'Devilled Eggs' with a filling spiced by chilli vinegar. The eggs are served cold and not cooked further, an infrequent feature of stuffed egg recipes of the time. One interesting note is the reference to 'à la Columbus' as a preparation method which appeared earlier in American cookery books. Additional dishes featured Eggs la Bonne Femme, another cold preparation, as well as the elaborate hot dish, Eggs à la Dauphine. Despite the presence of several stuffed egg recipes, quartered eggs topped with cayenne-laced gravy were termed 'Devilled Eggs' in *Cassell's Household Cookery* in 1909 departing from the stuffed form favored by vegetarians.[19]

Beginning in 1940 and lasting for fourteen years, World War II rationing limited the availability of eggs in urban areas and resulted in fundamental changes in the cuisine of England. Recipe formulation and consumption patterns moved away from egg intensive uses such as stuffed eggs during these years.

Other European cuisines offer variations of stuffed eggs today. In modern Spain, shrimp stuffed eggs are baked as a brunch dish while *tapas* include deep-fried salmon stuffed eggs and egg halves topped with sour cream, shrimp, olive and anchovy. A traditional Swedish recipe, *Fyllda ägghalvor*, is often a part of the smörgåsbord, and recipes for the eggs include a rich early 1950s version featuring an ample measure of anchovies in the yolk filling.[20] More recent versions of the dish include curry, gravlax and mayonnaise as additions to the filling.

In the Pacific region, Australians not only enjoy the classic deviled egg but also bring to us the most unique foundation for the dish, the deviled emu egg. Noting that the hefty, greenish black eggs are plentiful, Paul Tessmer the creator of the recipe suggests boiling the grapefruit sized egg for 70 minutes. Given that the shell will support the weight of a 150-pound bird, cracking the egg requires the use of a crab mallet or heavy kitchen knife. The large egg white is cut into one-inch squares onto which a classic mixture of yolk, mayonnaise, ketchup, Worcestershire sauce and relish is piped.[21] Thailand's stuffed egg variation is *Kai Kwam* in which the egg white cups are filled with a mixture of seafood and pork. Either crabmeat or a mixture of crabmeat and raw shrimp are chopped and mixed with cooked pork then seasoned with fish sauce, coconut milk and cilantro. The egg halves are mounded with this mixture, dipped in batter and deep fried until golden. This preparation may be a part of Thai cuisine due to sixteenth- and seventeenth-century influences of the French, Dutch and Portuguese.

Deviled eggs in America

In America's early years, the principal food influence was British, but French cuisine was well known to Thomas Jefferson and other leading figures of the time. Additionally, the presence of the French during the Revolutionary Period created great receptivity to French influence on the part of Americans. As in Europe, the natural cycle of egg production resulted in large quantities of eggs in springtime following little or no fresh egg availability during late fall and winter. All of these factors resulted in cooking practices for eggs that resembled those of Britain and France with eggs playing a significant role in the diet of the nation.

The history of stuffed egg recipes in American cookbooks appears to begin in 1857 with Eliza Leslie's recipe Columbus Eggs.[22] American recipes of the late nineteenth and early twentieth centuries often reprise the French in such recipes as the 1883, Eggs à L'Aurore[23], from *Our New Cook Book and Household Receipts*. Fanny Farmer's *Boston Cooking-school Cook Book* provides two recipes for stuffed eggs but does not term either Deviled.[24] The first recipe, Stuffed Eggs in a Nest uses 'devilled ham' and melted butter in the yolk filling then tops the filled eggs with white sauce and crumbs before browning. The second, Egg Farci, is one of the earliest to mention mayonnaise as a possible binder of the yolk filling which also includes chicken or veal as well as cayenne and other seasonings. This recipe is also one of the earliest to be served cold without further cooking. By 1897, both Stuffed Eggs and Deviled Eggs are cited in two recipes contained in *Hood's Practical Cook's Book*.[25] In both recipes, fillings contain olive oil, minced ham, salt, pepper and parsley; the Deviled Eggs contain French mustard as a differentiator.

The author explored the possibility that deviled eggs were sourced from Mexican cookery.[26] The first use of the term deviled eggs in the British *Cassell's Vegetarian Cookery*[27] as well as the similarity to recipes in the earliest American cookbooks suggests that stuffed eggs and deviled eggs predate the period in the late nineteenth century when Mexican cuisine influenced American foods. Additionally, the recipes cited as deviled contain mustard or cayenne but lack the chili-based ingredients common to Mexican-Indian cooking.

During the early part of the twentieth century, Hungarians migrating to the United States brought with them paprika which came into 'wide use' in the 1920s.[28] In 1929, *The International Cook Book* offered cold stuffed eggs with prepared salad dressing as the binder for the yolk filling and represents an early mention of paprika as topping.[29] Mustard, olives, nuts, caviar and anchovy paste are noted as potential additions to the filling. Stuffed eggs are also the basis of salads with the egg halves on lettuce and served with mayonnaise. Numerous cookbooks from this period offer variations on cold stuffed eggs still rarely employing mayonnaise as the primary binding agent. While mayonnaise was commercially distributed beginning in 1912, it does not appear frequently in recipes until the 1940s.

In November 1914, *The New York Times* advised its women readers to appreciate the few fresh eggs available by enjoying new recipes, and stuffed eggs were featured in the article, 'What Every Woman Wants to Know.'[30] Once fewer than 14 hours of daylight were present, egg production faltered, and New York City cooks of the time were reduced to cold-storage eggs which many chose to avoid. Conversely, these housewives were challenged to take advantage of the relatively large quantities of affordable eggs resulting in the spring when daylight hours became longer.[31] In 1935, half of the year's egg production occurred between March and June[32] coinciding with other spring delights such as asparagus and strawberries in the markets. Of course, the popularity of deviled eggs was not without controversy as erupted in 1904 in Fort Washington, Pennsylvania. The all-male officers of the Reformed Church voted against permitting deviled eggs and angel cake at the June fete.[33] In their view, having deviled eggs, would bring profane objects within the sacred edifice while angel cake would be sacrilegious. Women planning the fete cancelled the event in a fit of pique refusing to bow to the will of the sanctimonious menfolk. Similar issues arose in the southern states sometimes requiring a change in the dish's name.[34]

Picnicking instructions offered in 1908 by *The New York Times* provided details of the perfect portable meal.[35] Citing eggs as the basis for any picnic luncheon, the article notes that making the eggs attractive is a requirement and that a stuffed egg is more palatable than a plain 'hard boiled egg.' The article instructs the cook to place the stuffed egg halves together and then to wrap them in oiled paper, twisted at the top. An additional tip was to have an extra coachman and horses to convey the food and drinkables.

African-Americans in the south-eastern United States had different reasons for packing the stuffed egg in lunches during the first six decades of the twentieth century. Since they were unable to enter dining establishments while traveling to work or on longer journeys, these travelers included stuffed eggs wrapped in paper and tied securely as an antidote to hunger.

As the Depression deepened in the United States, egg dishes were promoted as nutritious and economical protein sources. On May 21, 1933 in the depths of the Great Depression, President and Mrs. Franklin Roosevelt enjoyed lunch at the White House featuring stuffed eggs topped by tomato sauce as the entrée. Touted for its economy and nutritional content, the meal was prepared by Cornell University's Home Economics Department at a cost of only 7½ cents per serving. The President declared the luncheon 'good.'[36]

Mid-twentieth century recipes demonstrate the vogue which stuffed eggs enjoyed during this period. They are prominently featured by James Beard in his 1940 *Hors D'oeuvre and Canapés*.[37] He notes that 'No matter what else is served at a cocktail party, you will always find that a tray of stuffed eggs … will be one of the most popular items. These disappear more rapidly than anything else.' Mayonnaise is used liberally in most of his variations which include foie gras, anchovy, curry, seafood and steak tartare. In 1975, *The Joy of Cooking* provides a broad range of potential fillings and toppings for deviled or stuffed eggs.[38] Elaborate entrée preparations including shrimp or sweetbreads join the cold hors d'oeuvre of filled egg whites garnished with olives, capers or truffles.

Twenty-first century eggs

Deviled eggs have gained significant visibility in the new century. In 2004, The Southern Foodways Alliance invited cooks to submit their favorite recipes and recollections of deviled eggs.[39] Men and women from all parts of the United States shared their recipes, and the winner, Rick Ellis, became known as the King of Deviled Eggs. Rather than reflecting only southern U.S. recollections of deviled eggs, the contest contributions evoke the broader social context of the eggs. Church potlucks, family gatherings, and simpler lifestyles are all celebrated along with extraordinary creativity by the chefs. Also marking the heightened interest in the dish, the book *Deviled Eggs: 50 Recipes from Simple to Sassy* contains a dizzying array of recipes ranging from traditional preparations to dessert eggs filled with chocolate and fruit fillings.

For those who don't enjoy the preparation journey, deviled eggs have reappeared on menus in upscale American restaurants. With quail eggs occasionally providing an even more elegant package, they come filled with Crabmeat Ravigote or flavored as a favored cocktail, rising above nostalgia to take their rightful places as worthy beginnings of special meals.[40] Restaurant news in Washington, San Francisco and New York notes the fresh appeal of the dish whether in nostalgic, traditional form or one of its more rarified incarnations.

The deviled egg plate

The precarious transport of the filled eggs together with their habit of rolling about on serving plates produced special purpose deviled egg plates, serving dishes that continue to be viewed as a necessity in Southern homes today. As Susan Perry, a contributor to the Southern Foodways Deviled Egg Competition stated, 'Years ago someone at my annual New Year's party said that all Southern women should be given a deviled egg plate at birth. I could not help but take such a delightful remark to heart. I have been giving egg plates to newborn girls and as house-warming gifts for years. I am working to fulfill my own notion that every household should have at least one deviled egg plate. Plates adorned with a chicken or chicks or egg motif are my favorites and matching salt and pepper shakers designed to fit on the plate itself are a definite plus. The necessity of having such a plate or indeed any deviled egg plate cannot be downplayed. As we who celebrate deviled eggs know, they disappear quickly thus leaving an empty plate on the table long before other offerings are gone; so it better be an attractive empty plate.'[41]

Tupperware's deviled egg transporter was a great improvement over other methods such as tying the halves up in paper or the inevitably sat-upon cardboard boxes. This rescue from the disappointment of eggs squashed by bad fortune or careless children made the carrier an additional must-have for every household. While today, beds of parsley or herbs may cushion the eggs gently on any serving dish, the deviled egg plate with its gentle oval indentations was a required serving piece for hostesses when a full dinner service indicated your station in life.

Deviled eggs: the business

Commercial promotion of deviled eggs is rooted in the recipes' very intense consumption of the egg product. Few other recipes approach the deviled egg for commodity use especially with the recipe warning so often given, 'Boil two or three extra just in case.' The United States offering in the International Egg Commission's International Cookbook[42] is 'Deviled Delight,' while Canada's Egg Board and regional associations promote 'Devilled Eggs' heavily.[43] Egg producers now offer deviled egg kits, a twenty-first-century shortcut to the classic dish. Touted as taking 'the Devil out of deviled eggs' the kits are sold in grocery stores containing 24 or 48 egg halves along with a filling bag to snip and press for filling the egg cups. The filling may be purchased with or without sweet green pickle relish. Billed as 'always fresh, always tasty' the product appeals to those who may not know the simple techniques required to produce deviled eggs or who are simply unwilling to devote the time to preparation.[44] Commercial success of the product has not been validated.

Finally, the little-observed National Deviled Egg Day is November 2 for those who lack adequate opportunities for celebration. Invented by egg producers to drive up demand, the day provides another opportunity to wear that Deviled Egg costume one might have bought for Halloween.[45] Since parades or other recognition of the day may be in short supply, celebrants may also wish to purchase the Deviled Egg Bowl, a handy game selling online for only $8.99.[46] According to the website, both kids and adults love trying to hit the jumping eggs while avoiding a devil who seeks to interfere with their bowling balls. Whip up a batch of deviled eggs for fellow-gamers to top off a successful day.

Conclusion

Call them what you will, deviled or stuffed, these little bites are seductive and satisfying, evoking the past in their traditional forms while enabling self-expression by their makers. Although today's dish is normally associated with post-World War II cocktail parties and picnics, the dish's history has great dignity grounded in the foundations of Renaissance cookery. Interestingly, the greatest challenge to their preparation is a very fundamental one, achieving the perfect hard-cooked egg. While earliest preparations began as heavy dishes with dense fillings, rich sauces and heavy frying, stuffed egg preferences of the modern age tend toward a cool, light yolk mousse filling the egg white.

In the 2004 *Gourmet Cookbook*, the advice to cooks of deviled eggs sums up the approach best taken to preparation, 'Make these your own by embellishing them with your favorite herbs and spices.'[47] The recipe below from the author's family invites the reader's additions, and the reward for this effort is assured. Echoing a similar sentiment to that of James Beard, Richard A. Brooks, another Southern Foodways contributor notes, 'Deviled eggs are eaten first – an appetizer of sorts – less from fear of microbes than the understanding that damn soon there won't be any left.'[48]

The Deviled Egg

Deviled Eggs Nance

12 hard-cooked eggs
½ cup mayonnaise (may use low-fat versions)
2 tablespoons sugar
2 teaspoons yellow prepared mustard
2 teaspoons vinegar
salt & pepper to taste
paprika

Halve eggs lengthwise, and remove the yolks to a shallow bowl. Mash yolks with a fork or sieve as desired. Mix in remaining ingredients by hand adding mayonnaise to achieve desired consistency. Spoon yolk mixture into egg whites and garnish with a light dusting of paprika. Refrigerate if not to be served immediately.

Make them your own: stir in pickle relish or minced onion. Omit the sugar and add curry powder reducing or eliminating the mustard as desired. Add chopped fresh herbs such as dill (which is amazing), omit the sugar and top with herb sprig.

Bibliography

A. W., *A Book of Cookrye* (London, printed Edward Allde, 1591, originally published 1584) Transcribed by Mark and Jane Waks, <http://jducoeur.org/Cookbook/Cookrye.html>.

An Anonymous Andalusian Cookbook of the 13th Century, translated by Charles Perry, <http://www.daviddfriedman.com/Medieval/Cookbooks/Andalusian/andalusian_contents.htm>.

Anonimo Veneziano, *Libro di Cucina/Libro per cuoco* (14th/15th c.), trans. Helewyse de Birkestad, OL (MKA Louise Smithson) from the transcription of Ludovico Frati (ed.): *Libro di cucina del secolo XIV*. Livorno 1899 prepared and made available online by Thomas Gloning. Last updated March 28th 2005. <http://www.geocities.com/helewyse/libro.html>.

Beard, James, *Hors D'Oeuvre and Canapés* (New York, William Morrow and Company, Inc., 1940 revised 1971).

Casas, Penelope, *The Food and Wines of Spain* (New York, Knopf, 1982).

Casteau, Lancelot de, *Ouverture de Cuisine* (Liege, Leonard Steel, Licensed Printer, 1604).

Child, Julia, *The Way to Cook* (New York, Alfred A. Knopf, 1989).

Edwards, John, translated and adapted to the Modern Kitchen, *The Roman Cookery of Apicius: A Treasury of Gourmet Recipes & Herbal Cookery* (Point Roberts, Washington: Hartley & Marks, 1984).

Farmer, Fanny Merritt, *Boston Cooking-school Cook Book* (Boston, 1896, facsimile ed. New York: Weathervane Books, 1986).

Frost, S. Annie, *Our New Cook Book and Household Receipts* (Boston, People's Publishing Company, 1883).

Heritage, Lizzie, *Cassell's Household Cookery* (London, Cassell & Co. Ltd., 1909).

Heywood, Margaret Weimer, *The International Cook Book* (Boston, Merchandisers Inc., 1929).

Hood's Practical Cook's Book for the Average Household (Lowell: C. I. Hood & Co. 1897).

Hooker, Richard J., *Food and Drink in America A History* (New York, The Bobbs Merrill Company, Inc. 1981).

James, Alice L., *The Chafing Dish and Sandwiches* (New York, The Knickerbocker Press, 1912).

Leslie, Eliza, *Miss Leslie's New Cookery Book* (Philadelphia, T. B. Peterson, 1857).

Moose, Debbie, *Deviled Eggs: 50 Recipes from Simple to Sassy* (Boston, The Harvard Common Press, 2004).
Payne, A. G., *Cassell's Vegetarian Cookery: A Manual of Cheap and Wholesome Diet* (London, B. A. Cassell & Company, Ltd., 1891).
Pellaprat, Henri Paul, *Modern French Culinary Art*, Second Edition, Third Impression (London, Virtue & Company Ltd., 1984).
Pepin, Jacques, *The Apprentice: My Life in the Kitchen* (New York, Houghton Mifflin, 2003).
Platina: *On Right Pleasure and Good Health*, trans. Mary Ellen Milham (Tempe, Medieval & Renaissance Texts, 1998).
Rombauer, Irma S., Becker, Marion Rombauer, *The Joy of Cooking* (Indianapolis, Bobbs Merrill Company, Inc., 1975).
Stanley-Wrench, Mollie, *Hors D'Oeuvres How to Make Them* (London, Herbert Jenkins, Ltd., 1952).
The Art of French Cooking, trans. Joseph Faulkner, Edited Bart Winer (New York, Simon & Schuster, 1958).
The Gourmet Cookbook, ed. Ruth Reichl (New York, Houghton Mifflin, 2004).
Varenne, Francis Peter, *The French Cook*, Trans. I.D.G. (London, Charles Adams, 1653).

Notes

1. James p. 235.
2. Herbst, Sharon Tyler, *The Food Lovers Companion*, 2nd edition. , epicurious.com <http://www.epicurious.com/cooking/how_to/food_dictionarysearch?query=devil>.
3. Moose pp. 53–55.
4. Child pp. 62–63.
5. Edwards p. 186.
6. *An Anonymous Andalusian Cookbook of the 13th Century* #148.
7. Milham p. 182.
8. Anonimo Veneziano XLVII.
9. Varenne p. 178.
10. Casteau p. 134 & 278.
11. *The Art of French Cooking* p. 261.
12. *The Art of French Cooking* p. 261.
13. *The Art of French Cooking* p. 269.
14. Pellaprat pp. 298–299.
15. Pellaprat pp. 300–301.
16. Pepin p.13.
17. A. W., *A Book of Cookrye*.
18. Payne pp. 78–95.
19. Heritage pp. 592–599.
20. Stanley-Wrench p. 39.
21. Tessmer, Paul, 'Deviled Emu Egg,' International Recipes Online, <http://www.internationalrecipesonline.com/recipes/view.pl?1041>.
22. Leslie pp. 92–93.
23. Frost p. 303.
24. Farmer pp. 7–8.
25. *Hood's Practical Cook's Book for the Average Household*, p.167.
26. Hooker p. 239.
27. Payne p. 61.
28. Hooker p. 290.
29. Heywood pp. 245–246 29.

30. 'What Every Woman Wants to Know,' *The New York Times*, 8 Nov 1914, p. X3.
31. Fact Sheet 35, Animal Science Department, Florida Cooperative Extension Service, Institute of Food and Agricultural Sciences, University of Florida. Original publication date April 1998. Revised June 2003.
32. Beaver, Dorothy, 'Fresh Eggs Roll to Market,' *The New York Times*, 19 May 1935 p. SM16.
33. From the *Chicago Tribune*, 'Angel Cake and Deviled Eggs Barred,' *New York Times* 13 June 1904, p. 6.
34. 2004 Deviled Egg Recipe Competition. Southern Foodways Alliance, 3 Jul. 2006. <http://www.southernfoodways.com/oral_history/eggs/02basics.shtml>.
35. Rittenhouse, Anne, 'Be Sure to Take It in a Box That You May Throw Away–The Faithful Eggs and Sandwiches,' *New York Times* 16 August 1908, p. X9.
36. Associated Press, '7 ½-Cent Economy Luncheons Served to the Roosevelts', *New York Times* 22 March 1933, p. 9.
37. Beard pp. 49–55.
38. Rombauer & Becker p. 225.
39. 2004 Deviled Egg Recipe Competition. Southern Foodways Alliance, 3 Jul. 2006. <http://www.southernfoodways.com/oral_history/eggs/index.shtml>.
40. Patronite, Rob. Raisfield, Robin. 'The Devil You Say', *New York Magazine*, 21 November 2005. <http://newyorkmetro.com/nymetro/food/features/15056/>.
41. Susan Perry, 'All About the Plate.' 2004 Deviled Egg Recipe Competition. Southern Foodways Alliance, 3 Jul. 2006. <http://www.southernfoodways.com/oral_history/eggs/01theplate.shtml>.
42. International Egg Commission, USA – Deviled Delight. 3 Jul. 2006. <http://www.thinkegg.com/recipes/details.asp?id=30&cid=1>.
43. Canadian Egg Marketing Agency, All Recipes D, 3 Jul. 2006. <http://www.eggs.ca/recipes/allrecipes.asp?currentletter=100>.
44. Sauder's Eggs. Our Products. 3 Jul. 2006. <http://www.saudereggs.com/products.html#Deviled Eggs>.
45. Costumes by Scavenge. Deviled Egg Costume. 27 Jun. 2006. <http://www.costumesbyscavenge.com/deviled-> egg-costme-0.3711.html>.
46. Handango. Deviled Egg Bowl, 27, Jun. 2006. <http://www.handango.com/PlatformProductDetail.jsp>.
47. *The Gourmet Cookbook*, p. 27.
48. Richard A. Brooks, 'The Legend, The Lore.' 2004 Deviled Egg Recipe Competition, Southern Foodways Alliance. 3 Jul. 2006. <http://www.southernfoodways.com/oral_history/eggs/05legendlore.shtml>.

The History of Eggs in Irish Cuisine and Culture

Máirtín Mac Con Iomaire and Andrea Cully

Which came first, the chicken or the egg? The argument has gone on for generations, and has never been settled. However, the answer is to be found nesting in the history of food; the egg was first, for the very good reason that the chicken, as the latest addition to the poultry yards of Greece and Italy in the fifth century BC, found geese, ducks and guinea fowl already installed, laying eggs and hatching them.[1]

Introduction

Eggs are one of the most basic and versatile ingredients used throughout the world. Their culinary uses include aeration, emulsifying, enriching, thickening, colouring, binding, and clarifying, not to mention the numerous ways of cooking them on their own. Without eggs, the disciplines of pastry, baking, and sauce cookery would be much less sophisticated. In Ireland today, hens' eggs are the most commonly used but in bygone days the eggs of ducks, geese, quails, plovers, gulls and other wild birds were widely used.

Eggs have played an important role in the Irish culture. For centuries, eggs have done so much more than simply nourish the body; they have soaked up mythological and folk belief, and have been used to celebrate certain religious festivals. They were also an early form of income or means of barter, often contributing far more to the family income than the commonly-used term 'pin money' suggests. Initiatives sponsored by successive governments and the rise in the co-operative movement led to improvements in the poultry and egg industry from the end of the nineteenth century to the 1960s when intensive production in 'battery farms' commenced. Today's hybrid hens can lay up to 330 eggs a year on a daily feed of 120g. Enriched feed produces value added eggs rich in Omega 3 and other nutrients. This paper traces the development of egg production and consumption in Ireland. It includes mythology and folklore, the type of eggs and the breed of hens used, the government schemes which influenced the Irish egg economy, and gives examples of how eggs were consumed in the different strata of Irish society.

History

Ireland's culinary traditions have been evolving since prehistoric times. The story of Irish food is as complex as the many cultural, political and economic forces that have shaped Ireland's existence.[2] There is a debate about when hens were first introduced to Ireland. Archaeologists tend to agree that they arrived via Roman Britain, where hens' eggs were an everyday part of people's lives and diet.[3] Popular legend has it, however, that hens were introduced by the Danes.[4] In early Ireland goose eggs were a very sought-after luxury served at banquets on dishes of silver and gold. The beauty of the hen's and the goose's attractive plumage is immortalised in *The Book of Kells*, an illuminated ninth-century manuscript containing the Latin text of the four gospels, housed in Dublin's Trinity College.[5] Cereals and dairy produce were two staples of the early Irish diet. Oats, barley, wheat and rye were used to make coarse flat breads and porridge. Eggs, milk and butter were used to enrich the widely eaten porridge.[6] A section in the Brehon Laws – the legal system of early medieval Ireland, deals with poultry and lists the fines for trespass of fowl and the measures that should be taken to ensure that poultry did not stray.[7] 'Dry eggs' formed part of the rigidly sparse diet of the extreme penitent monks in the late-eighth-century monastic movement 'Céilí Dé' based at the monastery of Tallaght, near Dublin.

Ireland was subject to a forceful wave of conquest and colonisation from the twelfth to the seventeenth centuries. Prior to this, the diet of Gaelic Ireland was bland, based on 'white meats' – milk and dairy products – coarse cereals and occasional meats – principally pork or bacon. New culinary techniques and recipes were introduced in the twelfth century by the Anglo-Normans, including the masonry oven and the use of spices and sweet and sour combinations. By the fourteenth century there was a fusion of Gaelic Irish and Anglo-Norman food patterns. Culinary innovation and change followed the Tudor and Stuart conquests of the sixteenth and seventeenth centuries, with the introduction of the pheasant, turkey and most significantly the potato. An Anglo-Irish gentry class emerged with a rich and varied cuisine, influenced by the professional French chefs who had become a fashionable addition to their kitchens.[8] Diet varied considerably with social status, the basic peasant staples of oats and dairy produce co-existing with the acquired traditions of the gentry. By the nineteenth century the potato had established itself as a staple of one third of the population, an over-dependence which led to the devastation of the Famine in the 1840s when successive harvests failed.

Ireland underwent a period of rapid commercialisation during the latter half of the nineteenth century. Egg consumption increased during this time but was rarely referred to in dietary surveys.[9] Eggs provided farm families with a domestic economic enterprise directly tied to the marketplace, which required little initial capital.[10] Eggs were not eaten by the poor in the West of Ireland in the 1821–1851 period, but sold to pay the rent or 'put a shoe on our foot or a spade in our hand. We sell them now, we used to eat them'.[11]

Mythology and folklore
Hens and eggs feature strongly in Irish mythology and folklore. The Middle Irish tale of 'Fled Dúin na nGéd', dating probably from the twelfth century tells of a battle where good, represented by King Domnall mac Aeda, prevails over evil. The king of

The History of Eggs in Irish Cuisine and Culture

Ulster, Congal Cláen, attends a feast prepared by Domnall at which goose eggs are served, some of which were stolen from Bishop Erc Sláine and others provided by two monstrous giants. Erc and the giants place a curse on whoever eats the eggs. When the first goose egg, which was served on a silver platter, was placed before Congal, the power of the curse turned the platter to wood and the goose egg into a hen's egg. The men of Ulster took the happenings as a great insult and a ferocious battle was fought. The storyteller concludes 'What is the difference at all between the egg of the red feathered hen and the egg of the white winged goose. Alas for him who destroyed all Erin for dispute over an egg'.[12]

Legend also has it that the pairing of eggs and bacon is of Irish origin. An old Irish peasant woman was frying bacon for her man when a hen roosting on the cross-beams above the open fireplace dropped an egg, hitting the side of the pan and spilling its contents into the sizzling fat. The woman served the egg and bacon to her man who consumed the lot and went forth to the monastery where he laboured, marvelling at the combination. Thus the fame of bacon and eggs entered the monastery walls and spread from monastery to monastery, from country to country, as the dish came to be relished by rich and poor 'all by the grace of God and the irregular proclivities of the lazy old hen'.[13] Cohabiting with poultry had its perils. Hens foraged for themselves during the day and were always housed at night to protect them from predators, often spending the night on ropes hung across the kitchen of a labourer's cottage.[14] A Blasket Islander recalls a young chicken dropping out of the roof and into his father's mug of milk during his childhood in the 1870s. Further investigation revealed over ten chickens and a hen nesting in the thatch roof.[15] Eggs are central to an anecdote collected by folklorists in the four provinces of Ireland concerning the meanness of employers and the cleverness of servants or workers with regard to the food they received. When asked how they would like their egg boiled, the answer was 'along with one or two others'. When asked whether they liked them hard or soft the answer was 'doesn't make one bit of difference, ma'am; if they are too soft, I'll harden them with butter, and if they are too hard I'll soften them with butter'.[16]

Irish food customs

On Shrove Tuesday, a night of feasting took place before the black fast of Lent began. Pancakes were always made that night using up all surplus butter, eggs, milk and cream before Ash Wednesday. It was customary to let the eldest unmarried daughter toss the first pancake. If the pancake fell to the floor she had no hope of marriage during the coming twelve months.[17] In medieval times people believed that the barnacle goose did not constitute meat, since it spent most of its time at sea, and therefore their flesh and eggs could be eaten during times of fasting. The week of Good Friday, known as Holy Week, marked the end of the Lenten fast at its most severe. Eggs, which were laid on Good Friday were marked with a cross and kept aside until Easter Sunday when they could be eaten. Eggs hatched on Good Friday were believed to produce healthy birds.[18] Eggs were consumed in large amounts for breakfast on Easter Sunday, with men eating an average of six eggs each.[19] Eggs were dyed by boiling them with herbs, plants and traditional dyestuffs and these coloured eggs were a symbol of luck. Today, chocolate Easter eggs have replaced birds' eggs.

May Day was the time of year that the *sióga* or fairies were believed to change their residence and their magic was supposedly at its most potent. To counteract fairy magic each family set up a May bush before their door. Eggshells, especially those that had been dyed for Easter Sunday, were used along with ribbons, bunches of flowers and coloured paper to decorate the May bush.[20]

Role of eggs in the Irish economy

The value of eggs in the Irish economy in 2006 is approximately 30 million Euros. Ireland produces in excess of 569 million eggs annually, predominantly for the Irish market.[21] The Irish egg business was not always as buoyant. The names of two politicians, Horace Plunkett and James Dillon, stand out in the story of the Irish egg industry. In his Land Act of 1891, Arthur Balfour established the Congested Districts Board, of which Plunkett was a member. It encouraged a huge range of cottage industries and employed instructors who taught farming families the skills of poultry and egg production. Many of the small nondescript fowl found in Irish farmyards were inbred for generations and laid small white eggs. Poor stocks and the practice of hoarding eggs prior to sale combined to give Irish eggs a very poor reputation in the lucrative English marketplace. Efforts were made to improve the breeding stocks and the quality of eggs produced. The Congested Districts Board's scheme for improving poultry was calculated to benefit the poorer classes of small occupiers on the western seaboard. The scheme distributed pullets and cockerels and recommended distributing sittings of eggs of the Andalusian and Leghorn varieties.[22]

Horace Plunkett founded the Irish Co-operative Movement in 1889,[23] and also founded The Irish Agricultural Organisation Society (IAOS) in 1894 to co-ordinate and promote the co-operative movement. In 1895 the weekly *Irish Homestead* was established to publicise the movement and its ideas.[24] The IAOS had 778 affiliated societies,[25] and employed poultry experts from England and Denmark to educate and advise its members on how to select and pack eggs for the English market. The Recess Committee, also formed by Plunkett to urge the establishment of a Department of Agriculture and Industries, reported in 1896 that the total value of eggs imported into the United Kingdom in 1894 was £3,786,329 – coming mainly from France but also from as far away as Russia. They argued that

> there is no reason why every penny of this £3,786,329 might not be earned in Ireland, if the suppliers learn the secret of getting their eggs to market fresh, if they are helped to do so by railway and steamboat facilities and if good breeds of poultry be introduced and proper principles of rearing and keeping inculcated.

Thom's Directory shows an increase in the number of poultry kept in Ireland in 1891 and values them at £381,309, but they give no figures or value for eggs.[26] The value of the sale of eggs to the County Mayo economy in 1880 was calculated at £42,500.[27] This figure had more than doubled by 1892 according to the Congested Districts Board's baseline reports.[28]

Egg production may be viewed as a substitute for the pre-Famine domestic linen manufacture, since it employed the same family members, and like domestic spinning it produced a similar cash income necessary for the maintenance of a small farm economy.[29] The production and selling of eggs, principally women's work, contributed up to a quarter of the total family income.[30] This is far more substantial than the commonly-used term 'pin money' suggests.

Co-operative poultry societies

By 1902 there were 31 special poultry societies with a turnover of £29,914. Some of these societies were absorbed by agricultural co-operatives which increasingly started to sell eggs for their members.[31]

> 'The Irish egg', said Plunkett, 'has acted as a depreciated currency. In its too long life it became as dirty as a one pound note, and the process of securing for it its proper place in the English wholesale trade, aroused the wrath of those who profited by its humble place in Irish retail trade'.[32]

The co-operatives faced resistance from the established traders. It was the local shopkeeper's system of bartering eggs for groceries that had led to the crisis of dirty, stale, un-graded eggs being refused by the British merchants. A persistent problem facing the early efforts to improve the quality of the Irish egg was that cheap, low-grade, foreign eggs were sold in England as 'Irish', whilst the good Irish eggs supplied by Irish co-operatives were passed as English or French. A similar fate befell Irish whiskey in America during Prohibition from which it never fully recovered. In order to overcome the fraud and deep-rooted prejudice against Irish eggs, the IAOS introduced a trademark – a diamond shape with an odd looking shamrock and the letters IAOS. In 1910 this was superseded by the trademark KARKA, a phonetic rendering of the Gaelic word for 'hens'. The co-operative bought eggs by weight rather than by number, and children would often take the day's laying of eggs to the co-op on their way to school, thus ensuring freshness. The IAOS calculated that in 1899 40 hens gave as much profit as one cow, but revised the figure by 1906 to 20 hens.

Many housewives regarded the new system of selling to the co-op rather than bartering with the shopkeeper as an intrusion into their jealously guarded domain. This sentiment impeded the growth of co-ops' involvement in the egg trade. By 1914 only 12 strong poultry societies remained, most of which had added grocery supply to their business, as they could not otherwise compete with the 'huxters'.

Government schemes

Government policy during much of the twentieth century actively promoted domestic egg production until economies of scale led to the intensive production of eggs. The Department of Agriculture established a poultry fattening station in 1905 at Avondale, County Wicklow. A profitable table poultry industry, the forerunner of the modern broiler chicken industry emerged. Chickens were luxury food that enjoyed a steady market demand except during the game season. The Poultry Advisory Service was initiated in 1908 and continued following Irish Independence in 1921 by the Department of Agriculture and Technical Instruction. Instructors travelled the country visiting farms that kept a large number of hens, teaching poultry management skills. The main concentration of the instructors was in the counties of Cavan, Monaghan, Limerick and Cork where the industry was most prevalent.[33] In 1924 the Agricultural Produce (Eggs) Act laid down definite standards for grading and packing export eggs.[34]

Irish egg exporters enjoyed a boom period during the First World War. In 1930 Ireland exported £3,750,000 worth of eggs, but by 1937 this figure had fallen dramatically to £750,000. Countries such as Denmark and Holland whose production had been affected by the war were pushing Ireland out of the egg market. By 1940 only three specifically poultry co-ops had survived: North Kilkenny, Athlone and Clonbrock & Castlegar.[35] Deputy James Dillon, foresaw the need for action and encouraged the Irish public to engage in extensive egg production. Dillon urged the then Minister for Agriculture, Patrick Hogan, to take measures to stimulate the production of eggs. The 'day old chick scheme' was introduced to produce a better class of fowl for laying eggs, particularly for the British market. Eggs were provided for hatching, either free or at a reduced rate, and grants were provided for building proper poultry houses. Dillon suggested widening the use of Hover and Putnam lamps, as the average country house had no suitable accommodation for the maintenance of day-old chicks. He also suggested that poultry instructors take vigorous measures to familiarise farmers' wives with the use of these lamps. Rural electrification helped the winter production of eggs as lights could be left on to fool the hens into thinking it was still summer.

Production of eggs increased but the advent of the Second World War also increased export demands, which remained long after the war had ended. There was plenty of meat, fish and eggs in neutral Ireland, which was like the land of milk and honey to visitors from war-ravaged Britain. Jimmy Kilbride,[36] a chef in Dublin's Gresham Hotel during the war years, remembers a party of sailors ordering two Porterhouse steaks and six fried eggs each. Johnny Opperman[37] who was head chef at the City Hotel in Derry in 1939 recalls Donegal women crossing the border with eggs hidden in special pockets under their shawls to sell on the 'black market'. An Egg Agreement with Britain had been secured in January 1947 requiring Ireland to supply a stated quantity of eggs regardless of season. In 1950, a sum of £1,350,000

The History of Eggs in Irish Cuisine and Culture

was made available by the British Ministry of Food to subsidise the price of Irish eggs in an effort to encourage Irish people to go into greater production of eggs to supply the British market. A similar amount of money was put up by the Irish Government but Ireland didn't exploit the export opportunity that existed and the establishment of British Egg Marketing Board (BEMB), which guaranteed a profitable price for all British eggs, put an end to the export market. A thriving egg industry grew in England particularly around Lancashire. The number of laying hens in Northern Ireland rose from 2 million to 9 million in five years. Eggs were now being smuggled across the border from the north to the south.[38] In 1956 the Co-operative Poultry Products Ltd. was founded by a group in the Cavan/Monaghan area and played an important part in the development of modern intensive poultry keeping which began in the early 1960s.

James Dillon served for almost 40 years in and out of Government, sitting as Minister for Agriculture on two occasions. Since the inception of the 'day old chick scheme', young chicks have been known as 'Dillons óga' or 'young Dillons' in the West Galway Irish speaking 'Gaeltacht' area. The Poultry Advisory Service evolved over the years, but still exists to advise new entrants into the now specialist egg industry. The Irish egg industry suffered from the 1988 salmonella scare in England. Although there was little or no salmonella in Ireland, public confidence was affected by the negative press coverage. The egg industry working with Bord Bia, the Irish food marketing board, and experts from relevant state agencies developed the Egg Quality Assurance Scheme (EQAS) in 2000. Ireland is one of only four European Union countries with an EU-approved salmonella plan.

Types of eggs

Domestic fowl were bred from at least the early Christian era. The following birds are mentioned by name in the *Lives of the Saints*: blackbird, wren, duck, lark, swan, cuckoo, crane, raven, partridge, kite, hawk, sparrow, eagle and stork.[39] Turkeys were introduced in the wake of the Stuart and Tudor settlements but like the guinea fowl that followed they were more valued for their flesh than their eggs. Little is published about Irish wild egg consumption; most records deal with domesticated birds – hens, ducks and geese.[40] Wild birds' eggs supplemented the diet in spring and early summer when food was scarce and crops had yet to ripen. Seabirds' eggs were eaten frequently by the Blasket and other west coast islanders, though their consumption often resulted in bad breath.[41] The eggs of larger fowl were usually roasted whilst those of smaller birds were often sucked out of the shell – a practice which is preserved in the saying 'don't teach your granny how to suck eggs'. Goose eggs were known to be a luxury, hen's eggs were preferred by women and children as sweeter, whereas duck eggs were considered more substantial food for men, and hard-boiled, provided a portable lunch whilst at work in the field or cutting turf.[42]

Since egg production slowed or ceased in winter months, it was customary in

Ireland to preserve eggs when they were plentiful. The most common method was to butter the eggs. As soon as the hen laid the egg, the warm egg was rolled between palms that had been smeared in fresh butter. The butter formed an air-tight seal around the egg and kept them fresh through the winter months. Buttered eggs are still sold in Cork's famous English Market. Another method found in an 1851 county Limerick manuscript book preserves eggs in a mixture of water, saltpetre, salt and lime (Sexton 1998:101). Eggs preserved in this way were mostly used for baking.[43]

Breeds of hens

Today's laying hens are all hybrids that have been developed by geneticists in a few elite centres around the world for the quality and quantity of their eggs. Commercial laying breeds used in Ireland today include Hy-line, Lohman Brown, I.S.A. Brown, Shaver and Babcock.[44] Among the earlier breeds were the Leghorn (white, black, and brown), Wyandotte, Sussex, Dorking, and the Old Irish Bare Neck hen – a hardy breed popular on small hill farms introduced from Transylvania in the nineteenth century.[45] The ordinary fowl at this time were small and nondescript, mostly comprising of poorly fed mongrel hens which virtually ceased egg production in winter.[46] In the late nineteenth and early twentieth centuries there appeared a number of fancy breeds such as the Bantam hens, Peking Ducks and Indian Runner Ducks.[47]

A distinctive dual purpose breed – the Hibernia – was established following nine years of intensive work by Isaac Varian of Stillorgan, Co. Dublin.[48] This new breed, exhibited in 1904 at the Royal Dublin Society, was described as 'an excellent layer of large brown eggs and a large shapely fowl which can readily be fattened'.[49] One of the most common breeds used to be the Rhode Island Red, which was first introduced to Ireland in 1904. The Rhode Island Red breed was improved in the first two decades of the twentieth century. A dual-purpose hen, they are excellent layers of mid-brown eggs and are also known to be strong foragers. With dual breeds the male birds were reared as broilers and the females for laying. Co-ops remained active in the broiler industry, but dual-purpose breeds declined as the egg industry specialised and specific laying breeds like Warren Studler, Babcock, and Hysex became common.[50] Among today's hybrid layers all male birds are destroyed at hatching, the pullets begin laying eggs at 17 weeks and continue egg production for around 14 months.[51] Production has reached nearly 100% with birds producing up to 330 eggs a year on a daily feed of 120g.[52] They are effectively 'egg machines'.

Intensive production

Farmers seemingly never realised the monetary value of eggs, dismissing it as women's work, so much so that in the 1960s when production intensified with the modern battery industry, it was businessmen rather than farmers who took the lead. The pioneers were the Phillips family who set up the 'Ballyfree Farm' brand.[53] Ballyfree were the first to market their eggs to supermarkets and engaged in advertising their brand in the press and on the television. Prior to this, eggs were mostly sold door to door in urban areas. Corby Rock Eggs were one of the early companies that diversified into milling animal feeds. They sold their egg operation in recent years to Greenfield Foods. There has been a growth in recent years in free-range, barn and organic egg production. Clonard Clover Ltd have specialised in free-range eggs for the last ten years. An EU directive has set the year 2012 for the complete phasing out of the battery system. A new 'aviary' system is currently being developed. Profit margins in egg production are very tight, squeezed by the power of the supermarkets. Many producers dream of selling directly to the consumer and a machine for automatic farm-gate sales has been recently invented by an Irishman.[54]

Code	Production	Number of hens	Dozens of eggs	Total Eggs	Average eggs in dozens	Average eggs per bird
0	Organic	15,576	397,335	4,768,020	26	306
1	Free Range	554,421	14,563,530	174,762,360	26	315
2	Barn	53,019	1,329,851	15,958,212	25	301
3	Cage	1,342,118	31,095,906	373,150,872	23	278
Total		1,965,134	47,386,622	568,639,464	24	289

Figure 1. Annual Egg Production for 2003[55]

Eggs today

The leading producers of eggs in Ireland, mostly based in County Monaghan, are Greenfield Foods, Annalitten, Mac Fresh Eggs, and the Nest Box Company.[56] In 2003 the annual per capita consumption of eggs in Ireland was 151. Japan (329 eggs) and Mexico (321 eggs) are the world leaders in egg consumption, with India (40 eggs) bottom of the list.[57] Figure 1 shows the annual egg production for 2003. Free-range hens produce on average the most eggs, but the majority of birds are in cage production. In the past number of years the Irish egg market has seen the introduction of a number of new added-value branded egg products. Corby Rock Eggs, have developed two such products; 'Eggcel' and 'Eggsmart'.[58] 'Eggcel', is high in Omega 3 and selenium, due to the enriched diet of the laying hens. First introduced in 2000, it now accounts for 14 per cent of the company's business. In 2004 'Eggsmart' was launched, which is high in lecithin and carotene helping to keep the brain active and aid eyesight. Greenfield Foods have also introduced an egg rich in Omega 3, called 'O-Megga' free-range eggs.

The egg in Irish cookery

Where would the rich Irish home baking tradition be without eggs? Pancakes, Porter cake, Simnel Cake, Caraway seed cake, Plum cake or indeed the most important of all, Christmas cake would not exist without them.[59] Eggs are most commonly consumed today as part of the Irish breakfast, mostly fried, but also poached or scrambled. Fried egg and bacon are mentioned in 1732 as the favourite food of the Dean of Down.[60] Soft-boiled eggs were either breakfast or supper food, often served with toast or chopped up in a cup for younger children. Boiled eggs were often served with a mixture of mashed potatoes and chopped onion called 'Kala' in West Galway.[61] Hard-boiled eggs, the ultimate convenience food, became portable lunchtime snacks, and were also served in salads or sandwiches, often mixed with mayonnaise or salad dressing.

Social stratification influenced how the eggs were cooked. The Clonbrock manuscript book from Castlegar, Co. Galway provides evidence that curried eggs were eaten as part of the late nineteenth and early twentieth century upper-class diet. Alfred Suzanne, in his 1905 publication *Egg Cookery* describes more than 200 ways of converting eggs into dainty and appetising dishes.[62] Suzanne, born in Normandy in 1829, was apprenticed in the kitchen of the Earl of Clarendon, then Lord Lieutenant of Ireland, before spending four years in the position of head pastry cook at Dublin Castle in the mid-nineteenth century. The Irish twentieth-century culinary repertoire included Coulibiaca, Kedgeree and Haddock Monte Carlo, all of which combine eggs with fish. I heard a Dublin woman recall ordering an omelette in Dublin's Metropole Restaurant in the 1950s because it was the only item of the French menu she understood. The poet Patrick Kavanagh used to eat a boiled egg each morning for breakfast and used the boiling water to shave. He explained his unshaven appearance one day to an enquirer thus: the egg cracked. Ireland in 2006 is a truly multicultural, cosmopolitan society where egg consumption is as likely to be in the form of egg fried rice from a Chinese takeaway or in a goat's cheese and sun-dried tomato quiche from Marks & Spencer, as in the form of the traditional boiled egg.

Conclusions

Eggs have long been part of Irish cuisine and culture. Goose eggs were the most highly prized in ancient Ireland. Duck eggs were considered more suitable for men and sea birds' eggs consumed by the west coast islanders reportedly led to bad breath. Different breeds of hens have been introduced over the centuries culminating in today's hybrids. During the Great Famine (1845–47), eggs were not eaten by the poor but sold to pay the rent. Research has shown that egg production, predominantly women's work, generated up to a quarter of the family income in poor farming households. Eggs were a form of cash, as they were bartered with local shopkeepers for items such as tea, bread and sugar. The practice of shopkeepers hoarding eggs prior to exporting them led to Irish eggs gaining a poor reputation in the British market. The work of the Congested Districts Board, the co-operative movement and the Department of Agriculture led to the improvement of breeds and poultry management. Exports were helped by both World Wars, but the egg industry gradually became more and more specialist. It was businessmen, not farmers, who developed modern intensive battery farming in Ireland. Eggs are now moving from a basic food to a functional food with the new Omega-3 enriched eggs gaining market share. Ireland is one of only four European Union countries with an EU approved salmonella plan, and the Irish egg business is valued at 30 million Euros annually. There is an old expression used in Dublin when someone is doing well financially 'they must be keeping hens'.

Bibliography

Allen, D. (1998), *Irish Traditional Cooking*. London, Kyle Cathie.
Almquist, E. L. (1977), *Mayo and Beyond: Land, Domestic Industry and Rural Transformation in the Irish West*. Ph.D. thesis, Boston University.
Anon (1896), 'Celebrated Chefs No. IX: Alfred Suzanne', *The Chef: A Journal for Cooks, Caterers & Hotel Keepers* 1(9): 1–2.
Bode, W. K. H. (2000), *European Gastronomy: The Story of Man's Food and Eating Customs*. London, Hodder and Stoughton.
Bolger, P. (1977), *The Irish Co-operative Movement: Its History and Development*. Dublin, Institute of Public Administration.
Clarkson, L. A. and E. M. Crawford (2001), *Feast and Famine, Food and Nutrition in Ireland 1500–1900*. Oxford, Oxford University Press.
Jordan, D. E. J. (1994), *Land and Popular Politics in Ireland: County Mayo from the Plantation to the Land War*. Cambridge, Cambridge University Press.
King, C. (2003), 'Sir Horace Curzon Plunkett', in *The Encyclopaedia of Ireland*, ed. B. Lalor. Dublin, Gill and Macmillan: 879.
King, C. (2003a), 'Irish Agricultural Organisation Society (IAOS)', *The Encyclopaedia of Ireland*, ed. B. Lalor. Dublin, Gill and Macmillan: 537.
Langan-Egan, M. (1986), *Women in Mayo 1821–1851: A Historical Perspective*. 2nd edition; Westport, Berry's.
Mac Gearailt, U. (2003), 'Fled Dúin na nGéd', in *The Encyclopaedia of Ireland*, ed. B. Lalor. Dublin, Gill and Macmillan: 398.
Mahon, B. (1991), *Land of Milk and Honey: The Story of Traditional Irish Food and Drink*. Cork, Mercier Press.
Mc Kenna, M. (2003), 'Food of the Blasket Islands', in *The Encyclopaedia of Ireland*, ed. B. Lalor. Dublin, Gill and Macmillan: 406.
Ní Éineacháin, S. (2000), 'The Congested Districts Board in Erris, Co. Mayo – Part 1', *Cathair na Mart: Journal of the Westport Historical Society* 20: 90–117.
O' Dowd, A. (1991), *Spalpeens and Tattie Hokers: History and Folklore of the Irish Migratory Agricultural Worker in Ireland and Britain*. Dublin, Irish Academic Press.
Ó Crohan, T. (1990), *The Islandman*. Oxford, Oxford University Press.
Quinn, D. (1996), 'Mayowomen and Politics of the Land in the latter half of the Nineteenth Century: Part 1', *Cathair na Mart: Journal of the Westport Historical Society* 16: 92–111.
Sexton, R. (1998), *A Little History of Irish Food*. Dublin, Gill and Macmillan Ltd.

Sexton, R. (1998a), 'Foreword: The History of Food in Ireland', *Irish Traditional Cooking*. D. Allen. London, Kyle Cathie: 10–15.
Stokes, W. (1995), *Lives of the Saints from the book of Lismore*. Llanarch, Felinfach.
Toussaint-Samat, M. (2001), *A History of Food*. Maldon,MA, Blackwell Publishers Inc.
Wilson, C. A. (1973), *Food and Drink in Britain*. London, Constable.

Notes

1. Toussaint-Samat 2001, p. 355.
2. Sexton 1998a, p. 15.
3. Wilson 1973, p. 139.
4. Allen 1998, p. 31.
5. Mahon 1991, p. 114; Sexton 1998, p. 52.
6. Sexton 1998a, p. 11.
7. Mahon 1991, p. 116.
8. Sexton 1998a, p. 12.
9. Clarkson and Crawford 2001, pp. 106–7.
10. Jordan 1994, p. 143.
11. Langan-Egan 1986, p. 28.
12. Mahon 1991, p. 120; Mac Gearailt 2003, p. 398.
13. Allen 1998, p. 118.
14. Ibid., p. 31.
15. Ó Crohan 1990, pp. 28–9.
16. O' Dowd 1991, pp. 161–2, 326.
17. Mahon, 1991, p. 125.
18. Ibid., p. 127.
19. Ibid., p. 128.
20. Ibid., p. 128.
21. Personal Communication with Martin Freeman, Department of Agriculture 29 June 2006.
22. Ní Éineacháin 2000, pp. 99,110.
23. King 2003, p. 879.
24. King 2003a, p. 537.
25. Number of affiliated societies in 1904.
26. Bolger 1977, p. 277.
27. Almquist 1977, p. 258.
28. Jordan 1994, p. 143.
29. Almquist 1977, pp. 254–259.
30. Quinn 1996, p. 97.
31. Bolger 1977, pp. 278–9.
32. Ibid., p. 278.
33. King 2006.
34. Bolger 1977, p. 287.
35. Ibid., p. 283.
36. Interview with Jimmy Kilbride 18th October 2003.
37. Interview with Johnny Opperman 24th April 2004.
38. Ennis 2006.
39. Mahon 1991, p. 114; Stokes 1995.
40. Quinn 1996, p. 96.
41. Mc Kenna 2003, p. 406.
42. Mahon 1991, p. 119.

43. Ennis 2006.
44. Ibid.
45. Interview with Jonathan Bell, retired curator of Ulster Folk and Transport Museum 22 June 2006.
46. Bolger 1977, p. 279; Ní Éineacháin 2000, p. 99.
47. Bell 2006.
48. Bolger 1977, p. 283.
49. *The Irish Homestead*, 17 December 1904.
50. Personal Communication with John Mohan 26 June 2006.
51. Interview with Nuala King, Poultry Advisor, Teagasc, Athenry Co. Galway 26 June 2006.
52. Interview with Arthur Ennis, poultry expert 28 June 2006.
53. Ibid.
54. Ibid.
55. Department of Agriculture figures.
56. Freeman 2006.
57. *Poultry International 2005* Volume 1.
58. www.farmersjournal.ie/2004/0515/agribusiness/companycoop.
59. Wilson 1973, p. 147.
60. Allen 1998, p. 32.
61. A dish often prepared by my father Liam Mac Con Iomaire for the family when my mother was visiting her parents (MMCI).
62. Anon 1896; Bode 2000, p. 123.

Scrambled Class: Eggs and Refinement in Nineteenth-century America

Mark McWilliams

In the middle of the nineteenth century, American homemakers struggled to balance a commitment to simple, wholesome food with increasing desires for culinary sophistication. One answer to this dilemma was the egg. The only food that is both 'elegant and frugal', according to cookbook author Marion Harland, the versatile egg worked equally well in quick dishes and more complex fare.[1] Even Catharine Beecher, who scoffed at the overly 'stylish' dinner parties of New York and Boston, frequently recommended eggs as a garnish to elevate dishes for 'proper' entertaining. Eliza Leslie, one of the first American popularizers of French cuisine, went even farther, almost daring ambitious home cooks to attempt soufflés. For both Beecher and Leslie, the egg epitomizes 'niceness', that treasured quality of delicate richness central to refinement. In this paper, I trace the egg's treatment by American cooks, real and fictional, as a surprisingly complex marker of social class.

American attitudes toward food were shaped during the Revolution, when simple, wholesome food became coded as a sign of republican virtue and European cuisines were condemned as overly luxurious and hence morally suspect. As foodways became one site for expressing late eighteenth-century anxieties over national identity, an ideal of republican simplicity emerged to counter what was increasingly seen as the social decadence and moral decay of Europe. Drawing on an ideal agrarianism that combined Jefferson's sense of natural aristocracy with a kind of frontier egalitarianism, republican simplicity reinterpreted the necessities of often harsh colonial life as a model for a new society that rejected the luxuries and hypocrisies of the Old World. After the Revolution, even after the nation began to move toward prosperity, the myth of republican simplicity gained powerful force. In foodways, this myth is associated with the simple, wholesome food of the colonies – with, for example, baked beans, cornbread in all its forms, roast game and pork, and the New England boiled dinner. As republican simplicity helped form a national culture, colonial foods like corn, originally substituted for more expensive English staples, became signs of patriotic virtue.[2]

Even as Americans continued to fear being seen as provincial, however, their culture was becoming more refined, as Richard Bushman has claimed, and increasing numbers of Americans sought the pleasures of cosmopolitan sophistication.[3] These desires can be tracked in cookbooks, as the implicit appeal to the plain, wholesome food valorized in the myth of republican simplicity of the early books shifted, during the middle decades of the nineteenth century, to more complex preparations designed, at least in part, to display a woman's social status. This slippage between individual morality and class status frequently occurs in these texts' insistence on the importance of the domestic space and emphasis of the housewife's role in providing the best for her family, especially as the meaning of 'the best' moved from simplicity to refinement. Whether or not writers believed their own rhetoric – Lawrence Buell has pointed out that many authors 'found it to their economic advantage to present themselves as harbingers of moral uplift' in this period – the moral dimension of domestic rhetoric effectively legitimated the rush toward emulating the upper class that would culminate in Gilded Age conspicuous consumption.[4]

As desires for cosmopolitan sophistication increasingly challenged commitments to republican simplicity, shifting views of French cuisine became one of the best indicators of changing American attitudes. Even early in American history, a taste for French cookery was often seen as un-American. From Patrick Henry's famous 1793 charge that Jefferson's love of *haute cuisine* led him to 'abjure his native victuals' to William Henry Harrison's 1840 portrayal of Martin Van Buren's French meals in the White House as effete and out of touch, charges of cosmopolitan sophistication could be politically powerful.[5] And yet, as the nineteenth century progressed, even some of the staunchest defenders of republican simplicity recognized the quality of French cuisine. For example, in 1869 Catharine Beecher and her sister, Harriet Beecher Stowe, offered the following assessment in their influential *The American Woman's Home*: 'In France, one never asks in vain for delicious *café-au-lait*, good bread and butter, a nice omelet, or some savory little portion of meat with a French name. But to a tourist taking like chance in American country-fare, what is the prospect? What is the coffee? what the tea? and the meat? and above all, the butter?'[6]

The Beecher sisters' choice of 'a nice omelet' to characterize the advantages of French cookery is telling. American cookbook writers were well aware of the versatility of the egg in French cuisine. In 1852, for example, Sarah Josepha Hale, the culturally powerful editor of *Godey's Lady's Book*, wrote hopefully in *The Ladies' New Book of Cookery*, 'They reckon 685 ways of dressing eggs in the French kitchen; we trust our more limited number will be sufficient for Americans'.[7] By the end of the century, Delmonico's chef Charles Ranhofer's encyclopedic volume *The Epicurean*, the closest thing to an authority on *haute cuisine* in America, included one hundred egg dishes.[8]

While no American cookbook approached the variety of egg preparations in French cuisine, many shared an appreciation for the versatility and character of the egg. Consider this story with which Marion Harland introduces her *Breakfast, Luncheon and Tea*:

'Give me half-a-dozen eggs, a few spoonfuls of gravy and as much cream, with a spoonful of butter and a handful of bread crumbs, and I can get up a good breakfast or luncheon,' said a housekeeper to me once, in a modest boastfulness that became her well, in my eyes.

For I had sat often at her elegant, but frugal board, and I knew she spoke the truth.

'Elegant and frugal!' I shall have more hope of American housewives when they learn to have faith in this combination of adjectives. Nothing has moved me more strongly to the preparation of this work than the desire to convert them to the belief that the two are not incompatible or inharmonious. Under no head can practice in the endeavor to conform these, the one to the other, be more easily and successfully pursued than under that which begins this section.

Eggs at sixty cents per dozen (and they are seldom higher than this price) are the cheapest food for the breakfast or lunch-table of a private family. They are nutritious, popular, and never (if we except the cases of omelettes, thickened with uncooked flour, and fried eggs, drenched with fat) an unelegant or homely dish.[9]

This rare combination of qualities – elegance and frugality – helped eggs bridge the American home cook's conflicting desires for both republican simplicity and cosmopolitan sophistication.

The egg epitomized 'niceness'. In cookbooks of this period, 'nice' is high praise indeed. As the *OED* notes, in this context 'nice' means 'refined, cultured; associated with polite society', 'delicate', and even 'virtuous'. Ascribing this treasured quality to the egg seems fitting given its appearance, as Hale's instructions for poached eggs emphasize: 'The beauty of a poached egg is for the yolk to be seen blushing through the white, which should only be just sufficiently hardened, to form a transparent veil for the egg'.[10] Eliza Leslie agrees that the white should only 'thinly cover' the yolk.[11] These cooks insist on achieving such results even though extra effort is required; both Hale and Leslie strain boiling water before poaching eggs in it. As Leslie explains, 'by observing this process the eggs will be nicer and more easily done than when its impurities remain in the water' – nicer because, Marion Harland adds, 'The least impurity will mar the whiteness of the eggs'.[12] Such attention to detail matters with the egg. Leslie guides cooks to gently 'slip' the eggs into the water.[13] And note how Hale's presentation emphasizes the poached egg's delicate beauty: 'take it up with a slice, and neatly round off the ragged edges of the white; send them up on bread toasted on one side only, with or without butter'.[14] Leslie also instructs her readers to 'trim off all the ragged edges from the white' and to serve them on 'thin slices of buttered toast with the crust cut off'.[15]

Other recipes also stress the egg's niceness. In Hale's instructions for cupped eggs, for example, the gravy in which the eggs poach must be 'very nice' and the seasoning (mace, nutmeg, or salt) must be ground 'very fine'.[16] Even omelettes, though sometimes 'judiciously varied by mixing minced ham or tongue with them', are 'more delicate' when made 'of eggs alone'.[17] Perhaps the best example of taking extra steps to season the eggs without marring their delicate beauty can be found in Harland's recipe for toasted eggs:

> Cover the bottom of an earthenware or stone-china dish with rounds of delicately toasted bread. Or, what is even better, with rounds of stale bread dipped in beaten egg and fried quickly in butter or nice dripping, to a golden-brown. Break an egg carefully upon each, and set the dish immediately in front of, and on a level with a glowing fire. Toast over this as many slices of *fat* corned pork or ham as there are eggs in the dish, holding the meat so that it will fry very quickly, and all the dripping fall upon the eggs. When these are well 'set,' and a crust begins to form upon the top of each, they are done. Turn the dish several times while toasting the meat, that the eggs may be equally cooked.
>
> Do not send the fried pork to table, but pepper the eggs lightly and remove with the toast, to the dish in which they are to go to the table, with a cake-turner or flat ladle, taking care not to break them.[18]

While the pork fat is crucial to the flavor here, the scraggly appearance of the fried meat would mar the presentation. In this case, Harland's technique is certainly elegant, but hardly frugal. More often, she includes the pork, but works to make sure it matches the egg, as when she trims the 'rough edges' off of fried eggs and serves them with carefully selected 'neat slices of fried ham … cut … evenly in oblong pieces'.[19] Leslie also prepares ham and eggs separately before serving them together: 'This is a much nicer way than the common practice of frying the ham or bacon with the eggs'.[20]

The niceness that makes eggs so suitable for such preparations also makes them perfect as a garnish to elevate other, less nice dishes. For Catharine Beecher, who rejected the urge for sophistication she recognized in trends toward increasingly 'stylish' dinner parties in Boston and New York, the egg offered a way to dress a dish in a simple yet elegant way – a compromise, in other words, between the republican simplicity she sought to integrate into domestic ideology and the cosmopolitan sophistication desired by many of her readers. (Beecher's allegiances are clear: she aims to 'set forth a large variety of what is both healthful and good', though she also includes 'a good supply of the rich and elegant dishes demanded at entertainments' – 'demanded' here suggests that she has considerably less enthusiasm for such fare.)[21] As she puts it in her first hugely popular cookbook, the 1846 *Miss Beecher's Domestic Receipt Book*, 'There are modes of *garnishing dishes,* and preparing them for table, which give an air of taste and refinement, that pleases the eye'.[22] Such garnishes could be quite simple: 'On *Broiled Ham,* or *Veal,* eggs boiled, or fried and laid, one on each piece, look well'.[23] Others were slightly more ornate: '*Greens* and *Asparagus* should be well drained, and laid on buttered toast, and then slices of boiled eggs be laid on the top, and around'.[24]

Other cookbook writers shared Miss Beecher's use of the egg as the ideal garnish. For Eliza Leslie, one of the first to try to popularize French cookery in America as well as the author of standard works like the successful 1840 volume *Directions for Cookery, In Its Various Branches*, eggs offered a number of possibilities. Consider these variations for garnishing fish: boiled salt cod is 'garnished … with hard-boiled eggs, either cut in half, or in circular slices, yolks and whites together'; broiled rockfish is decorated with hard-boiled eggs, cut in half, laid 'closely on the back of the fish in a straight line from the head to the tail'; and fried sea bass comes to table in a dish ringed 'with hard-boiled eggs cut in round slices'.[25]

Like garnishes, egg dishes ranged from simple to elegant, from quick fried eggs to complex presentations, although these dishes seem to become increasingly elaborate as the century progresses. Many cookbooks of the period include at least one omelette recipe. Leslie, for example, recommends one made with four whole eggs enriched with two more egg yolks. As with other egg dishes, the recipe strives for niceness: straining the beaten eggs, frying it 'gently', and adding only carefully minced ingredients – if any – to 'flavour' the dish.[26] Some cookbook authors go so far as to recommend soufflés – almost always sweet rather than savory – though their recipes hint at the precariousness of the preparation. Note, for example, the concern in Hale's instructions for serving the soufflé: 'it must be served the *instant* it is taken out; carried, indeed, as quickly as possible to table from the oven. It will have risen to a great height, but will sink and become heavy in a very short space of time: if sugar be sifted over it, let it be done with the utmost expedition'.[27] Leslie, recognizing that 'an omelette soufflé is a very nice and delicate thing when properly managed; but if flat and heavy it should not be brought to table', offers an alternative to the tricky preparation: 'If you live in a large town, the safest way of avoiding a failure in an omelette soufflé is to hire a French cook to come to your kitchen with his own utensils and ingredients, and make and bake it himself, while the first part of the dinner is progressing in the dining room'.[28] Soufflés are not the most ornate egg dish in this period, however, though they may be the most difficult to prepare. Several cookbooks include recipes for some variation on what Hale calls 'A Hen's Nest':

> 6 or 8 eggs boiled hard.
> 1 cup minced chicken, or other fowl, ham, tongue, or, if more convenient, any cold firm fish.
> 1 cup of drawn butter into which have been stirred two or three table-spoonfuls of good gravy and a tea-spoonful of chopped parsley.
> When the eggs are quite cold and firm, cut the whites from the yolks in long thin strips, or shavings, and set them aside to warm in a very gentle oven, buttering them, now and then, while you prepare the rest.

Pound the minced meat or fish very fine in a Wedge-wood mortar, mixing in, as you go on, the yolks of the eggs, the parsley, and pepper and salt to taste. When all are reduced to a smooth paste, mould with your hands into small, egg-shaped balls. Heap in the centre of a dish, arrange the shred eggs around them, in imitation of a nest, and pour over all the hot sauce.

A simple and delightful relish.[29]

In *Common Sense in the Household*, Harland calls this preparation 'Chinese Bird's-Nest of Eggs', and Ranhofer includes a similar recipe in *The Epicurean*.

The varying degrees of elegance in these dishes come to mark class status. For example, Leslie's suggestion that the urban housewife hire a French chef for the occasional soufflé is clearly aimed at an upper-class audience. (Lydia Maria Child even refers wealthy readers to Leslie's works in her influential *The Frugal Housewife*, which, unlike Leslie's, is written explicitly 'for the poor'.)[30] And the ornate hen's nest dishes would certainly be ostentatious in most working-class and even many middle-class homes. What is interesting here is the way the egg's extraordinary range can be adapted across the economic spectrum, with dishes increasingly emphasizing the egg's 'niceness' as one climbs the socio-economic ladder. Beecher's garnishes offer an example of the egg's ability to transform everyday dishes into something more elegant, something suitable for entertaining meant, in part, to showcase a family's status.

One way to see the way eggs could function as a class marker is to examine its use in fiction of the time. Like other authors of the mid-nineteenth century, Susan Warner uses the development of culinary skill to measure the growth of her heroine in *The Wide, Wide World*. Warner's book was a wild success – until the publication of *Uncle Tom's Cabin* the best selling American novel. Warner follows young Ellen Montgomery through a succession of domestic situations, from comfortable city life with her sickly but adoring mother to the harsh farm routine with her Aunt Fortune, from the spiritual guidance of the kind Humphreys to the worldly ways of Ellen's rediscovered relatives in Scotland. Throughout her tale, and particularly during the crucial and lengthy stay at Aunt Fortune's, food and cookery are central to young Ellen's development. But it is her preparation of a 'nice' egg dish that best signals her future as an admirable middle-class housewife.

Ellen has (at least) three female teachers in her struggle to learn cookery. Her mother instills in her a love for cooking through demonstrating the way food preparation can express emotion; Aunt Fortune provides an example of effective kitchen management – and I might note briefly here that Fortune, whose skill in the 'mysteries of cooking' is as legendary as her cold, furious nature, marks rare moments when her heart softens toward Ellen by serving food; and Alice, her friend and mentor, who shows her that cooking can be a joy as well as drudgery and reinforces the lessons of Ellen's mother.[31] The midpoint in Ellen's development comes when she has to take over the kitchen when Aunt Fortune falls sick; in her lack of knowledge and skill (reflected in burnt eggs and weak tea) she shows herself still a child, but in her willingness to work and eagerness to master each aspect of kitchen management the reader sees the promise of the woman she will become.

Ellen must pass two tests during her aunt's illness: one of her skills and one of her temperament. These tests are often simultaneous: 'Ellen warmed some gruel and carried it with a plate of biscuit up stairs to her aunt. But Miss Fortune said she was tired of gruel and couldn't eat it; she must have some milk porridge; and she gave Ellen very particular directions how to make it. Ellen sighed only once as she went down with her despised dish of gruel, and set about doing her best to fulfill her aunt's wishes'.[32] Here we see Ellen tested in both ways, and even readers concerned about the lack of cooking skill in a girl who must be told how to make milk porridge would surely be sympathetic to one with such quiet determination.

Yet Ellen's perseverance is stretched by her lack of skill. Aunt Fortune is not only notoriously difficult to please, but also teaches only by example. Until her sickness, Fortune neither demands nor allows Ellen to work in the kitchen proper; jealous of her own reputation as a cook, she confines Ellen's labors to the seemingly endless work of dairying and cleaning. During Fortune's illness, however, Ellen seeks to follow her aunt's example as a cook and finds two unexpected helpers in Nancy Vawse, a trouble-making but practical local girl, and Mr Van Brunt, Fortune's kindly hired man. Nancy, helping Ellen keep house until Fortune's health returns, steps in when the prepared food donated by neighbors runs out and Ellen is at a loss as to what to serve for dinner:

> 'I tell you what, Ellen, – we'll just boil pot for to-day; somebody else will send us something by to-morrow most likely.'
>
> 'I don't know what you mean by "boil pot,"' said Ellen.
>
> 'Oh, you don't know everything yet, by half. *I* know – I'll fix it. You just give me the things, Miss Housekeeper, that's all you've got to do; I want a piece of pork and a piece of beef, and all the vegetables you've got.'
>
> 'All?' said Ellen.
>
> 'Every soul on 'em. Don't be scared, Ellen! you shall see what I can do in the way of cookery; if you don't like it you needn't eat it.'[33]

What Nancy 'can do in the way of cookery' is prepare a traditional New England boiled dinner – a meal representative of republican simplicity – which follows in short order, ready not long after Ellen finishes churning the butter. Yet Nancy does more than take over dinner. She also places herself and Ellen in the socially prescribed roles of their respective classes: Nancy acts as cook while explicitly addressing Ellen as Miss Housekeeper, the manager of the domestic scene – a predicted role the novel's development confirms.[34]

Eggs and Refinement in Nineteenth-century America

Watching Nancy's easy skill in preparing this rustic meal, Ellen is inspired to develop her own abilities in a way that confirms Nancy's prediction that she is suited to be Miss Housekeeper. A couple of nights later, she is worrying about dinner while ironing when a neighbor arrives to steam and fold for her, and the break 'gave Ellen spirits to carry out a plan she had long had, to delight the whole family with some eggs scrambled in Margery's fashion'. But while she tries to follow the examples she has seen, her inexperience shows when 'instead of acting right the eggs maliciously stuck fast to the spider and burned'. She has failed to grease the pan with butter, as Mr Van Brunt gently points out as he encourages here to try again. Before she can, however, she must overcome another obstacle; Aunt Fortune smells the burning eggs and forbids her to use any more. Again Mr Van Brunt comes to Ellen's aid: 'That ain't fair play, … you and I are the head of the house now, as I take it. You just use as many on 'em as you've a mind; and all you spile I'll fetch you again … Now, Ellen, here's the spider; try again; let's have plenty of butter in this time, and plenty of eggs too'. Ellen's repeated effort meets with success: 'the eggs were scrambled to a nicety, and the supper met with great favour from all parties'.[35] In a way, this scene sums up Ellen's development as a cook – and as a young woman – during this period. She has the best intentions and an admirable model in the dish she has eaten at Alice's, but her lack of skill ruins her attempt. Aunt Fortune, who has served as a daunting example in the kitchen, works both to limit what she sees as the wastefulness of Ellen's attempt and to blunt the fulfillment of her plans. Mr Van Brunt both helps Ellen directly, by his carefully phrased question about the butter and by directing Nancy to assist, and indirectly, by overruling Fortune's commands and quietly restoring Ellen's confidence through his faith in her eventual success. And success there is, with Ellen drawing on the help provided her to overcome obstacles and put a fine meal on the table.

Ellen's choice of eggs 'scrambled to a nicety' separates her from Aunt Fortune, who serves a well-prepared but humble farmhouse fare of what Charles Frazier has called 'brown' food, and from Nancy's hearty boiled dinner.[36] The meal reminds readers that Ellen is suited for more than the rustic chores of the farm. Like Nancy, characters in the book recognize this as well, as when the wealthy Mr Marshman, for example, promises to 'take her away' from the constant work of Fortune's farm or, more importantly, when Alice's brother John, a promising minister, sees in Ellen the potential of an ideal wife.

Just as Warner's fictional heroine displays her status through a 'nice' dish of scrambled eggs, real American women seem to have used the egg's astonishing versatility to help them balance the conflicting demands of republican simplicity and cosmopolitan sophistication. Like Brillat-Savarin's roast turkey – a dish he finds served for special occasions across class boundaries, with different preparations marking class status – the egg's rare combination of simplicity and elegance led to a range of dishes from hard-boiled to hen's nest. Unlike the turkey, though, the egg could also be used to transform other dishes, to make everyday dishes nice enough for company. With such easy social mobility, the egg met American desires for both the wholesome fare of a wholesome people and the culinary riches of a growing nation.

Notes

1. Marion Harland (Mary Virginia Terhune), *Breakfast, Luncheon and Tea* (New York: Scribner, Armstrong & Co., 1875), p. 18. Subsequent references are cited as *BLT*.
2. For example, while many colonists developed a real taste for molasses, the colonial boycott of imported sugar following the Sugar Act of 1764 transformed the use of molasses into a political act; John Adams called molasses "an essential ingredient in American independence" (quoted in Anne Willan, *Great Cooks and Their Recipes from Taillevant to Escoffier* (London: Pavilion, 1992), p. 138).
3. Though I think he compresses the chronology of these changes, see Bushman's *The Refinement of America: Persons, Houses, Cities* (New York: Vintage, 1992).
4. Lawrence Buell, *New England Literary Culture: From Revolution through Renaissance* (Cambridge: Cambridge UP, 1986), p. 63.
5. Waverly Root and Richard de Rochemont, *Eating in America: A History* (Hopewell, NJ: Ecco, 1995), pp. 112–114.
6. Catharine Beecher and Harriet Beecher Stowe, *The American Woman's Home: Or, Principles Of Domestic Science; Being A Guide To The Formation And Maintenance Of Economical, Healthful, Beautiful, And Christian Homes* (New York, J.B. Ford And Company, 1869), pp. 168–169.
7. Sarah Josepha Buell Hale, *The Ladies' New Book of Cookery* (New York, H. Long & Brother, 1852), p. 258.
8. Charles Ranhofer, *The Epicurean: A Complete Treatise of Analytical and Practical Studies on the Culinary Art* (New York: Charles Ranhofer, 1894).
9. Harland *BLT*, p. 18.
10. Hale, p. 256.
11. Eliza Leslie, *Directions For Cookery, In Its Various Branches* (Philadelphia: E.L. Carey & Hart, 1840), p. 189.
12. Leslie, p. 208; Harland, *Common Sense in the Household: A Manual of Practical Housewifery* (New York: Scribner, Armstrong & Co., 1873), p. 254. Subsequent references are cited as *CS*.
13. Leslie, p. 208.
14. Hale, p. 256.
15. Leslie, p. 208.
16. Hale, pp. 256–257.
17. Hale, p. 258.
18. Harland *BLT*, p. 18.
19. Harland *CS*, p. 254.
20. Leslie, p. 124.
21. Catharine Beecher, *Miss Beecher's Domestic Receipt Book: Designed As A Supplement To Her Treatise On Domestic Economy* (New York: Harper, 1850), p. xi.
22. Beecher, p. 246.
23. Beecher, p. 246.
24. Beecher, p. 246.
25. Leslie, p. 49, p. 52, p. 54.
26. Leslie, p. 209.
27. Hale, p. 259.

28. Leslie, p. 210, p. 209.
29. Harland *BLT*, pp. 27–28.
30. Lydia Maria Child, *The Frugal Housewife Dedicated to Those who are not Ashamed of Economy* (Boston: Carter, Hendee and Babcock, 1830), p. 7.
31. Susan Warner, *The Wide, Wide World*, ed. Jane Tompkins (New York: The Feminist Press, 1987), p. 137, p. 106, p. 112.
32. Warner, p. 367.
33. Warner, p. 365.
34. Nancy recognizes the incongruity of her pairing with Ellen earlier in the book when she asks, 'I say, Ellen, any one would think I was Miss Fortune's niece and you was somebody else, wouldn't they?' (pp. 249–250).
35. Warner, pp. 368–369.
36. Charles Frazier, *Cold Mountain* (New York: Vintage, 1997), p. 150.

'Balut', the Fertilised Duck Eggs of the Philippines

Margaret Magat

Once there were two rival towns in the countryside outside of Manila. One day, the larger town burned the smaller town to the ground. After the battle, the warriors were hungry and the only food left in the small town were these incubating duck eggs, which had been roasted by the burning which levelled the smaller town. So the warriors ate the balut eggs and found them tasty.[1]

Though this legend may not or may not be true, there is no question about the Filipinos' liking for embryonic duck eggs, known as *balut*. The enormous appeal of balut has been described by some as being 'popular in Manila as hotdogs in the United States.'[2] Despite the fact that balut may have been at one point prevalent only in the Luzon region, and not considered a delicacy in the Visayas, it has now reached the status of 'national street food of the Philippines.'[3] Balut is so deeply embedded in Philippine culture that it has inspired everything from a hit record song about the distinctive howling calls of balut vendors in the late night and early morning, to recently influencing Filipino *haute cuisine*. Indeed, the love affair of Filipinos with fertilised duck eggs has been carried by those emmigrating to the United States.

Eaten as a snack, balut is also a familiar food for Chinese, Laotians, Cambodians and Thais. In Vietnam, it is called *hot vit lon*. Based on the closest Thai transliteration, balut is called *khaj luuk* or *khay luuk* (same in Laotian). For Cambodians, the closest transliteration in the Khmer language that refers to embryonic eggs is *pomtiakhong* or *pomtiakong*. Another spelling based on the sound of the word is *poomgpiakoong*. Socio-cultural factors dominate its consumption, not just nutritional reasons. Using historical and literary sources, as well as fieldwork data culled from 25 balut eaters, a nutritionist, two balut distributors and a duck farmer as well, I explore what it is about balut that makes eating it desirable. Why ingest something that may already have bones, feathers and a beak? For Filipino and other Asian-Americans, there are alternative sources of protein.[4] In the Philippines where balut is generally sold late at night or early morning, Filipino males consume it for its alleged aphrodisiac properties while women eat it for reasons such as energy and nutrition, but never as a sexual stimulant. As one male informant put it bluntly, balut as an aphrodisiac is 'para lang sa lalaki ito' (it is just for men).

The number of balut businesses in the U.S. is difficult to estimate. But where there are Filipinos, one can usually find balut. In California and Hawaii, there are businesses catering specifically to balut eaters. It is also easy to make balut in homes where it is sold to friends and co-workers. Filipinos sometimes introduce the food and its accompanying beliefs to other cultural groups. In Hawaii, it has become popular with Micronesian immigrants, while in California, Vietnamese eaters also believe in its aphrodisiac qualities.

California, with its large percentage of Filipino-Americans, is a leader in balut production. During the course of my fieldwork for my master's thesis, from which this article is derived, I visited Metzer Farms, which supplies an estimated 50 percent of the balut sold in the Bay Area.

What is balut?

Fertilised duck eggs sold as balut in the U.S. ranges from 16 to 20 days in age. The older the egg, the larger the chick and the more pronounced its feathers, bones, and beak. An embryo at 17 days has beak and feathers that are more developed at 20 days. Normally, after being fertilised, a chick hatches after 26 to 28 days of incubation.

The taste of the egg also depends on the breed of the laying duck. Different breeds of duck supposedly produce balut varying in taste, with Muscovy ducks being hailed by some as 'cream of the crop.'[5] The kind of balut sold in the U.S. is made from duck eggs. Chicken eggs may be made into balut as well, but duck eggs are preferred by the majority of Filipino-Americans since they are larger and thought to be better in taste.

But whether the fertilised egg is chicken or duck, there are two types of balut. One is called *mamatong* by Filipinos. *Mamatong* balut has the embryo floating on top of the white and yolk and the consumer can easily detect it. Roughly translated to mean 'the float,' *mamatong* occurs between 14 to 16 days. The second is *balut sa puti* where the embryo is wrapped by a thin, whitish membrane and one cannot tell whether there is an embryo or not. In *balut sa puti*, the embryo is hidden by the albumen's white film. *Balut sa puti* is 17 to 18 days old and it is the preferred favorite of Filipinos in the U.S. and in the Philippines. A folk belief in the Philippines lets people know if an egg develops into *mamatong* or *balut sa puti*. One takes a balut egg and drops it in water. If it floats, it is not *balut sa puti*, but when it sinks, it is.

Eating balut

In the U.S., balut is usually sold uncooked in Asian markets and sometimes cooked in Filipino restaurants. Once bought, raw balut is prepared by cooking in boiling water for 20 to 30 minutes. It is eaten warm and never cold, and can be eaten by itself or accompanied by condiments. Filipinos eat it with salt, vinegar or soy sauce, while Vietnamese Americans accompany the egg with a green, mint-like herb called *rau ram* as well as salt and pepper. Alcoholic beverages tend to be the drink of choice when eating balut, especially during Filipino drinking sessions.

In general, balut and other *pulutan* (snack) items do not make a complete meal, since rice is not served. But it now appears that balut can be eaten either as a snack or as part of the meal. Although a majority of my informants stated they ate balut as a snack, several admitted they ate it with rice, and this may grow more common as balut exceeds its street food reputation.

A good duck balut has four parts. There is the yolk, the white part called *bato* (rock) that is the tough-to-eat albumen, the embryo, and some liquid which aficionados sip with gusto before opening the egg. If the balut has a crack or if it is a chicken balut, it tends to not have the soup or liquid that is naturally present in duck eggs even after they are cooked.

There are numerous ways to eat the egg, but the usual method involves tapping the broad base of the egg on the table or with a spoon. Then the consumer removes the small cracked shell and breaks the delicate membrane to sip the liquid of the balut. As one sips the soup, one continues breaking the shell to expose the yolk, embryo and albumen. At this point, one can separate the pieces on a plate and salt them before eating. Others prefer to eat the egg straight from the shell, in two to three bites in order to not see the duck or chicken embryo. For those who like the taste of balut but cannot chew the embryo, they swallow it whole.

In his 15 years of distributing balut to stores as well as Filipino-Americans and other Asian-Americans in the Bay area, Butch Coyoca estimates that he has sold hundreds of thousands of eggs. Twice a week, he handles 5,000 to 10,000 fertilised eggs. Not surprisingly, he has come up with his own observations on why people eat balut. According to Coyoca, the majority of people who buy balut from him believe that there is some medicinal value in eating it or that it creates sex drive in males. When delivering balut directly to consumers during parties, he observes most balut eaters are males. This is similar to the Philippines. Of his customers, roughly 75 percent of Filipino-American males and 25 percent Filipino-American women eat balut. Most of the Filipino-American males who eat it are over 15 years old to seniors aged 55 and above.

Preferences for the age of the balut differ from group to group, although individual choices play a role as well. Vietnamese-Americans generally prefer their eggs to be at least 17 days and they along with Cambodians find 19-to-20-day-old balut to be more desirable unlike Filipinos. In general, women prefer younger eggs with smaller embryos like 14 or 16 days old or *penoy* eggs. Penoy eggs range from 8 to 10 days of the incubation period, and they generally have no embryo.

Traditionally, men are what Coyoca terms the 'hard-core balut eater.' This is the case for men no matter what race. Male customers usually want a bigger embryo aged 17 to 20 days. They tend not to be bothered with the appearance of the developed embryo.

A cheap, 'super' food

Balut is categorised in Filipino culture as a 'hot' food, and therefore, those with a fever are told not to eat it. A few informants mentioned limiting their balut consumption for fear of cholesterol. But for many, balut's reputed benefits more than outweigh its proscriptions.

'Balut', the Fertilised Duck Eggs of the Philippines

The following is a nutritional breakdown of a fertilised duck egg.[6] Embryonated duck egg – 188 calories, 13.7 grams of protein, 14.2 grams of fat, 116 milligrams of calcium, 176 milligrams of phosphorous, 2.1 milligrams of iron, 875 micrograms of retinol, 435 micrograms of B-carotene equivalent, 0.12 milligrams of thiamine, 0.25 milligrams of riboflavin, 0.8 milligrams of niacin, 3 milligrams of ascorbic acid.

For Coyoca and countless other Filipinos, balut is the cheapest nutritional substitute available. Instead of buying vitamins, Coyoca says that one can buy balut. 'It's like a powerbar, a superfood,' he said. 'If you stay up late at night and it's already morning, like 2 a.m., a lot of people would eat one or two before they go to bed because they would believe that (balut) would compensate for whatever losses they incurred for not sleeping enough.' It is also easy to transport balut, which makes it a convenient food to eat during long journeys when one cannot have a regular meal with rice, fish and vegetables. Since balut is covered in its own shell, one can consume it whenever needed.

In addition to its nutritional value and ease in transport, the stark poverty in the Philippines is another factor in the consumption of balut. 'Because most Filipinos have low incomes, they have learned to use all edible parts of a plant or animal product … the internal organs of chicken, hogs, cattle, which may look unappetising, can be made into savoury dishes.'[7] A list of the items available as barbecued street foods shows this to be the case, with many of the barbecued parts giving rise to their own folk names. Beside grilled bananas, one can find barbecued chicken feet, nicknamed 'Adidas,' chicken wings called 'PAL' (Philippine Airlines), chicken intestines called 'IUD' for its appearance, pig's ears that are known as 'walkman' and the combs on roosters, which are referred to as 'helmet.'[8]

The consumption of balut may in recent times be more tied to the economic situation in the Philippines since it is a relatively inexpensive source of protein and calcium. However, this alone cannot be the reason as to why Filipino-Americans continue to eat balut. Other factors must be present. The fact is Filipino-Americans choose willingly to eat a food that others consider exotic in a country full of steak and chicken. Besides the cultural taste for fertilised eggs, the continued consumption of balut is likely due to its reputation as an aphrodisiac, a psychological belief that I explore elsewhere.

History of Balut

It is impossible to date accurately when the custom of eating balut first began since pre-Spanish records written in syllabic writing by early Filipinos have not survived the burning zeal of the Spanish missionaries. This has forced scholars to consult ancient records of neighboring countries to find references regarding the Philippines. What is known is that long before the Spaniards set foot on the Philippine islands in 1521, Filipinos were already conducting maritime trade with Persia, Arabia, and India especially China beginning in 300 AD.[9]

'Balut', the Fertilised Duck Eggs of the Philippines

Theorising that much of the modern world's eating habits are a result of Columbus' journey to the New World in 1492 and the subsequent growth of the Spanish empire which involved the exchange of goods as corn, tomatoes, chillies and livestock, Raymond Sokolov points to the Philippines as being one of the main 'centers for gastronomic change.'[10] Spain controlled the Philippines through Mexico, enabling the Spaniards to also partake in commerce with China. The effects of Spanish colonisation as well as the history of exchanges with neighbouring countries can be seen in Philippine cuisine with its Spanish, Chinese and Malay-influenced dishes that have been indigenised by the use of local ingredients and Filipino seasoning tastes. Popular dishes like *adobo* betray their Spanish-Mexican origin with their names. *Adobo* refers to chicken or pork simmered with vinegar, soy sauce and bay leaves. But the Philippines owes its noodle dishes, as well as its *lumpia* (egg roll) and *siopao* (*char su bao*, a white bun filled with meat), to the Chinese.[11]

The influence of the Chinese may perhaps explain the presence of balut in the country. Many books on Chinese food mention salted duck eggs, tea eggs and century-old duck eggs,[12] but only a sprinkling of works mention fertilised eggs. In *Food in China: A Cultural and Historical Inquiry*, geographer Frederick Simoons provides a clue regarding fertilised duck eggs. 'Perhaps also of nutritional relevance is the Chinese liking for fertilised eggs in which the embryo is well-developed, a preference they share with certain peoples in Southeast Asia and the Pacific region. Embryonated duck eggs ... are substantially higher in calcium than ordinary ones.'[13] In addition to confirming that fertilised eggs are consumed in some level by the Chinese, Simoons also verifies the widely held belief in the Philippines that balut is an important source of calcium, which explains why pregnant women and sick people are urged to eat it as well.

The earliest citation I was able to find regarding balut is an 1830 report on Siam and Cochin China. It seems that 'hatched eggs' were being eaten during great parties. The eggs 'formed a delicacy beyond the reach of the poor, and only adapted for persons of distinction;' after 10 to 12 days when an egg is being hatched, they are 'exactly in the state most agreeable to the palate of a Cochin Chinese epicure.'[14] M. Duval also mentioned incubated duck eggs in 1885[15] and so did geographer Friedrich Ratzel in *The History of Mankind*. 'The Tagals are said to have learnt from the Chinese to eat eggs that have been sat upon, with the chick in them, as tit-bits.'[16] In 1905, Jenks took note of the Igorots' liking for developing eggs and how they preferred to wait 'until there is something in the egg to eat.'[17] A few other works mention balut consumption.[18] Simoons speculates balut-eating may have arisen long ago 'when people gathered the eggs of wild fowl, any of which contained half-hatched birds, or it may be related to some primitive fear of undeveloped eggs. As eggs are widely considered to be a fertility symbol, primitive man may have been afraid to eat them before they had developed into some recognisable form of life, when their dangerous quality was presumably eliminated.'[19]

'Balut', the Fertilised Duck Eggs of the Philippines

I do not agree with this theory, for in my search through historical records of the Spanish chroniclers dating from 500 years ago, there is no mention of a fear of 'undeveloped' eggs by early Filipinos, instead; there was plenty of evidence that they enjoyed eating all kinds of eggs. For example, both Pigafetta and Loarca remarked on the tabon bird whose eggs in the sand were prized by Filipinos.[20] Describing his fascinating encounter with a native chief, Pigafetta writes in 1521 that the chief 'was eating turtle eggs which were in two porcelain dishes, and he had four jars full of palm wine in front of him covered with sweet-smelling herbs and arranged with four small reeds in each jar by means of which he drank … then the king had us eat some of those eggs and drink through those slender reeds.'[21] Diego de Bobadilla also remarked on how he enjoyed eating those eggs as well.[22]

As these records show, the early Filipinos were not afraid of eating eggs. Eggs for Filipinos were not things to fear but things to savour. Although there is no mention that the eggs were fertilised, it may well be that Filipinos may have been eating them long before the Spanish arrived. Filipinos have the most adventurous palates and consume many items which others, especially Westerners, may fear. It is my contention that balut-eating developed because it is an easy and relatively cheap protein source for people to eat. I also believe that the aphrodisiac belief attached to it was not originally a reason for people to eat balut, but I suggest that this belief in balut as an aphrodisiac for men only came about when the Spaniards introduced the concept of 'machismo.'

In light of the brief historical mentions above, it may be assumed that the Chinese truly did influence the Filipinos regarding the eating of balut.

Chinese consumption of fertilised eggs does not appear to be as pervasive as Filipino consumption, which some of my informants confirmed as well when answering the balut survey. Several of them were firm in their opinion that the Chinese did not eat balut. The lack of Chinese recipes mentioning fertilised duck eggs may mean that it is not as popular in China as salted eggs, tea eggs, soy sauce eggs or thousand-year-old eggs. It is worth noting, however, the many similarities between the production of thousand-year old eggs and fertilised eggs.

The process of making thousand-year-old eggs involves the duck eggs being coated in lime clay and then wrapped up in rice husks.[23] In the Philippines, the traditional way of incubating balut involved the eggs being surrounded by heated rice husks. Now, however, mechanical incubators likely warm the balut. Some claim that eggs from an incubator do not taste as good as eggs incubated with rice husks which they say gives balut a sweeter taste.

It may well be that balut originated in China and was taken up by the Filipinos, but whatever the case, balut is now considerably more popular in the Philippines than in China. 'Balut is sold all the time and everywhere – on streets, at stalls, outside movie houses, outside night clubs and discos, in markets; by vendors walking, sitting, or squatting; at midnight and early dawn, at breakfast, lunch, merienda, and dinner time.'[24] The newly cooked balut are sold with twists of rock salt in baskets covered with cloth to keep them warm, as the vendors walk the streets hawking loudly about their wares. Worth noting is the fact that tea eggs in China were sold by vendors at night who call out in a 'sing-song' manner.[25] This is much like the way balut is sold, usually at night and accompanied by a vendor's own style of calling 'bal-uuuut!' which can vary from person to person.

Balut is also sold at food stalls and in restaurants, where they have transcended their street food status and have become haute cuisine. It can now be ordered in restaurants 'as an appetiser (rolled in flour, fried, and with a vinegar-chilli dip), *adobado* (cooked in vinegar with garlic), or baked in a ramekin with olive oil or butter and spices ('Sorpresa de balut').'[26] One can visit a five-star hotel in Manila to eat *adobong balut*. This is balut without the shell, and then cooked with garlic, soy sauce and vinegar instead of using the usual chicken or pork.

The notion of balut as a street food and a food for the masses takes on special meaning when linked to the idea that the Chinese dishes brought to the Philippines have flourished in the food stalls, small eateries, and as street vendors' wares; not in the meals of the rich. They point out that 'the Chinese, who first came as traders, merchants, and then settlers, had their food absorbed into lower and middle-class cuisine.'[27] If taken into account this observation that the Chinese food in the Philippines is the food of the streets, this certainly lends further credence to balut originating in China, with Chinese salted and century duck eggs appearing to be distant cousins of balut.

A Philippine company called Andoy's Best now bottles balut in gourmet sauces and vacuum seals the products to last up to two years. There are three different sauces available, with one featuring balut in brine. The brined balut can be used in recipes like *adobo* and oven-baked Balut Supreme. Other flavors are Balut Afritada, made with tomato sauce and bell peppers and the other is Balut Caldereta, which has been described as a meaty and spicy tasting dish.

The very fact that balut is now featured in rich, Spanish-influenced dishes is a sign that the once-humble snack has metamorphosed into a main dish and has entered the meals of the upper classes. Indeed, balut has become so emblematic of Filipino culture that it has become the ultimate test of being Filipino. It is usually the first thing Filipino friends urge their foreign visitors, and refusing it may be construed as a refusal not just of the food itself, but of everything Filipino. This is because balut has evolved from economical street snack to a proud symbol of national identity.

Supernatural beliefs and balut

Many of my informants expressed strong feelings of disgust at seeing the embryo or catching a glimpse of the developed little chick. The majority of my informants preferred to swallow the balut whole. If they do bite the embryo, they try not to look at the embryo. Some people take apart the egg and eat it piece-by-piece. P.P. described eating balut 'like eating an Oreo cookie – you eat it in sections.' But another informant, A.G., disagreed. 'If you eat it piece by piece, it's gross. So I'd rather eat the whole egg in two bites, including the chick.'

I believe that the feelings of revulsion experienced by many at the sight of the fetus may be due to the idea of ingesting something that is clearly on the verge of being born. The notion of eggs as symbols of life can be demonstrated by the fact that many places impose prohibitions on the eating of eggs including parts of Africa, Europe and Australia. Eggs were not to be consumed or destroyed because they had 'universal significance … as an image of life force.'[28] This idea of eating something and ending its life as a chick seems to be a deeply disturbing issue even for those who choose to eat balut as well as for those who do not.

Several of the informants I interviewed mentioned that eating balut makes a person like an *aswang*. Also known as a *manananggal*, an *aswang* is a supernatural creature who craves human flesh and is afraid of salt and spice. 'The Filipinos' decided preference for salt, sour, and spicy foods is likely due to their fear of the *manananggal* and similar preternatural beings.'[29] I am not, however, insinuating that balut eaters are *aswang*. Rather, there seems to be a symbolic relationship between the belief in balut's invigorating powers and the belief in the *aswang*. Perhaps the beliefs regarding balut may have been an effect or a result of the belief in the *aswang*.

P.P., a mother of three children, ate balut daily for almost three years in the Philippines, when she was pregnant. She still eats balut occasionally in the U.S. She compares the inside appearance of an open balut egg as similar in looks to a human fetus with its skin and veins. 'It's almost like cannibalism,' P.P. said. 'When you look at balut, you see the veins, the skin, the fetus inside. It's like you're eating a human fetus.' P.P. believes that balut is something that would empower an *aswang*, whose favourite meals include eating fetuses from pregnant women. 'I can see where eating balut could empower an *aswang*, since *aswangs* like to eat the fetuses of human babies,' she said.

The idea that eating balut will transform a person into an *aswang* caused a lot of childhood agony for one Filipina informant, Issandra Yap, a visiting student in U.C. Berkeley. Yap was born and raised in Quezon City, Luzon. She recalled the intense teasing she was subjected to whenever others saw her eating balut. 'Oh, *aswang ka, aswang ka!! Kadiri ka, kadiri ka!!*' (Oh, you're an *aswang, aswang*!! You're gross, you're gross!!) was a common taunt that was directed at her. She would retort back that since she was eating balut, it would make her strong and if she was going to be an *aswang*, she would catch them as soon as she could. According to Yap, this was a popular response to the common taunt linking balut-eating to the *aswang*. She learned this from other children.

It is significant that in Filipino beliefs, salt and seasonings play an important part in warding off creatures like the *aswang* or placating others like the *dwende* (dwarves) who prefer food without salt.[30] For example, ghoul *aswang*s, who are believed to feed on dead bodies that they often steal during wakes, are terrified of salt, spices, and vinegar. Vampire *aswang*s and viscera suckers are also driven away by the use of salt and spices like garlic.

Salt also plays an essential role in eating balut. The overwhelming majority of balut eaters preferred salt to sprinkle on their eggs. Other spices included pepper and vinegar with chillies. Perhaps salt is being used by people as a sort of neutralising agent when eating balut, with people unconsciously warding off the '*aswang*' effects from eating balut. After all, salt and spices are reputed to scare off various types of the *aswang*. If salt is used, then presumably the person eating balut would not turn into an *aswang*.

In addition to being a neutralizer, salt may also be used unconsciously as a sort of purifying agent, to cleanse the balut eater from the impure action of eating and therefore ending the life of the baby chick. I speculate that if this is the case, the sprinkling of salt may be for the balut eater a way of atoning for the 'sin' of ending another's life for the sake of continuing his/her own. The notion that a life must be ended to ensure that others may live could be applied here with salt acting as an offering to the sacrificed life. However, salt should not be taken too seriously as an extension of the fear of the *aswang* or as a purifying agent; after all, supernatural beings aside, salt does tend to make everything taste better.

Several interesting practices that have to do with the *aswang* utilize eggs. If one swallows an unhatched egg of a chicken with its shell on, it will enable one to fly as an *aswang*.[31] Another fascinating belief involving eggs is that a new balbal (ghoul *aswang* as called by the Tagbanua), can once again become a normal person if made to vomit a yolk-like substance. If the *aswang* is already in the advanced stages, then a 'chick-like creature' is vomited.[32] This belief in developed chicks being the harbinger of evil may have influenced Filipino balut eaters in their preference for balut aged no more than 17 days, since they do not want to see, much less eat a developed embryo.

It is interesting to note that in transportation hubs in the Philippines such as bus and train stations, balut vendors purposely sell 19-day-old or older balut to customers they never will see again, customers who are *not* their '*suki*' (regulars). These balut eggs being sold are described as 'chicks almost ready to be hatched' and are sold by vendors 'who will never see their customers again, will not hear recriminations, or form friendships with them.'[33] This deliberate sale of items considered by many Filipinos as culturally unwanted and undesirable can be construed as a hostile act since the vendor is foisting upon a unsuspecting customer an egg that is a 'chick-like creature.' One can even venture to say that the vendors are in effect, treating their customers like an *aswang* or forcing them to be an *aswang* in that the customers are 'swallowing' what in essence is a chick.

In my study of balut, I have attempted to show that cultural values of the Filipinos and Filipino-Americans can be seen in the beliefs regarding the consumption of fertilised eggs.

I believe that these observations can have further implications on the study of

Philippine worldview. 'Worldview, the way a people perceives the world and its place in it, permeates all aspects of a given culture and this is why the pattern of the whole is to be found even in that whole's smallest part.'[34] Although the custom of balut may be considered by some as an inconsequential item of study, I have tried to illustrate otherwise. According to Dundes, 'it is not always easy to discern patterns of worldview, especially when one attempts to look at a culture as a whole ... it makes more sense to examine microcosms, and from these examinations, one may have better access to the corresponding macrocosm.'[35] In choosing a topic that can be considered a 'microcosm,' I hope to have shed some light on the 'macrocosm' that is Philippine culture and society today.

Bibliography

Blair, Emma Helen & James A. Robertson eds., *The Philippine Islands 1493–1898* (Cleveland: The Arthur H. Clark Co., 55 vols., 1903–1909).

Claudio, Virginia S., *Filipino-American Food Practices, Customs, & Holidays* (Chicago: American Dietetic Association, 1994).

Crawfurd, John, *Journal of an Embassy from the Governor-General of India to the Courts of Siam and Cochin China; Exhibiting a View of the Actual State of Those Kingdoms*, 2nd edition, vol. 1 of 2 (London: Henry Colburn & Richard Bentley, 1830).

Demetrio, Francisco, *Dictionary of Philippine Folk Beliefs and Customs*, 4 vols. (Cagayan de Oro City, Philippines: Xavier University, 1971).

Dundes, Alan, 'Pecking Chickens: A Folk Toy as a Source for the Study of Worldview', in *Folklore Matters* (Knoxville: The University of Tennessee Press, 1992), pp. 83–91.

Fernandez, Doreen G., *Tikim: Essays on Philippine Food and Culture* (Pasig: Anvil Publishing, 1994).

——, 'Balut', in *Oxford Companion to Food*, ed. Alan Davidson (Oxford University Press, 1999).

Fernandez, Doreen & Edilberto Alegre, *Sarap: Essays on Philippine Food* (Manila: Mr. & Mrs. Publishing Co., 1988).

Freeman, Nancy, 'Balut Brokering: Embryonic Enterprises', in *Filipinas Magazine* (July 1996), pp. 53–56.

Jenks, Albert E., *The Bontoc Igorot* (Manila: Bureau of Public Printing, 1905).

Leung, Mai, *The Classic Chinese Cook Book* (New York: Harper's Magazine Press, 1976).

Leung, Woot-Tsuen Wu & R.R. Butrum and RH. Chang, *Food Composition Table for Use in East Asia*. Part 1. DHEW Publication No. (NIH) 73–465 (Bethesda: U.S. Dept. of Health, Education and Welfare and the Food and Agricultural Organization of the United Nations, 1972).

Magat, Margaret, *Balut: Caviar of the Philippines. Fertilized Duck Eggs and Their Role in Filipino and Filipino-American Sexuality and Culture*. Thesis, University of California, Berkeley, 1997.

Maness, Hubert, 'Balut – a Duck Egg Delicacy', in *World's Poultry Science Journal* (June 1950), pp. 10–13.

Newall, Venetia, *An Egg at Easter: a Folklore Study* (London: Routledge and K. Paul, 1971).

Ramos, Maximo, *Legends of Lower Gods* (Quezon City: Phoenix Publishing House, 1990a).

——, *Philippine Demonological Legends and their Cultural Bearings* (Quezon City: Phoenix Publishing House, 1990b).

Ratzel, Friedrich, *The History of Mankind*, vol. 1 (London: Macmillan, 1896–1898).

Simoons, Fredrick J., *Eat Not This Flesh: Food Avoidances in the Old World* (Madison: University of Wisconsin Press, 1961).

——, *Food in China: A Cultural & Historical Inquiry* (Boca Raton: CRC Press, 1991).

Sokolov, Raymond, *Why We Eat What We Eat: How the Encounter between the New World and the Old Changed the Way Everyone on the Planet Eats* (New York: Summit Books, 1991).

Notes

1. From the UC Berkeley Folklore Archives, collected in 1988 from 68-year-old Walter Hamilton, retired army officer, by Annette Ivens.
2. Maness, p. 10.
3. Fernandez (1994), p. 11.
4. But there are many in the Philippines who do not have the luxury of choosing their food. If they can afford it, balut is one of the more economical sources of protein.
5. Freeman, p. 53.
6. According to the *Food Composition Table for Use in East Asia* by W. Leung et al., p. 111.
7. Claudio, p. 6.
8. Fernandez, p. 10.
9. see for example, Garcia, Mauro ed., *Readings in Philippine Prehistory* (Manila: The Filipiniana Book Guild, 1979), pp. 8–34. Also Jocano, F. Landa, *Philippine Prehistory. An Anthropological Overview of the Beginnings of Filipino Society and Culture* (Diliman: Philippine Center for Advanced Studies, 1975), pp. 135–158.
10. Sokolov, pp. 14–22.
11. Fernandez & Alegre, p. 17.
12. see for example, see Chang, K.C. ed., *Food in Chinese Culture: Anthropological and Historical Perspectives* (New Haven: Yale University Press, 1977); Barer-Stein, Thelma, *You Eat What You Are: A Study of Canadian Ethnic Food Traditions* (Toronto: McClelland & Stewart, 1979); Anderson, E.N., *The Food of China* (New Haven: Yale University Press, 1988).
13. Simoons (1991), p. 365.
14. Crawford, p. 408.
15. Duval, Mathias. 'Sur les œufs pourris comme aliment en Chine', *Bulletins de la Société D'Anthropologie de Paris,* troisième série vol. 8, (1885), pp. 209–300.
16. Ratzel, p. 432.
17. Jenks, p. 143.
18. see for example, Verrill, A. Hyatt, *Strange Customs, Manners and Beliefs* (Boston: L.C. Page & Co., 1946), p. 211; Schwabe, Calvin W. *Unmentionable Cuisine* (Charlottesville: University Press of Virginia, 1979), p. 399.
19. Simoons (1961), p. 68.
20. Blair & Robertson vol. 33, p. 133; Blair & Robertson vol. 5, p. 167.
21. Blair & Robertson vol. 33, p. 149.
22. Blair & Robertson vol. 29, p. 303.
23. Simoons (1991), p. 364.
24. Fernandez (1994), p. 10.
25. M. Leung 1976, p. 21.
26. Fernandez 1999.
28. Fernandez & Alegre, pp. 17–18.
28. Newall, p. 113.
29. Ramos (1990b), p. 148.
30. Ramos (1990a), pp. 40–41, p. 58.
31. Demetrio, p. 241.
32. Demetrio, pp. 247–248.
33. Fernandez (1994), p. 10.
34. Dundes, p. 83.
35. Dundes, p. 83.

Eggs, the English Breakfast and the Biography of a National Meal

Kaori O'Connor

The anthropology of food

The English breakfast is the best-known national meal in the world, a unique cultural and culinary symbol of England and Englishness, in edible form. As Countess Morphy (1936) put it: 'Breakfast is the English meal par excellence … one of the great national institutions of England'. But how did it attain this elevated status, and what can a national meal tell us about the nation that eats it? These are the questions that led me to write my book, *The English Breakfast, the Biography of a National Meal, With Recipes*.

The anthropology of food has been summed up in just four words by the great Mary Douglas (1997), a pioneer in the field – 'food is not feed'. Anthropologists are usually thought of as experts in extreme eating practices and exotic table manners – such as the guinea pig cuisine of South America or the proper use of the cannibal fork in the South Seas. Long before the current popularity of exotic edibles, anthropologists were exploring the significance of particular foods in communities of which they are emblematic, such as the jerk pork of the slave-descended Maroons of Jamaica (B. Kopytoff 1997) or the salmon prepared by Native Americans of the Pacific Northwest Coast (Dick 1997). Increasingly, however, anthropologists are moving beyond traditional, small-scale societies to explore the larger relationships between food and national identity. Definitions of nation, nationality and national identity have always been elusive and contentious, ranging from the conventional view of a nation as sovereign state in the modern sense to one to a wider definition that includes communities that exist only in the political imagination of their constituents (Anderson 1991). However, as Palmer (1998:177) points out, whatever criteria are employed, there is agreement that 'an idea of nation is inextricably tied to a sense of history, to the memories and traditions that have been handed down from one generation to the next'. Prime among these are culinary traditions, for it is through food rather than political rhetoric that most people experience the nation in everyday life.

As Douglas (1975) has demonstrated, to decipher a society's meals and cuisine is to understand the society itself. As the English food writer P. Morton Shand (1929) put it, 'The cookery of a nation is just as much part of its customs and traditions as are its laws and language.' In all cultures and periods of history, national cuisines have been believed to be intimately linked to a nation's character, health and fortunes. Once again, Brillat-Savarin (1825) had an aphorism for it – 'The destiny of nations depends on the manner in which they eat.' Anthropologists have come to appreciate Brillat-Savarin's insight into the close links between nations and their food. It is said that, in any conflict, the victors rewrite history. They certainly rewrite menus. The literature of colonialism is full of examples of foreign cuisines being imposed on subaltern peoples. As Thomas Sankaru, a former President of Burkina Faso wrote, 'So you do not know where imperialism is to be found? Look on your plate' (in Cusack 2000:207). Food politics are just as pervasive in non-colonial settings. What seem to be national cuisines often turn out on closer inspection to be the cuisines of particular groups, classes or regions that became dominant at a significant point in a nation's development. For example, what outsiders think of as the traditional and representative national cuisine of Japan is actually the cuisine of a particular geographically-situated class at a specific point in historical time – the samurai (warrior) and merchant elite of the urban centres of Edo (Tokyo), Kyoto and Osaka in the mid-nineteenth century, when they seized political power and brought about the modernising Meiji Restoration under which Japan rapidly turned from a feudal state into a modern nation. Subsequently, the growing Japanese middle class adopted the culture and cuisine of the politico-military Meiji elite, a process that Ashkenazi and Jacobs (2000:31) call 'samuraisation'.

Regionality presents nationality with the challenge of conflicting identities and loyalties, one example of which is the proliferation of regional food products which compete with each other, emphasising difference rather than community. As an exasperated Charles de Gaulle once complained when President of France – 'How can one govern a nation that makes two hundred and forty six kinds of cheese?' Different cooking styles, dialects and domestic ideologies can also be divisive, so the making of a new nation can rest on the successful construction of a national or official cuisine in which the culinary practices of a particular region and group are imposed on the others, as in Japan, or in the creation of a new cuisine that can successfully weld regional and ethnic identities and cuisines into a diverse yet unified national whole. In India, Appadurai (1988) has traced the emergence of a post-colonial national 'Indian' cuisine that was fuelled by the expansion of the Indian middle classes and spread through the parallel growth of literacy and the print media, particularly cookbooks. In newly independent India, food became the medium for the spread of new middle class ideology, public culture and domestic values that cut across the boundaries of India's many regional and ethnic groupings. Instead of the cuisine of one group or region becoming dominant, India's evolving national identity was best served by incorporating middle-class values and practices into existing regional cuisines, in an ongoing double process that used diversity to both enrich and consolidate the whole. So the new 'national' cuisine of India was a polyglot practice in which distinct regional and ethnic culinary traditions play an important part, the rich meat curries of the north, the coconut-flavoured fish dishes of the tropical south, and the many forms of vegetarian cuisine, breads, rice dishes and chutney all helping to spread new unifying middle class ideas of nationhood, nutrition and domestic values, while also providing a means by which citizens from one part of the country could become familiar with those of others through recipes and cookbooks. Helstosky (2003) has shown how cuisine played a similar role in the creation of the modern Italian nation. And sometimes a single meal or dish can become a unifying emblem of nationality, as with the Jordanian *mansaf,* or lamb with rice (Howell 2003).

Studying national cuisines and meals
Some food historians, notably Flandrin and Montanari (1999) have questioned the validity of the concept of a 'national' cuisine, arguing that long-established regional cuisines do not stop at shifting political borders, and that many traditions involving the origins of national cuisines – the belief that Marco Polo introduced pasta to Europe after visiting China being a case in point – are no more than gastronomic myths perpetuated for narrow nationalistic purposes. Instead, in the manner of the *Annales* school, they aim to illuminate the relationship between society and food by focussing on the *problematiques* of broad themes such as the economic and demographic factors that influence the relationship between production and consumption, the effects of technology, the difference between the urban and the rural, and what food can tell us about the structures of everyday life and changes in those structures. There can be no quarrel with this, but they locate their studies in different historical periods, such as 'the Classical period' and 'the Late Middle Ages', and often in broad geographical areas such as 'the Mediterranean' and 'the Arab Empire', with most of the work to date concentrating on Europe (but see Matsuyama 2003 for a pioneering study of the formation of South East Asian dietary culture). This regional approach is appropriate in Europe where borders have always been fluid and there is an extensive array of documentary sources that pre-date the establishment of the present nation states. It is less successful in the case of island nations like Japan and Great Britain where identity has been consolidated by a degree of geographical isolation, and in younger nations like America, where the development of regionality and city states did not precede nationality in the same way as it did in Europe. The use of historical periods is also problematic. As the Japanese anthropologist Naomichi Ishige (2001:1) points out, 'Historians tend to take changes of political system as the dividing points for historical eras, yet a change in government does not lead to any rapid change in people's eating habits ... divisions in the history of dietary life differ from the periods into which historical events are generally classified'. In the social study of food, it is not historical eras *per se* that are important, but those junctures in time and space when dietary life and historical events and processes coincide in meaningful ways.

An extremely productive approach to the study of food is one that combines anthropology with the kind of cultural history that is exemplified by the work of David Hackett Fischer, who seeks to build on the achievements of the *Annales* school while overcoming what he sees as its excessive rationalism. In *Albion's Seed*, his study of the cultural making of America, Fischer uses the term 'folkways' to designate social values, beliefs and their associated material culture, tracing the formation of America by charting changes and continuities in values and material culture over time and space. These 'ways' (Fischer 1989:8–9) include power ways (attitudes toward authority and power), social ways (conventional patterns of migration, settlement, association and affiliation), dress ways (customs of dress, demeanour and personal adornment) time ways (attitudes toward the use of time, time-keeping and the conventional rhythms of life) and food ways – patterns of diet, nutrition, cooking, eating, feasting and fasting. Archaic though the term 'folkways' may seem, Fischer purposely employs it to suggest the persistence of culture in history, noting 'the more advanced a society becomes in material terms, the stronger is the determinant power of its folkways, for modern technologies act as amplifiers, and modern institutions as stabilizers, and modern elites as organizers of these complex cultural processes'. In *Albion's Seed*, Hackett focuses on what he calls the 'canonical dish' of New England Yankee society – the baked pie – tracing its origins and showing how it, the other dishes that made up Yankee cuisine along with practices such as table manners, embodied a moral order based on Puritan values, and also served as defining emblems of Yankee-ness. Material culture also plays a central role in the anthropology of food. As Douglas (1979:38–9) put it, material goods 'make visible and stable the categories of culture … goods have another important use: they also make and maintain social relationships. This is a long-tried and fruitful approach to the material side of existence which yields a much richer idea of social meanings than mere individual competitiveness'. The most significant way in which anthropology and Fischer's cultural history differ from the *Annales* approach is this. The interest of anthropologists and cultural historians in the symbolic means that, instead of disregarding gastronomic myths, they make them the positive focus of study. What matters is not whether something is 'true', but what people *choose* to believe is true, even in the face of contradictory evidence. Why, for example, they may choose to go on believing that Marco Polo introduced pasta to the west after visiting China (see Wood, 1995).

Despite the reservations of the regionalist food historians referred to above, it is seemingly impossible to separate nations from what they think of as their national cuisines, whether or not the cuisine is truly representative and even if it is entirely invented, as can be the case with new nations. The challenge is how to come to grips with the subject. The development of cuisines as Goody (1982, 1998), and others have shown, is a long and complex process. The process through which edible materials take on meaning and associations and are transformed into national cuisines is one that anthropologists call 'the cultural biography of a thing' (I. Kopytoff 1986). Once achieved, a culinary identity can be maintained over time, even though some of the ingredients, recipes and culinary techniques and practices may change (Wilk 1999). Many aspects of the process by which a national cuisine is formed and a useful method of approaching it can be seen in Ishige's *The History and Culture of*

Japanese Food (2001). Ishige begins in the Palaeolithic era before rice was cultivated in Japan, and presents a cultural account that continues down to the present, tracing the development of Japanese food through the study of typical dishes of all periods, including condiments, beverages, ingredients, methods of preparation, etiquette, the aesthetics of presentation, eating implements, cooking utensils and cookbooks, placing these objects and techniques of material culture in the social, political, and economic contexts of their consumption and use. He shows, for example, how the switch from the traditional method of serving meals on small individual tables to the new practice of sitting around a central table reflected the shift from a purely Japanese to a Westernized style of eating and also a change in household constitution, from the extended to the nuclear family, and how the frequency and timing of meals reflected changes in employment practices. By starting in the distant past, it is possible to construct a culinary stratigraphy that shows how the various edible elements came to be present in a particular location, and then how and when they began to take on cultural meaning. Ishige is able to avoid many of the problems of regionality because Japan, like Britain, is an island nation. In both Japan and Britain it is possible to see how nationhood developed, and how national cuisines, dishes and meals emerged to reflect it. This is the approach I took when writing *The English Breakfast*.

Eggs And the English breakfast

As the research proceeded, my book became a cultural biography of the English breakfast, a culinary detective story and a cookbook rolled into one. A nearly universal aspect of national cuisines, dishes and meals is that they are believed to have their roots in antiquity, although very often they do not. By beginning with the archaeological record, I was able to see how most 'typically English' flora and fauna were not indigenous, but were introduced in relatively recent times. Similarly, the emblematic meal of 'eternal England', like so much else that is considered to be 'traditional' in Britain today, was largely a construct of the Victorian era. I discovered that, as a formal substantial early morning meal, breakfast appeared only in the nineteenth century as an outcome of complex processes of social and cultural change, although it drew upon much older beliefs and values. Because meals of this kind had not existed before, at least not for most of the population, the elevation of breakfast to special status was marked by the appearance of a new kind of popular book – cookbooks devoted exclusively to breakfasts, and how to make and serve them. There were handsome volumes for the well-off, plainer editions for the middling market and cheap paper-covered sixpenny editions for readers of the poorer sort bent on self-improvement. And what a revelation they proved to be.

The English breakfast of today – even the delectable version consisting of bacon, sausage, tomato, black pudding, mushroom and eggs of choice served at the Wolseley café-restaurant in London's Piccadilly – is a pale shadow of the meals enshrined in these culinary volumes. The most splendid were the great Victorian and Edwardian country house breakfasts, like this one of 1870 recalled by Lady Raglan, granddaughter of the Earl of St Germans, in *Memories of Three Reigns*:

> I always remember what a great feature was made of the breakfasts at my grandfather's house parties at Port Eliot, and of the numerous courses that succeeded each other. There would be a choice of fish, fried eggs and crisp bacon, a variety of egg dishes, omelettes and sizzling sausages and bacon. During the shooting parties, hot game and grilled pheasants always appeared on the breakfast menu but were served of course without any vegetables. On a side table was always to be found a choice of cold viands; delicious home-smoked hams, pressed meats, one of the large raised pies for which Mrs Vaughan (the cook) was justly famous, consisting of cold game and galantine, with aspic jelly. The guests drank either tea or coffee, and there were the invariable accompaniments of home-made rolls, piping hot, and stillroom preserves of apple and quince jelly, and always piled bowls of rich Cornish cream. The meal usually finished with a fruit course of grapes or hothouse peaches and nectarines.

Meals like this were of course only enjoyed by the elite, but they inspired very passable and palatable imitations across the social scale. There are many accounts of breakfasts like this one served in the Plumstead rectory in Trollope's *The Warden (1855)*:

> The tea consumed was the very best, the coffee the very blackest, the cream the very thickest; there was dry toast and buttered toast, muffins and crumpets, hot bread and cold bread, white bread and brown bread, home-made bread baker's bread, wheaten bread and oaten bread, and if there be breads other than these, they were there; there were eggs in napkins, and crispy bits of bacon under silver covers, and there were little fishes in a box, and devilled kidneys frizzling on a hot water dish … Over and above this, on a snow-white napkin spread upon the sideboard, was a huge ham and a huge sirloin; the latter having laden the dinner table on the previous evening.

And as this essay is being written for the Oxford Symposium on Food History 2006, in the home-city of Oxford marmalade, mention must be made of the breakfast parties once held in Oxford colleges, although sadly not in my time there, such as this one that took place in 1884 (*Cassell's Family Magazine*, in Aylmer 1995:10):

> The feast commences with two enormous dishes of whiting and soles. After the edge of appetite has been blunted on these trifles, the serious business of the day begins. A couple of 'spread eagles' i.e. Fowls squashed flat and embellished with mushrooms, face a mound of sausages enclosed in a rampart of mashed potatoes, and are supported on either hand by a regiment of boiled eggs and a

solid square of beefsteak. These are backed up by a reserve of omelettes, sweet and savoury, anchovy toast, more graphically than elegantly known as 'dirty Toast' – and 'squish' – a synonym for marmalade.

Across the land, breakfast was so important that those who could afford to do so set aside chambers – breakfast parlours or breakfast rooms – specially devoted to the meal. New kinds of china appeared – breakfast services with specialised pieces like porridge bowls with lids, covered bacon dishes and sardine boxes. Many words were written on the importance of dressing and setting the breakfast table in an attractive manner, *The Young Ladies' Journal* devoting an Extra Supplement (No. 4) to the subject. But what exactly was eaten off pretty plates set on snowy linen? What Victorian and Edwardian breakfast cookbooks reveal is that, in this era when food was relatively cheap and servants plentiful, eggs – the mainstay of today's English breakfast – played a comparatively minor role amid the other delights on offer such as shrimp pie, hashed mutton, devilled bones and pheasant soufflé.

It was after World War I, when economic conditions became less favourable, domestic service went into decline and many middle-class women had to cook for themselves for the first time, that eggs began to dominate the breakfast table for three reasons: cheapness, speed and ease of preparation. Inevitably, the grand variety of the English breakfast began to fade, and monotony reared its head. The complaint with which *What Shall We Have For Breakfast* by Agnes C. Maitland (1926) opens is representative of the period:

> In most English middle-class households breakfast is of all meals the most uninteresting. The monotony of fried bacon and boiled eggs is seldom varied, except by an occasional dish of fish, or bacon and eggs fried together. This, no doubt, is partly due to the early hour at which breakfast must be taken in most homes, and partly to the want of resource and knowledge of an ordinary English cook.

World War II struck the English breakfast a blow from which it has never fully recovered. For one thing, at least in the cities, bacon and fresh eggs were hard to come by. Foodstuffs were strictly rationed, and people ate what they could get. Rationing continued for years after the war ended, and when breakfast foods finally came off rationing, many people had got out of the traditional breakfast habit. Or, indeed, any breakfast habit at all.

In the course of researching the biography of the English breakfast, I was struck by how little we know today about just what was in those covered silver dishes on sideboards during the Victorian and Edwardian heyday of the English breakfast and – more importantly – how to cook it. Period cookbooks cannot be fully appreciated without their historical, social and anthropological context. Equally, context alone is not enough. When reading or writing about food, you should also be able to make and taste it. My book *The English Breakfast: The Biography of a National Meal With Recipes* therefore combines both. The first part presents the cultural biography of the English breakfast, while the second part consists of three original Victorian and Edwardian cookbooks that between them embrace the theory and practice of the English breakfast in elite households, modest homes and middle-class establishments. The earliest and most elaborate is Georgiana Hill's (1865) *The Breakfast Book*. The second, Miss M. L. Allen's (1884) *Breakfast Dishes for Every Morning of Three Months* is a bright and bustling work aimed at housekeepers of homes in which economy was a consideration. Finally, the pukka Colonel Kenney-Herbert's (1904) *Fifty Breakfasts* is the epitome of the manly, no-nonsense approach to cookery, sprinkled with a few colonial dishes, the legacy of his years in India. Taken together they offer a feast of lost dishes that richly deserve rediscovery. These three cookbooks are presented in facsimile in order to show readers how the original editions look. They have not been amalgamated because the comparison between them is instructive, and they are published in their entirety because, when reading edited period cookbooks, I always wonder what the editor has left out.

I conclude by sharing with you three egg recipes from a book of which I am immensely fond, Major 'L's' (Major James L. Landon's) 1887 *Breakfasts, Luncheons and Ball Suppers* which I could not include because it dealt with meals other than breakfast. Major 'L' divides breakfasts into three types – those suitable for large parties; those for breakfasters of robust constitution; and those for ladies and for gentlemen of sedentary occupation and a certain age. Whether you cook these, the breakfast recipes in my book, or others that you may have, remember – the future of the English breakfast is in your hands.

Recipes (all from *Breakfasts, Luncheons and Ball Suppers* by Major 'L'.)

Eggs Aux Fines Herbs À La Crême (For Ladies)

Small earthenware cups with handles are made especially for serving eggs cooked in the following way: Put into each cup a quarter of an ounce of butter, put the cup in the oven and melt the butter; take the cups out and break an egg into each, dust with pepper and salt, put them into the oven until the whites are set, and if the bottom should get cooked before the top, which is sometimes the case if the heat in the oven is not equal, pass a salamander over the top which will have the desired effect; mask with *Fines Herbs* Sauce or Béchamel Sauce, sprinkle with some fried bread-crumbs, and serve hot.

Buttered Eggs Aux Tomates (For Robust Appetites)

Melt in an enamelled saucepan two ounces of butter, add a table-spoonful of cream, remove it from the fire, and break into the saucepan four eggs; flavour with pepper and salt, put the saucepan on the fire, and mix the whole with a wooden spoon until the mixture mixes like custard, being careful it does not curdle. Fry in butter some toast in squares of three inches, and put a table-spoonful of the mixture on each, and mask with a *purée* of fresh tomatoes.

Bouchées of Buttered Eggs Au Gratin, Champignon, Asparagus, etc
(For Large Parties)

The inside of some small halfpenny rolls can be taken out and the rolls put in the oven again until crisp, when they can be filled with the buttered eggs, and either shrimps, truffles, mushrooms, asparagus points, or a spoonful of *Maitre d'Hôtel* butter put in the centre, and masked with a few fried bread-crumbs and served very hot.

References

Allen, Mrs. M. L. 1884, *Breakfast Dishes for Every Morning of Three Months,* J. S. Virtue, London.

Anderson, Benedict 1991, *Imagined Communities: Reflections on the Origin and Spread of Nationalism,* Revised Edition, Verso, London

Appadurai, Arjun 1988, 'How to Make a National Cuisine: Cookbooks in Contemporary India', in *Comparative Studies in Society and History*, Vol 30, No. 1:3–24.

Ashkenazi, Michael and Jeanne Jacob 2000, *The Essence of Japanese Cuisine,* University of Pennsylvania Press.

Aylmer, Ursula with Caroline McCrum 1995, *Oxford Food: An Anthology Chosen and Edited by Ursula Aylmer, with Recipes from the Colleges,* edited by Caroline McCrum, Bodleian Library, Oxford.

Brillat-Savarin, Jean-Anthelme 1970, *The Philosopher in the Kitchen* (originally published as *Physiologie du Goût* in 1825, translated from the French by Anne Drayton), Penguin Books, London.

Cusack, Igor 2000, 'African Cuisines: Recipes for Nation Building?' in *Journal of African Cultural Studies*, Vol 13, No 2: 207–223.

Dick, Annette with Thelma Dick and Edward Dick 1997, 'Songhees Salmon: The Dick Family Recipes', in Kuper, Jessica (ed.) 1997, *The Anthropologist's Cookbook,* 2nd edition, Kegan Paul, London, New York and Bahrain.

Douglas, Mary, with Baron Isherwood, 1979, *The World of Goods: Towards an Anthropology of Consumption,* Routledge, London and New York.

Douglas, Mary 1995, 'Deciphering a Meal', in *Implicit Meanings: Selected Essays in Anthropology,* Routledge, London and New York.

Douglas, Mary 1997, 'Introduction', in Kuper, Jessica (ed.) 1997, *The Anthropologist's Cookbook,* 2nd edition, Kegan Paul, London, New York and Bahrain..

Fischer, David Hackett 1989, *Albion's Seed: Four British Folkways in America,* Oxford University Press.

Goody, Jack 1982, *Cooking, Cuisine and Class: A Study in Comparative Sociology,* Cambridge University Press, Cambridge and New York.

Goody, Jack 1998, *Food and Love: A Cultural History of East and West,* Verso, London and New York.

Flandrin, Jean-Louis and Massimo Montanari 1999, 'Introduction', in Flandrin, Jean Louis and Massimo Montanari (Eds) 1999: *A Culinary History of Food,* Columbia University Press, New York and London.

Helstosky, Carol 2003, 'Recipe for the Nation: Reading Italian History Through *La Scienza in Cucina* and *La Cucina Futurista*', in *Food and Foodways,* 11: 113–140.

Hill, Georgiana 1865, *The Breakfast Book,* Richard Bentley, London.

Howell, Sally 2003, 'Modernizing Mansaf: The Consuming Contexts of Jordan's National Dish', *Food and Foodways,* 11: 215–243.

Ishige, Naomichi 2001, *The History and Culture of Japanese Food,* Kegan Paul, London New York and Bahrain.

Kenney-Herbert, Colonel Arthur Robert 1904, *Fifty Breakfasts,* Edward Arnold, London.

Kopytoff, Barbara 1997, 'Maroon Jerk Pork and Other Jamaican Cooking', in Kuper, Jessica (ed.) 1997, *The Anthropologist's Cookbook,* 2nd edition, Kegan Paul, London, New York and Bahrain.

Kopytoff, Igor 1986, 'The Cultural Biography of Things: Commoditization as Process', in Appadurai, Arjun (ed.) 1986, *The Social Life of Things: Commodities in Cultural Process,* Cambridge University Press, Cambridge and New York.

Maitland, Agnes C. 1926, *What Shall We Have for Breakfast?* John Hogg, London.

L, Major (Landon, Major James L.) 1887, *Breakfasts, Luncheons and Ball Suppers,* Chapman and Hall, London.

Matsuyama, Akira 2003, *The Traditional Dietary Culture of South East Asia: Its Formation and Pedigree,* Kegan Paul, London New York and Bahrain.

Morphy, Countess 1936, *British Recipes: The Traditional Dishes of England, Scotland, Ireland and Wales,* Herbert Joseph, London.

O'Connor, Kaori 2006, *The English Breakfast: The Biography of a National Meal With Recipes,* Kegan Paul, London, New York and Bahrain.

Palmer, Catherine 1998, 'From Theory to Practice: Experiencing the Nation in Everyday Life', in *Journal of Material Culture,* Vol 3(2): 175–199, Sage Publications, London, Thousand Oaks and New Delhi.

Shand, P. Morton 1930, *A Book of Food,* Jonathan Cape, London.

Wilk, Richard 1999, 'Real Belizean Food': Building Local Identity in the Transnational Carribean', *American Anthropologist* June 1999, Vol 101, No. 2: 244–255.

Wood, Frances 1995, *Did Marco Polo Go To China?* Secker and Warburg, London.

Moorish Ovomania

Charles Perry

Take fatted hens and capons ... Add water, salt, much oil, pepper, coriander, some chopped onion, peeled almonds, pine nuts, fresh acorns, fresh chestnuts and peeled blanched walnuts. Put on the fire to cook.

Then take 30 eggs per bird ...

So begins a recipe in the thirteenth-century Moroccan book *Fadālat al-Khiwān*.[1] It proceeds to beat 20 of the yolks and all 30 whites (per bird) with spices. When the jointed birds are done in the pot, they are taken out and cooked in another pot with the beaten eggs (the individual pieces being separated with a knife when the eggs are about to congeal) and then served, with the cooked eggs caking them, along with the reserved 10 yolks, which have been fried, and then even more eggs: quartered hard-boiled eggs and a thin omelet (*isfiriyya*) flavored with chicken livers.

'Some people put small pieces of good dry cheese in this stuffing,' the recipe concludes, using the word 'stuffing' loosely, as a number of the recipes do, for any stew accompaniment containing eggs. 'Eat it in good health, God the Most High willing.'

No other medieval Moorish recipe calls for quite such heroic quantities of eggs, but eggs are used lavishly in *Fadāla* and the other thirteenth-century Moroccan/Andalusian recipe collection, known as the *Manuscrito Anónimo*.[2] Eggs often appear as garnishes the way they do at the end of the recipe quoted above; 25 stews have an egg garnish in *Fadāla*, 45 in *Anónimo*. They also figure in dozens of stuffings in both books, especially for fowl, and also serve sundry other purposes, such as stiffening meatballs or making a batter for frying fish. In a small handful of cases they are used to thicken a sauce.

Mostly, however, they appear as the *takhmīr* ('covering'), which was a topping or crust of eggs cooked on a dish as the finishing touch. In *Anónimo*, just over 125 recipes have a *takhmīr*. That's a quarter of the 500-odd dishes in the book, one third of the 375 savoury dishes. There are only 24 *takhmīrs* in the manuscript of *Fadāla* I have been able to study, but one of them appears on a dish of eggs; poached eggs are actually covered with more eggs and then sent to the oven until they stiffen.[3]

This word *takhmīr* has puzzled the authors of the published translations of these books (the late Rudolf Grewe's translations have not yet appeared). Perhaps because *takhmīr* can also mean 'the act of causing to ferment' – certainly the sort of instruction one would expect to find in recipes – and because scribes may sometimes have misspelled it as *khamīra* 'sourdough,' Ambrosio Huici-Miranda, Mohamed Mezzine and Laila Benkirane usually render it as 'to thicken' or 'to bind' ('se espesa'; 'épaissez-le', 'faire liaison'). Or perhaps the reason is that the translators could not imagine adding eggs to a stew for any other reason than to thicken it.

Sometimes a scribe left off a dot and misspelled the word as *tahmīr* 'the act of making something red or brown,' also a common word in recipes, and Mezzine-Benkirane translate the related verb form *yuhammar* as 'on colore' or 'colorez-le'. But passages such as 'when the *ta(k)hmīr* browns and becomes wrinkled' leave no doubt that 'covering' is the correct translation. The verb form of *takhmīr*, *yukhammar* ('cover it'), appears frequently in recipes. In a few cases, eggs are added to a dish with the instruction *yughmar* ('flood it'), perhaps a scribal error for *yukhammar*.

The simplest way to give a stew a *takhmīr* was to break whole eggs on its surface when the stew was done and slip the pot into a bread oven until the eggs cooked. (Sometimes a stew would be left on euphorbia embers or a hot stone, and in a few recipes the residual heat of the dish was apparently enough the cook the eggs.)

Breaking eggs onto a stew was not unique to Spain and North Africa in the Middle Ages; it was also done in the eastern Arab world. In the thirteenth-century cookbook *Kitāb Wasf al-At'ima*,[4] for instance, 11 stews are garnished by 'dotting' them with eggs. But it was a much rarer practice – 11 recipes out of 420, and in three of them the eggs were optional. In Syria or Iraq, an egg topping was considered something out of the ordinary; two dishes in *K. Wasf* take their names from it (*nujūmiyya*, 'starry' and *narjisiyya*, 'narcissus' because the eggs were thought to resemble poet's narcissus, with its white petals and yellow center).

But merely breaking eggs onto a stew was not the usual *takhmīr*. More often, Moorish cooks would beat the eggs with spices or other flavorings, such as ground nuts or chicken giblets or livers (most of the dishes identified as Jewish use a liver *takhmīr*). Frequently they would thicken it with flour or breadcrumbs.

Why this craze for covering stew with eggs? The manuscripts do not suggest an answer; they never say, for instance, 'cover it with eggs so that it will be more savory' or 'to counteract cold and dry humours'. The *takhmīr* was evidently just the fashion of the day – more marked in Moorish Spain than in Morocco, if the higher proportion or *takhmīrs* in *Anónimo* reflects Andalusian usage.

It's true that medieval recipes are generally party food, rather than everyday dishes, so this ovomania could have been a way of enriching dishes for a special occasion, or perhaps the marker of a class of special-occasion treats, but again, the recipe books give no clue. The half-dozen dishes that call for 20 or 30 eggs (which come out as egg cakes of one description or other) do sound like extravagant productions for a rare occasion, but *takhmīrs* occur promiscuously, even on quite plain dishes; on meatless eggplant dishes, for instance.

The impression the recipes give is that the Moors just considered eggs a proper finishing touch. One recipe in *Anónimo*[5] suggests a conceivable reason. It is lamb stewed with cabbage and flavourings; when the dish is done, you take lean meat from the pot and 'beat it in a bowl with eggs, breadcrumbs, almonds, pepper, coriander and caraway. Cover the pot with this little by little and leave it on the coals until the sauce dries and the grease comes to the top, and serve.' The name of the dish is 'a *baqliyya* (potherb dish) of Ziryab'. Ziryab was a ninth-century Persian connoisseur who was driven from the court of Baghdad by a jealous rival and became the arbiter of taste in Granada. He was known for introducing elegancies, such as an added string on the *oud*; perhaps this was one of his innovations that caught on in Moorish Spain.

Was this craze for eggs just a medieval aberration, or has it left traces on food in the modern world? In Spain and Portugal, there is a class of sweets, traditionally made by nuns, composed of sugar and egg yolks. These are regularly ascribed to Moorish influence, but the only Moorish contribution I can see is the sugar. Not one sweetmeat in either of these Arabic books is made from sugar and egg yolks; the combination of sugar and yolks seemed to revolt the Moors. When eggs do figure in one of their sweets, only the whites are used. This was also the practice in the eastern Arab world, as one would expect, because sweets were the area of cookery in which east and west differed least during the Arab Middle Ages.

One possible consequence of Moorish ovomania does occur to me, however. *Anónimo* records the first recipe for a food fried in an egg batter, *bādhinjān muʻaffar* (eggplant).[6] This is probably the origin of both tempura (known to have been introduced to Japan by the Portuguese) and the fried fish of a fish and chip shop (a recipe brought to England by Sephardic Jews and long known as Jewish fish). A cuisine less giddy about throwing eggs into everything might not have invented egg batter.

At least our doctors can be grateful that the Moors never sold anybody else on their dish of chicken with 30 eggs.

Notes

1. Ibn Razin al-Tujibi, *Fadālat al-Khiwān*, MS We 1207, Staatsbibliothek Preussischer Kulturbesitz, Berlin; *laun ākhar*, p. 57a.
2. Ambrosio Huici Miranda, *Traducción Española de un Manuscrito Anónimo del Siglo XIII sobre la Cocina Hispano-Magribi* (Madrid: Imprenta y Editorial Maestre, 1968); Arabic text ed. Ambrosio Huici Miranda, in *Revista del Instituto (Egipcio) de Estudios Islámicos en Madrid*, vol. 9, 1961, pp. 14–255.
3. *Fadālat al-Khiwān*; *laun ākhar*, p. 70b; Fudalat al-Khiwan 'Les Délices de la Table et les Meilleurs Genres de Mets,' translated by Mohamed Mezzine and Laila Benkirane (Fez: Publications Association Fès-Saïs, 1997); *un autre genre*, p. 200.
4. *Kitāb Wasf al-Atʻima al-Muʻtāda*, translated by the author in *Medieval Arab Cookery* (Totnes: Prospect Books, 2001).
5. *Traducción Española de un Manuscrito Anónimo*, p. 80; Arabic text, p. 146.
6. Op. cit., p. 86; Arabic text, p. 155.

'The Ultimate in Cookery': the Soufflé's Rise Alongside Feminism in the 1960s

Phyllis Thompson Reid

In April 1967, a soufflé rose grandly from its dish, positioned in front of a rustic wire basket of eggs, commanding the cover of *Gourmet;* the accompanying recipe opened with the words, 'Culinary reputations frequently rise or fall on the making of a soufflé, the delicate and utterly delicious creation that is one of the great glories of French cuisine.'[1] Six months later, President Lyndon Johnson signed new legislation to prohibit discrimination based on gender; six months previous, 300 middle-class women had founded the National Organization for Women. Although the women's movement is widely blamed (or credited) with releasing millions of women from their kitchens and into the workplace, it took place at a moment of new emphasis on the production and consumption of complex French food in the home. The culture of elaborate cookery that sprang up in the 1960s functioned as a counter-discourse to feminism, helping to articulate the tricky compromise between self-expression and traditional gender conformity. Middle-class American women were cooking ever-more sophisticated food, but for better or worse they were still in the kitchen.

During periods of social unrest one often sees the reassertion of traditional gender roles: a presumed continuity of gender *difference* can seem to anchor unstable worlds. Food proves a useful medium for this negotiation. Gender inevitably interfaces with food, which, as anthropologist Carole Counihan has argued, 'is a product and mirror of the organization of society on both the broadest and most intimate levels.'[2] Daily food preparation is repetitive and pragmatic, the performance of routine and entrenched ritual. For this reason it produces culture, inexorably, if almost invisibly.

This simultaneous invisibility and prominence make food and culinary norms particularly valuable as transmitters of cultural values. Did the raising of the culinary bar during the Women's Movement serve to reassure America that Mom was still in the kitchen? Or did it create a new kind of cook, one empowered by a new sense of mastery? What did it mean to emphasize the status-reaping aspects of cooking at this moment? And what implications did this have beyond the kitchen?

Paradoxically, while the notion of women's subordination within the home was key for second-wave feminists – those active in the final third of the twentieth century – neither they nor academic historians of women have written more than glancingly about kitchens and cooking during the period; the issues arising from the relation-

The Soufflé's Rise Alongside Feminism in the 1960s

ship of gender and food that have received consistent scholarly attention are eating disorders and body image, and the gendered aspects of nutrition and famine. Arlene Avakian suggests that, 'Because cooking has been conceptualized as part of [women's] oppression, "liberation" has often meant freedom from being connected to food.'[3] This comment might be extended to encompass 'liberation' from a fully articulated intellectual relationship to food as well. Second-wave feminism was so focused on improving public roles for women, or, for radical feminists, on repudiating traditional forms of private life altogether, that the mechanics of women's relationship to food-production during the period have gone largely unexamined. This is striking, as the class of women – white, educated, and middle class – most visible in the movement is the same one for whom cooking expectations and aspirations changed most notably, and to whom elaborate kitchen techniques were marketed most aggressively.

Cooking has had a dual status in women's lives. Firstly, it is a duty. Women continue to be associated symbolically with kitchens, as well as to be to be responsible for the vast majority of all parts of food preparation, including menu planning, cookbook and ingredient purchasing, preparation, serving, cleaning up, and the maintenance and stocking of the kitchen itself.[4] Sociologist Marjorie DeVault has suggested that

> Activities such as feeding, which members of the society have learned to associate strongly with gender, come to seem like 'natural' expressions of gender. This observation does not imply that all women engage in such activity… but as long as feeding is understood, collectively, as somehow more 'womanly' than 'manly,' the work stands as one kind of activity in which 'womanliness' may be at issue.[5]

Secondly, cooking is a forum for self-expression and the exhibition of craft. Many see it as a compensation for the more tedious aspects of housework. Creativity can be a way of transforming what is otherwise at risk of being invisible labor. The soufflé – ethereal, often sweet, and based on that most female of symbols, the egg – and with its reputation as a risky undertaking, requiring finesse and expertise, and its potential to produce social status through its ephemeral glory, is an apt metaphor for the fragility of that dual status.

******

Soufflés first appeared in the 1750s; the great nineteenth-century French chef Antonin Carême called them 'the queen of hot pastries.'[6] Eliza Leslie, in her immensely popular 1840 *Directions for Cookery*, included an omelette soufflé, with the accompanying suggestion that 'the safest way of avoiding a failure in an omelette soufflé is to hire a French cook to come to your kitchen with his own utensils and ingredients, and make and bake it himself, while the first part of the dinner is progressing in the dining room.'⁷ Isabella Beeton's 1861 guide (published in England but widely available in America) warned that soufflés 'are the prettiest, but most difficult of all entremets.'⁸ Fannie Farmer's 1896 *Boston Cooking-School Cook Book* was the first major homegrown volume to introduce the soufflé proper to Americans: 'serve at once,' it noted crisply.⁹ Future publications, including later editions of that very cookbook, were less restrained in their instructions, and the formula of praising the soufflé's virtues, ventriloquizing warnings about its trickiness, and then offering assurances has followed its recipes well beyond the period when oven temperatures became reliable – in fact, up until the present day. A 2006 *New York Times Magazine* article titled 'Recipes for Disaster' refers to the soufflé as a 'moody beauty' which is 'among the most feared kitchen failures.'¹⁰ Myra Waldo's 1954 cookbook, *Serve at Once: The Soufflé Cookbook*, follows this program paradigmatically. Waldo calls the soufflé 'the one dish that invariably excites both the appetite and the imagination … Perfectly prepared, properly presented, it is one of the high points of culinary art.' Then she issues the customary warning-cum-reassurance: 'Most people assume that soufflé preparation is beyond their abilities [but] … it can be mastered by anyone who can cook even simple dishes.'¹¹

Her actual advice, however, is less soothing. 'How long to beat the whites? Actually, there is no way to tell except by examination of the whites as the beating continues.'¹² Because of the variance in ovens, she warns that the 'times specified in the recipes can be only approximate … Thus, when you come to the last five minutes of baking time, an inspection is in order. The kitchen window or outside door should be closed when you open the oven door. Open it slowly and do not let it slam shut … Have your guests at the table, ready to eat the soufflé; a soufflé will not await the guests.'¹³ But it will all be worth the anxiety: 'There is apparently no other dish that pleases the guest as does a soufflé – the ultimate in cookery!'¹⁴

Julia Child, who owned a copy of Waldo's book, echoed her rhetoric for the second-wave generation: 'The soufflé is the egg at its most magnificent. How glorious it is when borne to the table, its head rising dramatically out of its dish, and swaying voluptuously as it is set down … a loving treat for your most favorite dinner guests.'¹⁵ But she is far more clinical in her methodology. A soufflé, Child wrote, is simply 'a sauce containing a flavoring or purée into which stiffly beaten egg whites are incorporated. It is turned into a mold and baked in the oven until it puffs up and the top browns.'¹⁶ You will be 'the boss of the big cheese soufflé,' Child promised on her TV show.¹⁷

Even the assurances about soufflés are in fact warnings: they reinscribe an anxiety that the individual cook did not necessarily have to begin with. Why not just give good directions? Why do so many recipes repeat the admonitions, so few echo Childs's note that the dish can be completely assembled and left for an hour before baking? The 'boss' of the soufflé remains watchfully in the kitchen; she is quiet, knowledgeable, and, most of all, obedient, following directions precisely and alert to the specter of failure. The idea of flopped soufflé as the archetypal kitchen disaster was so well established as to provide the subtitle for a self-help book in the seventies, *How to Keep Your Soufflé Up and Your Depression Quotient Down*.[18] Even Harold McGee's scientific treatise *On Food and Cooking: The Science and Lore of the Kitchen* (2004) feels obliged to give a disclaimer for the soufflé's 'reputation for being difficult.'[19] 'Beware of drafts,' warned the 1964 *Joy of Cooking*, which also directly characterized the soufflé itself as a troublesome woman, a 'prima donna.'[20]

******

Divvying up the world of food by gender is neither new nor specific to America. Claude Lévi-Strauss suggested that there is a universal binary distinction between roast and boiled food, which correlates to gender: in Western culture, men cook food that directly contacts the fire (and this they do outdoors, in public) and women are responsible for more mediated cooking that takes indoors in a domestic space and separates food from the primal element of fire.[21] Barbecue indeed was codified in 1950s America – a complement to the spurt in competitive female cookery – as the ultimate in *male* cookery. To barbecue meat means a special occasion, a treat and celebration. Barbecues take place outside the house, and require special male equipment and expensive ingredients, most notably steak. Women tend to prepare salads, desserts, and to do the washing up – in other words, the majority of the work.[22] James Beard wrote in his *Complete Book of Outdoor Cookery* that grilling 'is primarily a man's job and … a woman, if she's smart, will keep it that way. The ladies can do the planning and the marketing, the preparation and the hostessing, but the man will do the actual cooking over the coals.'[23] By 'smart,' Beard surely means non-confrontational and hard-working.

The flip side of that set of associations is that Victorian etiquette books prohibited 'young ladies' from eating cheese, game, and savories, as well as from drinking, most likely so that their breath would be fresh, 'pleasing to men.'[24] Even today, Americans associate 'lighter' foods like lettuce and yogurt with femaleness, and 'heavier' or more pungent ones like smelly cheeses, beef, beer, and potatoes with maleness; similarly, hearty eating is male-coded; picky, sparing, or 'dainty' eating female. When one takes cultural representations into account, as well as personally-reported preferences, the strongest associations are of men with red meat and women with sweets.[25]

The 1964 *Joy of Cooking* made the comparison of soufflé and woman literal: 'If your guests are assembled, prepare a soufflé. If not, it may be like the beauty Horace Walpole commented on: "She is pretty with the bloom of youth but has no features and her beauty cannot last."'[26] The 1951 edition too had made this equation, 'The soufflé is the "misunderstood woman" of the culinary world. This simple and useful everyday dish is held in awe by many people who hold an exaggerated idea of the difficulties of its composition … It is at all times delicate and tempting, so take your courage in your hands and try it out.'[27]

The Soufflé's Rise Alongside Feminism in the 1960s

******

Why *were* so many women willing to take that courage – and whisk – in hand? What would this mean within the context of a country swept by mass-movement feminism? The answer most readily to hand is that there was (and is) enormous variety in the expression of feminist impulses. Some women found it satisfying to research their food, to make it with learned skill. Some cooked elaborately because of the sensory pleasures afforded by doing so. Most – doubtless, for it is rare to theorize one's own daily life exhaustively – simply cooked because they had to. Some, I'd like to suggest, were soufflé-ing eggs rather than boiling them because new cultural pressures asked them to participate in competitive social-class production via the kitchen.

Little in the public discourse suggested that there might be great meaning in *how* women did their cooking. In one of the few second-wave feminist tracts to address domestic details, Alice Rossi proposed that a woman raised in an equal society would both recognize the 'intrinsic pleasures' found in 'fine cooking or needlework' and see domestic work on the whole as 'best gotten done as quickly and efficiently as possible;' this theoretical woman's brother would be able to 'cook with the same easy skills.'[28]

On the whole however, liberal feminists were more focused on eliminating discrimination in the workplace than in the home. Second-wave feminism recognized the insufficiency of formal political equality and called for juridical and social equality as well, focusing on male control of economic life. The solutions they proposed focused on the public arena, and on ending discrimination and improving opportunities for women. Conscious too of the consequences of the unequal division of labor within the home, second-wave feminists had a 'passion to free themselves from exclusive domesticity' and insisted they could have both work and a family.[29] The ideal of female altruism was also dismantled by feminists: women's selflessness, so lauded by men and women alike in the earlier fight for the vote, came to be seen as the result of socialization (not as an essential, biological characteristic). In other words, women were not better suited by nature to housework and child care, but had been taught those skills and attitudes.

For their part, American radical feminists were opposed to assimilating women into the mainstream. They believed that NOW's narrow focus on formal equality with men both ignored 'the fundamental problem – women's subordination within the home' and 'assumed that equality in an unjust society' was a worthwhile goal.[30] A few radical groups did focus on re-imagining domestic life entirely, in many cases advocating for wages for housework.[31] The re-socialization efforts of radical feminists, however, like those of liberal feminists, failed; most men did not pick up the burdens of child care, cleaning, or cooking, and neither did the state. By the end of the decade many women radicals who had experimented with shifting the responsibilities of housework had resumed their prior roles. As historian Barbara Haber observed,

The Soufflé's Rise Alongside Feminism in the 1960s

'Sheer survival often seems to dictate that we return to jobs, aspirations, relationships, and living arrangements that resemble those from which we once fled in self-righteous and passionate rejection.'[32] Many feminists left the issue of housework alone, contenting themselves with asserting that privatized, female-performed housework served to maintain women's isolation and men's pre-eminence in the public arena, but seldom examining the specific material expectations of sub-categories of housework in a fine-grained way. 'Feminist' and 'housewife' seemed opposite poles and domestic work went under-theorized. This is surprising, as while in developed countries today, women still spend twice as much time as men at housework, in the 1960s, they spent six times as much time on housework on men.[33]

However, between 1926 and 1968 women came to spend about three hours a week less on *food* preparation (time spent on managerial tasks accounts for the lack of dip in the overall figures.) Processed foods did save time.[34] A community cookbook put together by members of NOW contained no soufflés. It was community cookbook along standard Junior League lines: A-B-C Dessert Salad, Beef Stroganoff, and Low Fat Swedish Meatballs. The compendium as a whole showed a notable reliance on time-saving processed ingredients such as cake mix and canned pimentos.[35] 'Five Can Hot Dish' recipes and the like still dominated not just feminist, but community and commemorative cookbooks throughout the 1970s. One headnote for this delicacy read 'This is a good recipe for a career lady or one involved in community service. If the ingredients are in the kitchen, the recipe is quick and easy!'[36] The combination of such concoctions and ready-made dinners led the likes of food critic John Mariani to complain that women and some men had taken up cooking with 'a real passion' in the early 1970s, but that then 'the Women's Liberation Movement shamed their sisters out of the kitchen and into the workforce.'[37]

******

It was not always the case that feminism turned its back on the kitchen. Alongside the late-nineteenth- and early-twentieth-century suffrage movement – which asserted that giving women the vote would necessarily result in social improvements across the board, thanks to women's presumably elevated moral natures – existed an entire home economics branch of feminist thinkers, known as the Domestic Science movement, which held that all household activities should be approached scientifically. Ideally, this would have increased the efficiency of households and the prestige according to housewives and other domestic workers, and caused specialization. Charlotte Perkins Gilman, one of the movement's originators, cultivated a particular disdain for '"fancy cookery," – a thing as far removed from true artistic development as a swinging ice-pitcher from a Greek vase.... human labor and time and skill are wasted in producing what is neither pure food nor pure pleasure, but an artificial performance, to be appreciated only by the virtuoso.' Gilman found the training of 'both the wife and the servant' to be wasteful, and called for a socialist-style collectivization of household work. In such an arrangement she argued, 'the food would be better, and would cost less.'[38]

Collective living never took off, but Domestic Science did open the door for 'efficiency experts' who advocated a reliance on technology, not female work hours. Ironically, as technology improved, expectations increased apace, and the time women devoted to housework remained relatively steady throughout the century.[39] Yet at the same time a discourse on the '"fun" and "glamour"' of housework attempted to reconstitute it as somehow *not* labor, but rather a creative pleasure.[40]

Cookbooks from the 1910s onward defined cooking in particular as a creative act. These books were aimed at middle-class white women, who had en masse recently found themselves to be without domestic help.[41] The food suggested was creative indeed. Victorian Americans were already convinced that women's food should be dainty and delicate, but the idea became a 'craze' in the early twentieth century. The food advocated by the popular press as suitable for women's consumption was enormously complex, hopelessly fussy, and nutritionally inconsequential – for example, rose petal or violet sandwiches, an enormous variety of cunning teacakes, elaborate Jell-O molds.[42] Culinary accounts of this period have not noted the irony that women campaigning for political citizenship were being urged to snack upon flowers. The Domestic Science movement's emphasis on 'dainty' meals created out of sanitary ingredients in modern, 'scientific' kitchens not incidentally helped create a market for processed commercial food products – billed as the ultimate in science and sanitation.[43]

These 'improvements' did not convince everyone. No matter how attractive and hygienic food might be, women were still making it, in their own kitchens, every day. Simone de Beauvoir, for example, complained of the 'sordid materialism' that was woman's lot. 'Few tasks are more like the torture of Sisyphus than housework, with its endless repetition.' Cooking was the high point of this drudgery, mostly because it allowed the housewife out into the world to do her shopping, but also because it had the potential for 'revelation and creation; and a woman can find special satisfaction in a successful cake or a flaky pastry, for not everyone can do it: one must have the gift.' Yet even these small triumphs were fated for consumption: 'a continual renunciation is required of the woman whose operations are completed only in their destruction.'[44]

During the period in which Beauvoir was writing, actual cooking became less burdensome, or debased and unfulfilling, depending on one's perspective. Packaged, frozen, and semi-prepared foods were available in unprecedented quantity (if notoriously low quality.) The TV Dinner, the ultimate convenience food, was introduced under that brand name by C. A. Swanson & Sons in 1953, appeared, as if in cahoots, the same year Beauvoir's text appeared in English. Drudgery-diminishing as such inventions may have been, they seriously impacted taste. Mary McFeely suggests that the era's willingness to accept canned and processed ingredients and ersatz substitutions stemmed from 'ignorance of the real thing.'[45] (Yet it is possible some palates might have adjusted, or women have found the liberation from measuring spoons a bonus worth retaining.) These tendencies, however, led journalist Leslie Brenner to

The Soufflé's Rise Alongside Feminism in the 1960s

finger 1957 as the 'nadir' of American cooking, despite a climate of 'increasing cultural sophistication' including a new appreciation of the foreign.[46]

Despite the era's reliance on processed foods, the 1950s media continually trumpeted cooking as a creative outlet. Furthermore, ensuring solidarity by cooking a good dinner for one's family every night was constructed specifically as the fulfilling, patriotic duty of a Cold-War wife, whose proper life centered entirely on her home.[47]

******

Under pressure from prominent Democratic Party women, President John F. Kennedy appointed a Commission on the Status of Women in 1961. Not surprisingly, although its language was conciliatory, the report identified significant sex discrimination throughout the employment sector. On its heels, the Congress finally passed the Equal Pay Act, which had been pending for two decades. Into this climate burst Betty Friedan's polemic, *The Feminine Mystique,* in February 1963. Friedan argued that the 'system,' not women themselves was sick: kitchens were prisons, housework demoralizing, and women unfulfilled, suffering from 'the problem with no name.'[48] In her autobiography, Friedan claimed that her book had proved 'threatening to women,' more so than to men, inferring that women felt more implicated by its claims.[49] Whether women were unsettled or not, they bought it: *The Feminine Mystique* became the best-selling non-fiction book of the year in 1964. Friedan was deeply opposed to housework; indeed, she went to great lengths to avoid it in her own life. One of her proposals was to simply hire out the work to maids – in other words to shift the unwelcome burden to working-class women without correcting the low status of the work whatsoever. (Although Friedan generalized about all women in her polemical statements, her data dealt primarily with findings from her class of Smith College classmates – overwhelmingly white, middle-class, and, obviously, educated.) A few years later, Germaine Greer, in *The Female Eunuch,* suggested that women 'represent the most oppressed class of life-contracted unpaid workers, for whom slaves is not too melodramatic a description.'[50]

Cooking itself came under specific fire. In her tirade of a poem 'What's that Smell in the Kitchen?' Marge Piercy defended bad cooking, declaring that 'burning dinner is not incompetence but war.'[51] More mundanely, the era's best-selling cookbooks continued to emphasize 'modern short-cut recipes' and 'jiffy meals' suitable for the 'busy lady.'[52] Culinary historian Jessamyn Neuhaus discusses Peg Bracken's *The I Hate To Cook Book* (1970), a runaway bestseller that sold three million copies within its first decade, as articulating the female 'discourse of discontent' with the domestic role. Bracken declared that 'some activities become no less painful through repetition: childbearing, paying taxes, cooking.' She advocated a return to convenience foods and set the bar low on kitchen achievements. Tellingly, she assumed her female readership bore daily responsibility for meals and never suggested getting help with the labor from other household members as a solution.[53]

The Soufflé's Rise Alongside Feminism in the 1960s

Not everyone felt like Bracken, obviously. One psychologist noted that 'many a housewife is *saddened* to learn that with a package mix she can make an angel food cake two inches higher than the one she had previously made from one cookbook and twelve left-over egg whites.'[54] This essay was published in 1963, the same year Julia Child – a figure just as dynamic as Friedan – first appeared on public television as *The French Chef* with a counter-proposal: cooking ought to be elevated, not eliminated.

Child didn't offer any help in making cooking either quick or easy. She did promise that she could make good, true, French cooking understandable. 'Anyone can cook anything with the right instruction,' she promised in the introduction to *Mastering the Art of French Cooking*, which sold more than one hundred thousand copies in its first year of publication, 1961, and was reprinted forty times.[55] The ground had been prepared for her message. Since the eighteenth century, French food had dominated professional high-status cooking throughout Europe, a prejudice exported to America with the invention of the restaurant, and more widely disseminated with its proliferation in the first half of the nineteenth century.[56] French *haute cuisine* 'reoccupied its place at the pinnacle of status' when the Kennedys hired a French chef for the White House, a fact which Child herself credited with having created the environment for her success.[57] Child made this elevated cuisine accessible via descriptive headnotes, authoritative, clear, and precise discussions of classical technique, and a guarantee that practice made perfect. She was not interested in nutrition, family harmony, household budgets, or speed of preparation. Rather, she insisted upon top-quality ingredients, professional technique, time, close attention, and confidence. For those dependent on convenience foods this was something of a shake-up. But America was poised for it: observing that supermarkets now carried 'fancy foods from ... kangaroo tails to pickled rooster combs,' *Time* suggested in 1966 that 'Julia is just right for the times.'[58]

As sociologist Gary Fine explains, because 'no widely accepted "theory" of food exists; food talk is not privileged discourse. As a result, cooks must continually construct and reconstruct culinary meanings for an unknowing or skeptical audience.'[59] Cookbooks and cooking shows are a kind of prescriptive literature, suggesting the proper technique for performing class and gender positions, in addition to being instruction manuals. They, and Child's productions were no exception, tend to presume the same middle-class audience. Child's books and programs constructed a very particular type of cook: competent, calm, and sophisticated. She did not intend to construct a gendered cook, but given the environment of the time, that could not be helped.

While Child herself was a staunch Cambridge Democrat who personally supported Planned Parenthood, even doing cooking demonstrations as fundraisers for them, she refused the label of feminist throughout her life and repudiated suggestions that her work addressed women in particular. Beyond this blind spot, she also insisted that men were better cooks: 'A man in a chef's apron is a fine sight ... They are marvelous.

The Soufflé's Rise Alongside Feminism in the 1960s

They're more daring, while women are often timid and tend to get bogged down in detail. I think one can see from history that the great creators are men.'[60]

But to her credit, unlike the bestselling Betty Crocker cookbooks of the 1950s, Child never mentioned husband-pleasing as a goal for cooking. Her goal was more direct: make the food according to proper technique, and make it delicious. She reminded a reporter that her attitude was entirely gender-neutral: 'We never talk about women cooking. It is PEOPLE who like to cook, and we don't care who they are – race, color, sex, animals, ANYBODY.'[61] Her program, she insisted, was not aimed at 'plain old housewives [who] get plenty of encouragement and recipes from the daily newspapers.'[62] But who did she think had sufficiently flexible time to cook her recipes on a regular basis? Of course Child was not acknowledging that although she did inspire a handful of well-documented men, it was women who were buying her books, women doing the cooking – the fancy cooking she taught them, as well as the more daily drudgery 'encouraged' by newspaper food columns. Whether she liked it or not, the whisk-wielders of the 1970s were overwhelmingly female.[63]

But if Child's message to housewives was not particularly encouraging unless one truly enjoyed the process of fine French cooking (or simply read her books or watched her shows for entertainment value), the example she set was without a doubt especially meaningful for women. The only woman in her Cordon Bleu class, she went on to make her career in a world that could be quite hostile to women. The Culinary Institute of America (CIA), the most prestigious culinary school in the United States, only began admitting women in 1970, fifty years after it opened. In the 1970s, many professional kitchens refused to hire women altogether, other than the odd woman in a pastry department, and their machismo-heavy climates were often hostile to women.[64] It is crucial though to remember that Child never ran a restaurant – she was a well-trained home cook with a professional life in food.

Child's books and shows both helped create and responded to a growing culture of culinary sophistication. She did not enter the field alone – most prominently Craig Claiborne and James Beard accompanied her crusade for better cooking in America. Writers such as M. F. K. Fisher and the Englishwoman Elizabeth David also elevated the level of discussion of food, emphasizing its connections to *terroir*, as well as to sensuality and pleasure of all sorts. The circulation of *Gourmet*, which had been founded as a general interest magazine with an emphasis on travel in 1941, boomed after it refocused more exclusively on food in the 1960s.

The sort of eating detailed by *Gourmet* and its ilk functions as a class marker: to both pursue hedonistic pleasure yet retain a disciplined relationship to one's body differentiates the middle class from both the conservative restraint of their forebears and a working-class looseness. Classical French cooking was ideally suited to this project: as Pierre Bourdieu put it, 'the taste for rare, aristocratic foods points to a traditional cuisine, rich in expensive or rare products (fresh vegetables, meat) ... the very refinement of the things consumed, with quality more important than quantity ... shift[s] the emphasis from substance and function to form and manner.'⁶⁵ This shift in focus, it must be stressed, required great quantities of time to create. This cuisine is not the simple salads Alice Waters later made famous: this is highly processed food – the hand of the cook is necessary at every stage, ingredients are *transformed* through work. A soufflé bears little resemblance to a boiled egg.

The usual explanation offered by both food historians and feminists is that women who pursue elaborate cookery do so because they like to do it. However, sociologist Marjorie DeVault's work in the 1980s showed that the emphasis on creativity and experimentation was correlated to professional households, as was relying on textual sources for cooking knowledge. But although cooking is usually classed as the second-most enjoyable kind of domestic work (after caring for children), there is no correlation between the performance of complex cookery and individual women's enjoyment of cooking: that is, wives of the professional class feel obliged to produce 'interesting' food regardless of whether they like to cook. DeVault's surveys found that husbands of this class are both more likely to share cooking labor to some degree and to 'pressure their wives toward more elaborate routines.'⁶⁶

One group that fell famously prey to the late 1960s emphasis on fine cooking was that of academics. Literary critic Elaine Showalter recalls that in the early Sixties an interest in food was considered 'crass and anti-intellectual' on the East Coast; but in California the 'hedonism' of an academic lifestyle with 'many-coursed dinner parties of elaborate dishes' had already caught on. It soon spread East, and at Princeton Showalter and her female cohort of faculty and faculty wives 'slaved over *tians*, *confits*, *bombes glacées*, and foods puréed, marinated, caramelized, glazed, steeped, tossed, and poached.'⁶⁷ Betty Fussell's account of her life as an academic wife concurs with Showalter's: women competed via elaborate dinner parties, and 'when a hostess set forth a *salmis de faisan*, she supplied footnotes on what a *salmis* was … The ritual of presentation required responsive *aaahs*.⁶⁸ … Cooking – the one activity, besides tennis, in which housewives were encouraged to excel – had become a magnificent obsession.'⁶⁹ Writer Nora Ephron similarly reports, 'Food acquired a … gloss of snobbery it had hitherto possessed only in certain upper-income groups … Hostesses were expected to know that iceberg lettuce was *déclassé* and tuna fish casseroles *de trop*.'⁷⁰ And cooking teacher Joyce Goldstein recalls that in the 1960s, 'the only thing people wanted was gourmet French. If you wanted to learn to cook, that's what you had to do.'⁷¹

Women's work was very much at stake in these productions. As Fussell puts it, 'All dishes, especially showpieces like soufflés, must appear as if by miracle … although it was understood among the women guests that each would assist from time to time in shuttling dishes to and fro, no one knew better than we did who'd done the work, and just how much work it was.'⁷² In short, a new cultural imperative calling for more intricate food, requiring both greater skills and more time to produce, was behind women's production of showpieces. It is fitting both that the ever-symbolic egg featured so prominently, and that the *ur*-dish, the soufflé, was figured as so tricky, so fraught with peril. As the 1965 edition of *Fannie Farmer* put it, 'Serve a soufflé the moment it is baked. A soufflé sturdy enough to stand without falling is not delicate enough to be perfect.'[73] A soufflé, it can and has been said, is ladylike.

******

Feminism drove some women away from cooking and also allowed others to take it more seriously: yet this latter accomplishment, though much heralded in food histories, has a conflicted legacy. Without shifting the labor, or the culture at large taking food preparation more seriously as an endeavor, re-conceptualizing this form of work as self-fulfillment merely makes it more tolerable without clearing the way for other choices of work. Engaging in elaborate home cooking is a voluntary activity, but it takes place within a discursive context, one which nags its readership about the perils and glories of participation, and then cheerily encourages such labor for the professional class (and especially for women) and associates it with status, but which does not reward it in the market. Drawing 'distinctions' in the arena of food has been a form of labor consistently accorded overwhelmingly to women; yet the ironies of this labor remain little noticed. It surfaces only in memoir. As Betty Fussell recalled,

> The ... soufflé [was] the piece de resistànce of our show-off menus, and the emblem of our paradox. Literally, the French phrase meant the climax of a series, or a piece of artillery with staying power. A dessert soufflé was a good climax, all right, but its staying power was nil. It held only two or three minutes before collapse. And what was it, after all? An airy nothing, inflated for a momentary display ... time's victim, not its resister.[74]

As Child noted on her show on the soufflé, 'the important thing is to time it so neither one of you collapses.'[75] In contrast, a perfect inch-thick steak is grilled in seven minutes, and holds up quite nicely.

Bibiliography

Avakian, Arlene Voski, ed. *Through the Kitchen Window: Women Explore the Intimate Meanings of Food and Cooking*, Boston: Beacon Press, 1997.
Avakian, Arlene Voski, and Barbara Haber, eds., *From Betty Crocker to Feminist Food Studies: Critical Perspectives on Women and Food*, Amherst: University of Massachusetts Press, 2005.
Beauvoir, Simone de, *The Second Sex*, New York: Vintage Books, 1989.
Beeton, Isabella, *Beeton's Book of Household Management*, A First Edition Facsimile ed., New York: Farrar Straus and Giroux, 1969.
Bourdieu, Pierre, *Distinction: A Social Critique of the Judgment of Taste*, London: Routledge & Kegan Paul, 1986.
Brenner, Leslie, *American Appetite: The Coming of Age of a Cuisine*, New York: Avon Books, Inc., 1999.

Child, Julia, Louisette Bertholle, and Simone Beck, *Mastering the Art of French Cooking*, Vol. 1, Updated, New York: Alfred A. Knopf, 1992.

Child, Julia, and David Nussbaum, *Julia's Kitchen Wisdom: Essential Techniques and Recipes from a Lifetime of Cooking*, New York: Alfred A. Knopf, 2000.

Cooper, Ann, *A Woman's Place Is in the Kitchen: The Evolution of Woman Chefs*, New York: Van Nostrand Reinhold, 1998.

Counihan, Carole, *Food in the USA: A Reader*, New York: Routledge, 2002.

——, *The Anthropology of Food and Body: Gender, Meaning, and Power*, New York and London: Routledge, 1999.

Counihan, Carole, and Penny Van Esterik, *Food and Culture: A Reader*, New York: Routledge, 1997.

Cowan, Ruth Schwartz, *More Work for Mother: The Ironies of Household Technology from the Open Hearth to the Microwave*, New York: Basic Books, 1983.

Dalla Costa, Mariarosa, and Selma James, *The Power of Women and the Subversion of the Community*, 2nd ed. Bristol, Eng.: Falling Wall Press, 1973.

Davis, Dawn, *If You Can Stand the Heat: Tales from Chefs and Restaurants*, New York: Penguin Books, 1999.

DeVault, Marjorie, *Feeding the Family: The Social Organization of Caring as Gendered Work*, Women in Culture and Society, Chicago: University of Chicago Press, 1991.

Dornenburg, Andrew and Karen Page, *Becoming a Chef*, New York: John Wiley and Sons, Inc., 1995.

Echols, Alice, *Daring to Be Bad: Radical Feminism in America, 1967–1975*, American Culture, Minneapolis: University of Minnesota Press, 1989.

Ferguson, Priscilla Parkhurst, *Accounting for Taste: The Triumph of French Cuisine*, Chicago and London: University of Chicago Press, 2004.

Fine, Gary Alan, *Kitchens: The Culture of Restaurant Work*, Berkeley: University of California Press, 1996.

Fitch, Noel Riley, *Appetite for Life: The Biography of Julia Child*, New York: Doubleday, 1997.

Freedman, Estelle B., *No Turning Back: The History of Feminism and the Future of Women*, New York: Ballantine, 2002.

Friedan, Betty, *Life So Far*, New York: Simon & Schuster, 2000.

——, *The Feminine Mystique*, New York: W.W. Norton, 2001.

Fussell, Betty Harper, *My Kitchen Wars*, New York: North Point Press, 1999.

Gilman, Charlotte Perkins, *Women and Economics: A Study of the Economic Relation between Men and Women as a Factor in Social Evolution*, Berkeley: University of California Press, 1998.

Greer, Germaine, *The Female Eunuch*, London: MacGibbon & Kee, 1970.

Haber, Barbara, 'Is Personal Life Still a Political Issue?' *Feminist Studies* 5, no. 3, 'Toward a New Feminism for the Eighties' (1979): 417–30.

Hochschild, Arlie Russell, and Anne Machung, *The Second Shift: Working Parents and the Revolution at Home*, New York: Viking, 1989.

Inness, Sherrie A., *Dinner Roles: American Women and Culinary Culture*, Iowa City: University of Iowa Press, 2001.

Johnson, Lesley, and Justine Lloyd, *Sentenced to Everyday Life: Feminism and the Housewife*, Oxford and New York: Berg, 2004.

Kuper, Jessica, *The Anthropologists' Cookbook*, London: Routledge and K. Paul, 1977.

Leslie, Eliza, *Directions for Cookery, in Its Various Branches*, 11th ed., Philadelphia: Carey & Hart, 1840.

Lévi-Strauss, Claude, *The Raw and the Cooked: Introduction to a Science of Mythology*, Chicago: University of Chicago Press, 1983.

MacLauchlan, Andrew, *The Making of a Pastry Chef: Recipes and Inspirations from America's Best Pastry Chefs*, New York: John Wiley and Sons, Inc., 1999.

Mariani, John, *America Eats Out: An Illustrated History of Restaurants, Taverns, Coffee Shops, Speakeasies,*

The Soufflé's Rise Alongside Feminism in the 1960s

  and Other Establishments That Have Fed Us for 350 Years, New York: William Morrow and Company, Inc., 1991.
May, Elaine Tyler, *Homeward Bound: American Families in the Cold War Era*, New York: Basic Books, 1988.
McFeely, Mary Drake, *Can She Bake a Cherry Pie?: American Women and the Kitchen in the Twentieth Century*, Amherst: University of Massachusetts Press, 2000.
McGee, Harold, *On Food and Cooking: The Science and Lore of the Kitchen*, completely revised and updated, 1st Scribner rev. ed. New York: Scribner, 2004.
Mendelson, Anne, *Stand Facing the Stove: The Story of the Women Who Gave America the Joy of Cooking*, New York: H. Holt, 1996.
Mintz, Sidney Wilfred, *Sweetness and Power: The Place of Sugar in Modern History*, New York: Penguin Books, 1986.
National Organization for, Women, and Chapter Greater Champaign Area, *Now We're Cooking*, Champaign, Ill.: National Organization for Women Greater Champaign Area Chapter, 1965.
Neuhaus, Jessamyn, *Manly Meals and Mom's Home Cooking: Cookbooks and Gender in Modern America*, Baltimore: The Johns Hopkins University Press, 2003.
O'Neill, Molly, 'Food Porn,' *Columbia Journalism Review*, September/October 2003, 38–45.
Oakley, Ann, *The Sociology of Housework*, London: Robertson, 1974.
Piercy, Marge, *Stone, Paper, Knife*, New York: Knopf, 1983.
Rombauer, Irma S., and Marion Rombauer Becker, *Joy of Cooking*, Indianapolis, Ind.: The Bobbs-Merrill Company, Inc., 1964. Reprint, 1967.
———, *Joy of Cooking*, 3rd ed. Indianapolis, Ind. and New York: Bobbs-Merrill Company, 1951. Reprint, 1952.
Root, Waverley, and Richard De Rochemont, *Eating in America: A History*, Hopewell, N. J.: The Ecco Press, 1995.
Rosen, Ruth, *The World Split Open: How the Modern Women's Movement Changed America*, New York: Viking, 2000.
Schenone, Laura, *A Thousand Years over a Hot Stove: A History of American Women Told through Food, Recipes, and Remembrances*, New York and London: W.W. Norton, 2003.
Shapiro, Laura, *Perfection Salad: Women and Cooking at the Turn of the Century*, New York: Farrar Straus and Giroux, 1986.
Showalter, Elaine, 'My Dinner with Derrida,' *The American Prospect*, January 1, 2002, 36–39.
Spang, Rebecca L., *The Invention of the Restaurant: Paris and Modern Gastronomic Culture*, Cambridge, Mass.: Harvard University Press, 2000.
Visser, Margaret, *The Rituals of Dinner: The Origins, Evolution, Eccentricities, and Meaning of Table Manners*, New York: Grove Weidenfeld, 1991.
Waldo, Myra, *Serve at Once: The Soufflé Cookbook*, New York: Crowell, 1954.
Watson, James L., and Melissa L. Caldwell, *The Cultural Politics of Food and Eating: A Reader*, Blackwell Readers in Anthropology, 8, Malden, MA: Blackwell Pub., 2005.
Zanger, Mark H., *The American History Cookbook*, Westport, Conn.: Greenwood Press, 2003.

Notes

1. 'Soufflés on the Rise,' *Gourmet*, April 1967, 30.
2. Carole Counihan, *The Anthropology of Food and Body: Gender, Meaning, and Power* (New York and London: Routledge, 1999), 6.
3. Arlene Voski Avakian, ed., *Through the Kitchen Window: Women Explore the Intimate Meanings of Food and Cooking* (Boston: Beacon Press, 1997), 5.
4. Marjorie DeVault, *Feeding the Family: The Social Organization of Caring as Gendered Work*, Women

in Culture and Society (Chicago: University of Chicago Press, 1991). See also Counihan, *The Anthropology of Food and Body*. Women purchase 2/3rds of all cookbooks sold. Leonard Wood, 'Who's Buying the Cookbooks?' *Publisher's Weekly,* August 26, 1988, 29, cited in Sherrie A. Inness, *Dinner Roles: American Women and Culinary Culture* (Iowa City: University of Iowa Press, 2001). A recent telephone survey of women who shop in grocery stores found that 45 per cent of them are responsible for preparing dinner a full seven nights a week. Food Marketing Institute, 'Self-Care and the Grocery Store,' *Supermarket Research* 4, no. 2, March/April 2002.
5. DeVault, *Feeding the Family*, 118–19.
6. Harold McGee, *On Food and Cooking: The Science and Lore of the Kitchen*, 1st Scribner rev. ed. (New York: Scribner, 2004), 110.
7. Eliza Leslie, *Directions for Cookery, in Its Various Branches*, 11th ed. (Philadelphia: Carey & Hart, 1840), 210.
8. Isabella Beeton, *Beeton's Book of Household Management*, A First Edition Facsimile ed. (New York: Farrar Straus and Giroux, 1969), 696.
9. Fannie Merritt Farmer, *The Original Boston Cooking-School Cook Book, 1896*, facsimile edition (New York: New American Library, 1988, 320. True traveling sophisticates had access to more than enough recipes – Escoffier included eighty variations on the soufflé (his definitive *Guide Culinaire* was published in 1902).
10. Christine Muhlke, 'Recipes for Disaster,' *The New York Times Magazine*, May 21, 2006, 135.
11. This cookbook may be the century's sole soufflé-only volume, and it was owned by Julia Child. The copy at Harvard's Schlesinger Library is stamped 'Paul Child, 3 Steubenring Apt. 5, Plittersdorferaue, Bad Godesberg, Deutschland. Myra Waldo, *Serve at Once: The Soufflé Cookbook* (New York: Crowell, 1954), 1.
12. Ibid., 2.
13. Ibid., 6.
14. Ibid.
15. Julia Child and David Nussbaum, *Julia's Kitchen Wisdom: Essential Techniques and Recipes from a Lifetime of Cooking* (New York: Alfred A. Knopf, 2000), 71.
16. Julia Child, Louisette Bertholle, and Simone Beck, *Mastering the Art of French Cooking*, vol. 1, Updated (New York: Alfred A. Knopf, 1992), 157.
17. Julia Child and WGBH Video, *The French Chef with Julia Child*, WGBH, 1972.
18. Louis Parrish, *Cooking as Therapy: How to Keep Your Soufflé Up and Your Depression Quotient Down* (New York: Arbor House, 1975).
19. McGee, *On Food and Cooking*, 109.
20. Irma S. Rombauer and Marion Rombauer Becker, *Joy of Cooking* (Indianapolis, Ind.: The Bobb-Merrill Company, Inc., 1964; reprint, 1967), 204. Mendelson notes that Rombauer was well aware of the rhetorical ironies of the soufflé. It was 'her idea of the perfect company dish – a creation surrounded by a rarified mythos but in fact a simple, cheap, and nearly foolproof vehicle for all sorts of leftovers.' Anne Mendelson, *Stand Facing the Stove: The Story of the Women Who Gave America the Joy of Cooking* (New York: H. Holt, 1996), 130.
21. Jessica Kuper, *The Anthropologists' Cookbook* (London: Routledge and K. Paul, 1977), Claude Lévi-Strauss, *The Raw and the Cooked: Introduction to a Science of Mythology* (Chicago: University of Chicago Press, 1983).
22. Margaret Visser, *The Rituals of Dinner: The Origins, Evolution, Eccentricities, and Meaning of Table Manners* (New York: Grove Weidenfeld, 1991), 229.
23. Helen Evans Brown and James Beard, *The Complete Book of Outdoor Cookery*, Garden City, N.Y.: Doubleday, 1955), 8.
24. Visser, *The Rituals of Dinner*, 279.
25. For a review of the literature, see Carole Counihan, 'Food Rules in the United States: Individualism, Control, and Hierarchy,' in Counihan, *The Anthropology of Food and Body*, 124. This association

carries through even in cookbooks aimed at children. See also Inness and Neuhaus. For associations in cultural mythologies see Roland Barthes, 'Toward a psychosociology of contemporary food consumption,' in Carole Counihan and Penny Van Esterik, *Food and Culture: A Reader* (New York: Routledge, 1997). For the association of women and sweetness see Sidney Wilfred Mintz, *Sweetness and Power: The Place of Sugar in Modern History* (New York: Penguin Books, 1986).

26. Rombauer and Becker, *Joy of Cooking*, 203–04.
27. Irma S. Rombauer and Marion Rombauer Becker, *Joy of Cooking*, 3rd ed. (Indianapolis, Ind. and New York: Bobbs-Merrill Company, 1951; reprint, 1952), 217.
28. Alice S. Rossi, 'Equality between the Sexes: An Immodest Proposal,' *Daedelus*, Spring 1964.
29. Ruth Rosen, *The World Split Open: How the Modern Women's Movement Changed America* (New York: Viking, 2000), 320.
30. Alice Echols, *Daring to Be Bad: Radical Feminism in America, 1967–1975*, American Culture (Minneapolis: University of Minnesota Press, 1989), 139.
31. This debate was especially pronounced in the U.K. where intellectual and Marxist feminists banded together under the call of 'Wages for Housework,' an effort which has spawned chapters worldwide, many still extant. For the argument see especially Mariarosa Dalla Costa and Selma James, *The Power of Women and the Subversion of the Community*, 2d ed. (Bristol, Eng.: Falling Wall Press, 1973). The earliest complete articulation of the burdens of modern housework was Ann Oakley, *The Sociology of Housework* (London: Robertson, 1974).
32. Barbara Haber, 'Is Personal Life Still a Political Issue?,' *Feminist Studies* 5, no. 3, Toward a New Feminism for the Eighties (1979).
33. Estelle B. Freedman, *No Turning Back: The History of Feminism and the Future of Women* (New York: Ballantine, 2002), 133. Strikingly, figures from 1912, 1935 correspond very closely to those for the 1960s – amounting to about four hours a day on housework, and three-and-a-half on child care. These averages were not notably affected by income or education levels. Ruth Schwartz Cowan, *More Work for Mother: The Ironies of Household Technology from the Open Hearth to the Microwave* (New York: Basic Books, 1983), 199. The situation was not entirely remedied by the passage of time. In 1989, Arlie Hochschild found that 70 per cent of the men she studied did only between a third and half of their family's housework, while 10 per cent of men did even less than a third, and only 20 per cent took on a portion equal to that done by their wives. However, she found that men spend a greater proportion of their housework time on child care, women proportionally less. She found that most parents indicated a preference for child care over cooking and cleaning, indicating that men do more of the work they enjoy than women do. Notably, 'Even when couples share more equitably in the work at home, women do two-thirds of the *daily* jobs at home, like cooking and cleaning up – jobs that fix them into a rigid routine.' Arlie Russell Hochschild and Anne Machung, *The Second Shift: Working Parents and the Revolution at Home* (New York: Viking, 1989), 8.
34. Laura Schenone, *A Thousand Years over a Hot Stove: A History of American Women Told through Food, Recipes, and Remembrances* (New York and London: W.W. Norton, 2003), 271. Schenone notes however that 'Food companies understood that if their products took away all labor and work, women would no longer care about cooking at all. And so, countless advertising campaigns reminded women of their emotional connections to food, even if the products came in boxes and tins,' 274.
35. Women National Organization for and Chapter Greater Champaign Area, *Now We're Cooking* (Champaign, Ill.: National Organization for Women Greater Champaign Area Chapter, 1965).
36. *Missouri 1821–1971 Sesquicentennial Edition Cookbook*, reproduced in Mark H. Zanger, *The American History Cookbook* (Westport, Conn.: Greenwood Press, 2003), 427.
37. Quoted in Noel Riley Fitch, *Appetite for Life: The Biography of Julia Child* (New York: Doubleday, 1997), 388.
38. Charlotte Perkins Gilman, *Women and Economics: A Study of the Economic Relation between Men and Women as a Factor in Social Evolution* (Berkeley: University of California Press, 1998), 114–20.
39. For the full argument, see Cowan, *More Work for Mother*.

40. See discussion in Lesley Johnson and Justine Lloyd, *Sentenced to Everyday Life: Feminism and the Housewife* (Oxford and New York: Berg, 2004), 66–68.
41. Jessamyn Neuhaus, *Manly Meals and Mom's Home Cooking: Cookbooks and Gender in Modern America* (Baltimore: The Johns Hopkins University Press, 2003), 220.
42. This passion for ornamentation was picked up again by cookbooks in the 1950s, which also tended to include ideological messages about the role of a good housewife. Inness, *Dinner Roles*, 55, 130–43.
43. See Laura Shapiro, *Perfection Salad: Women and Cooking at the Turn of the Century* (New York: Farrar Straus and Giroux, 1986).
44. Simone de Beauvoir, *The Second Sex* (New York: Vintage Books, 1989), 451–55.
45. Mary Drake McFeely, *Can She Bake a Cherry Pie?: American Women and the Kitchen in the Twentieth Century* (Amherst: University of Massachusetts Press, 2000), 112.
46. Leslie Brenner, *American Appetite: The Coming of Age of a Cuisine* (New York: Avon Books, Inc., 1999), 31–35.
47. Neuhaus, *Manly Meals*, 223. This creature was, of course, a figment: 40 per cent of married women in the 1950s worked full-time outside of the home. Elaine Tyler May, *Homeward Bound: American Families in the Cold War Era* (New York: Basic Books, 1988), 84. For a discussion of the emphasis on the mother-cooked family meal as a patriotic value and as a transmitter of gender socialization during World War II, see Amy Bentley, 'Islands of Serenity, Gender, Race, and Ordered Meals During World War II,' in Carole Counihan, *Food in the USA: A Reader* (New York: Routledge, 2002).
48. Betty Friedan, *The Feminine Mystique* (New York: W.W. Norton, 2001).
49. Betty Friedan, *Life So Far* (New York: Simon & Schuster, 2000), 141.
50. Germaine Greer, *The Female Eunuch* (London: MacGibbon & Kee, 1970), 328.
51. Marge Piercy, *Stone, Paper, Knife* (New York: Knopf, 1983).
52. *Better Homes and Gardens New Cook Book*, rev. ed. (Des Moines, Iowa: Meredith Pub. Co., 1965), 2. The book contains a recipe for cheese soufflé made with American processed cheese food: 'Whisk to table!,' 217.
53. Quoted in Neuhaus, *Manly Meals*, 251–52.
54. Lois Hoffman, 'The Decision to Work,' in *The Employed Mother in America*, ed. F. Ivan Nye and Lois Hoffman (Westport, Conn.: Greenwood Press, 1963), 26–27, cited in Laura Shapiro, 'Betty Crocker and the Woman in the Kitchen, in Arlene Voski Avakian and Barbara Haber, eds., *From Betty Crocker to Feminist Food Studies: Critical Perspectives on Women and Food* (Amherst: University of Massachusetts Press, 2005), 39.
55. Child et. al.
56. Rebecca L. Spang, *The Invention of the Restaurant: Paris and Modern Gastronomic Culture* (Cambridge, Mass.: Harvard University Press, 2000), John Mariani, *America Eats Out: An Illustrated History of Restaurants, Taverns, Coffee Shops, Speakeasies, and Other Establishments That Have Fed Us for 350 Years* (New York: William Morrow and Company, Inc., 1991), Priscilla Parkhurst Ferguson, *Accounting for Taste: The Triumph of French Cuisine* (Chicago and London: University of Chicago Press, 2004).
57. Harvey Levenstein, *Paradox of Plenty: A Social history of Eating in Modern America* (Oxford: Oxford University Press, 1993), 140. See also Brenner, *American Appetite*, 52.
58. 'Everyone's in the Kitchen,' *Time*, November 25, 1966, 74–87: 74. Another group to reject convenience foods and the ethos of minimizing kitchen time were the countercultural. As Mark Zanger puts it, such things had been 'long associated with women taking a larger role outside the home – and the hippie period was initially quite antifeminist.' Zanger, *The American History Cookbook*. The classic statement of a more hopeful view was Frances Moore Lappé's *Diet for a Small Planet* (1971), which identified meat-loving culture as the source of injustice and argued that eating lower on the food chain could solve hunger problems worldwide. Her solutions, and those of various alternative collectives involved sustainable farming and living close to the land. One was to bake one's own bread,

and even, perhaps to grind one's own flour. Milling flour takes time, of course. Whose time? The usual answer should not come as a surprise. For a good accounting of the ideals of the movement (an account which does not take gender into account at all, however), see Warren Belasco, 'Food and the Counterculture: A Story of Bread and Politics,' in James L. Watson and Melissa L. Caldwell, *The Cultural Politics of Food and Eating: A Reader*, Blackwell Readers in Anthropology, 8 (Malden, MA: Blackwell Pub., 2005).

59. Gary Alan Fine, *Kitchens: The Culture of Restaurant Work* (Berkeley: University of California Press, 1996), 202.
60. 'Everyone's in the Kitchen,' 86–7.
61. Fitch, *Appetite for Life*, 387.
62. Quoted in McFeely, *Can She Bake a Cherry Pie?*, 122.
63. Restaurants were beginning to relieve the pressure. In 1965 one meal in four was eaten outside the home; in 1973 one in three. Reporting in 1976 on these statistics, food writer Waverly Root used the term 'Mom's kitchen' to refer to the alternative to the restaurant, which shows how thoroughly naturalized the role of woman-as-cook continued to be. Waverley Root and Richard De Rochemont, *Eating in America: A History* (Hopewell, N. J.: The Ecco Press, 1995), 447.
64. Pastry is an interesting exception to the gender rule. Because baking isn't tied to the service of the restaurant, it can begin and end earlier in the day, and is more predictable in its hours. Dornenburg, *Becoming a Chef*. This makes it a more family-friendly niche. Women quickly advanced as pastry chefs in top restaurants in the 1980s, while still being shut out of executive chef positions. Schenone, *A Thousand Years over a Hot Stove*, 332. For anecdotal support see Andrew MacLauchlan, *The Making of a Pastry Chef: Recipes and Inspirations from America's Best Pastry Chefs* (New York: John Wiley and Sons, Inc., 1999), 127. See also Dawn Davis, *If You Can Stand the Heat: Tales from Chefs and Restaurants* (New York: Penguin Books, 1999), 7–8. And see 'Sexism in the Kitchen,' on *The Leonard Lopate Show*: WNYC, 2003. Finally, see Ann Cooper, *A Woman's Place Is in the Kitchen: The Evolution of Woman Chefs* (New York: Van Nostrand Reinhold, 1998), 65.
65. Pierre Bourdieu, *Distinction: A Social Critique of the Judgment of Taste* (London: Routledge & Kegan Paul, 1986), 185–96.
66. DeVault, *Feeding the Family*, 224–25.
67. Elaine Showalter, 'My Dinner with Derrida,' *The American Prospect*, January 1, 2002.
68. Betty Harper Fussell, *My Kitchen Wars* (New York: North Point Press, 1999), 127. This work all went on while her husband, Paul Fussell, was composing his monumental work of literary criticism, *The Great War and Modern Memory* (Oxford: Oxford University Press, 1975).
69. Ibid., 152.
70. Nora Ephron, 'The Food Establishment,' in *Wallflower at the Orgy*, 1967, quoted in Molly O'Neill, 'Food Porn,' *Columbia Journalism Review*, September/October 2003, 40.
71. Brenner, *American Appetite*, 70.
72. Fussell, *My Kitchen Wars*, 153.
73. Fannie Merritt Farmer and Wilma Lord Perkins, *The Fannie Farmer Cookbook*, 11th ed. (Boston: Little Brown, 1965), 372.
74. Fussell, *My Kitchen Wars*, 157.
75. Julia Child and WGBH Video, *The French Chef with Julia Child*, WGBH, 1972.

Eggs in Art

Gillian Riley

Eggs appear in works of art for many reasons. They can have symbolic or cosmological significance, or they can tell us about everyday eating habits. Weird creatures concealed within or emerging from eggs in the works of Hieronymus Bosch do not stimulate the gastric juices, but the earthenware dish of fried eggs in a still life by Munari are appealing, even though we cannot be sure what their significance was to the painter and his clients. Velasquez's *Old woman frying eggs* is a social comment on different levels, telling us about eating habits of the time. Later Meléndez was to include eggs in compositions which can be read as recipes. Still lifes of Easter meals show eggs in their symbolic role and as prepared foods and bread. Genre scenes from the Low Countries deploy eggshells among the litter on the floors of kitchens and taverns, realism and symbolism combined in decorative confusion.

The egg as cosmos, the source of all life, the symbol of renewal, birth and growth, since time immemorial, and later an important item in Christian iconography, is not the subject of this paper, I present a selection, not an exhaustive survey, of images of eggs in paintings. These concepts did however influence painters and their clients, and it is thanks to this that we have some delightful images of eggs as part of Easter celebrations. We also have eggs in the context of seventeenth- and eighteenth-century still-life paintings in Spain and Italy, where their presence seems to be more secular. Eggs appear in genre scenes in the Low Countries, where they can be interpreted in different ways. When they might be part of a mixture, pancakes, a *frittata*, in cakes or pastry, as a glaze on bread and biscuits, the eye of faith can call up the recipe as witnesses, but cannot claim any deliberate intent to portray eggs in a significant role. Considering the significance of the egg as symbol, and its ubiquity as an ingredient, it is strange that it appears so rarely in Dutch paintings. Perhaps the symbolism was too heavy a load, and its role in the kitchen so lowly, the egg was ignored or avoided, for as we shall see, eggs could also have quite obscene connotations.

An early sighting of an egg to eat is in a third-century mosaic from Antioch. On a platter sit two boiled eggs on neat little egg cups, with two bunches of cooked asparagus, upright in containers, and two Bath chaps, or cooked pig's jowls, with a bowl of dipping sauce in the centre. Perhaps Martial had a simple meal like this in mind when he wrote *et sua non emptus praeparat ova cinis*, 'and cooked his egg in his own [that is, not bought] ashes', a way of getting a cheap meal, but as Pomponio Leto pointed out in the 1460s, a high-risk form of frugality, for the egg might crack into the hot ashes and be wasted.

Eggs as food appear in the *Tacuina Sanitatis*, illustrated versions of a text translated from the Arabic in northern Italy in the mid-fifteenth century, a sort of health handbook describing the properties of foodstuffs. Poultry are shown being fed by the mistress of the house, and on another page a woman with a basket of eggs holds up a fresh egg, newly laid and still warm, while another intrepid housewife gathers their large eggs from belligerent geese. This reinforces what we know of the domestic economy of the time – that eggs were a cash crop under the wing of the female head of the house, the *resdora*, who sold them for money to buy essentials she could not produce herself, like salt or sugar, or exchanged them for other foodstuffs. This might have some bearing on our interpretation of later still-life paintings where a pan of fried eggs might be more of a luxury than they appear.

Munari, from Reggio Emilia, worked for the dukes of Tuscany in the second half of the seventeenth century, giving them sumptuous images of luxury goods and food, a jumble of musical instruments, fragile imported china, Venetian glasses, fine wines and exquisite pastries, but he also celebrated more ordinary local products, cured hams and salami, bread and fruit, an earthenware pan of fried eggs and great hunks of parmesan cheese, here the eggs, glowing gold and white in the translucent oil, reflect the sunshine bouncing off the rich yellow cheese. But this cannot surely be a rustic meal, for a peasant's wife would not have squandered the precious eggs on a quick snack. This is more a celebration of the everyday meals of the affluent when not showing off, than a comment on the food of the poor. A pair of paintings probably executed for Ferdinando de' Medici in 1704 show robust but not frugal local food – some deliciously fatty cured ham, cardoons, bread, salami, and an earthenware pot one hopes might contain beans, and in its companion painting a fine roast guinea fowl, a bitter orange to squeeze over it, a dish of fried eggs, a flask of wine, an elegant glass and some bread, the components of a modest meal that must have brought joy to the jaded baroque palate. Another canvas from about the same time again celebrates the luxury of a simple meal, with bread, ham, a dish of fried eggs, and various rustic pots are on a ledge above a watermelon, its red flesh vying with the lean of the ham, a deep orange melon with rugged peel, a flask of wine and plums and cherries scattered among fragile Chinese porcelain, all apart from the china, high quality local products. These paintings seem to be more part of the Medici economic policy of promoting of Tuscan products than any kind of gastronomic slumming.

In *The old man of Artimino* painted by Giovanna Garzoni in the 1640s shows an elderly peasant surrounded by the products of the Tuscan countryside, carrying a cockerel and hen, a basket of eggs, which are out of all proportion to the rest, adding to the surreal quality of the scene. Hams, cured meats, fruit and vegetables crowded together, seem to be arranged in an arbitrary grouping, balanced on the rugged rocks from which the old man emerges like Neptune from the waves. It is to be hoped that Garzoni's client, possibly the Grand Duchess Vittoria della Rovere, wife of Ferdinand II Medici, provided her with all these good things, so painstakingly reproduced. Like a later painter Jacopo Chimenti da Empoli, whose greed inspired some lush kitchen scenes painted in the 1620s for the Medici grand dukes, the subject matter later devoured by his studio staff and eager guests, earning him the nickname of 'Empimi!' – 'Fill me up!' Vittoria was almost certainly the owner of the soppy dog leaning into Garzoni's picture from the left.

Velasquez, in some of his early work, was depicting everyday life, low life, as one might see in a tavern or *bodegon*, from which the genre gets its name, *bodegones*. One of his *bodegones* shows an old woman frying eggs. I have dealt with this elsewhere. Briefly we are more concerned here with what the old woman is doing – frying eggs in an earthenware pot over an improvised pan of coals resting on a huge storage jar, than any possible interpretation of any hidden meaning. Thanks to Alicia Rios, who came up with an overview of the many subtle ways of frying eggs in Spain, we can see that the sulky child had a lot to learn, and the once-beautiful old woman a lot to tell. Another painting by Velasquez shows eggs in a different context, an equally sulky girl, perhaps the not unreasonably resentful Martha, preparing a meal for the unexpected guest while her sister sits inactive at his feet. Admonished by an old woman, she is about to fry two gilt-headed bream and serve them with a sauce made of garlic and some dried hot chilli pounded with salt and oil in a mortar. This is for us a welcome glimpse of daily life, which we appreciate probably more than the bible story, whatever the intention of the painter.

A century later Luis Meléndez was producing still-life paintings of everyday food, some of which represent recipes or the components of whole meals. A hunk of fatty bacon and some eggs point to the *duelos y quebrantos* of Don Quixote, 'mourning and lamentations' as a humble version of fried or scrambled eggs and bacon.[1] The conjunction of eggs, oysters and garlic promises another tasty fry-up, and Meléndez also shows eggs in conjunction with salmon, possibly to use in a sauce.

In Portugal, about the same time, we get a sight of eggs as part of offerings of festival food at Easter time; the painter Josefa de Óbidos, whose devotional works had the same sugary sweetness as her not unrelated still lifes of flowers and sweetmeats, shows whole eggs enclosed in a lattice work of twisted bread dough in a composition which includes ripe cherries, spring flowers, fresh young cheeses, a crock of some cooling drink and a bowl of probably savoury eggy tarts and pasties; in the background a basket of fresh peas and broad beans, springtime delicacies, are rated alongside this luxury confectionary, as they should be. Its companion is a composition of sweet things, also celebrating Easter, which includes a large silver platter resting on a wooden box of *membrillo*, piled with at least a dozen different little cakes, pastries and biscuits, nestling under a white linen cloth, and adorned with the decorated filigree wands or large toothpicks sometimes seen in Netherlandish banquet scenes. To the right of this display is a honeycomb in a blue and white porcelain dish resting on a silver salver, next to a box of sugar pastilles in the shape of seashells, which are also strewn all over the table top, along with crinkly sugared comfits enclosing fennel and anise seeds, nuts and spices, while an elaborate glazed covered jar, probably full of a milky drink similar to *horchata* or distilled perfumed water, is festooned with flowers and ribbons looped through the handles of little drinking cups. Eggs and sweetmeats as devotional offerings are not as hedonistic as they sound, for much confectionary was made in religious establishments, as part of the round of work and worship, and a nice little earner as well. Eggs enclosed in interwoven strands of dough are still today a feature of traditional Easter baked goods in Spain and parts of Italy.

Another pair of Easter meals by Tomaso Realfonso from early eighteenth-century Naples show a cold snack of hard-boiled eggs, cheeses and various salami, with a pitcher of decorative flowers, some citrus fruit, and a large ring of twisted and cut bread, like an Easter garland – a savoury meal. Its pair is a collection of cookies and sweetmeats, not as sweetly pretty as the Portuguese version, but with a strong Spanish influence, on the left a bowl of knotted and braided pretzel-like objects, deep fried and dusted with sugar, and some slices of possibly fruit paste, with a sliver of candied fruit on top of each, and the same beribboned wands that we saw in Josefa de Óbispa's Easter paintings.

A totally secular meal from the mid-seventeenth century by an unknown artist in Lombardy (once attributed to Carlo Cane) is of a hunt picnic, featuring 15 men and boys, a grown woman and two little girls, and four dogs. The dominant figure is the formidable lady of the house, presiding over a huge composed salad, sometimes known as an *olla podrida*, a loose term also applied to the *gran bollito* of Piedmont and Lombardy, but here a cold dish with perhaps some relationship to the *capon magro* of Liguria. If hers were the hands that arranged the salad the painting might be an implied tribute to female powers of organisation, for although the men in the party all carry emblems or instruments of hunting, they seem somewhat cowed, and the food appears to have been carefully pre-prepared in the domestic kitchen by a regiment of women. The decorative properties of hard-boiled eggs are exploited here to give a liveliness to the assembled vegetables and roots, with glimpses of possible layers of bread, *bottarga*, anchovies, and bright crayfish beneath. A still life by Carlo Magini shows hard-boiled eggs as part of a composition of objects on a kitchen table, including spring vegetables, lettuce, broad beans and artichokes, some bread, with a deep chestnut coloured surface and a golden interior, the crumb holding what might be nuts (a kind of sweet Easter *pannetone*, or possibly the famous bread from the Marche – Magini was from Fano – containing lumps of cheese) imply a modest but exquisite snack, if it were not for the disturbingly realistic calf's head looking at us in mild reproach.

Georg Flegel, working during the late sixteenth and early seventeenth centuries, has a delightful image of a boiled egg sitting on its side in an oval pewter egg cup, pierced to hold a 'soldier' of bread. Although at first sight merely a glimpse of everyday life, this like most of the artist's work invites, and gets, complex layers of interpretation. If the egg represents the purity of new life and renewal, the fly dabbling in the runny yolk reminds us of the sins and corruption of this world which threaten it.[2]

Eggs in Art

A commentary on this quotes a contemporary remark that the horizontal egg cup is characteristic of Germany and the Low Countries, while Italians eat their boiled eggs upright. The easy way was to plonk a boiled egg in a mound of salt, saving the cost of an egg-cup, an image used by Hogarth to point out the meanness of a penny-pinching but ostentatious City alderman.

In another work by Flegel we see more cooked eggs, four of them, neatly poached and trimmed, sitting in a little earthenware skillet, rather pallid and humdrum compared with the glowing fried eggs of Munari. They are part of what looks like an inconsequential jumble of items on a kitchen table but which yield to the enquiring mind a plausible welter of interpretations. The leg of veal symbolises the pleasures of the flesh, food that according to the theory of the four humours generates heat and unruly passions, so the melon and cucumber, the grapes and citrus fruits, which are cold and wet are brought in to counteract this. For we must, with food as in life, seek to achieve a just balance between moderate enjoyment and gross over-indulgence, as one regulates the ingredients of a dish or the components of a meal. This image, flaunting the contents of a well-stocked larder while imposing order and restraint on the greed and unruly desires of a hungry household, is all part of what Simon Schama describes as a 'mixture of the moral and the merry'. But giving such pictorial scope to the moralising of a repressive parent is surely a form of child abuse. Mercifully the commentator gave up on the eggs, but can they be read simply as useful items in a non-meat diet or, balefully, as the four horsemen of the apocalypse? There are only two works by Flegel with these skillets of eggs, both part of displays of food so heavily loaded with symbolism that it seems unlikely that only the eggs would have escaped. They remain a mystery.

There are not many eggs in the still lifes of the Netherlands, although egg and mussel shells litter the floors of Jan Steen's untidy homes and taverns. Genre scenes of the sixteenth and seventeenth centuries show that weird pastime, the Egg Dance, usually part of tavern scenes or raucous rustic weddings. The performers had to dance all around an egg on the floor, which was also strewn with things like flowers, spring onions and so forth, none of which should be trampled underfoot. Having deftly slid the egg from its bowl with his foot, the dancer would push it gently in and out of a circle chalked on the floor before returning it to the bowl. Difficult enough to perform when sober, and a cause of much merriment when attempted drunk. This sort of association with uncouth peasant revelry, as opposed to Catholic imagery of resurrection and rebirth, perhaps did not fit comfortably into the didactic representation of everyday things that could be used to point a moral. Jan Steen, himself a Catholic, was unfazed by eggs and used them frequently, not just in his rendering of the Egg Dance, but in scenes where eggs and eggshells could mean lasciviousness and sexual transgression, as in a tavern scene where a lewd man (a self portrait) lifts the skirts of a blowsy possibly pregnant woman, contemplating the floor littered with broken eggs. In *The game dealer's shop* the obvious equation of the word for hare [to come]…

with that for sexual intercourse [to come]... is reinforced by a couple embracing in the background, while in the foreground two rosy-cheeked children (probably Steen's own) are a picture of smiling innocence, the little girl holding up a pure white egg, the little boy a live duck. But other painters show eggs in a more equivocal role, in *A couple in a kitchen interior* by Abraham Bloemaert is a seduction scene with a difference; an already sozzled youth is fondled by a maidservant with one hand, while she extracts coins from his purse with the other, a licence for us to put the sleaziest interpretation on every innocent item littering the kitchen table, where two eggs, elegantly described as in 'testicular formation'[3] combine with drooping sausages and onions, to re-enforce the message. In Peter Wtewael's *Kitchen scene* a buxom kitchen maid smiles fondly at a hopeful youth, holding a dead bird, a basket of eggs and a jug of wine, whose intentions are obvious. The erotic and phallic connotations of kitchen equipment and activities can become irritating after a while, but might explain the rare appearances of eggs. Since they had this libidinous significance in kitchens and taverns, they never figure in the 'breakfast' snack still lifes which glorify the simple 'fatherland' fare of the virtuous common man. We see bread, fish, especially herrings, cheese and onions, which could all be used to point religious and patriotic morals – but never eggs.

It is a relief to escape into the harmonious world of Chardin, where he appears to take his eggs for granted, and paints them in several still lifes which seem to represent things one might find in larder or kitchen without straining to impose any moral message. What might have been the intrusive presence of a male painter into calm, domestic, female environment, is neutralised by his technique and composition. 'The goal of this lazy, peripheral focus is non-invasive participation in the spaces of the household' is how Norman Bryson puts it.[4] These immensely skilful compositions, where every object, its colour, form and position, have a precise geometric function, do not seem to have a moral message, or even the agenda of a meal or recipe, that we can detect in the work of Meléndez. *Les aliments de la convalescence*, also known as *La garde attentive*, where a maid is seen peeling a freshly cooked egg, is a calm domestic moment, all hazy pinks and whites, not a symbolic gesture. In Chardin's *Fast day meal*, the assembly of eggs, salt fish, spring onions, a wooden pestle and mortar and various pots and pans say more about calm domesticity than religious observance. Eggs just happen to be there, and we love them and Chardin for this.

And so, from cosmic symbol to ordinary ingredient, the egg has a part, though strangely minor, in the broad spectrum of still-life painting throughout history.

Notes

1. Bryson, Norman, *Looking at the overlooked* (London: Reaktion Books, 1990), p. 167.
2. Wettengl, Kurt (ed.), *Georg Flegel, 1566 – 1638, Stilleben* (Stuttgart: Verlag Gerd Hatje, 1993), pp. 119 and 138.
3. Rios, Alicia, and March, Lourdes, *El arte dela cocina española* (Barcelona: Blume, 1993), p. 79. Calderón de la Barca:
   '...para una cuitada,
   triste, mísera, viuda,
   huevos y torreznos bastan
   que son duelos y quebrantos.'
4. Barnes, Donna R., and Rose, Peter G. *Matters of Taste* (Albany: 2002), p. 42.

Eggs in the Moon Shine With Cream. A Selection of Egg Recipes 1500–1800

William Rubel

This cookbook is divided into four sections: *Simple Eggs, Elaborations, French Elaborations*, and *Dessert Eggs*.[1]

The simple egg

This first section on 'Simple Eggs' concerns egg dishes that are the least transformed by the cook. It is the section with recipes that most often emphasize the inherent quality of the eggs. When you prepare these recipes you will find that the less the egg is cooked the more you will be rewarded by using new-laid eggs from barnyard or backyard chickens. I have emphasized recipes that utilize the open hearth – and specifically roasting – a significant early method for cooking eggs, but one that was not transferred to the modern kitchen.

The New-laid Egg

149. These old laid Eggs taste ill.
150. This is a new-laid Egg.
151. That's a rotten one.
152. So an Egg be fresh, I care not whether it be soft or hard.
153. I care not whether it be boile'd or roasted, or potch'd.

149. Hæc ova requiete matè sapiunt.
150. Hoc ovum recens natum est.
151. Illud est putre.
152. Modo ovum sit recens, nil curo molle an durum sit.
153. Nil curo, sive elixum, sive assum, sive coctillatum.[2]
   No Author, *Familiar Forms of Speaking*, 1701

This Latin exercise published in 1701 proclaims the first rule of egg cookery – new-laid eggs are best.[3] In a northern European farmyard in the eighteenth century chickens laid eggs seasonally. While cookery books include many egg storage systems, none prevented deterioration as effectively as refrigeration. For much of the year a new-laid egg, if available, was a delicacy, the treasure amongst the dross of tired, old-laid eggs.

Thanks to modern chickens, and modern egg rearing techniques, every season is now egg laying season. There is no seasonal variation in production and thanks to refrigeration and efficient transportation networks no egg purchased in a market is ever stinky.

While our eggs are always outwardly fresh, they are never new-laid.

The new-laid egg has a firm internal structure, and a pleasant taste. As eggs age the albumen and yolk become watery; they begin to taste acidic, and then horrible. New-laid eggs have remarkable leavening properties, whether beaten into a foam, or just stirred into a batter. They are always the baker's best friend, and always the best choice for simple eggs.

The perfect egg, the egg culinary dreams can be made from, is the new-laid egg of a barnyard fowl that scratches for its living. This was the egg of the Latin primer and it is an egg that stands on its own as a food of distinction. The yolk of a chicken that scratches for its living is deeply colored, and often deeply flavored. It is this egg that best reveals the recipes in this work. New-laid eggs from foraging chickens can sometimes be purchased at farmers' markets, but one's most reliable source is usually one's own backyard chickens, or those of a friend.

Sucking Egg

Here I found upon the Ground a Nest of Eggs, about the Bigness of a Duck-Egg, yet I could not discover what fowl own'd them, but I took 'em all away and ventured to Suck one of them, which I found as pleasant as new-laid Hen-Egg.[4]

William Rufus Chetwood, *The Voyages, Dangerous Adventures and Imminent Escapes of Captain Richard Falconer*, 1720

The sucking egg is at once a natural object and a cultural artefact. Because wild eggs are no longer collected,[5] and because few of us have access to the eggs of barnyard fowl, the sucking egg is now a rarity. While for millennia it would have seemed ridiculous to teach adults formally how to prepare a sucking egg, we now all need instruction.

Select an egg from under a chicken. Candle[6] it to be sure it is fresh – sometimes a barnyard egg is missed for days and even weeks when the others are gathered, and you don't want to suck an old-laid egg – and of course you have to be sure there is no embryo. Immediately after candling, wash the egg in warm soapy water and then use a sharp object, such as a nail, to poke holes in either end of the egg,[7] then suck out the contents. The holes should be big enough that one doesn't have to strain while sucking. If you can't get a new-laid egg while it is still warm, then after candling and washing, heat it as described in the following recipe for Rear Egg.

Rear Egg

Hard Egges, Soft Egges, Rere Egges. For in the regiment of health, egges should in no wise be eaten hard. But being in a meane between rere and hard, which Galen calleth Ouatremula: yet rere egs, named Ouaforbilia, that is to say, little more than through hot, are good to clere the throate and breast, and they doe ease the griefes of the bladder.

Thomas Cogan, *Haven of Health*, 1584[8]

As our own culture has its many obsessions with eggs and health it should come as no surprise that since the first European dietary texts were written nearly two-thousand years ago they usually had something to say about the healthfulness of eggs. While it now seems laughable to ascribe medical consequences to the outward state of a cooked egg, it would behoove us, so fearful of the raw egg, to refrain from too precipitously laughing at earlier dietary beliefs.

The rear egg is an egg that is heated until it is hot through but still liquid. It is a form of sucking egg. While the rear egg is now virtually unknown, for millennia it was the beginner-cook's first egg. The rear egg is a taste revelation. It surprises me to say it, but I cannot think of any other food as satisfying as a new-laid barnyard egg roasted rear. While rear eggs can be boiled, you are less likely to solidify the white when roasting in front of the fire. The method is simple. Place a room-temperature new-laid egg within a few inches (10 cm) of a hot fire. This can be a fire in a fireplace or a campfire. Stand the egg in ashes beside the fire or just lay it on the hearth in front of the fire. Turn as needed to heat it evenly. Aim to heat the egg through in exactly three minutes. To develop a sense for the method, heat one, taste it, and if necessary, for subsequent eggs, make adjustments in the distance of the eggs to the fire. If you don't have access to live fire, place the egg for three minutes in a hot oven – 450°F to 500°F (230°C to 260°C).

If you cool the shell in water, then the hot egg can be sucked, like a new-laid egg, otherwise, break into a bowl and served like a poached egg. If the egg was stored for a day in a container with black winter truffles it will taste especially delicious.

The Torturer's Warm Eggs

At last, my Head being by their Arms advanced, and my body taken from the Rack, the water regushed abundantly from my Mouth; then they recloathing my broken, bloody, and cold and trembling Body, being all this Time stark naked, I fell twice in a swooning Trance; which they again refreshed with a little Wine, and two warm Eggs, not for Charity done, but that I should be reserved to farther Punishment; and if it were not too truly known these Sufferings to be of Truth, it would almost seem incredible to many, that a Man, being brought so low, with starving Hunger, and extreme Cruelites, could have subsisted any longer reserving life. [9]

Joseph Morgan, *Lithgow's Racking at Malaga*, 1731

Eggs in the Moon Shine With Cream

What more lovely way to meet the day than with an egg taken from under a hen and sucked empty, right there, or taken into one's hut and roasted rear on the morning fire? But less obvious, but upon reflection, as obvious, is that eggs will have been used to brutalize as well as to succor – that the warm egg will have been eaten against the interests of the eater – that the egg will have been the torturer's friend. In the looking-glass world of Spain's eighteenth-century torture chambers, eggs, nearly raw, were served to their victims with wine[10] so they could extend the hours of torment, forestalling what for many would have been a welcome death.

Soft-boiled Eggs
Two Rere Yolks in a Shell

[T]hen I say there is nothing better, than a couple of Egges potched, or the yolkes of two Egges sodden[11] rere and put into one shell, seasoned with a little pepper, Butter and Salt, and supped off warme, drinking after it a good draught of Claret wine. [12]

Thomas Cogan, *Haven of Health*

Eggs, poached or soft-boiled, need no introduction. This simple variation on the soft-boiled egg was, according to Thomas Cogan, a favorite of the most influential men of his time. By combining the hot yolks, and jettisoning the solidified white, the recipe highlights the creamiest, warmest, most sensual part of the egg. If you follow Thomas Cogan's suggestion you will find that a good swallow of claret makes for a nice contrasting chaser, perfect for a rainy morning sitting before the fire.

Roasted Egg

I got many Birds Eggs, and striking a fire, I kindled some Heath and dry Sea Weed, by which I roasted my eggs.[13]

Jonathan Swift, *Travels into several remote nations of the world*, 1727

Throughout the era of the open hearth, eggs were roasted in front of the fire, on the embers beside the fire, and buried in hot ash. [14] Egg roasting encompasses a complex world of culinary experience that has been dropped from practice. Egg roasting could have been adapted to the modern oven, but wasn't.[15] Roasted eggs range from the egg that is roasted to just hot – the rear egg – to eggs that acquire a caramel color and deep taste from a night spent in embers, and to every state in between.

Getting roast eggs to turn out exactly the way one envisions them is one of the most difficult of any culinary skill, hence the proverb 'There is reason [thoughtfulness] in roasted eggs'. [16] In Dryden's expansive translation of Ovid's line in *Metatmorphoses* regarding roasted eggs he emphasizes the need to pay attention, even for the simple rear egg.

Eggs in the Moon Shine With Cream

> Then Curds and Cream, the Flow'r of Country Fare,
> And new-laid Eggs, which *Baucis'* busie care,
> Turn'd by a gentle Fire, and roasted rare. [17]

Many challenges face the egg roaster. An egg exposed to high heat for too long explodes. Platina describes a roast egg dish in which an exploding egg is a common risk – and thus says that his friend Pomponius never makes the dish because in his poverty he cannot afford to recklessly lose eggs.[18] The careless roaster may produce the ill-roasted egg, the one that is cooked on one side, and raw on the other, or burnt on one side while perfect on the other. As Shakespeare put it in one of his more cutting insults,

> Truly, thou art damn'd, like an ill-roasted egg, all on
> one side. [19]

Alexander Pope, like Shakespeare, assumed that his audience understood the mechanics and difficulties of roasting eggs. Pope expressed the idea that the sophisticated reader wants to see the poet exerting skill in the development of poetic ideas, to see ideas turned this way and that in the transformative focus of the poet's imagination, and not, metaphorically speaking, to be formulaically dropped in boiling water and cooked to a state of mechanical perfection with these lines,

> One likes the Pheasant's wing, and one the leg;
> The vulgar boil, the learned roast an egg.[20]

The charm of roasted eggs is not just that it is a challenge. Particularly at the two extremes – the rear egg and the long-roasted egg – one achieves a product that cannot be had through boiling.

Always begin roasting eggs with eggs that are at room temperature. Use every relationship possible between egg and fire, hot ash, and embers. The egg may sit fully in the open, or it may rest on or be half or fully buried in ash or embers. Time and temperature are the variables. Although experience will be your best guide you will find an infrared thermometer helpful in judging the temperature of ash for long-buried eggs.

You may use an oven to simulate roasting eggs with an open fire. An oven at 225°F (107°C) simulates the slow-roasted egg, and an oven at 450°F (232°C) provides the high heat for rear eggs, and, of course, there are all the gradients in between. An egg roasted in an oven in a bowl of ash at 225°F (107°C) for 6 or 8 hours will give you an egg of requisite beauty and taste. As always, run eggs under cold water immediately upon removing from the heat in order to facilitate peeling.

Eggs in the Moon Shine With Cream

Eggs on a Spit

Pierce eggs lengthwise on a well-heated spit, and roast near the fire as if it were meat. They have to be eaten hot. This is a stupid concoction, one of the absurdities and games of cooks.[21]

Platina, *On Right Pleasure and Good Health*, c. 1467

Who cannot love a cookbook-author as opinionated as Platina? In his own time, eggs on a spit must have been all the rage in the finest Roman [Italian Renaissance] kitchens[22], otherwise, his dig at the games of cooks would have made no sense. Cooks could have gamed the dish by roasting extra large or rare eggs, like goose or ostrich. But I rather think that Platina considered spit-roasted eggs to be a stupid concoction because he knew one could achieve the same results with less drama by simply burying eggs in hot ash. So, why did the cooks do it?

In seventeenth- and eighteenth-century English 'to have eggs on a spit' was a proverbial expression denoting something that absorbed one's attention and prevented one from doing anything else.[23] Bringing a spit to table threaded with a line of perfectly shelled perfectly-roasted eggs demonstrated more than culinary accomplishment – it demonstrated that unlike mere mortals, one could simultaneously do a host of demanding things, in addition to roasting eggs on a spit.

Here is what to look out for when you make this recipe. The hot skewer must seal the eggs shut by cooking the albumen that leaks out as you thread the eggs. If you roast them too hot the eggs will both leak and also begin to explode, cracking the shells, and to make matters worse, you won't be able to peel them because the shell will stick to the white. If you roast the eggs too cool the yolks won't be solid. Serve hot as Platina suggests, perhaps with a little vinegar and salt.[24]

Elaborations

I include here three simple elaborations of familiar egg preparations. *Puffed Eggs* use the same ingredients as fried eggs, but with a little processing, to create a dish that is utterly new – if several hundred years old. *Eggs in the Moon Shine with Cream* reminds us that we can sometimes reinvent a dish simply by paying acute attention to its ingredients, and Robert May's oven-peel broiled egg memorializes an unfamiliar cooking method and reminds us that the ubiquitous fried egg can be taken as a beginning, rather than an end in itself.

Oeufs au Zephir Puffed Eggs

Separate the yolks and whites of eight or ten eggs without breaking the yolks, beat the whites to a snow, wrap each yolk in spoonful of the snow, and so on as you please; slide them gently off into hot hog's-lard, one after another; fry of a fine gold colour, and serve with a little cullis made pretty sharp, with the juice of a lemon.[25]

George Dalrymple, *The Practice of Modern Cookery*, 1781

This is a delightful egg recipe that has gone out of fashion, but that would easily find favor with a modern audience. The lemon-accented broth called for in the recipe is delicious – appropriate for a lunch or light dinner. The recipe lends itself to many variations. If served without the sauce, then you might consider flavoring the whites with salt and herbs to give more flavor to the dish. If you substitute another fat for lard, use one, like olive oil, or butter, that will contribute its flavor to the eggs. The lard called for in the recipe would have been from a pig that had eaten a varied diet, and is likely to have grazed in a field. It would therefore have had a distinctive flavor. Lacking lard of this quality, one could render fat with onion or fresh herbs, a custom in Normandy, France, [26] and thus create a flavorful pork fat in which to fry these eggs.

Eggs in the Moon Shine with Cream
Make a bed of butter in your dish, and break your eggs over it; after they are broken season them with salt. Then put some cream to them until they be hidden, or some milk so that it be good. Seethe them, and give them colour with the fire-shovell red, then serve. [27]

La Varenne, *The French Cook*, 1653

Eggs in the Moon are what English speakers now usually refer to as 'fried eggs.' *Eggs in the Moon Shine with Cream*, falls into the group of egg dishes now called shirred, or *oeufs cocotte*. This particular recipe appeared in La Varenne's *Cuisinier françois*, the most influential French cookbook of the seventeenth century, and one of the most influential cookbooks of all time.

In our contemporary reading of this recipe it is one for any day of the year. We always have reasonably fresh eggs, sweet butter, and cream at our disposal. But each of these ingredients had a seasonal aspect in La Varenne's time. La Varenne and his contemporaries will have seen this as a seasonal recipe. While it is hard to know what role this dish played in a seventeenth-century household, it would surprise me if its first reintroduction into the household after the winter had not been seen as one of the first sure indications that spring had arrived. Farmyard chickens don't lay in the winter. Eggs are plentiful in the spring, and to those raised on farm products, the taste of butter and cream from spring pastures was distinct from the taste of butter and cream produced later in the season. [28]

This recipe does not specify the type of egg. In addition to chicken egg, it will also have been made with duck and goose egg. Of these three choices, my own favorite is goose egg. Its large yolk is creamier than that of chicken or duck and because of its size, twice that of a large chicken egg, it gives the dish a festive aspect. La Varenne specifies for preparing this recipe a dish that can be put directly over flames and also presented at table. A silver dish would meet these conditions.

To Broil Eggs

Take an oven peel, heat it red hot, and blow off the dust, break the eggs on it, and put them into a hot oven, or brown them on top with a red hot fire shovel; being finely broil'd, put them into a clean dish, with some gravy, a little grated nutmeg, and elder vinegar; or pepper, vinegar, juyce of orange, and grated nutmeg on them.[29]

Robert May, *The Accomplisht Cook*, 1684

I know of no other reference to a heated oven peel as the preferred cooking utensil. As with first-sightings of rare animals it is hard to know what this reference means. Is this Robert May's own eccentricity, a peek into a baking guild secret, or a method so common that there was no point in mentioning it? Did Robert May have a reason for specifying the hot oven peel that his readers would have recognized? As with Lost Eggs,[30] this method obviates the use of frying fat which, in the health manuals of the day – as in the health manuals of our own – was considered unhealthful.[31]

Robert May takes what might have been a baker's recipe – eggs fried on a red-hot peel seasoned with salt – and transforms it into a refined course by suggesting the eggs be finished with gravy, elder vinegar or orange juice, and spices – nothing ruinously expensive – but certainly not a worker's meal taken in the bakery on the fly.

To make this dish, thrust an iron peel into a bread oven when it is being fired, or into the fireplace, or use a steel frying pan. If you use a frying pan, you may want to drop the egg onto the bottom of the pan. A thin spatula is helpful for removing the eggs. If using a fireplace shovel to brown the eggs, then it needs to be heavy enough to retain sufficient heat to brown them.

French elaborations

French seventeenth-century egg cuisine is one of unparalleled imagination, inventiveness, and vigor. It provides the underpinnings for the egg dishes in modern French classical cooking. Many of the egg recipes recorded by Escoffier in *Le Guide Culinaire* (1903) come directly from this literature, even to the extent of retaining original names, such as *Oeufs à la Huguenote*.

The egg recipes from this period of French cooking are so varied – from simple omelets that we can easily relate to – to complex amalgams of eggs, meat broths, and other flavors that are distinctly alien to the current Anglo-American palate – that it would take a book in itself to fully represent the cuisine. I include here just two recipes to stand as windows into this complex cuisine – an egg poached in sugar syrup and an egg scrambled with sour orange juice. To more fully step into this world of egg cookery I suggest the Prospect Books editions of La Varenne and Robert May.[32] Though recipe details may change as these recipes are repeated by different authors over the course of the next one-hundred plus years, between these two works you will be able to appreciate the innovative qualities of this extraordinary cuisine.

Robert May places English egg recipes, like like eggs and collops[33] in a different part of his book from his French-inspired egg section. A review of egg recipes in the index of English seventeenth- and eighteenth-century cookbooks offer a quick way to get a sense of the author's attitude towards French cuisine. Authors such as Elizabeth Smith, Hannah Glasse, and Elizabeth Raffald did not have egg chapters, and offer their readers only a comparative few egg recipes compared with the many dozens typical of the Francophilic-English cookbook authors.

Eggs in Moon shine Otherways
Make a sirrup of rose-water, sugar, sack, or white-wine, make it in a dish and break the yolks of the eggs as whole as you can, put them in the boiling sirrup with some ambergriece,[34] turn them and keep them one from the other, make them hard, and serve them in a little dish with sugar and cinnamon.[35]

Robert May, *The Accomplisht Cook*, 1684

In this recipe we move away from the almost universal poaching of egg in water[36] to something completely different – egg yolk poached in an aromatic sugar syrup. In our dining sequence this is a recipe for a dessert egg. Drop the yolks into a syrup that has reached the soft-ball stage. The yolk flattens out as it cooks. If the syrup becomes too thick, add more wine, sack, or rose-water. Unfortunately, ambergris is difficult to come by,[37] so most of us will have to enjoy this version of Eggs in Moonshine without it. A very similar, though modernized version of this recipe was published by John Nott in 1724 as 'To dress eggs in the Italian way'.[38] John Nott's recipe has a more elaborate and festive garnish – pistachio, orange flowers, and lightly candied lemon peel – but for a practical everyday recipe I prefer the warmth and simplicity of Robert May's version.

To Butter a Dish of Eggs
Take twenty eggs more or less, whites and yolks as you please, break them into a silver dish, with some salt, and set them on a quick charcoal fire, stir them with a silver spoon, and being finely buttered put to them the juyce of three or four oranges, sugar, grated nutmeg, and sometimes beaten cinnamon, being thus drest, strain them at the first, or afterward being buttered.[39]

Robert May, *The Accomplisht Cook*, 1684

Orange juice and eggs is a common pairing in French-inspired seventeenth- and eighteenth-century egg recipes. This is a simple recipe with which to make the orange juice taste break through. Use one orange to five eggs, or half an orange for two. Robert May assumes that you will use your judgment on the ratio between whites and yolks. I stick with the natural ratio of 1:1. The eggs are strained prior to service so the precise amount of orange doesn't really matter. While the English knew the sweet orange (*Citrus sinensis*), which is the orange of the egg-enriched Mexican street-stall beverage,[40] this recipe is written for the Seville orange (*Citrus aurantium*)[41] and thus introduces into these eggs the element of sweet-and-sour. The call for orange juice implies that this was a seasonal recipe. In the northern hemisphere Seville oranges can be purchased in late fall and early winter. As oranges store well, they would still have been on-hand for spring eggs. I tested the recipe with sour sweet oranges.

It is worth keeping in mind that butter is in the title of the dish. The taste butter imparts to these eggs is so important that I would think of it as a condiment and select the butter accordingly. Robert May offers the option of modulating the butter's influence on the dish by adding the butter enrichment either before or after the eggs are strained.

You will find an optimum blend, based on your personal taste, between the butter, sour orange, sugar, salt, nutmeg, and optional cinnamon. My advice is to make this once with two eggs and the juice of half an orange to get a sense of the balance that will please you before making it for company.

Dessert eggs

I end this small work on eggs with two dessert recipes – *Oeufs au Caffe* to wake you up, and *Opium with Rear Yolks* to put you to sleep.

> *Oeufs au Caffe*
> *Coffee Eggs, or with Coffee*
> Make some good strong Coffee, let it rest to clear as usual, and sweeten to discretion; beat up six Yolks of Eggs, with about four cups of Coffee, and sift it; pour this into little moulds in the form of Eggs, or of any other, (do not fill them quite) and bake in a mild Oven, or a Dutch one, or with a Brazing-pan Cover between two Fires. They are made after this manner, in the shape of any Fruits or Birds, if you have proper moulds, either of copper or china, &c.[42]
> Menon, *The professed cook*, 1769

This is a lean molded coffee-flavored egg custard. Because this custard is water-based it goes down well, even after a heavy meal. It is a dessert to close out a long lunch, or made with decaffeinated coffee, a dessert even the most fearful guest will be able to enjoy, no matter how late at night the dinner has ended. As a rule, more lightly roasted coffees show off their varietal characteristics.

While this custard is a worthwhile addition to one's egg repertoire, I selected this recipe over other choices because of the recipe's instructions. This is a Rosettastone recipe that establishes an equivalency between a slow oven, an English Dutch oven,[43] and a brazing pan with embers on its lid.[44] These instructions establish what is implicit in other cookbooks, but nowhere else so clearly stated.[45]

The smaller one interprets a cup of coffee, the firmer the custard sets up. A two-ounce cup (60g) molds perfectly. I advise using three-quarters of an ounce (20g) of coffee for 8 (225g) to 16 ounces (500g) of water. The custard can also be steamed.

Opium with Rear Yolk
Dissolution of Opium in the *Yolk of a rear new-laid Egg*, by pounding the Dose that you intend to take, with a little Quantity of the *Yolk*, till both be thoroughly mixed, and then taking it in the remaining Part of the Yolk.[46]
John Jones, *The Mysteries of Opium Reveal'd*, 1700

John Jones considered egg yolk to be the ideal carrier for opium. He thought that it would bind the opium, keeping it from sticking to the stomach, thus improving its absorption into the body. A *rear* egg is an egg that is hot, but the whites and yolk are both still liquid (see *Rear Egg*). As opium is both exceedingly illegal, and not a drug to play around with, I tested this recipe with *Cannabis sativa*, a drug that is more readily available, safer to experiment with, and in small quantities, legal in some countries. As *Cannabis sativa* is variable in its potency, it is advisable to start with a small quantity. An easy way of obtaining a rear yolk is to boil a room temperature egg for two and a half minutes. Adding a little salt helps grind up the herb, and improves the flavor. This makes a lovely green egg with a pleasant slightly resinous taste. Its psychoactive properties vary depending on the potency of the herb, how much you add, and your own physiology. In my own experience this makes for a gentle nightcap, and sweet dreams. I advise pounding the *Cannabis sativa* with salt in a warmed mortar, and then adding the rear yolk. Serve with a horn spoon as soon as the herb and yolk are mixed.

Notes

1. From August 15, 2006, selected primary documents will be posted on my web site at williamrubel.com.
2. *Familiar Forms of Speaking, Compos'd for the Use of Schools. The Fourteenth Edition, Corrected and Amended, and Somewhat Enlarged. To Which Are Added Short Forms for Parsing a Lesson (Familiares Colloquendi Formulæ, in Usum Scholarum Concinnatæ. Editio Decima Quarta, Etc.)* (London: Printed by J. M. for Tho. Helder, 1701), p. 82.
3. The new-laid egg a high-status food which is why Charles Dicken's aspiring Miss Tox always had 'one egg new-laid (or warranted to be)' on her breakfast table. Charles Dickens, *Dombey and Son*, 2 vols., vol. 1 (Charles E. Lauriat Company, 1923), ch. 29.
4. William Rufus Chetwood, Francisco Alcaforado, and Richard Falconer, *The Voyages, Dangerous Adventures and Imminent Escapes of Captain Richard Falconer: Containing the Laws, Customs, and Manners of the Indians in America. Intermix'd with the Voyages and Adventures of Thomas Randal. Written by Himself [or Rather, by W. R. Chetwood], Etc* (London: W. Chetwood), p. 14.

5. The cookbook literature universally assumes the chicken egg is the egg of the kitchen. One exception is Mrs. Beeton who refers to many wild eggs including plover, lapwing, and ruff. Isabella Mary Beeton, *Mrs. Beeton's Dictionary of Every-Day Cookery* (London: S. O. Beeton, 1865), p. 112.
6. Hold an egg near a candle, or interpose the egg between your eye and the sun. The egg should be clear. A good period explanation is found in *The Accomplish'd Housewife; or, the Gentlewoman's Companion: Containing I. Reflections on the Education of the Fair Sex, Etc.* (London: J. Newbery, 1745), p. 160.
7. A hole around one-quart inch in diameter (½ cm) is usually large enough.
8. Cogan, in the *Haven of Health*, spells it *rere*, which being close to our *rare*, makes it easy to remember his definition, an egg that is 'little more than through hot.' Thomas Cogan, *The Hauen of Health. Chiefely Gathered for the Comfort of Students, and Consequently of All Those That Haue a Care of Their Health. Hereunto Is Added a Preseruation from the Pestilence, with a Short Censure of the Late Sicknes at Oxford* (London: Henry Middleton for W. Norton, 1584), p. 151.
9. Joseph Morgan, *Phoenix Britannicus. Being a Miscellaneous Collection of Scarce and Curious Tracts. Also. Some Choice Originals. On. Useful and Entertaining Subjects. By J. Morgan, Gent. Nos. 1–5* (London: For the Compiler and T. Edlin, 1731), p. 201.
10. Heated or lightly cooked eggs are often associated with wine, though when fed to horses farriers usually associated eggs with ale. S., a Gent., *The Gentleman's Compleat Jockey: With the Perfect Horseman, and Experienc'd Farrier* (London: Henry Nelme, 1697), p. 57.
11. Boiled.
12. Cogan, *The Hauen of Health*.
13. Lemuel Gulliver and Jonathan Swift, *Travels into Several Remote Nations of the World* (Dublin: Dublin, 1727), p. 4.
14. Joannes de Mediolano, *Regimen Sanitatis Salerni*, trans. Thomas Paynell (London: Thomas Berthelet, 1528), pp. 19–21.This work seemes to have been Thomas Cogan's primary source for the egg section in *Haven of Health* and includes numerous technical culinary details. For even more detailed instructions see Platina and Mary Ella Milham, *Platina, on Right Pleasure and Good Health: A Critical Edition and Translation of De Honesta Voluptate Et Valetudine* (Tempe, Ariz.: Medieval & Renaissance Texts & Studies, 1998), pp. 402–07.
15. For a rare example of adapting egg roasting to the modern kitchen see Paula Wolfert, *The Slow Mediterranean Kitchen: Recipes for the Passionate Cook* (Hoboken, NJ: Wiley, 2003), p. 49. See also William Rubel, *The Magic of Fire: Hearth Cooking: One Hundred Recipes for the Fireplace or Campfire* (Berkeley, California: Ten Speed Press, 2002), pp. 80–81.
16. Ebenezer Cobham Brewer, *Dictionary of Phrase and Fable*, new ed. (London, New York: Cassell and Co. Ltd., 1898) accessed June 10, 2006 http://www.bartleby.com/81/5663.html.
17. Publius Ovidius Naso et al., *Ovid's Metamorphoses in Fifteen Books* (London: J. Tonson, 1717) VIII 285. The original line was simply, and from a cook's perspective, ambiguously, *ovaque non acri leviter versata favilla*. Publius Ovidius Naso, Jan Minell, and Nathan Bailey, *Ovid's Metamorphoses, in Fifteen Books, with the Arguments and Notes of John Minellius Translated into English.*, sixth ed. (London: London: printed for J. Rivington and Sons; T. Longman; B. Law J. Johnson; G.G.J. and J. Robinson; W. Goldsmith; T. Evans; Scatchard, 1778), p. 292.
18. Platina and Milham, *Platina, on Right Pleasure and Good Health: A Critical Edition and Translation of De Honesta Voluptate Et Valetudine*, p. 407.
19. William Shakespeare, *As You Like It*, Act III, Scene 2.
20. *The Works of Alexander Pope*, vol. 3 (Edinburgh: Martin & Wotherspoon, 1770), p. 89.
21. Platina and Milham, *Platina, on Right Pleasure and Good Health: A Critical Edition and Translation of De Honesta Voluptate Et Valetudine* p. 405.
22. Platina copied most of his recipes, including this one, from Maestro Martino of Como. Maestro, Martino, Luigi Ballerini, Jeremy Parzen, and Stefania Barzini, *The Art of Cooking: The First Modern Cookery Book*, Berkeley: University of California Press, 2005, p. 97.

23. In a letter to Mrs Dingley in 1713, Jonathan Swift explained a change in his writing this way, 'I write short journals now. I have eggs on the spit.' Cob, at the end of the third act in Ben Johnson's *Every man in his Humour* explains he cannot be distracted because, 'I have Eggs on the Spit. Now am I for some and fifty Reasons hammering, hammering Revenge.'
24. While spit-roasted eggs have fallen out of fashion in Western cooking, they are found in modern Thai cookbooks and make a great campfire entertainment.
25. George Dalrymple, *The Practice of Modern Cookery; Adapted to Families of Distinction, as Well as to Those of the Middling Ranks of Life* (Edinburgh: Printed for the Author, 1781), p. 418.
26. Gilles et Bleuzen du Pontavice, *La Cuisine Des Châteaux De Normandie* (Rennes: Editions Ouest-France, 1998).
27. François Pierre de La Varenne and I. D. G., *The French Cook*, trans. I. D. G. (London, 1653), p. 169.
28. Pellegrino Artusi, *The Art of Eating Well*, 1st ed. (New York: Random House, 1996), p. 107.
29. Robert May, *The Accomplisht Cook, or, the Art and Mystery of Cookery* (Totnes: Prospect Books, 1994), p. 440.
30. *Le Mesnagier De Paris*, ed. trans. Karin Ueltschi Georgina E. Brereton and Janet M. Ferrier (Paris: Librarie Générale Française, 1994), p. 717. Lost Eggs, *Œufs Perdus*, are eggs fried directly on embers or hot ash.
31. Thomas Cogan wrote in favor of poaching rather than frying eggs for collops and eggs (eggs and bacon), a healthful method adopted by Robert May (1684) and Hannah Glasse (1747).
32. Sieur de la Varenne, François Pierre, *La Varenne's Cookery*, ed. Terence Scully (Totnes: Prospect Booksk, 2006). May, *The Accomplisht Cook, or, the Art and Mystery of Cookery*.
33. May, *The Accomplisht Cook, or, the Art and Mystery of Cookery*, p. 437 (To dress a dish of Collops and Egg the best way for service, p. 169).
34. Natural ambergris is difficult to acquire and, in the United States, illegal to possess.
35. May, *The Accomplisht Cook, or, the Art and Mystery of Cookery* p. 437.
36. One rarely sees recipes for egg poached in broth or flavored liquids.
37. In the United States it is illegal to possess. There is a synthetic substitute.
38. See recipe 40 in John Nott, *The Cooks and Confectioners Dictionary: Or, the Accomplish'd Housewives Companion. The Second Edition with Additions. [or Rather, Compiled] Revised and Recommended by John Nott, Etc* (London: C. Rivington, 1724) n. p.
39. For another version of this dish – one that is more modern – see *Eggs with Orange-juice*, in Vincent La Chapelle, *The Modern Cook*, vol. 3 (London: the Author, 1733), p. 173.
40. Fresh eggs – quail or chicken – broken into a glass of freshly squeezed orange juice is a common Mexican street food.
41. This is a sour fruit and is the preferred orange for marmalade and was the primary orange of seventeenth- and eighteenth-century English cooking, including when orange was used as a garnish.
42. Menon, *The Professed Cook; or, the Modern Art of Cookery, Pastry and Confectionary Made Plain and Easy. Second Edition*, trans. B. Clermont from *Soupers de La Cour* of Menon (London, 1769), p. 479.
43. A reflector oven – a three-sided metal box set in front of the fire and heated by radiant heat. This meaning was common in America up to the twentieth century.
44. The brazing pan was usually used on a stove over coal or charcoal and tended not to have legs – the primary difference between it and an American Dutch oven.
45. For a similar comparison between a slow oven and a pan with embers on the lid see *To make leauened bread* in Anon, *A Good Huswifes Handmaide for the Kitchin* (London: Imprinted by Richard Iones, 1594), p. 50.
46. John Jones, M. D., Chancellor of Llandaff, *The Mysteries of Opium Reveal'd, Etc* (London: 1700), p. 287.

The Encyclopaedic Egg

Barbara Santich

In 1751 the most ambitious publishing project of the eighteenth century was launched with the first volume of the *Encyclopédie,* edited by Denis Diderot and Jean le Rond d'Alembert. Its aim was to encompass the entire knowledge of the time, not only in the noble domains of philosophy and theology but also in the more practical areas of *arts et métiers,* crafts and trades. Unusually, its plan allowed a place for entries on food and cooking to be included in a variety of categories, from *Matière médicale & Diete* to *Agriculture & Economie rustique,* from *Cuisine exotique* to *Jardinage.*

According to Jean-Claude Bonnet, while the *Encyclopédie* does not 'give a clear picture of eighteenth-century eating habits' but rather is more interested in 'food practices throughout the world and throughout the ages', it nevertheless 'reflects, above all, the state of knowledge at the time, as well as the authors' wide-ranging and pluralistic learning'.[1] Thus the humble egg enters into a diverse range of entries; its role as a culinary ingredient is by no means the most significant.

It is salutary to realise that, even in mid-eighteenth-century France, knowledge of the female anatomy and the reproductive processes was still quite rudimentary, and other biological processes were not well understood (for example, concerning the hatching of eggs). Nevertheless, the *Encyclopédie* can be assumed to offer a trustworthy and reliably accurate representation of practices, beliefs and ideas current at the time in relation to the nutritional and therapeutic value of eggs, the preservation of eggs, and their culinary and non-culinary uses.

Curiously, one of the most frequent uses of the egg in the *Encyclopédie* was as a comparative measure – for size (size of a pigeon egg, or of a hen's egg; aubergines were described as being about the size of an egg or of a cucumber); for viscosity – 'a little thicker and more viscous than egg white'; and for appearance – as fine as the thin layer of skin inside an egg.

Characteristics of the egg

The *Encyclopédie* was nothing if not encyclopaedic! While noting that hens' eggs were the most commonly used as food in Europe, it added that goose, duck, guinea fowl, pheasant and peahen eggs were also eaten and that ostrich and crocodile eggs were eaten in Africa, turtle eggs in the Caribbean.

Eggs were considered a good, wholesome food, highly nourishing and useful for both healthy and ill individuals. They were believed to increase the quantity of sperm produced, promote the sexual appetite, and were very efficient at predisposing individuals to satisfy such appetites. The aphrodisiac properties were considered to belong

The Encyclopaedic Egg

to the yolk which had different qualities to the egg white; while the egg white was more nourishing, the yolk had heating properties.

Culinary uses

According to the *Encyclopédie,* there were many ways of preparing eggs, and many different dishes; the simpler these were, the healthier they were deemed to be. 'For all these refined preparations in which eggs are combined with dairy products, sugar and flavourings so disguise the true nature of the egg that it loses all its good qualities. It has even been observed that when eggs are added to dairy products [milk and cream], these start to undergo the changes they are naturally susceptible to, transmit these to the eggs, and the resultant spoiling is worse than would have happened to dairy products by themselves. One can therefore state that these delicate mixtures of eggs and milk, such as *crèmes* [custards] etc. are foods which are at least suspect, as is milk.' This report concerned whole eggs; the *Encyclopédie* attributed different dietary properties to the white and the yolk separately. The egg white was considered more nourishing; the yolk was less nourishing but more heating, and it was the yolk that was supposed to confer aphrodisiac properties to eggs.

By themselves, eggs were considered a good food, though deciding how well they were to be cooked posed certain problems. In general, according to the *Encyclopédie* and citing Louis Lémery (a Paris physician, 1677–1747), eggs should be moderately cooked, 'd'une substance molle et humide', soft and moist; if undercooked, they remain slimy and are difficult to digest. Equally, if overcooked they also become difficult to digest.

The *Encyclopédie* repeated the accepted wisdom that eggs had a heating effect when they were old, and while there were no obvious symptoms of this, it was well known that old eggs had a disagreeable taste and were more likely than fresh eggs to become corrupted in the stomach. The worst of all, it reported, were old hard-boiled eggs such as those sold at Easter in Paris and in other countries. These, wrote le Chevalier de Jaucourt, weigh heavily on the stomach, cause colic, and generally cause genuine indigestion which is even more annoying for being accompanied by constipation. 'We cannot,' he continued, 'approve the practice, based on this property, of using hard-boiled eggs as a popular and household remedy for diarrhoea.'

This was almost the extent of the *Encyclopédie's* summary of the culinary uses of eggs, though it also included a generic recipe for the culinary term, *ramequin*, a preparation of finely chopped kidneys with parsley, garlic and egg yolk which was spread on bread, subsequently cooked in a frying pan or on the grill. There is no recipe for *ramequin* in *La Cuisinière Bourgeoise*, but *ramequins* do figure in La Varenne's *Le Cuisinier françois* (1651); this entry represents one of a number of borrowings from La Varenne's book.[2] The entry added that *ramequins* could be made with cheese or sugar in the same way.

Much more about the variety of ways of cooking and using eggs in the kitchen can be learnt from *La Cuisinière Bourgeoise* (1774 edition; first ed. 1746).³ They were poached; boiled; hard-boiled and served in salad; grilled; scrambled (with variations, such as with a *ragoût de celeri* or lettuce); fried; cooked *au plat* or *au miroir*; as an omelette; as *œufs au gratin*; *en timbales* (cooked in a bain-marie). Omelettes seem to have been served relatively frequently. Accounts of meals provided to the military in Provence at the end of the eighteenth century frequently mention omelettes. For example, when the national guard of Mormoiron stopped at Entraigues, they were offered for supper three omelettes each of 12 eggs – in addition to bread, salad, 30 bottles of wine and 24 pounds of mutton; their prisoner was allowed three eggs, one and a half pounds of bread and one bottle of wine.

Eggs and egg yolks also served to thicken soups, sauces, ragoûts and fricassées, and the *Encyclopédie* explained how: egg yolks served to unite the melted fat which comes to the surface with the aqueous part which lies below, therefore seeming to render the fat invisible. This particular property of egg yolks was explained by their analogy with bile, which made them able to bind oily and watery substances together.

They were also ingredients in fritters and *bisquits* (small, dryish, individual cakes); they were brushed on pastry to give it a golden brown colour; they were essential to a variety of *crèmes* – the very dishes disparaged by the *Encyclopédie* – chocolate, coffee, caramel-flavoured, *crème brûlée*, some with bread or crushed macaroons, some set with rennet. Eggs were also essential to what *La Cuisinière Bourgeoise* called *Fromage à la Montmorency* and what the *Encyclopédie* called syllabub, a drink made of white wine and sugar to which was added fresh (new) milk. It could also be made with the sweet white wine from the Canary Islands (in which case sugar was omitted, and lemon juice and nutmeg added as flavourings). Egg whites entered into the whipped syllabub; the mixture of wine, egg whites and sugar was whipped and the froth that rose to the surface was skimmed off as it formed and transferred to a separate dish, allowed to stand for two or three hours and then eaten.

Egg whites had a role in *confiserie* (confectionery). For sugared almonds (*amandes glacées*) blanched almonds were coated in an icing of powdered sugar, egg white and orange-flower water then slowly dried in the oven at low temperature. *Amandes soufflées* were similar but apparently not baked; the blanched almonds were dipped in egg white and powdered sugar alternately until the coating was sufficiently thick, after which they were presumably left to dry.

The *Encyclopédie* noted that eggs were used in the preparation of chocolate in the French colonies of the Caribbean, a practice apparently not common in France itself. Grated chocolate, powdered sugar and ground cinnamon were mixed together in a chocolate pot with a whole egg, hot liquid (milk or water) was added, and the mixture was frothed over heat. This method of making chocolate had several particular advantages which make it preferable to other methods, reported the *Encyclopédie*, but did not elaborate as to the nature of these advantages.

The Encyclopaedic Egg

Preservation

The variety of methods proposed for the preservation of eggs is an indication of their importance in the diet, and for culinary and medicinal purposes. By the eighteenth century people had realised that the egg shell is porous and that, as the egg ages, the air sac at one end of the egg gradually enlarges; this, according to the *Encyclopédie*, was because moisture was lost through the shell. (Evidence for the existence of this air sac was that the cheeping of the chick can be heard inside the egg even before it hatches.)

The principle for preserving eggs was therefore to prevent this transpiration. The common way of keeping eggs in good condition was to arrange them in a barrel and completely surround them with compressed ashes, or bran, or sawdust. These are the same methods as suggested in the 1774 edition of *La Cuisinière Bourgeoise*, 'For storage: store in a place neither too warm nor too cold (the cellar is good), in summer put them in a barrel, with straw; in winter with hay; some people use sawdust, others thatching, others ashes' and apparently had been known for many centuries, since they are mentioned by the Ménagier de Paris in the fourteenth century.

The *Encyclopédie*, however, reported an improved technique attributed to M. de Réaumur (French physician, 1683–1757), namely to paint the eggs with a waterproof varnish composed of gum lacquer plus turpentine dissolved in wine spirits. Having suggested this method, Réaumur came up with a much simpler and cheaper technique using fresh mutton fat. This fat costs hardly any more than tallow, reported the *Encyclopédie* (but it seems that people found the idea of tallow disgusting). Wax, or resined pitch, would also work. The instructions were to melt the fat, strain it into an earthenware pot, and keep it warm near the fire; then dip the eggs in this and withdraw immediately. The *Encyclopédie* suggests using tongs, or simply to tie a thread around the middle of the egg and lower it into the melted fat. According to the *Encyclopédie*, mutton fat does not taint the egg in the slightest; and is easily removed by dipping the coated egg in boiling water then rubbing lightly with a cloth. It was suggested that eggs preserved in this way would last for about a year.

Oil would also serve for sealing the eggs and allowing them to be stored, but the *Encyclopédie* suggested that this would not be as effective as the more solid fats and the resins. Further, it would be easier to remove a coating of mutton fat than a coating of oil, and therefore the mutton fat process was recommended for eggs that were to be kept for hatching. The author of this entry, le Chevalier de Jaucourt, seemed surprised that neither the varnish nor the mutton fat techniques were more popular in France.

Le Chevalier de Jaucourt even hypothesised that, by using the mutton fat method of preservation, it might be possible to take to other countries the eggs of various species of bird not present in those environments, to hatch them, and thus to naturalise the species in a new country. In this suggestion he was anticipating the efforts of the Acclimatisation Societies of the nineteenth century.

The Encyclopaedic Egg

If all these efforts were made to preserve them, or to ensure a reliable supply throughout the year, eggs must have been valued relatively highly, if not as a luxury then at least as a culinary essential. Accounts for the household of Gaspard II de Fortia de Montréal in Avignon in 1772 and 1773 show that eggs were bought in large quantities two or three times a week and, at 10 to 16s per dozen, were relatively cheap, though slightly more expensive in winter than in summer. Really fresh eggs, however, the new laid '*œufs du jour*', cost as much as £2 2s per dozen, more than twice as much as standard eggs, though at these prices they were bought in ones and twos. They seem to have been valued for their therapeutic properties, having been bought for the sick coachman and for the Count in his final days.

Medicinal uses

As mentioned earlier, day-old eggs were significantly more expensive than other eggs in eighteenth-century Avignon and were credited with therapeutic properties. None of the preparations cited in the *Encyclopédie*, however, specifies day-old eggs, though its general advice is that eggs be as fresh as possible, and preferably white and long ('bien blanc & longs').

According to the *Encyclopédie*, a very common preparation based on egg yolks and used for coughs was *bouillon à la reine*. The same was also used to treat bilious colic, although this treatment seems to have been less widely practised. This preparation seems to have been the same as the *lait de poule* – fresh egg yolk mixed with a little sugar and hot water, drunk just before going to bed – recommended for the flu by *La Cuisinière Bourgeoise*.

Egg yolks were an essential component of soothing emulsions, typically based on oils plus sugar. One particular category of emulsions were called *looch*, thick emulsions to be slowly sipped, made of sweet almond oil, syrup and distilled (flavoured) waters) emulsified with egg yolk. Mixed with turpentine or other natural balsams, egg yolks yielded digestives with similar properties, the egg yolk softening the harsh burning properties of the balsams.

Egg whites were valued in medicine for their astringent and glue-like properties. Mixed with Armeniac (a pale red-coloured earth from Armenia, used medicinally, and in the composition of tooth-powders) they were used on bruises to prevent swelling; egg whites also entered into compounds applied to recent wounds and to control bleeding. Similarly, *La Cuisinière Bourgeoise* suggests egg white whisked with *eau de plantin* as being good for inflammation of the eyes.

Cinnamon oil, reputedly one of the most effective stimulants and fortifying tonics, also effective for women in prolonged labour, was administered by means of a poached egg, 1–6 drops per egg. Clove oil was given in carmelite water (*eau de mélisse*) after being first mixed with a little sugar or egg yolk.

Finally, egg shells also had a medicinal use. Crushed on porphyry (a very hard rock, slabs of which were used for grinding and triturating drugs), they were an absorbent exactly analogous to the crushed oyster shell, pearls and mother of pearl. 'It is purely for fickle fashion,' reprimanded the author of this entry, 'that certainly people have recently been advised to carry in their pockets a tin of ground eggshell sent from Louvain.'

According to *La Cuisinière Bourgeoise*, burnt and crushed eggshell was good for whitening the teeth; if the shells were burnt, reduced to ashes and drunk with wine, this was reputed to prevent the spitting of blood.

Other uses of eggs

One important use of egg whites was in clarification, especially in chemistry and for pharmaceutical extracts, as well as in medicinal jellies, for example in hartshorn jelly (*gelée de corne de cerf*), a nourishing restorative, and in viper jelly, made from viper soup (*bouillon de vipères*); both these remedies are also mentioned in the eighteenth century by the English author Richard Bradley. They were also used in the clarification of whey intended for pharmaceutical use.

Egg whites also had important roles in a number of trades, according to the *Encyclopédie*. In the preparation of canvasses, the final stage involved giving a coating of pure walnut oil then, when this had dried, brushing on egg white. In wineries, egg whites were used to moderate the fermentation process. Bookbinders and gilders used egg whites to make the spine or other parts of the book sticky before applying the gold leaf when the egg white had dried. Egg white was also used to give a lustrous shine to book covers; a cloth dipped in egg white was very lightly rubbed over the surface which was allowed to dry then finished with a smoothing iron. Leather workers soaked the high heels of delicate ladies' shoes in egg white before reddening them with red ochre, *rouge d'Inde* or Indian red. Finally, egg whites entered into some of the preparations for removing the natural lanolin from woollen cloth. One method used a mixture of three parts hot water and one part urine; another used saltpetre; and a third applied sal ammoniac (ammonium chloride), egg white, alum and vinegar.

Conclusion

While the *Encyclopédie* is not very informative on the culinary uses of eggs in the eighteenth century – and this lack of attention to what the Chevalier de Jaucourt might have considered a frivolous purpose is quite characteristic of the work – it compensates for this with a wealth of information on the *useful* uses of eggs, in accordance with the intentions of the project as conceived by Diderot and d'Alembert. In so doing, it demonstrates vividly the importance of this barnyard staple in eighteenth-century French life.

Bibliography

L'Encyclopédie de Diderot et d'Alembert [electronic resource] : *ou, Dictionnaire raisonné des sciences, des arts et des métiers* (Marsanne : Edition Redon, 1999).

Le Cuisinier François: Textes présentés par Jean Louis Flandrin, Philip et Mary Hyman (Paris: Editions Montalba, 1983).

La Cuisinière Bourgeoise, Facsimile of 1774 edition, with postface by Alice Peeters (Poitiers: Temps Actuels, 1981).

Notes

1. Bonnet, Jean-Claude, 'The Culinary System in the Encyclopédie' in *Food and Drink in History: Selections from the Annales*, eds. Robert Forster and Orest Ranum, trans. Elborg Forster and Patricia Ranum (Baltimore: Johns Hopkins University Press, 1979), pp. 139–165.
2. *Le Cuisinier François: Textes présentés par Jean Louis Flandrin, Philip et Mary Hyman*. Paris: Editions Montalba, 1983.
3. *La Cuisinière Bourgeoise*, facsimile of 1774 edition, with postface by Alice Peeters. Poitiers: Temps Actuels, 1981.

Turkey Eggs

Andrew F. Smith

Over the last 10 million years, North America and Asia have been intermittently connected by land bridges. At times, these bridges extended vast distances, permitting animals to migrate freely between the two continents. The ancestors of the modern horse and camel, for instance, originated in North America. Conversely, the ancestors of the American buffalo and turkey originated in Asia and traveled over the land bridge to populate North America.

Turkey-like birds have inhabited North America for the last 7 million years or longer. From these progenitors, the modern turkey emerged about 50,000 years ago; by the pre-Columbian era it was widely dispersed throughout North and Central America. By any standard, the turkey is an unusual bird. Perhaps its most peculiar characteristic has to do with the hen's reproductive system. Like some lizards, snakes, and a few other animals, the turkey hen has the ability to reproduce by parthenogenesis: under certain conditions, hens can produce fertilized eggs without having mated. All chicks produced from these eggs are male, but only about 20 per cent of them will be able to reproduce as adults. Although parthenogenesis has only been documented in domesticated turkeys, it is thought that wild turkeys have this ability as well.[1]

Numerous descriptions of wild turkeys have survived from earlier centuries, but the ornithologist John James Audubon offers some of the best. Observing wild turkeys in the early nineteenth century, he reported that in a single clutch, wild turkey hens lay between 8 and 15, and sometimes as many as 20 eggs. When the hens begin to lay, 'they separate themselves, in order to save their eggs from the male, who would break them all, for the purpose of protracting his sexual enjoyments.' She makes her nest with some leaves in a hollowed-out depression in the ground, preferably by the side of a log or in a thicket preferably on an isolated island. The eggs range from white to a cream color, with brown speckles; the hen carefully conceals them on the ground. When the hen seeks water and food, she covers the eggs with leaves, making them difficult to spot. She leaves the nest with extreme caution, reports Audubon, scarcely ever taking the same course twice. The hen incubates and turns the eggs for 28 days. Hatching takes place over a 24-hour period, during which the hen does not leave the eggs under any circumstances. Even when an enemy, such as a crow, eagle, snake, skunk, fox or raccoon, passes within sight, the hen does not move. If the eggs have been destroyed for some reason, the female soon yelps again for a male and females can produce one or two additional clutches during a season.[2]

Turkey Eggs

American Indians

The last land bridge occurred during the Pleistocene era, permitting people to traverse from Asia into North America sometime between 30,000 and 15,000 years ago.

Early humans were evidently excellent hunters, as a number of species, such as the horse, the mastodon, and the sabre-toothed tiger, disappeared after their arrival. Despite these disappearances, the New World was particularly well endowed with birds. Thousands of species of migratory and gallinaceous birds – heavy-bodied fowl that roost and feed mainly on the ground – were widely dispersed throughout North and South America, and virtually all were likely eaten by pre-Columbian peoples. Some – such as the wild turkeys inhabiting the west coast of North America – disappeared from the fossil record at the time of early human habitation. Wild turkeys, however, survived in prodigious numbers in Mexico and North America east of the Rockies, and they were an important food source for those American-Indians who inhabited modern-day Mexico and eastern North America. In addition to eating the birds' flesh, early humans also ate their eggs, as evidenced by shells found at archeological sites.

According to many European travelers, American Indians 'much sought after and relished' wild turkey eggs, according to the Moravian Bishop George Henry Loskiel.[3] In the American south-west, the Hopi also enjoyed them whenever they could be found, and some considered turkey eggs a delicacy.[4] On the other hand, the Navajo, also in the south-west, ate turkey flesh, but for unexplained reasons never ate the eggs.[5]

Europeans ran into domesticated turkey in Mexico in the early sixteenth century and brought them back to their home countries; from there, the turkey soon traveled to the rest of the world. In addition to turkey flesh, Europeans also ate their eggs. The sixteenth-century French writer Charles Estienne, however, had nothing good to say about them: 'The housewife shall not make any great account of Turkie egs: at least he that loueth his health, shall not esteeme of them for to use them: for phisitions hold, that egs of Turkies engender grauell, and minister cause to breede the leprosie.'[6] On the other hand, the seventeenth-century English cookbook author Gervase Markham found turkey eggs 'exceeding wholesome to eate, and restore nature decayed wonderfully.'[7] Estienne's and Markham's statements regarding turkey eggs were repeated regularly throughout the seventeenth and eighteenth centuries by both American and British authors. In the mid-seventeenth century, the early American explorer and settler John Josselyn reported that turkey eggs were 'very wholesome and restore decayed nature exceedingly' but he also reported that 'the French say they breed Leprosie.'[8] In the early eighteenth century John Mortimer and other English agricultural experts heralded turkey eggs as 'very wholsome, and a great Restorer of Nature.'[9] One hundred years later, English cookbook writers were still heralding the wholesomeness of turkey eggs.[10]

In America, European colonists, particularly on the frontier, ate wild turkey eggs whenever they could be found. James Nourse, for instance, went out hunting in

Turkey Eggs

Kentucky in 1775 and was able to bring back nothing more than three turkey eggs.[11] In 1791, Israel Donalson, a New Jersey native who became a Kentucky pioneer, made meals of wild turkey eggs while fleeing from Indians.[12] In 1797 Pennsylvania missionary John Heckewelder reported that turkey eggs were more 'palatable than wild goose or wild duck eggs.'[13] In 1848, Sarah Brewer-Bonebright, an early settler in Iowa, agreed: turkey eggs were 'more palatable than those of wild goose or wild duck eggs.'[14] By the late nineteenth century, turkey eggs were sold on the market for ten cents per dozen in Arkansas.[15]

In general, turkey eggs were prepared in many of the same ways as chicken eggs, since turkey eggs taste like chicken eggs (although they are one-and-a-half times larger). Turkey eggs contain on average 135 calories, 9 grams of fat, and almost 740 mg of cholesterol – much more than the largest chicken eggs. These differences can make it somewhat tricky to substitute turkey eggs for chicken eggs in recipes.

Recipes using turkey eggs do occasionally appear in British and American cookbooks. Jennie June's *American Cookery Book* (1866), for instance, includes one for a sauce made with them:

Turkey's Eggs Sauce
Turkey's eggs are superior to others for sauce. Boil three eggs gently in plenty of water twenty minutes. Break the shells by rolling them on the table; separate the whites from the yolks, divide all the yolks into quarter inch dice pieces, mince one and a half of the whites rather small, mix them lightly and stir them into a pint of white sauce, and serve hot. The eggs of common fowl may be prepared for sauce according to these directions, using four yolks and two whites, and boiling four or five minutes less. The eggs of guinea fowl also make a good sauce after ten minutes.[16]

This appeared in *Cassell's Dictionary of Cookery* published about 1874:

Eggs, Turkey's, to Dress.
Choose those of the young bird for cooking in the shell. They may be known by their pale, almost white colour. The larger ones are excellent for poaching, and to serve in the composition of any dishes where eggs are required. Time, six minutes, to boil, four to poach.[17]

In the 1880s, Juliet Corson, founder of the New York Cooking School, offered a system for boiling duck, geese and turkey eggs:

Turkey, Geese, and Duck Eggs
Put the eggs into a bowl filled with boiling water for five minutes, keeping the bowl covered tight and in a hot place; then pour off the first water, replace it

with more boiling water, and let them stand for five minutes longer; serve them like ordinary boiled eggs; or, actually boil the eggs for five minutes: either of these methods will cook the eggs medium hard. From ten to fifteen minutes boiling will cook the eggs hard, according to size. Duck eggs will cook in less time than turkey or goose eggs.[18]

In the mid-nineteenth century, Alexis Soyer, a French chef and author who lived most of his professional life in England, proclaimed that, 'Turkey eggs are good boiled, and are preferred to those of hens for pastry; mixing them with common eggs makes an omelette more delicate.'[19] Chef Charles Ranhofer, chef at Delmonico's in the late nineteenth century, believed that turkey eggs were 'much liked either boiled or cooked in an omelet.'[20] As long as wild turkey eggs could be found, Americans continued to eat them throughout the nineteenth century.[21]

According to the mid-nineteenth century butcher and historian Thomas F. De Voe, turkey eggs were rarely sold in markets. When they did appear, they were 'usually mixed with the common fowls' when brought to us direct by the neighboring farmers or market-men.'[22]

Turkey breeding

In addition to being used for food, beginning in the eighteenth century wild turkey eggs were collected and placed under domesticated turkeys. Since wild turkeys were much larger than the domesticated turkeys of the time, those engaged in this experiment hoped that when the wild turkey eggs hatched, they would produce large domesticated turkeys.[23] Of course, the pre-natal 'nurture' of wild turkey eggs by domesticated hens could not change the genetic 'nature' of the resulting chicks, but continued attempts were made to raise wild turkey eggs in this manner through the nineteenth century.[24]

Although these experiments were doomed to failure, the long association of the wild eastern turkey with the domesticated turkey brought by European colonists to North America did bear fruit. Most farmers permitted their turkeys to roam freely about the farm, eating insects and plants and mating at will. The domesticated European birds bred with each other and also with the wild eastern turkeys (*M. g. silvestris*), creating a true 'melting pot' bird. Crossbreeds were mentioned by the Englishman John Mortimer as early as 1708: Mortimer 'knew a Gentleman that had a Hen-Turkey of the wild Kind from *Virginia*; of which an *English Cock* he raised a very fine Breed, that bred wild in the Fields.' It was much larger than the domesticated turkeys then in England.[25] Likewise, the English agricultural writer Richard Bradley reported in 1736 that there was 'a Breed in some part of the West of England, between the Turkey and the Virginia Bustard, which produces the largest sort I have yet seen. I have eaten part of one of them, which I judged to excell our common Turkey abundantly in Fineness of Flesh.'[26] In 1750 Englishman William Ellis reported that there were 'two sorts of this species, the common *Suffolk* or *Norfolk* turkey and the Blue Virginia sort,'[27] the 'Virginia bronze' turkey which was commonly raised in Virginia and in England by the mid-eighteenth century.[28]

Turkey eggs today

Turkey eggs are scarcely ever mentioned in twentieth-century cookbooks. The reason for this is mainly economic. Broodiness – the hen's instinctual desire to sit on eggs to hatch them – has not been bred out of turkey hens, as it has in chickens, and so they do not produce as many eggs as chickens. Domesticated turkey hens lay only about 100 eggs per year, depending upon the breed and conditions of the hatchery.[29] By comparison, a laying chicken can produce almost 300 eggs per year. In addition, turkey hens take longer to mature, so more costs are incurred in raising them to laying age. Because of the limited supply, virtually all turkey eggs are used for production of more turkeys. In addition, breeders are not usually licensed to sell the eggs as food. Indeed, in the United States, the Department of Agriculture (USDA) has no inspection or grading regulations for turkey eggs.

Still, turkey eggs are occasionally available in specialty markets and there is a small resurgence of interest in them. Some turkey egg recipes are now available upon the Internet. The new interest in preserving heritage turkeys, particularly by the Slow Food movement, has encouraged the reintroduction of turkey eggs into the diets of some enthusiasts. In 2004, Steven Saunders, a Master Chef of Great Britain, reported that, 'The egg white made wonderful soufflés, probably because of the amount of albumen, and the creamy yolk produced superb pastry sauces.'[30]

Notes

1. M. W. Olsen, 'The Sex of Parthenogenetic Turkey Embryos,' *Journal of Heredity* 48 (1957): 217–8; M. W. Olsen, 'Performance Record of a Parthenogenetic Turkey Male,' *Science* 132 (December 1960): 1661; M. W. Olsen, 'Twelve Year Summary of Selection for Parthenogenesis in Beltsville Small White Turkeys,' *British Poultry Science* 6 (1965): 1–6; T. F. Savage, G. L. Bradley, and J. Hayat, 'The Incidence of Parthenogenesis in Medium White Turkey Hens When Fed a Breeder Diet Containing Yeast Cultures of Saccharomyces Cerevisiae,' *Poultry Science* (Supplement 1) 72 (1993), 80; Thomas F. Savage and Elzbieta I. Zakrzewska, 'A Guide to the Recognition of Parthenogenesis in Incubated Turkey Eggs,' at www.oregonstate.edu/Dept/animal-sciences/poultry/index.html.
2. John James Audubon, *The Birds of America, from Drawings Made in the United States and Their Territories* 7 vols. (New York: J. J. Audubon; Philadelphia: J. B. Chevalier, 1840–44) Volume 5, 54.
3. George Henry Loskiel, *History of the Mission of the United Brethren among the Indians in North America* (London: The Brethren's Society for the Furtherance of the Gospel, 1794), 91.
4. Don C. Talayesva [Leo W. Simmons, ed.], *Sun Chief: the Autobiography of a Hopi Indian* (New Haven: Published for the Institute of Human Relations by Yale University Press; London, H. Milford, Oxford University Press, 1942), 55.
5. Willard W. Hill, *The Agricultural and Hunting Methods of the Navaho Indians* (New Haven: Published

for the Department of Anthropology by the Yale University Press, 1938), 174.
6. Charles Estienne [Richard Svrflet, trans.], *Maison Rustique, or the Covntrie Farme* (London: Edm. Bollifant, 1600), 117.
7. Gervase Markham, *Cheape and Good Husbandry* (London: Roger Jackson, 1614), 127.
8. John Josselyn, *An Account of Two Voyages to New-england* (London: G. Widdows, 1674), 99.
9. J[ohn] Mortimer, *The Whole Art of Husbandry* (London: Printed by J. H. for H. Mortlock, 1708), 197 (quote); John Laurence, *A New System of Agriculture* (London: T. Woodward, 1726), 152.
10. Charles Millington, *The Housekeeper's Domestic Library; or New Universal Family Instructor* (London: F. Flint, 1810), 361.
11. *The History of Montgomery County, Ohio* (Chicago: W. H. Beers & Co., 1882), 293; James Nourse, 'Journey to Kentucky in 1775,' *Journal of American History* 19 (1925), 127.
12. Israel Donalson, 'Captivity of Israel Donalson,' *American Pioneer* 1 (December 1842), 430.
13. John Heckewelder, 'Notes of Travel . . . to Gnadenhuetten, 1797,' *Pennsylvania Magazine of History and Biography* 10 (1886), 146.
14. Sarah Brewer-Bonebright, *Reminiscences of Newcastle, Iowa, 1848* (Des Moines: Historical Department of Iowa, 1921), 76.
15. Octave Thanet, 'Plantation Life in Arkansas,' *The Atlantic Monthly* 68 (July 1891), 40.
16. J. C. Croly, *Jennie June's American Cookery Book* (New York: The American News Company, 1866), 100.
17. *Cassell's Dictionary of Cookery* (London: Cassell Petter & Galpin, [circa 1874]), 202.
18. Juliet Corson, *Miss Corson's Practical American Cookery and Household Management* (New York: Dodd, Mead, and Company, 1886), 253.
19. Alexis Soyer, *The Pantropheon or, History of Food, and its Preparation, from the Earliest Ages of the World.* London: Simpkin, Marshall, 1853), 166.
20. Charles Ranhofer, *The Epicurean* (New York: R. Ranhofer, 1894), 629.
21. Theodore Adolphu Babb, *In the Bosom of the Comanches* (Dallas: Press of John F. Worley Printing Co., 1912), 78; Sarah Brewer-Bonebright, *Reminiscences of New Castle, Iowa, 1848* (Des Moines: Historical Department of Iowa, Des Moines,1921), 77.
22. Thomas F. De Voe, *The Market Assistant* (New York: Hurd and Houghton, 1867), 406.
23. Thomas Pennant, 'An Account of the Turkey,' *Philosophical Transactions of the Royal Society of London* 71 (1781), 71.
24. *United States Democratic Review* 29 (September 1851), 279; John Lauris Blake, *The Farm and the Fireside: Or, the Romance of Agriculture. Being Half Hour Sketches of Life in the Country* (Auburn: Alden, Beardsley & Co., 1852), 79.
25. J[ohn] Mortimer, *The Whole Art of Husbandry* (London: Printed by J. H. for H. Mortlock, 1708), 196.
26. Richard Bradley, *The Country Gentleman and Farmer's Monthly Director* 6th ed. (London: D. Browne, 1736), 62–3.
27. William Ellis, *The Country Housewife's Family Companion (1750) with an Introduction by Malcolm Thick* (Devon, United Kingdom: Prospect Books, 2000), 218.
28. *The Farmer's Magazine* (London) 4 (1779), 372.
29. Carolyn J. Christman and Robert O. Hawes, *Birds of a Feather; Saving Turkeys from Extinction* (Pittsboro, NC: The American Livestock Breeds Conservancy, 1999), 7.
30. As quoted in: http://www.countrysideonline.co.uk/comment.php?comment.news.967

Creating with Arctic Eggs

Zona Spray Starks with Anore Paniyauraq Jones

Demographers predict that by 2050 the populations of developing countries will swell 50 per cent, and world food demands will more than double.[1] Asian populations are expected to increase food imports more than any other demographic group, pressing food manufacturers to augment existing products for worldwide consumption. Meeting protein requirements poses the greatest challenge, possibly solved by utilizing land and sea proteins more efficiently; something Asian and Arctic people have done for centuries. Inupiat and Yupik Eskimos, who inhabit Alaska's north-west and northern regions, employ every possible nutrient-filled food – including eggs and innards – to create healthy dishes.

Whether Western populations adopt Arctic's wild egg dishes is doubtful. But borrowing from ancient Arctic egg knowledge merits consideration. Subsistence foods are closely related to wealthy nation's dishes, though the ingredients may differ. Understanding how and why Arctic dishes were created will offer insight into a cook's creative process as she responds to food shortages and hopefully fuel new ideas for local and exportable foods.

Eggs: cultural influences
Prior to the early 1900s, lack of food was a constant threat in the Arctic. Some years, fish failed to run and cold cellars emptied long before summer's plants and berries appeared. Hunger slowly devastated villages, killing entire families. For survival, women living along Alaska's Kobuk River and adjoining areas – a wide swath of land skirting the Arctic Circle and reaching 200 miles east of Kotzebue Sound, described as Alaska's western Circle in this paper – became major food suppliers, harvesting spawning fish runs during summer fishcamp while men hunted land animals.

Catching enough fish to feed families through the winter requires numerous skills and a vast knowledge of migrating fish routes. Knowing where fish lay their eggs is vital information; including the month, the week and the day a species usually appears. From generations of shared information, Alaska's western Circle residents amassed enough detailed spawning information that researchers frequently ask villagers to confirm scientific fish migration data, which residents sometimes consider sloppy, lacking in detail.

Harvesting large fish quantities requires that traditional people be ready with nets, waiting for migrations before fish make their runs. Though summer fish harvests are the largest, Arctic fish lay eggs throughout the year, including months when ice covers swift flowing rivers. Salmon, all five varieties, spawn once in a 2–6 year lifespan. They travel summer through fall to their natal streams, deposit a new generation, and die.

In the upper Kobuk and Selawik rivers, sharpnose whitefish lay eggs upriver before freeze-up; sheefish travel to deep-water areas, spewing eggs on top of rivers when fall temperatures dip below freezing.[2] Broad whitefish deposit eggs directly under river ice with grayling following close behind, fattening up on whitefish eggs in preparation for their own spawning spree. Mudshark eggs float in ice-covered rivers until break-up, when river ice thaws. Along Kotzebue Sound, herring seek refuge for their young by laying eggs in seaweed-filled tidal beds. Depending upon water temperature and sunlight, some eggs hatch within days after spawning, others not until months later. The warmer the water and more hours of daylight, the quicker eggs develop.[3]

Understanding bird migrations and egg-laying patterns is as important for gathering bird eggs as the knowledge necessary to harvest fish. Birds, like fish, typically migrate and lay eggs at the same time each spring. And after a winter without eating bird eggs, gathering and eating newly laid eggs is tempting. But Arctic people prefer the flavor of eggs 14–16 days old, so nests are carefully monitored to ensure an egg's development. The number of eggs removed from a nest is also noted, for birds lay additional eggs when nest egg numbers decline. Hunters also know how many eggs to take from a nest. Depending upon the bird, when one or two eggs remain, production continues, ensuring a food supply – and plenty of baby birds. When the nest is empty, females stop laying eggs.[4]

Understanding yearly bird and fish migration patterns does not always guarantee a good harvest. For unknown reasons, there were years in the past when fish failed to run and birds ventured elsewhere, leaving villages without food. Hoping to control food supplies, taboos and rituals were established, although they usually applied to large animal hunting and preserving. Few fishing taboos exist along Alaska's western Circle, possibly because women traditionally controlled summer fishcamps. While women and children worked at fishcamp, men took to the mountains, hunting caribou for furs, believing that good hunters living at fishcamp caused inferior harvests. Yet women still pile fish, heads away from the water, to ensure future runs. And finding a large egg in a whitefish stomach is considered a bad omen for the fisherman's family.[5] Far off in Nunavut, previously Canada's north-eastern area, taboos during 1900 were far more rigid; but there, men were major fish harvesters. To promote continued fish runs, pregnant Netsilik women were banned from fishing areas, fearing they would frighten the fish away.[6]

Taboos also forbad Nunavut women from eating bird eggs, unless they had more than five children. And almost no one had five children: more than three were difficult to feed.[7] Nunavut men, however, ate bird eggs freely. While Josephine Peary waited for her husband to return from his attempted North Pole dash, she made a cake with wild eggs and shared it with the local Inuit women. They ate it, begging Mrs. Peary to keep their secret, more afraid of their husband's wrath than any mystical powers.[8]

Creating with Arctic Eggs

An effort to control food shortages, including eggs, also influenced Arctic values. Traditional people believe that respecting others ensures harmony: that all living beings respond to how they are treated. Improperly caring for food or wasting it shows disrespect, causing the animal or bird or fish's spirit to flee, forcing famine on the area. Similarly, when eating bird eggs, finding a chick-filled egg demands respect for the little bird's soul. Though only a veiny glob without a beak or feathers, the embryo's skin-covered eyes are carefully removed. Watching someone eat its body would displease the chick's soul, possibly causing the species to nest elsewhere in future years. For the same reasons, Kobuk River residents fear catch and release tactics practiced by fly-in sport fishermen. Equally upsetting, the tourists waste food when cleaning their catch, cutting the sides off fish and keeping the filets, throwing the rest into the river. Residents believe such disrespect disturbs the fish's well-being, including those fish living in the river. If fishermen want only filets, residents prefer the head, eggs and organs left on shore for the birds to eat. 'The river is not a dump', explained a resident from Shungnak, a tiny village 150 miles up the Kobuk River.[9]

Women's fishcamp

When temperatures warm, though snow might cover the ground, women and children load their boats and head to family camping areas along the Kobuk River. Tents are pitched for a four-month stay, sometimes longer, to take advantage of fish racing toward their spawning grounds. Once fish start running, women throw out their seine nets and haul them to shore, loaded with fish. A crew of eight, including two girls, who scale, rinse the cut fish and hang them to dry, can process 600 fish in a seven-hour period.[10] Within four months, the group can put-up the bulk of a year's food supply. In 2002 fish comprised 54 per cent of all Shungnak subsistence harvests: 297 pounds per person, 84,300 pounds altogether – versus the caribou harvest, which lagged 30,000-pounds behind.[11]

Without stopping to eat, moms slice open a fish while working and hand out raw caviar snacks to playing children. The young girls help by cleaning fish egg sacs, poaching them briefly in almost-boiling water to retain their tenderness and hand them out as is or dunked in seal oil for a flavor hit. The eggs are frequently preferred to fish filets and when a choice is available, elders consistently choose the most nutritious fish parts: eggs and livers first, then bones, skin, head, stomach and intestines.[12] Their aging bodies seem to have a second-sense, selecting the most nutritious food to maintain good health.

Flavor is one reason people prefer fish eggs; texture is another. No matter how fish is prepared, biting into an exploding egg is more exciting than biting into a filet. At fishcamp, when women and children are too busy working to stop and eat a meal, they poke a finger under the pectoral fin of a fecund fish, pull out the eggs and pop them into their mouth. They are a perfect food – nutritious, texturally pleasing, mild and slightly sweet. No wonder Spain's Ferran Adrià translated fish egg's distinct qualities into a restaurant dish, sporting transparent membranes filled with purées and infused oil.

Nutritionally, fish eggs provide more nutrition than the flesh surrounding them. Eggs contribute rich amounts of vitamin A, calcium, potassium, phosphorous and magnesium, plus supplying excellent sources of protein, vitamin C, selenium, and folates.[13] Their ample fat content helps keep bodies warm in cold climates. And each small egg provides all the nutrients found in a large adult fish.[14] For added nutrition, fermenting eggs elevates the B vitamins and Omega-3 fatty acids, plus supporting the body's immune system by promoting intestinal bacteria, which aids digestion.[15]

Drying

Once fish is cut, women rely on windy weather to process filets and eggs for winter storage. Drying racks line the riverbanks at fishcamp with fish hanging, suspended from horizontal poles like clothes on a clothesline. Drying filets seems like a simple task, but controlling wind and temperature pose constant challenges. Drying fish eggs is even more difficult because of the high fat content, which increases just before spawning. Eggs need dry, cool steady breezes to prevent turning rancid. They dry well in freezing winds during winter, too: called freeze-drying in modern society.

Though fish eggs popped from a freshly caught fish is a favorite Arctic snack, almost everyone prefers eggs a few days old. As they hang drying, their flavor and texture change daily, giving each successive meal a slightly different taste, like the nuances of an aging wine. When thoroughly dried, salmon eggs are hard, bright orange and sparkle in the sun. Lacking moisture, they keep well for a year; partially dried eggs require freezing. If almost fully dried, storing eggs in seal or fish oil is an excellent preserving method: the oil acts like a hermetic sealant. Over time, the eggs soften and turn into a delicately fermented dish. Too much moisture causes a stinky mess.[16]

In addition to a food source, dried eggs are utilitarian, especially salmon eggs. Moms smear barely cooked, sticky eggs on baby's little fingers, making clever pacifiers. And because some fish are cannibalistic, eating other fish eggs including their own, women today sprinkle borax over salmon eggs and lay them in the sun to dry for bait fishing.

'The fish like the taste?'

'Nooo', Esther Bourdon said smiling, 'they stay on fishhooks longer; keeps them a little soft'.[17]

When a sealing agent is needed, almost-dried salmon eggs are chewed until pasty and smeared on birch baskets to repair holes. Pitch can be used, too, but the eggy cement gives berries no unpleasant taste. The egg concoction is more durable, too. Or, if a screaming child needs quieting, hard shriveled eggs are handed out to eat. Mixed with saliva, they soon turn to glue, bonding the child's mouth shut. For sewing, women boil dried whitefish eggs, head, backbone and meat, using the broth to tan bull caribou skins for making socks. 'Don't use straight eggs. It would make socks so slippery you couldn't stand up'.[18]

Drying bird eggs is also an ancient preserving method, though hanging them takes ingenuity. About fifty years ago on Alaska's St. Lawrence Island, a barren island in the middle of the Bering Sea, women separated bird eggs and placed the yolks on rocks to dry in the sun. When firm, they were stored with rendered blubber in manageable-sized walrus stomachs, and stashed in cold cellars to freeze. In Nunavut, women altered the drying process, fitting it to their colder climate. Boys and girls were put to work cracking eggs, slurping-up the whites and dueling each other in spitting contests. After slipping a yolk from shell to mouth, they slid the unbroken yolks into inflated, dried seal intestines and hung the transparent cylinders in drying winds.[19] Their St. Lawrence Island sisters basically did the same with fresh fish roe, stuffing it into clean, blown-up walrus intestines, hanging them on racks to dry in the bitter cold air, ready to enrich soups.[20]

Freezing/fermenting/*quaq*

During cold wintry months, freezing fish and bird eggs is the easiest, most sensible preserving method. Inevitably, all foods freeze in the Arctic. Freezing also produces *quaq*, the Arctic's favorite protein dish made by freezing raw protein and eating it when partially defrosted. Fatty, about-to-spawn fish eggs make excellent *quaq*. When made with Arctic cod or tomcod eggs and their livers, *quaq* is an exciting textural dish – rich-flavored exploding eggs combine with mild-tasting, smooth fatty livers with an avocado consistency.[21]

Freezing bird eggs is not as easy and only possible in the Arctic's coldest areas, or where the deepest cold cellars exist, since birds migrate north during Alaska's warming spring months. Along the Kobuk River during fishcamp, women bury bird eggs in cold sandy gravel to keep them from spoiling. Dug up for meals, the eggs are placed in tubes made of willow bark and baked over hot coals.[22] In Nunavut's frigid northern coast, fresh eider duck eggs are stashed in shallow cold cellars or simple holes dug in the permafrost, ground temperatures registering freezing or colder. As the eggs freeze, their shells crack; the whites ooze out, forming a frozen froth ready to be nibbled away. Once eaten, the shell is picked away and the egg warmed briefly between two hands, then eaten like an apple – another form of *quaq*.[23]

A little fermentation, sometimes a lot, usually occurs before food freezes completely. Long fermentation periods involving whole fish with eggs, or fish parts mixed with eggs, demands high fat plus acidic conditions – and weeks to develop dishes with a heady aroma, which outsiders call putrid. A good example is a multi-layered *quaq* preparation made along Alaska's western Circle during fall fishcamp, when temperatures drop. Whole uncut fish are pulled from the river and piled in grass-covered mounds on rocks or acidic willow branches. Fish near the mound's exterior freeze quickly. The insulated center soon starts fermenting. In time, the mound develops various stages of preservation, ranging from fresh tasting raw-frozen fish to barely-fermented frozen fish, to rank-smelling fermented fish. The frozen fermented eggs, still inside the fish, are the most highly prized and last for months without turning rancid.[24] The same ancient method was described in the mid-1850s after discovering a two-year-old pile of fermented fish, explaining that the 'stinky smells and obnoxious flavors mellow and are infinitely more palatable than the one-year old [fermented pile]'.[25]

A similar traditional dish was often prepared with buried fish heads and eggs in Shungnak and as far west as Shishmaref along the Bering Strait. Still a favorite with Bering Strait elders, the dish is fermented 7–10 days and eaten alone or with other foods. If left until mushy, the juices are used as a condiment or a dipping sauce, similar to employing fermented Asian soy sauce to add flavor. And tasting much like an Asian fish sauce, small portions of fish heads and eggs flavor soups or cooked fish dishes. To mellow highly fermented fish egg or fish dish flavors, traditional women add cranberries or wild rhubarb.[26] Their acidity acts like sour tamarind or limes used with fermented Asian fish sauce in Pacific Rim dishes, pulling flavors together.

Arctic bird eggs

Although fish play the biggest dietary role along Alaska's western Circle area, spring bird eggs furnish a welcome taste when cold cellars are almost empty. Because the season is short, bird eggs are not a staple food, but they are an important one. Over one hundred-plus bird species live full-time or migrate yearly to the area.[27]

Everyone gathers eggs. But men typically risk their lives, and gain respect, by stealing newly laid eggs from nests amidst sheer cliffs along the coast. By the thousands, noisy migrating murres nest on the rocky ledges, one nest almost on top of another. Men climb the cliffs, secure a long rope at the top and throw it over the edge. One fellow watches the rope, checking its security. Another shinnies down, dangling with one hand clasped around the rope while the free hand grabs eggs. A third man waits in a boat below in case attacking birds force a misstep, sending the hunter into icy water. Gathering is a smelly job during rainfall when layers of wet defecation turn rank. Worse yet, footing turns slippery. And hands, searching for puffin eggs hidden in nests burrowed deep into the rocks, usually invite a hammerlock bite from tending parents. At the same time, scores of birds relentlessly attack.

Elders, women and children look in safer places for bird eggs, which vary in size, taste and texture depending upon the species. Seagull eggs are favorites: slightly tougher than chicken eggs when boiled, but rubbery when fried in hot oil and almost impossible to cut. Yet everyone loves them, possibly because gulls are the first to arrive and lay eggs, and the first eggs eaten. Loon eggs are less favored, tasting odd. Swan eggs smell like perfume. And though harvesting crane eggs is practical – one makes a meal – gathering them proves difficult. Cranes fiercely defend their eggs by using their beaks to stab holes in encroaching kayaks. The strange consistency and bland flavor of cormorant eggs makes them the least desired, and they barely coagulate when boiled.[28]

Creating with Arctic Eggs

The best time to rob a nest of its eggs is when eggs are at least two weeks old, edging near hatching time. The yolk and white turn into a veiny glob of flesh with a gelatinous texture, tasting like ever-so mild veal liver topped with a strong cheese. Tired and hungry, cliff-climbing hunters knock a hole in the eggshell and suck it clean – raw gelatinous egg-embryo and all. At home, wives briefly boil the eggs, though what's left of the egg white turns slightly rubbery. The fleshy yolk remains soft, albeit, with added texture. But the favorite preparation for embryonic eggs is raw-frozen for *quaq* and served with seal oil.[29]

The same embryo-in-a-shell is briefly boiled in the Philippines. Called *balut*, it's made with commercial duck eggs. Evidently the texture is gaining popularity outside the Philippines and the Arctic: farms in California and Oregon now produce duck eggs with a partially formed chick inside. They sneak onto restaurant menus, adding new taste and texture to dishes. For the daring, *balut* turns up fried and doused with fancy vinegars or a fiery sauce. Sometimes the chick-filled egg is baked *en croûte* and fashionably gives thick rich soup the name Balut Bisque. It supposedly includes the shelled featherless chick, though in an undetectable fashion.[30]

Little-known Arctic eggs

Utilizing all edible eggs in the Arctic mirrors the cultural value *no waste*, except for one insect. Inland, where winds frequently drift to a standstill, menacing blowflies threaten food sources by laying eggs – which develop into maggots. To prevent them, fish racks were historically covered with branches; today, plastic is used. Smudge pots smolder underneath, keeping flies at bay. After three days a seal forms on the surface of fish flesh and egg sacs, too thick for flies to penetrate and deposit eggs inside the filets. When hatched, maggots consume flesh from the center out and can destroy an entire harvest. In 1974, Shungnak lost 1500 drying fish to rainy weather and maggots, enough to threaten food supplies.[31]

Considering that Inupiat and Yupik historically ate everything edible, their resistance to eating maggots is surprising. Maggots are 50 per cent protein, low in fat and eaten dead or alive in Africa. In parts of Asia they are dry-roasted, adding flavor to fried rice seasoned with fish sauce and soy sauce. Australia goes so far as to encourage cultivating fly eggs, dispersing pictures of eye-appealing sautéed maggot dishes, usually with onions.[32]

Though Inupiats loathe fly larvae, they advocate eating botfly larvae found under the caribou's shaggy spring coat. The size of a small pecan shell, the easily removed lumps grow until they break through the molting skin and fly away. Soft and juicy with a slightly sweet taste, botflies are a treat when hunting. Frozen, the larvae make fine *quaq*, that raw-frozen protein eaten partially defrosted.[33]

Another egg, though inedible, was very important for Arctic women. Not really an egg, but an egg-producing organ, it was used as a teaching tool for first-time pregnant girls as late as the early 1900s. When nearing delivery, an elder woman summoned a pregnant girl to her house. Dissecting a seal, the woman pointed to the reproductive organs and the muscles surrounding them, explaining which muscles to relax and where to push on the baby to speed a delivery, hoping to aid birthing mothers when they delivered their babies – alone.[34]

Egg possibilities

Since gathering wild bird eggs is now illegal in many areas, turning them into a major food source is unlikely, unless birds producing eggs with good cooking potential are domesticated. Though possible, it's a doubtful venture considering environmental issues. But cooks daring enough to raid a wild bird egg nest can use the following information when creating dishes.

Alaska's modern Inupiat bakers substitute one gull egg for two chicken eggs in a recipe. Gull eggs mount well, raising a baked cake one-half inch higher than chicken eggs.[35] My mother, three quarters of a century ago in Shungnak, enriched homemade bread with duck eggs. She poached ptarmigan or little quail eggs and arranged them on toasted bread slices. Duck eggs were also whisked until the yolks and whites combined, and put over a hot wood stove to make a puffy omelet.

Further south, Chef John Pence in Portland, Oregon uses duck eggs to make home-made pasta in his restaurant, Caprial Bistro. The pasta is richer tasting and a pleasing yellow color, though 'customers are leery when they see the duck egg reference on the menu', Pence says.[36]

How customers will respond when seeing a menu listing salmon egg pasta is anyone's guess. But the dish may appear soon, for fish eggs have an edge over wild bird eggs as a viable commercial food. Fish egg farming is currently a US$9 million business in southern Alaska with exports distributed worldwide, and increasing yearly.[37] The downside to production is that most fish grow to a saleable size long before they produce eggs, making quicker inventory turnover in fish farms. More importantly, if major rivers and oceans host fish farms, they must have a pH between 6 and 8 to promote healthy fish. Keeping waters free of acid rain and other pollutants is essential; at pH 5, some fish species die.[38]

Because fish eggs in various colors are now sold wholesale, they serve as a popular garnish in high-end restaurants. When New York chefs adopted a family Greek dish of potato mashed with codfish roe, they popularized it, adding their own touch: *tobiko*, a garnish of red-tinted flying fish eggs covered with wasabi for a flavor bang. When readily available, fish eggs will also find their way into the kitchens of good home cooks. Sushi, for instance, was popular in Asian restaurants long before little packets of sushi with raw fish eggs appeared in specialty food stores. And for any cook interested, sushi classes are frequently taught in cooking schools.

But rather than using fish eggs as a garnish, they could easily function as a main ingredient. Hiding them inside a delicate membrane to resemble a little sausage, they could spill out with the first cut. Because fish eggs retain their shape when briefly

Creating with Arctic Eggs

cooked, dousing them in lemon oil and herbs, and shaping them into a little round before baking until hot on the outside and cool on the inside would turn them into an excellent sensory dish.

For cooks unaccustomed to working with fish eggs, they display the same cooking advantages as chicken eggs. When Anore Jones lived a subsistence life in the Kobuk Valley, she bound savory custards with sweet-tasting whitefish eggs, and did the same with pies. She beat sheefish eggs until light and used them to enrich quick bread batters, making muffins and hotcakes without a hint of a fish flavor. She could easily create tinted pasta dishes, pirogies and wontons with nothing more than flour and various colored fish eggs – and stuff them with lightly fermented fish eggs. And like chicken egg yolks, fish eggs give soups body and thicken fish sauces, heightening their natural flavors.

Whipping fish eggs into fluffy mounds also has endless cooking potential. Mature eggs ready to spawn, when their immature watery contents turn fatty and nutrient rich, whip-up best. Once individual egg membranes are broken to release their liquid contents, they mount like the whites of chicken eggs 4–8 times their original size, depending upon the fat content of each fish species. Women in Arctic Alaska whip fish eggs until light and fluffy and add mashed blueberries or cranberries for color, looking similar to a French mousse or the new foams. An ancient whipped creation that could easily be at home on a new-age menu is, in fact, a modern fish-egg gelato. Made during fall when spawning whitefish are pulled with nets through the ice, the fresh eggs are squeezed directly onto the ice-covered river. Whipped and mashed with bare hands or a piece of ice, snow is added until it's a white frozen froth.[39]

Ancient Inupiat pickled foods resemble modern cooked-with-acid dishes, too. Arctic cooks combine fish eggs and chunks of fish filet with acidic blueberries or cranberries, aging them for about five days until evenly colored, like pickled herring. Left one or two additional days until a little fizzy, the taste and texture is even more interesting.[40] The same idea lends itself to a *ceviche* of sorts, using fish eggs and lime juice marinated for about an hour. But a quickly cured fish egg *ceviche* lacks the Arctic's lengthier pickling qualities: color, textural variety plus flavor-depth. However, with the world clamoring for sensory dishes, consumers may soon want pickled dishes similar to those found in the Arctic.

But combining fish eggs with their accompanying innards – that is the Arctic cook's greatest gift for inspiring new products and extending valuable food from the sea. Fish innards are frequently discarded, though some are used in plant fertilizers. Employing clean fish stomachs and intestines is no different than cooking with chicken, beef or lamb innards. Poaching fish innards and frames, without the liver, deepens the flavor of stocks and soups. Cooked fish livers, as mild as the best veal liver, mashed with fish eggs and fish oil compositionally resembles a French liver pâté. Mixing fish livers with flesh, stomachs and intestines, and baking them, varies little from the usual country terrine ingredients. Substituting fish filets for fish liver fit the requirements of a classic terrine. For a mousse or a soufflé, folding frothy beaten fish eggs into minced innards is a good beginning. The same ingredients, ground together with fish filets and bound with fish eggs and a touch of cream is a mousseline. Molded into sausage shapes and sautéed or poached for an appetizer, or even a main dish, could be an excellent seller.

On the economical side, flavorful fish innards masquerading in fish dishes are potential profit makers, similar to hotdogs. They use body parts that wealthy nations prefer not to eat, or prefer eating in ignorance. And nutritionally, dishes made with fish stomach, liver and intestines add valuable sources of protein, Omega-3, iron, the B vitamins, plus vitamin A, D and E.[41]

In addition to innards, the fish egg theme could be extended to milt, that life giving creamy colored sac housed in male fish heading to spawning grounds. Called soft roe, milt is used with and/or substituted for fish eggs in traditional Arctic dishes. In northern Alaska's roadside restaurants, tourists eat a flattened 3–6 inch cylinder fried slowly in equal parts butter and oil for breakfast, thinking it's a nice sausage. And if chefs want to resurrect palace fare and present customers with new dishes, *Larousse Gastronomique* has a dozen recipes for milt.[42] It's also important nutritionally: high in protein, low in cholesterol and contains iron, calcium and vitamin C.

If fish eggs become an economically feasible food source, then surely fertilized fish eggs, like fertilized bird eggs, will also vie for the consumer's dollar. However, little fish clinging to their egg sac seems less appealing than their unfertilized cousins, and squeamish food fetishes take years to change. But then, marketing is a powerful tool, enticing restaurant-goers to experience the latest popular food.

Notes

1. Dr. Robert Thompson, 2007 Farm Bill Debate during 2006 International Food & Agriculture Trade Council. www.truthabouttrade.org/article.asp?id=4405
2. Georgette, Susan, and Attamuk Shiedt, *Whitefish: Traditional Ecological Knowledge and Subsistence Fishing in the Kotzebue Sound Region, Alaska*. No. 290 (Juneau: Alaska Department of Fish and Game, 2005), p. 75.
3. Jones, Anore, *IQALUICH NIGINAQTUAT, Fish That We Eat*. United States Fish and Wildlife Service, Office of Subsistence Management, Fisheries Resource Monitoring Program, No. FIS02–023 (Anchorage, 2002), pp. 98, 199, 210, 234.
4. Georgette, Susan, *Subsistence Use of Birds in the North-west Arctic Region, Alaska*. No. 260 (Juneau, Alaska: Department of Fish and Game, 2000), pp. 19 & 52.
5. Georgette, Susan, 2000, p. 75.
6. Balickci, Asen, *The Netsilik Eskimo* (Garden City, NY: Natural History Press, 1970), p. 218.
7. Cook, Frederick. 'Gynecology and Obstetrics Among the Eskimos', *Brooklyn Medical Journal*, 1894, Vol. 8, pp. 154–69.
8. Diebitsch-Peary, Josephine, *My Arctic Journal* (New York: The Contemporary Publishing Company, 1893), p. 164.
9. Georgette, Susan, *Subsistence and Sport Fishing of Sheefish on the Upper Kobuk River, Alaska*, No. 175

(Kotzebue: Alaska Department of Fish and Game, 1990), p. 29–31.
10. Magdanz, James S., Robert J. Walker and Ronald R. Paciorek, T*he Subsistence Harvests of Wild Foods by Residents of Shungnak, Alaska, 2002*, No. 279 (Juneau: Alaska Department of Fish and Game, 2004), pp. 9–11.
11. Anderson, Douglas B., Wanni W. Anderson, Ray Bane, Richard K. Nelson, Nita Sheldon Towara, *Kuuvanmiut Subsistence* (Washington, D. C.: National Park Service, 1998), p. 17.
12. Jones, p. 13.
13. USDA National Nutrient Database for Standard Reference, Release 18, 2005. <http://www.nat.usda.gov/fnic/foodcomp>
14. McGee, Harold, *On Food and Cooking: The Science and Lore of the Kitchen* (New York: Scribner, 2004), p. 239.
15. Mollison, Bill, *The Permaculture Book of Ferment and Human Nutrition* (Tyalgum: Tagari Publication, 1993), p. 15.
16. Jones, p. 72.
17. Bourdon, Esther, Personal Interview (Nome: 1996).
18. Jones, pp. 72, 201.
19. Freuchen, Peter, *Book of the Eskimos* (Cleveland, Ohio: The World Publishing Company, l961), p. 377.
20. Heller, Christine and Edward Scott, *The Alaska Dietary Survey 1956–1961*, No. 999–AH–2 (Anchorage: US Department of Health, Education and Welfare), p. 233.
21. Jones, pp. 31, 40.
22. Heller, p. 234.
23. Freuchen, Peter, *Arctic Adventure: My Life in the Frozen North* (New York: Farrar and Rinehart, Inc., 1935), p. 165.
24. Georgette, 2005, p. 20.
25. Zagoskin, L.A., *Lieutenant Zagoskin's Travels in Russian America, 1842–44* (Toronto: University of Toronto Press, 1967), p. 116.
26. Warbelow, Willy Lou and Hannah Miller, Personal Interviews (Tok and Shishmaref, 1994).
27. Anderson, p. 29.
28. Georgette, Susan, *Subsistence Use of Birds in the North-west Arctic Region, Alaska*. No. 260 (Juneau: Department of Fish and Game, 2000), p. 19 & 52.
29. Ray, Dorothy Jean, *The Eskimos of Bering Strait, 1650–1898* (Seattle: University of Washington Press, 1975), p. 117.
30. Hopkins, Jerry, *Extreme Cuisine: The Weird and Wonderful Foods that People Eat* (Singapore: Periplus Editions, 2004), p. 221.
31. Anderson, p. 189.
32. Hopkins, p. 165.
33. Brewster, Karen, Personal Interview, (Fairbanks, 1995).
34. Lucy Ayagiaq Jensen, 'Ayagiaq', in *Lore of the Inupiat: The Elders Speak*, ed. by Linda Lee and others (Kotzebue: North-west Arctic Borough School District, 1990), p. 43.
35. Georgette, 2000, p.20.
36. Pence John, Phone Interview, May 17, 2006.
37. Stockard, Lewis, 'Chile: A Fertile Market for US Fish Eggs', *AqExporter*, May 2002.
38. Watson, Craig, Artificial Incubation of Fish Eggs, FA–32, Department of Fisheries and Aquatic Sciences, (University of Florida: 2002), http://www.epa.gov/airmarkets/acidrain/effects/surfacewater.html.
39. Jones, p. 208.
40. Bourdon, 1996.
41. Nobmann, pp. 25–28.
42. Montagné, Prosper, *Larousse Gastronomique* (New York: Crown Publishers, 1961), pp. 884–5.

Egg Basket of the World

Dan Strehl

Petaluma, a small town in northern California, made surprising advances in poultry science, and became the largest egg production site in the world. It sits on a river about 38 miles north of San Francisco. Founded in 1850, the name of the town means 'flat back hills' in the language of the Miwok Indians. From the beginning, there was a lucrative egg trade with San Francisco. In 1857, 21,000 dozen eggs were sent in three months; in 1880, 95,000 dozen eggs were sent, all from small family farms.

Petaluma's poultry success was due to a number of factors: location, innovation, entrepreneurship. Because of it's location on the river, eggs could be safely shipped across the bay, without being subjected to the shaking (and breaking) of land transport. The soil, a light, sandy loam, was good for growing green feed in the summer, and absorbed chicken waste readily. There was an easy supply of oyster shell grit, and feed could easily be shipped up the river. The climate had a warm winter and cool summer, well adapted to poultry keeping.

Throughout the nineteenth century, most chicken eggs in America were produced by the farm wife's home flock. With a few exceptions, such as Petaluma, and Little Compton, Rhode Island, there was no intensive poultry industry in the U.S.[1]

Petaluma early on became a center for poultry innovation. In 1879, Lyman Byce, working with a local dentist, Isaac Dias, invented the first successful incubator for hatching eggs. Apparently Dias was issued the patent, but after his death in a hunting accident in 1884, Byce claimed the invention as his own. While there had been successful incubation in ancient Egypt and in eighteenth century France, Byce's work really advanced the science. His machines produced a hatch rate of 90 per cent, compared with the 60 per cent typical of machines being made on the East Coast.[2] Byce was a tinkerer, and had invented a potato digger, a spring lancet for surgery, and a telephone.

He began the sale of both incubators and brooders, and Petalumans began to purchase his machines. His Petaluma Incubator Company manufactured redwood incubators initially with a capacity of 460 or 650 eggs. By 1888, sales increased to 1000 units a year, and he introduced two smaller versions, with a capacity of 30 or 60 eggs. He promoted the machines heavily at trade fairs and agricultural exhibitions, hatching ostrich, silkworm and alligator eggs to garner attention. Hundreds of chicken farms dotted the landscape around town and with the price of eggs at 30 cents per dozen, profits from the egg business poured into Petaluma. In the 1902 catalog, there was a testimonial 'I have 12 Petalumas in use hatching Peking ducklings, and I have hatched over 40,000 ducks and 600 chickens in less than a year,' said Rosine Strehl,

Egg Basket of the World

proprietor of Mrs. Strehl's Duck Ranch, Arkansas & Solano Streets, San Francisco.[3]

Christopher Nissom was another important player in poultry innovation. An early adaptor of Byce's incubators, he had the first commercial hatchery. As he ran out of broody hens to raise his incubator chicks, he invented a brooder stove, a regular wood stove with a terracotta pipe buried in sand, where the chicks warmed themselves.[4] Nissom also devised a method for shipping live chicks.

Walter Hogan, a Bostonian, arrived in 1906 and announced his expertise with the Single Comb White Leghorn (which was to become the bird of choice in the area) and his ability to breed for capacity. While many were skeptical, his methods were proven to work. He came to write *The Call of the Hen*, which became the standard reference for poultrymen. The title was suggested by his friend Jack London, who said he'd had success with a similar title, *The Call of the Wild*.

Petaluma's population doubled between 1900 and 1920, from 3,871 to 6,266. New farmers swelled the population, and by 1915 an estimated 10 million dozen eggs were being shipped at an average rate of 30¢ per dozen. By 1917, Petaluma was the undisputed world leader of the chicken and egg industries. The U.S. entry to World War I caused eggs prices to soar to 46¢ a dozen, and the town was beginning to see real money. It soon became the richest city of its size in America.[5]

The Petaluma Chamber of Commerce was founded in 1906, and Lyman Byce was among the founders. In 1918, they hired H. W. 'Bert' Kerrigan as Secretary to bring new manufacturers to town (and paid him $50,000 for his fee and promotional projects). He was a public relations expert, who previously had come up with the slogan 'Milk from Contented Cows' for Carnation.[6] Kerrigan recommended against new manufacturing, instead suggested focusing on the poultry industry.[7] To capitalize on the chicken mania, he declared the town 'The Egg Basket of the World'. He then proceeded to market Petaluma, sometimes shamelessly, as the center of the Chicken Universe. The town helped launch National Egg Day on 13 August, 1918, which in Petaluma was celebrated with a parade led by the Egg Queen and her court of attendant chicks, with events ranging from the Egg Queen Ball to a Chicken Rodeo.

In 1919, National Egg Day was celebrated with an 'egg fiesta', featuring a chicken parade, chicken rodeo, egg scramble, egg race and contests, an egg ball, egg and chicken barbecues, and a horse race. The parade featured the world's largest egg basket, the largest White Leghorn ever made, the biggest egg on earth, and the dirty dozen dancing eggs. Twenty thousand eggs and 2,000 chickens were contributed for the barbecue.[8]

In 1921 three members of the San Francisco Ad Club were then initiated into the Order of Cluck Clucks Clan by Kerrigan, assisted by three female chickens from the Petaluma delegation. 'They were crowned with rooster caps, then instructed to give the Petaluma yell, which runs something like this: "We ain't got no well, but we can crow like hell, then crow."' The three gentlemen entered into the spirit of the stunt and crowed like good fellows.'[9]

During the 1923 Egg Day celebration, there was a 'playlet', *Princess Petaluma*, which celebrated the American business hen.[10] The same year the leading hotels in San Francisco offered special egg menus.[11] By 1927, they were shipping 1400 rail cars to the Eastern markets.[12]

One of the interesting aspects of Petaluma's history was the presence of a large colony of Jewish chicken farmers, documented in Kenneth Kann's *Comrades and chicken ranchers*. A film, *A Home on the Range: the Jewish chicken rangers of Petaluma*, was released in 2002. Details are available at http://www.jewishchickenranchers.com/history/. In 1925, the Jewish community of Petaluma built a Jewish Community Center, which was largely secular and focused on left-wing politics. Many in the community were labor zionists, or of related persuasions. In the 1950s McCarthyism brought a serious division in the community, with the founding zionists, socialists, Yiddishists and communists being banned from the Center.[13]

One of the stranger items on the internet is a short Petaluma chicken promotional film done in 1932 (at www.archive.org/details/Petaluma1932). It features a group of young ladies making a giant omelet in an oversized frying pan. The girls perform calisthenics in the frying pan.

Another great innovation was the discovery of how to sex chicks. By doing so, they could raise only the pullets, and eliminate feeding the cockerels once their gender was revealed. The Japanese had long known how to do this, but the U.S. government was unwilling to grant visas to commercial sexers. As a result, the Japanese opened a school in Vancouver, and a Petaluma woman, Gladys Hansey went there and learned the technique. She returned, and began training locals, a process which took about three months. Fifteen people graduated from her first course in 1934. Soon, local hatcheries were able to ship guaranteed pullet chicks. One of the first graduates, Heimer Carlson, would routinely sex 10,000 chicks a day. He sexed 56,000,000 birds during his career.[14]

Egg production peaked in Petaluma in 1945, with 42,415,000 dozen eggs.[15]

Innovation, which was responsible for Petaluma's rise to poultry success, was also the reason the industry faded. The development of the wire cage battery hen houses spelled doom. Wire cages made egg collection and cleanup much easier, and allowed many more chickens to be housed on the same property. There was a significant expense to converting to the battery farms, usually not affordable for a small grower. The addition of artificial lighting allowed the hens to lay year-round. At this point, there was no particular advantage in being in Petaluma, as the size of chicken ranches grew exponentially with the new technology. Farms in southern California and the Southwest housed 60–80,000 thousand hens. Small farms were no longer competitive, and the number of farms in the Petaluma area went from about 4,000 in the Twenties to under 300 in the 1960s.

While the egg industry has largely faded from Petaluma, there has been a specialized revival in the poultry industry. In 1986, Allen Shainsky, son of a Russian-Jewish immigrant and owner of Petaluma Poultry, introduced Rocky, America's first commercially available free-range chicken.[16] At the request of Bay-area chefs to develop a chicken with more flavor, he went to the Loire valley to study poultry husbandry. In 1988, he introduced Rocky Jr., a younger smaller bird. In 1989, they introduced organic birds. Rosie was the first USDA certified free-range organic bird available, and it's widely distributed in California and other major markets.

While the egg industry has shrunk from its once dominate position in Petaluma, there remains a small poultry industry in the area.

Bibliography

Biddle, G., *Western Poultry History* (Modesto, Pacific Egg and Poultry Association, 1989).

Bradley, F.A., 'Petaluma and the poultry industry as sentinel flocks for changes in rural America', *FAO World's Poultry Congress 2000*, August 20–24, Montreal, Canada (http://www.fao.org/AG/AGAInfo/subjects/en/infpd/documents/papers/2000/9BRADLE1.DOC).

Fishkoff, Sue, 'When left-wingers and chicken wings populated Petaluma', *Jewish Bulletin of Northern California*, May 7, 1999.

Heig, Adair, *History of Petaluma, a California River Town* (Petaluma, Scottwall Associates, 1982).

Hogan, Walter, *The Call of the Hen, or the science of the selection and breeding of poultry* (Petaluma, Petaluma Daily Courier, 1913).

Kann, Kenneth, *Comrades and chicken ranchers: the story of a California Jewish community* (Ithaca, Cornell University Press, 1993).

Lowry, Thea, *Empty Shells: the story of Petaluma, America's Chicken City* (Novato, Manifold Press, 2000).

Notes

1. Bradley, p. 1.
2. Biddle, p. 14.
3. Petaluma Incubator Company Catalog No. 48, 1902.
4. Heig, p. 110.
5. Heig, p. 115.
6. Heig, p. 115.
7. Golden, Dane. 'Petaluma Chamber of Commerce, a storied history', *Argus Courier*, June 8, 2005.
8. *Los Angeles Times*, Aug 29, 1919, p. II8.
9. Torliatt, Lee, 'Eggs in One Basket: How Bert Kerrigan Put Petaluma on the Map', *Petaluma Museum Newsletter*, April/May 1905, p. 5.
10. *Los Angeles Times*, Sep 9, 1923, p. Ix13.
11. *Los Angeles Times*, Aug 15, 1923, p. 17.
12. *Los Angeles Times*, May 3, 1927, p. A4.
13. Wall, Alexandra. 'Petaluma's historic center marks it's 75th anniversary', *Jewish Bulletin of Northern California*, August 18, 2000.
14. Lowry, p. 114.
15. Bradley, p. 2.
16. www.petalumapoultry.com/history.php.

Let's Have an Egg

Hervé This

Introduction
Created in 1988, Molecular Gastronomy is the scientific discipline that explores food preparation and consumption. This paper presents a systematisation of egg transformations as an example of the application of Molecular Gastronomy.

In his *Physiologie du goût*, French gastronome Jean-Anthelme Brillat-Savarin defined gastronomy as the intelligent knowledge of whatever concerns man's nourishment (knowledge, not cooking, contrary to what so many people think today!).[1] Accordingly, Brillat-Savarin explained that there could be historical gastronomy (the historical knowledge of whatever concerns man's nourishment); economic gastronomy (the economic knowledge…); scientific gastronomy, etc. And this is why, if the egg is to be considered, so many different perspectives can be used. Here, the 'molecular gastronomy' approach will be used, in particular, with a proposal to re-invent egg-cooking from scratch.

Molecular gastronomy
Before examining this re-invention, along with the discovery of a lot of new ways of cooking eggs, let's examine what Molecular Gastronomy is.

In 1988 (probably March), in preparation for the International Workshops on Molecular and Physical Gastronomy, the late Nicholas Kurti (1908–1998) and I came to the conclusion that although food science had drifted toward a better analysis of food ingredients and a better understanding of industrial food processes, the study of dishes and culinary transformations had been abandoned. This is why we thought that a new scientific discipline had to be created in order to examine culinary transformations and some related phenomena that occur between food's preparation and its consumption. While looking for a name for such a science, I proposed 'Molecular Gastronomy' because I thought that culinary transformations, with chemical and physical phenomena, could be well described as such. Because Nicholas Kurti, being a physicist, feared that too much emphasis would be given to chemistry, we decided upon 'Molecular and Physical Gastronomy,' the name which was indeed given to the workshops in Sicily. However, since its inception, the discipline's development proved that this fear was unfounded, and accordingly, in 2001, its title was reduced to Molecular Gastronomy.

The field's initial programme was to: (1) explore recipes; (2) collect and test culinary proverbs, old wives' tales, sayings, etc.; (3) invent new dishes; (4) introduce new tools, methods and ingredients into the kitchen; (5) use the appeal of cooking to show that the sciences are wonderful. It's strange that, when this programme was proposed in my PhD dissertation, none of the members of the jury committee (including not only Nicholas Kurti but also Jean-Marie Lehn, Nobel Prize in chemistry, and Pierre-Gilles de Gennes, Nobel Prize in physics) discussed the fact that aims 3, 4 and 5 do not pertain to anything scientific.[2]

In 2003, it was recognised that any recipe is composed of three parts: a technically useless one, a 'definition' (hard-boiled eggs are obtained by heating eggs in water), and 'precisions' (time, temperature, salt addition, proverbs, old wives' tales, etc.). Accordingly, a new programme proposed to: (1) model definitions; and (2) collect and test culinary 'precisions'.[3]

Alas, this new programme was also flawed because cooking not only consists of the technical act of producing food; it also includes some art (the food has to be 'good') as well as 'love' (caring about the well-being or the happiness of the guests). Of course, art is not science, and the study of love is more in the field of psychology, nevertheless the question can be asked: can we study art and love phenomena by way of 'molecular' explorations? These fascinating questions will not be considered here.[4] Concerning Molecular Gastronomy, let's simply conclude that the latest programme is to: (1) scientifically explore the love component of cooking; (2) scientifically explore the art component of cooking; (3) explore culinary 'definitions' and 'precisions'.

As with any other scientific discipline, Molecular Gastronomy has applications in technology and education.[5] Its technological application should be called 'culinary technology,' whereas new culinary trends produced by transferring technology from Molecular Gastronomy have already been given the name 'Molecular Cooking.'

Culinary precisions

In the context of the Oxford Symposium on Food & Cookery, one question should be discussed: what could the link between Molecular Gastronomy and food history be? Indeed, there could be none, except for the fact that cooking, being empirical until the 1980s, displayed its history as if it were someone living in an old manor house who cooked with the same tools and ingredients as the building's original inhabitants.[6]

In particular, one of the first objectives of the discipline, still important today, of collecting and testing culinary old wives' tales, proverbs, sayings, etc., is clearly related to culinary history. After twenty-seven years of work, the number of 'precisions' collected from French culinary books now exceeds 25,000, which makes it possible, specifically, to ask the question of why technically wrong recommendations were passed down.

In 2004, it was assumed that culinary 'precisions' arose when recipes failed and chefs of the past, looking for explanations without understanding the chemical and physical mechanisms behind the failures, proposed ideas that were later handed down and subsequently accumulated in culinary books until the present day. Indeed, the number of culinary precisions for mayonnaise – which can easily fail – is much higher than that for roast beef – which rarely fails.[7]

The study of this question needed a quantitative definition of the 'robustness' of recipes. In order to define such a concept, it was proposed to consider recipes as functions of many parameters and the production of dishes as paths in the multidimensional space having these parameters as their dimensions. Indeed, dishes are obtained from ingredients (when necessary, quantities can be considered as 'parameters'), which are transformed using a special protocol defined by technical parameters that describe the transformations being used. For example, mayonnaise is obtained by mixing egg yolk (defined quantity), vinegar (defined quantity) and oil (rate of addition, maximum quantity); the protocol is defined by the energy of mixing, the whisking energy, etc. At any time, the state of the sauce in creation can be represented as a point in the multidimensional space defined by the quantity of ingredients used and the protocol parameters; the making of the sauce is represented in this multidimensional space by a continuous path, whereas the successful recipe is a hypervolume within this space; points outside this hypervolume represent failed mayonnaise. Robustness is clearly linked to the minimum diameter of the hypervolume because the transformation path can most easily fall outside of the hypervolume corresponding to a successful product at the point where the diameter is smallest.

As diameter determination in multidimensional space is difficult, restricted robustness can also be used. Considering only one parameter of the culinary transformation (either ingredient quantity or process parameter), this is the ratio of the admissible interval for the parameter divided by the degree of uncertainty about this parameter. This can easily be understood when roast beef, for example, is considered. Let's assume that a roast is cooked at a fixed temperature of 180°C, and let's assume that the roast is 'successful' when the 'cooking' time is between 15 and 40 minutes. If time is measured with a very imprecise clock (for example, a precision of 60 minutes) it is difficult to get the proper result and the recipe is 'difficult' and fragile (robustness is then equal to (40–15)/60, i.e. 0.5). However, if a very precise clock (precision of 1 minute) is used instead, then the recipe rarely fails (robustness (40–15)/1 = 30).

Of course, only orders of magnitudes for robustness are worth considering in this way. However the quantitative determination of robustness has been useful in assessing the assumption concerning precision, appearance and transmission mentioned above.

Nevertheless, after calculating the robustness and a number of culinary precisions for some classical recipes it was discovered that this assumption was wrong! Indeed, Figure 1 shows that the observed law is very close to the theoretical one but one recipe clearly lies outside of the prediction. This point represents meat stock and the difference can easily be explained: meat stock was so important in the history of food that, although it is not difficult to make, its preparation was discussed in considerable detail.

Let's Have an Egg

Some culinary precisions with eggs

While culinary definitions found in antiquarian books are not generally very strange (and there will be much more about that in the following section), culinary precisions about eggs are of many types and sometimes quite peculiar.

For example, *La cuisinière du bon marché pour la ville et la campagne*, written *c.* 1850, states:

> Because chicken feed imparts flavour to eggs, one should be very cautious about the kind of food that chickens receive, so that it does not alter the eggs' goodness. In particular, it has been observed that during the insect season, eggs are very bad to eat, with a dull-coloured yolk; that pine-cones give them a turpentine flavour; and that barley makes them very fragile.[8]

Concerning egg transformations, one of the most frequently repeated 'precisions' is that of adding salt or lemon juice into whipped egg whites: 'In order to get rapidly whipped egg whites, add a small pinch of salt or some drops of vinegar or of lemon juice.'[9]

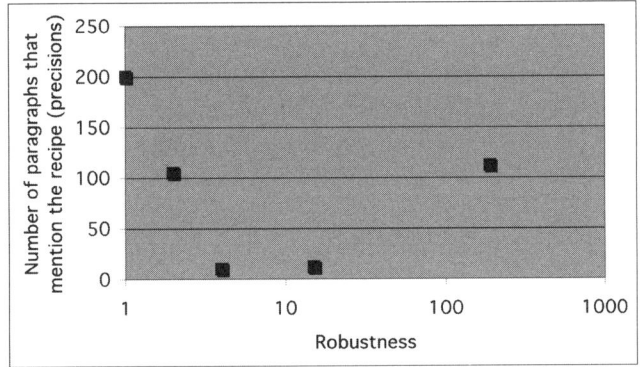

Figure 1.

More generally, 470 collected culinary precisions about eggs have been classified according to whether they apply to the yolk, to the white, to the yolk and the white together, are raw, or cooked. Are they are true or false? The methodology of the tests should be explained. In particular, it should be observed that the exact 'culinary conditions' should be kept during the tests so that the real precisions are examined, and not modified versions of them. This is a problem since ingredients can change, making currently observed test results inapplicable to a refutation of antiquated precisions. However, evaluation of an ingredient's chemical and physical description is useful in order to know whether the effect of such changes is important or not. Another important point, since only one refutation suffices to reject a general law:

some indications are so vague that many different tests are necessary. And, the sceptical eye of the chemist has to be benevolent because there is much to discover even behind apparently wrong precisions.

The importance of open-mindedness first became evident during a test of roast suckling pigs, in 1993, which investigated whether or not it was true that their skin is crisper when the head is cut immediately after roasting.[10] In this instance, the culinary precision proved to be true in spite of the advice of meat experts, who considered that there was no reason to loose any crispness of the skin on the leg, for example, when the head wasn't cooked. However, the experiment on four suckling pigs from the same parents and bred in the same farm indeed showed the effect. The interpretation was that vapour formed inside a pig's abdominal cavity and, flowing through the meat, softened crisp skin, but it escapes instead through the opening made when the head is cut. More recently, when examining whether wine sauces with butter are 'shinier' when only tossed instead of whisked, it was discovered that brilliance was not the real question, but rather that the droplet sizes of melted butter were very different between the two sauces, thereby producing different flavours.

Coming back to eggs, many culinary precisions have been tested since 1980: the importance of the temperature of eggs and oil while preparing a mayonnaise; the importance of womens' periods; of the moon's appearance in the sky; of the direction of whipping; of the introduction of egg white; of the maximum quantity of oil; of adding salt and lemon juice while whipping eggs; of the tools used; of the whipping speed, etc. Because the results of these tests have already been published, let's now move to previously unpublished work on 'culinary definitions' concerning eggs.

Let's invent 'cuisine'

In recipes, culinary definitions can be protocols, explicit definitions, etc. of any size (compared to the size of the recipe). Research remains to be done in measuring the definition/precision ratio in the various antiquarian recipes in order to find structures in the data (the influence of the historical period, of the author's personality, etc.). But what is also interesting is to find some relationship between the various definitions relating to egg transformations.

In order to envision these transformations comprehensively, a system can be constructed in a very logical way.[11] The full egg, made of a shell, yolk, egg white, is given a number (1), and put in the first row of a table (Figure 2).

Then the various possibilities of dividing it are now considered as cells of the second row. The full intact egg is assigned the label 1.1; the shell alone, 1.2; the unmixed yolk and white out of the shell, 1.3; the mixed yolk and white, 1.4; the yolk alone, 1.5; and the white alone, 1.6.

Let's now move to the next row, when these various 'parts' are transformed by culinary processes: we consider the addition of nothing (1), or gas (2), or 'water' (3), or 'oil' (4), or solids (5), ethanol (6), acid (7), alkali (8), or heat (9). Generally, the gas

1. Whole egg					
1.1. Whole egg in its shell	1.2. Shell only	1.3. Unmixed yolk and white, out of shell	1.4. Mixed yolk and white	1.5 Yolk only	1.6. White only
1.1.1 Nothing 1.1.2. Gas 1.1.3. Water 1.1.4. Oil 1.1.5. Solid 1.1.6. Ethanol: Eggs Baumé 1.1.7. Acid: Minus One Century Eggs 1.1.8. Alkali: One Century Eggs 1.1.9. Heat: *hard-boiled eggs*, eggs at 6X°C	1.2.1. Nothing 1.2.2. Gas 1.2.3. Water 1.2.4 Oil 1.2.5. Solid 1.2.6. Ethanol 1.2.7. Acid 1.2.8. Alkali 1.2.9. Heat	1.3.1. Nothing 1.3.2. Gas 1.3.3. Water 1.3.4. Oil 1.3.5. Solid 1.3.6. Ethanol 1.3.7. Acid 1.3.8. Alkali 1.3.9. Heat: *Fried egg, œuf cocotte,*	1.4.1. Nothing 1.4.2. Gas: *uncooked mixture* 1.4.3. Water: *Mayonnaise* 1.4.4 Oil: *mayonnaise* (version *ménagère*) 1.4.5. Solid 1.4.6. Ethanol: Thenard of yolks and whites 1.4.7. Acid 1.4.8. Alkali 1.4.9. Heat: *omelette, flans classique* or at 6X°C	1.5.1. Nothing 1.5.2. Gas 1.5.3. Water 1.5.4. Oil: *Mayonnaise* 1.5.5. Solid 1.5.6. Ethanol: Thenard of yolks 1.5.7. Acid 1.5.8. Alkali 1.5.9. Heat: *cooked yolk*	1.6.1. Nothing 1.6.2. Gas: *stiffened white* 1.6.3. Water 1.6.4. Oil: Geoffroy (emulsion of whites) 1.6.5. Solid 1.6.6. Ethanol: Thenard of whites 1.6.7. Acid 1.6.8. Alkali 1.6.9. Heat: *cooked white*
			1.4.3.9. Lavoisier (extreme royales), Avogadro	1.5.3.9. *Royale, flans, custards*	1.6.2.2. Chaptal (uncooked *cristal de vent*) 1.6.3.9. Avogadro of whites 1.6.4.5. Liebig (physically gelatinized emulsion) 1.6.4.9. Gibbs (chemically gelatinized emulsion)
					1.6.2.2.9. Cristal de vent 1.6.3.2.9. Vauquelin (*cristal de vent* cooked in the microwave).

Figure 2. As a general rule, each preparation is labeled 1.a.b.c...., with each indicator a, b, c comprising a number between 1 and 9, to designate the type of addition, in accordance with the indexation of the third row.

used in the kitchen is air but many possibilities exist. For example, during an educational dinner organized by the Institut des hautes études du goût, de la gastronomie et des arts de la table (The Institute for the Advanced Study of Taste, Gastronomy and The Arts of the Table), at the Cordon Bleu School in Paris, the dessert was made using helium so that the guests had strange, duck-like voices for some seconds (sound velocity changes depending upon the nature of the carrier gas, hence the modification of frequency when sounds are emitted in helium instead of air). Physical chemistry considers that the 'water' category can be any aqueous solution, as long as the concentration is low and the solutes do not noticeably change the properties of the solution. Similarly, 'oil' can be any liquid fat such as oil (olive oil, corn oil, sunflower oil…), melted butter, melted foie gras, etc. Of course, ethanol, acids and alkalis should be edible (Cognac, vinegar, baking powder…). And heat, finally, can be given in many forms, which means that more slots could be made if necessary. In particular, it is useful to consider systematically that heat can be given by a hot solid, a hot liquid (water or oil), a hot gas, or by radiations (microwaves, infrared, but also all kinds of electromagnetic radiations, as they transmit energy when they are absorbed).

Using these ingredients, new 'products' can be made and numbers can be used to describe what they are. For example, in the third row, three numbers describe the results. By way of illustration, 1.1.7 describes eggs that are put in, for example, vinegar and that coagulate after some time (about one month), making 'Minus One Century Eggs' (the 'opposite' of 'One Century Eggs,' which are prepared in parts of Asia by storing eggs in mixtures containing alkali such as lime or potash). Label 1.1.9 describes the hard-boiled egg as the full egg in its shell (1.1), which is heated (9). However, considering the various denaturation temperatures of proteins from the egg, many other possible sub-categories exist, such as 'eggs at 6X°C', i.e. eggs at 61°C, 62°C, 63°C… up to 100°C, with many different results between 61°C and 100°C. Label 1.3.9 corresponds to the fried egg, or *oeuf cocotte*. Already in this row unprecedented new products appear from this systematic description: 1.5.6 is a yolk coagulated by ethanol (and 1.6.6 is an ethanol coagulated egg white) that has been named a 'Thenard,' after the French chemist Jacques Thenard, who introduced the concept of 'osmazome.' Label 1.6.4. refers to an emulsion from egg white and oil, the oil being either ordinary oil (sunflower, soy, etc.) or melted butter (ordinary, clarified, brown…), or even melted foie gras or melted cheese, etc.; it is called a 'Geoffroy', after the French chemist Etienne Louis Geoffroy. Other products, differently labelled, can also be produced but they have never before received names.

If we move to the next row, products are now labelled with four figures. Again, some of them are known (but very few), and many new possibilities arise. The 'Liebig' and the 'Gibbs' (respectively labelled 1.6.4.5 and 1.6.4.9) are only two examples. They are obtained respectively by physical and chemical gelatinization of emulsions, such as are obtained, in the first case, by whipping oil in an aqueous solution of gelatine and waiting for it to gel, and in the second, by whipping oil in egg white and heating. The next line? There are more and more possibilities, such as 1.6.3.2.9., a product to which Vauquelin's name has been given. Which food product is it? Just read the figures: it's egg white, with the addition of air, then water, and then heat (in this case, using a microwave oven). Figure 3 shows such a dish, made by Denis Martin (Restaurant Denis Martin in Vevey).

Physical and chemical descriptions such as the ones proposed above are useful in order to understand culinary transformations, but their principal importance is that these systems can make it easier to create 'comparative gastronomy' between

Figure 3.

countries. Two other formalisms, the 'complex disperse systems formalism' and the 'non-periodical space organization formalism' are now used to describe dishes by their physical constitution rather than by recipes. In the first case, some 'phases' (gas, water, oil, solids) are described using 'connectors' such as /, +, @, σ, standing respectively for a random dispersion, a mixture, an inclusion, and a superposition. Formulas describe the physical composition of food material. The second formalism allows a description of dishes as arrangements of dots, lines, surfaces, volumes… and it was recently found that the same connectors as for the first formalism apply to these objects (indeed, this property led recently to the proposal that both formalisms could be mixed).

Using these formalisms, dishes from the past could be described and made into categories (in one category, all dishes would have the same formula), as it was done for the French classic sauces, which make 23 categories. What are we going to discover, then?

Notes

1. Brillat-Savarin, Jean-Anthelme, *La physiologie du goût* (Paris : A. Sautelet,1825).
2. This, Hervé, *La gastronomie moléculaire et physique*, Thèse de l'Université Paris VI (Paris: 1995).
3. Ibid., 'La gastronomie moléculaire', *Sciences des aliments*, vol. 23 no. 2 (2003), pp. 187–198.
4. Ibid., 'Modelisation of Dishes and Exploration of Culinary "precisions": The Two Issues of Molecular Gastronomy', *British Journal of Nutrition*, vol. 93 supp. 1 (April 2005).
5. Ibid., 'Cooking in Schools, Cooking in Universities', *Comprehensive Reviews in Food Science and Food Safety*, vol. 5 no. 3 (2006).
6. Ibid., 'Molecular Gastronomy: Scientific Explorations of Culinary Old Wives Tales and More, *Food & History* (forthcoming) and 'Les livres de cuisine anciens à l'épreuve du nouveau savoir culinaire', *Revue Critiques*, vols. 685–6 no. LX (June–July 2004), pp. 546–559.
7. Ibid., 'Molecular Gastronomy', *Nature Materials*, vol. 4 no. 1 (Jan. 2005), pp 5–8.
8. Author's translation of *La cuisinière du bon marché pour la ville et la campagne*, (Liège: Baudouin, Solédi), p. 164.
9. Fonty, Laura, *1000 trucs de grand-mère* (Paris: Marabout, 1996), p. 24.
10. This, Hervé, 'La cuisson : usages, tradition et science', *La cuisson des aliments*, 7e rencontres scientifiques et technologiques des industries alimentaires (Agoral: 5–6 Oct. 1994), pp. 13–21.
11. Ibid., 'Questions d'œuf', *Pour la Science*, no. 344 (July 2006), p. 4.

'Go to Work on an Egg'[1] is not the Same for All Cultures

Michelle Toratani

Even before the salmonella scare emerged in the United States in 1985 (when researchers from the Centers for Disease Control (CDC) found that the bacteria existed both on the shells and inside the eggs), most people who grew up in a Western country would have found the idea of eating raw eggs revolting, unless used for culinary purposes to make products such as mayonnaise, hollandaise sauce or salad dressings.[2] Today, for many, raw eggs probably conjure up an image of body builders or athletes whipping up a hefty protein shake with milk, protein powder and a few freshly cracked eggs made memorable by the Rocky (1976) movies.[3] Now with salmonella outbreaks often displayed in the media, this thought would probably be horrifying for most – unless you are Japanese. Although the risk of salmonella is real all over the world including Japan, why then, do the Japanese continue to eat raw eggs? Why do Western cultures find eating raw eggs so repulsive but the Japanese accept them as part of their culinary identity? Certainly, what is acceptable as edible in one culture is not necessarily accepted as such in another, but why?

In the 1960s, the British Egg Marketing Board launched a £12 million advertising campaign to entice the public to eat more eggs. The most famous advertising slogan was, 'Go to Work on an Egg' – aimed at busy working people. Eggs were advertised as quick, easy, inexpensive, nutritious and a perfect way to start the day.[4] Time-pressed workers would most likely have prepared them boiled, fried, scrambled, or poached but I can almost guarantee that no one ate their eggs raw.

On the other side of the globe, millions of Japanese have been waking daily to *tamago gake gohan* (literally, 'egg covered rice'), a bowl of hot white rice topped with raw egg seasoned with soy sauce and eaten with pickles or topped with other savoury Japanese condiments – it is quick, nutritious and incorporates Japan's main staple, rice.[5] The immensely popular cookbook author, restaurateur and television personality Harumi Kurihara, (often described as 'Japan's Martha Stewart'), even has a recipe for this traditional raw egg dish in the American version of her cookbook, *Harumi's Japanese Cooking*, claiming it as Japan's original 'fast food'.[6]

Having grown up in a Japanese family in the United States, my egg eating preferences vary anywhere from raw to hard-boiled. Knowing that I would receive objectionable reactions if I revealed to other people brought up in the United States and other Western cultures that I occasionally preferred eggs raw, I subconsciously kept my habit quiet. Growing up with immigrants from around the world, I instinctively knew since I was a child that what may be regarded as an acceptable food in one culture is not always considered so in another. One example is entomophagy (insect eating). Although many insects are highly nutritious and are widely consumed in countries such as Mexico, Japan, Nigeria and Indonesia (to name a few), most people from countries that do not practice entomophagy would find eating insects dirty and/or disgusting.[7]

Besides sauces and condiments, in countries like the United States, United Kingdom and Australia, raw eggs are consumed primarily as a drink, such as the 'Prairie Oyster,' touted to cure hangovers. One recipe calls for a raw egg, dash of Worcestershire sauce, salt and pepper with instructions to 'down in one,' assuming and not to mention ensuring, that no one will enjoy the drink.[8] It is advised to be drunk as quickly as possible to keep the experience with the raw egg to a minimum. In my experience, the closest to raw that is universally accepted in Western cultures would be a 'sunny-side up' fried egg that leaves the yolk in a liquid state.

On the contrary, in Japan, raw eggs are enjoyed and appreciated without the revulsion or squeamishness found in the West. Besides eating it over rice for breakfast, raw eggs are also mixed into curried rice, used as a dipping sauce for *sukiyaki* and garnished atop *tobiko* sushi.[9] Kurihara has another dish in her cookbook featuring raw egg: *Maguro no Tataki Don,* which is finely chopped raw tuna on rice topped with a raw egg yolk.[10] Kurihara should be commended for not removing the dishes featuring raw eggs in her cookbook printed for the Australian, American and British public – she instead shares her enthusiasm for this Japanese preference. To be safe (morally and legally), a warning on egg safety is included: 'Uncooked or undercooked eggs should not be eaten by young children or the elderly, or anyone with an illness that may have weakened the immune system. Uncooked eggs may contain salmonella bacteria that can cause food poisoning and serious illness. Salmonella is destroyed by cooking. Pasteurized eggs are available in some markets and are safe to eat uncooked. They are more expensive than regular eggs.'[11]

Salmonella poisoning or *salmonellosis* can be a serious disease for people with impaired immune systems – particularly the very young and elderly.[12] According to the WHO (World Health Organisation), *salmonellosis* is one of the most frequently reported food borne diseases worldwide with eggs and chickens as the primary transmitters for the *Salmonella* bacteria; yet, the bacteria can also be found in many other types of common foods including ice-cream, prepared sauces, chocolate bars and milk powders.[13] Because of their willingness to eat raw eggs, I assumed that *salmonellosis* incidence must be lower in the Japanese population but surprisingly, according to international data summarized by C.J. Thorns in 1997, the estimated incidence of *salmonellosis* per 100,000 people in the following countries are as follows: 14 in the USA, 38 in Australia, 73 in Japan and 120 cases in Germany.[14]

In Adelaide's daily newspaper *The Advertiser,* a recent front page headline read: 'EGG ALERT: Food poisoning outbreak hits 17 people'.[15] The headline was written in a large font intended to grab the public's attention, warning against eating raw eggs. Yet, at the time the article was printed, although no one had actually proved that infected eggs were the source of that food poisoning outbreak, the headline was still written to make people falsely believe that eggs were the culprit in the latest string of food poisonings.[16] This type of fear-causing hysteria over any *salmonella* outbreak would no doubt invoke trepidation and/or revulsion towards raw egg consumption.

Although the fear of food poisoning is probably one reason why people in Western countries have not incorporated raw eggs into their foodways, I believe that the main reason is its slimy, mucilaginous texture. Sliminess certainly causes negative reactions as it is not a well-accepted texture in most Western cuisines. According to psychologist Elizabeth D. Capaldi: 'The taste of food produces liking and disliking that appear to be genetically mediated, whereas, the other sensory characteristics of food (odour, temperature, texture, appearance) appear to produce their effect through learning.'[17] In other words, texture in foods is not a genetic but learned preference and a key principle of Japanese cuisine requires having a multitude of textures and flavours to create a balance. People in Japan are even encouraged to consume at least 30 different dishes a day for variety and balance.[18] For many foreigners travelling to Japan, the unfamiliar textures, odours and raw foods are some of the biggest culinary obstacles to overcome.

Although the definition of cooking is wide and encompassing, it is generally thought of as heat-based, in the form of fire. The ability to create fire is one of the many things that separate *Homo sapiens* from other animals in the kingdom. According to psychologist Paul Rozin, 'there is a common "theme" that "humans are not animals" and are to be clearly distinguished from animals.'[19] By eating foods that are uncooked, it may be looked upon as primitive and animal-like, thus separating the civilized from the uncivilized. The best advantage of cooking is that it protects humans from bacterial diseases. *Salmonella* is killed if the food is heated somehow. Perhaps the mucilaginous raw egg is too reminiscent of bodily fluids to eat?

The opposite is often true for Japanese cuisine – freshness is of the utmost importance. Eating raw foods is regarded as consuming it in its purest state without manipulation and adulteration. Fish is regularly eaten raw in Japan such as sashimi, sliced raw fish, sometimes prepared while the fish is still alive to ensure freshness. Abalone is a delicacy almost everywhere in the world but is often lightly cooked in Western countries before eating. In California, abalone divers often coat tenderized slices with corn flakes or crushed crackers before cooking in butter but my mother would consider this preparation as wasteful. Why cook a perfectly fresh abalone if it can be eaten raw in its most natural form? Culture definitely affects our food preferences by influencing how things are prepared and what types of things are considered appropriate to eat.[20]

Culture and experience influence what we find tolerable and edible. The neophilic attitude of the Japanese towards food is exemplified by striving for diversity in their cuisine. Raw foods in general are considered the norm in Japan and eggs are no exception. Although the risk of *Salmonella* infection may be statistically higher in Japan than in other industrialized nations, the acceptance of raw eggs in Japan's foodways was established before there was any real health risk. Whether it is the mucilaginous texture or the fear of illness that creates the revulsion Westerners have towards eating eggs raw, for the Japanese, culture seems to override the health and safety risks involved.

For me, eating breakfast is like playing Russian roulette but the creamy texture of a freshly cracked egg on steaming rice is still the perfect breakfast to start my workday.

Notes

1. BBC On This Day. Wikipedia, the Free Encyclopedia. 'Go to Work on an Egg,' 31 Oct. 2005 <http://en.wikipedia.org/wiki/Go_to_work_on_an_egg> [cited 13 April 2006].
2. Michele Bloomquist, 'Cracking Down on Eggs', in *WebMD,* 23 October 2000 <http://www.medicinenet.com/script/main/art.asp?articlekey=50728 > [cited 13 April 2006].
3. Ibid.
4. '1968: Egg board "should be scrapped"', in *BBC On This Day* <http://news.bbc.co.uk/onthisday/hi/dates/stories/june/21/newsid_2988000/2988175.stm> [accessed 10 July 2006].
5. Although more people today are having a slice of white toast for breakfast, many still eat *tamago gake gohan.*
6. Kurihara, 103. This does not suggest that the Japanese always eat all their eggs raw for breakfast or at other meals.
7. Logue, p. 7.
8. 'Basic Prairie Oyster' in *iVillage.co.uk: The Website for Women* <http://www.ivillage.co.uk/food/tools/recipefinder/display_recipe/0,,5523,00.html> [accessed 10 July 2006].
9. *Sukiyaki* is a dish usually cooked at the table and would probably be referred to as a 'hotpot'. It consists of thinly sliced beef, tofu, noodles and vegetables in a sweet, soy sauce broth. *Tobiko* is Flying Fish Caviar – it is orange in colour and has a lightly salty taste and very crunchy texture.
10. Kurihara, p. 66.
11. Kurihara, p. 66.
12. 'Salmonellosis' in Centers for Disease Control and Prevention, Division of Bacterial and Mycotic Diseases, 13 October 2005 <http://www.cdc.gov/ncidod/dbmd/diseaseinfo/salmonellosis_g.htm> [accessed 04 July 2006].
13. World Health Organization, p. 7.
14. World Health Organization, p. 7.
15. Jill Pengelley, 'Egg Alert: Food poisoning outbreak hits 17 people', *The Advertiser,* 17 June 2006, front cover, p. 1.
16. Ibid.
17. Capaldi, p. 53.
18. Kurihara, p. 16.
19. Rozin, p. 247.
20. Logue, p. 104.

Bibliography

Capaldi, Elizabeth D., ed., *Why We Eat What We Eat: The Psychology of Eating* (Washington D.C.: American Psychological Association, 1996).

Kurihara, Harumi, *Harumi's Japanese Cooking* (New York: Penguin Group, 2006).

Logue, A.W., *The Psychology of Eating and Drinking* (New York: Brunner-Routledge, 2004).

Rozin, Paul, 'Sociocultural Influences on Human Food Selection', ed. by Elizabeth Capaldi, ed., *Why We Eat What We Eat: The Psychology of Eating* (Washington D.C.: American Psychological Association, 1996).

World Health Organization, *Risk assessments of Salmonella in eggs and broiler chickens* (Geneva, Switzerland: World Health Organization, 2002).

More than One Way to Crack an Urchin

Christa Weil

Have you heard the one about the ancient dinner party, where a Spartan was presented with a serving of intact sea urchin? Demetrius of Scepsis tells it best: 'he grasped one, but not knowing how to deal with the viand, and not even observing how his convives disposed of it, he put it in his mouth, shell and all, and tried to crack the urchin with his teeth. Since he had a hard time with the bite and did not comprehend what its rough resistance meant he cried, "you rascally morsel, I won't be soft and let you go now, nor will I ever again take another."'[1]

The Spartan approach to cracking an urchin is the least effective of a roster of techniques mankind has devised ever since the first of our ancestors decided to discover what all those bristling spines were protecting. This experiment could have happened on any inhabited coastline on Earth, for approximately 800 species of urchin dwell in nearly every major marine habitat, ranging from the poles to the equator and from the intertidal zone to depths of more than 5,000 meters.[2] Today, sea urchin fisheries exist off the Atlantic and Mediterranean coasts of Europe, northern Asia, the Atlantic and Pacific coasts of North America, Chile, New Zealand, and Australia, harvesting the world's 22 primary edible species.[3] Should a Tlingit, a Barbadian and a Tasmanian seek common ground for conversation, they might swap stories about urchins they have known and loved.

Back in the mists of time, our proto-foodie, having observed the example of otters, starfish or gulls, knocked his or her urchin into bits with a rock, wrenched it apart with carefully curled appendages, or dropped it from a height to shattering effect. Revealed inside would be an unpromising mess of brownish digestive tract leaking bits of the half-digested kelp upon which the creature feeds, sullying the more rewarding generative parts discussed in greater detail a few paragraphs below.

The sea urchin is heartless, brainless, and otherwise lacking in organs that might inspire our empathy. The features it does have seem very alien indeed, most obviously the spines that are arrayed mace-like over the creature's globular shell, or test. While anyone unfortunate enough to accidentally tread on an urchin (driving the tip of a snapped spine into the skin, where, left untreated, it will lodge for several weeks or months until the body eventually gets around to expelling it) will find little fascination in the engineering, these spines are one of nature's most intriguing defensive systems. They attach to the test with ball-and-socket joints. When disrupted, they will swivel in unison to meet an attack. In calmer times, they act as multiple stilts upon which the creature scuttles over submerged rocks, coral and sand. Equally fanciful is the urchin's internal hydraulic system. This inflates a multitude of tube feet that extend beyond the spines and help the creature cling fast to the rocks and reefs it calls home. The appendages also snare drifting bits of food which they then pass foot-over-foot mouthwards, the orifice located on the creature's underside.

This peculiar assembly of five jaws around a central maw is known to insiders as Aristotle's lantern, in honor of the naturalist's fourth-century BCE description: 'In reality the mouth-apparatus of the urchin is continuous from one end to the other, but to outward appearance it is not so, but looks like a horn lantern with the panes of the horn left out.'[4] (The five-sided lantern to which Aristotle refers was not hornlike in shape, instead it bore panes of translucent horn, and was not dissimilar in configuration to the Victorian streetlamp housings still seen in parts of London.)

Compare the ancient naturalist's sober description of the mouthparts to that of the British diarist Bruce Cummings, writing as W.N.P. Barbellion in 1908: 'dissected the Sea Urchin (*Echinus esculentus*). Very excited over my first view of Aristotle's Lantern. These complicated pieces of animal mechanism never smell of musty age – after aeons of evolution. When I open a Sea Urchin and see the Lantern, or dissect a Lamprey and cast eyes on the branchial basket, such structures strike me as being as finished and exquisite as if they had just a moment before been tossed me fresh from the hands of the Creator. They are fresh, young, they smell *new*.'[5]

For those more inclined to say that the urchin smells *tasty*, the most significant aspect of the oral apparatus is what surrounds it – a ring of tissue unbuttressed by calcareous shell. Called the peristomal membrane, it is the equivalent of Achilles' heel. The creature hides it to the best of its ability, while its primary predator exploits it to the fullest.

Five are the beaks that munch kelp forests to barrens, five too are the plates that make up the creature's test. This pentacentric design marks the creature out as an echinoderm, kin to the starfish, sand dollar, and sea cucumber, which share the number as the organizing principle of their anatomical layout.

Once the test has been cracked, the principle is most clearly seen in the five tongue-like skeins of reproductive tissue that cling to the interior of the urchin's upper hemisphere. These well-girded loins, glistening in a palette ranging from bright orange to saffron to umber, are not only the wellspring of future generations, they are also the prime nutritive storeholds of the urchin, waxing and waning given the availability of food, and in times of abundance comprising up to one quarter of the creature's total weight. The Japanese, the primary consumers of urchin products, call these parts uni, which most English-speakers would translate as sea urchin roe. In this, most English-speakers would be wrong. The sexes are differentiated in the sea urchin, and uni are a hoard of either pre-ejaculated eggs or sperm. We consume it on an equal-opportunity basis, from both male and female alike. Therefore uni, properly speaking, are gonads.

Classical scholars and others might find a certain piquancy in the idea of speaking properly about sea urchin. The ancient Greek words *ekhinos*, *spatanges*, and *bryssos*,

More than One Way to Crack an Urchin

denoting various species found in the region, were synonymous with pubic hair,[6] the first term being put to licentious good use by Aristophanes in his *Lysistrata*. In Newfoundland and down the eastern seaboard to Maine, the local nickname for urchins is 'whore's eggs,' due to the creatures' propensity to foul fishing nets in the days before they were netted on purpose. In Asia, uni is widely regarded, for the obvious reasons, as an aphrodisiac.

For others, particularly those working in marine biology and embryology labs, the sex-appeal of sea urchin rests many degrees of magnification smaller, in the exhibitionistic flair of its gametes. The egg is large and transparent, and its outer layer swells within seconds following successful breach by a sperm. Within 90 minutes, the egg cleaves into the first of its many divisions, which can be followed microscopically well into the development of the embryo. Scientists are so taken with the viewer-friendly nature of the urchins' fertilization and subsequent zygotic splits that this creature's gametes are a stalwart of research and experimentation in the embryological field. Yet even Nobel-calibre PhDs, awash in saline tanks and grant money, cannot sex an urchin without a microscope.[7]

Uni is at its best during the spawning season, which generally takes place during the colder months of the year. Inconvenient for commercial harvesters, slightly less so for the beachcomber seeking an impromptu snack. 'Since sea urchins never try to run away or fight back, gathering them where they are abundant is about as much sport as pulling fruit from a tree.' This is famed food-forager Euell Gibbons, who is equally matter-of-fact in describing his preferred means to break and enter an urchin: 'To extract the roe, lay the urchin on its back, that is with Aristotle's lantern up, and crack the test all around with several sharp blows with a hammer. The lower part of the test and viscera can then be removed, showing the five-pointed egg sac, or gonads, against the upper part of the test. Reach in and loosen it from the points inward and it can be lifted out whole.'[8] The diver.net website, aimed at enthusiasts on the California coast, offers more insight for the casual harvester on the how-tos of sea urchin gathering: 'If you have had urchin, called Uni, in a Sushi Bar it may not have thrilled you … fresh is much better. Local urchin is going to have the most roe when there is the most kelp easily available, summer and fall. Pick your urchins from a healthy kelp bed where there is lots to eat. Bring a shallow plastic bowl and a plastic spatula. Like any wild game, urchin must be treated delicately. Find 5 or 6 large ones, though size does not determine content. The spines can be a nuisance, so the big ones can be broken off easily enough. I used to swim along with one in my hand, rubbing and breaking the spines as I swam, with my leather gloves. It makes it a bit safer when you put it in your bag and for when you go to open it up. … Hold the urchin and force it to break it open by putting your thumbs in the mouth and forcing the shell to break. Do this carefully or spines insert, things go flying and you lose roe. It may be necessary to use an iron or knife to carefully crack part of the shell, before pulling it open. It does increase the risk of mush though. … Carefully run the plastic spatula under the roe, along the inside of the shell, to loosen it. … Get the intact pieces of roe into the plastic bowl. There will be other things with it, such as partly digested seaweed and plumbing for the urchin. This must be carefully removed. I use my fingers, but tweezers work well for this too. … When they are cleaned, it is important to give them a quick rinse in fresh water or they will not taste right. They should be well drained, especially if they are not to be eaten immediately. They are good with a bit of lemon or lime. In Mexico, I had them with ketchup on Ritz crackers.'[9]

Do-it-yourself cracking provides rough-and-ready rewards for the hungry outdoorsman, but for the chefs in top-flight restaurants from Shinjuku to midtown Manhattan, the meticulous harvesting, extraction, preservation, and quality sorting methods used by specialists ensure that only intact, richly colored and glistening tongues of uni, the characteristic central groove and fine nubbly texture just discernible across the surface, reach their diners.

If the uni derives from red sea urchin commercially harvested from the waters off San Diego (*Strongylocentrotus franciscanus*, the species widely considered to be the tastiest in the world), the catch was likely taken by hand or rake, by a sole diver or a team of up to three breathing compressed air from hoses attached to tanks on the boat ('hookah gear'). Off the coast of Maine, divers harvest green sea urchin (*Strongylocentrotus droebachiensis*) typically utilizing standard scuba tanks, emptying a tank in about an hour's time given a depth of 15 feet of water, and carrying six tanks or more for a days' work. In both locales divers place the urchins in net bags capable of holding 200–350 pounds. The perils, according to Captain Bob Bernstein of the midcoast Maine fleet, include spines in the hands, oxygen tank issues, and getting the bends. An alternate harvesting method used on the East Coast is dragging the gravelly sea floor with what is known as a chain sweep or urchin drag. This, says Captain Bob, does not entirely eliminate the potential dangers of urchin fishing, for the drag can get hung up and pull the boat over.[10]

The catch is next trucked to onshore processing plants for cracking. Since uni is extremely friable stuff, given to liquefaction at the slightest hint of roughness, the techniques evolved for processing it on the large scale marry ample force to split the test with sufficient dexterity to slip the skeins out intact. To this end, special tools are used. 'The test or shell is cracked into halves using a duck-bill-like pliers that opens when the handles are squeezed. Cracking is accomplished by driving the duck bill into the peristomal membrane and mouth area in the bottom of the test to separate along the vertical axis. The cracked urchins are distributed to a group of 'spooners' who use long-handled spoons or spatulas to gently remove the 5 pieces of gonads from the test and place them in a plastic or metal mesh tray . . .' In plants where Asians are working, the roe may be extracted with chopsticks. It is next rinsed in cold saltwater to remove viscera and extraneous matter. Final cleaning of attached membranes is done with tweezers or small forks.[11] After extraction and cleaning, fresh uni is bathed in an alum solution to firm the flesh, and is then drained and packed in small wooden display-quality trays or larger perforated foam trays. After packaging, shipping the uni to its ultimate destination becomes a game of beat the clock. If that destination is the predawn uni auction at the Tsukiji fish market in Tokyo, 'air freight arrangements are made soon after sea urchins are received by the processing plants. Occasionally, fresh roe is shipped on passenger flights. Upon arrival in Japan, cargo is unloaded within 30 minutes to an hour. One or two hours are needed for clearing customs. Usually, it takes 6–7 hours after arrival before the cargo is released to truckers. Thus, the products will not be available for auction sale on the day of arrival, but rather on the following trading day.'[12]

In Japan, uni is most commonly consumed raw at a sushi bar, where it is placed atop rice balls and secured with a cuff of nori seaweed wrapper, or arranged *chirashi*-style atop a bowl of rice and garnished with shredded seaweed and pickles.

In other parts of the world, the striking shell of the creature is employed as the container for the rinsed tongues, most festively in the town of Carry-le-Rouet, located about 30 kilometers west of Marseille. Here the month of February hosts Sunday *oursinades,* which in this case roughly translates as 'urchin extravaganzas,' but also happens to be the name of a Provençal urchin soup described by Larousse. In Carry, quayside restaurants serve plate upon plate of the freshly-cracked creatures, which were hauled in by divers at work in the chilly waters from 2:00 a.m. until sunrise. Lemon slices are provided to heighten the flavor, chunks of baguette soak up the juices, and glasses of chilled Cassis wash it all down. According to Elizabeth Reichert's article for *France Magazine,* 'the Carry-le-Rouet sea urchin craze began in 1952 at the *calanque* (or water inlet) of cap Rousset. During a tasting, the local fishermen made a special set of scales so they could offer the mayor, Jean-Baptiste Grimaldi, his weight in urchins.'[13] In France, the creatures are frequently bisected by a formidable device known as a '*coupe-oursin*' (which resembles an oversized stainless-steel soft-boiled egg topper), that first clamps with opposing crescent-shaped blades, then cuts clean through with an effortful snap of the wrists. This tool is available off-the-rack at the Dehillerin kitchen supply store in Paris. More delicately (if less dramatically) the *oursins* are opened with stainless steel scissors, which do double-duty in the autumn as vine shears.

Across the Atlantic in Martinique, the shell also acts as a container, but in this case the '*chadron*' is cleaned and filled with a heap of rinsed tongues and roasted over a wood fire to create the dish *tête de chadron*. Another typical Martiniquaise recipe is the poetically named *blaff,* which mimics the sound the urchins make as they are tossed into a rolling court-bouillon.

In Italy, where *ricci di mare* has long been a staple, the tongues may be served as the topping of a bruschetta, or gently folded into pasta dressed with olive oil, garlic and herbs.

Cooking tends to diminish the custardy sweet richness of sea urchin, but this has not prevented ambitious chefs from trying their hand at various soups, panna cottas, tempuras, and sauces with uni as the signature ingredient. Possibly the most inventive of all urchin recipes was devised by Chef Rick Laakkonen for the now-defunct Ilo restaurant in Manhattan. Called the 'tidal pool,' this appetizer also featured percebes (goose barnacles), oysters, scallops, wakame, edamame, and mushrooms arrayed within a bowl and submerged tableside with a swell of bonito broth.

In 2003, an article published in the *U.S. Fishery Bulletin* reported that urchins are one of the longest-lived animals on Earth, and that it is possible to radiocarbon-date some particularly doughty specimens to over a hundred years of age.[14] If left to its own devices, uni is close to an endlessly renewable resource. But, given a taste that transcends all borders, that's unlikely to happen anytime soon.

Notes

1. Athenaeus, *The Deipnosophists*, iii.91 (English translation by Charles Burton Gulick, PhD, London: William Heinemann Ltd. New York, G.P. Putnam's Sons, 1927).
2. Natural History Museum, *The Echinoid Directory*, www.nhm.ac.uk/research-curation/projects/echinoid-directory/intro/introduction.html, p. 1/1.
3. Including the green sea urchins (circum-North Polar), red sea urchins (Alaska to California, Japan, China, Korea and Russia), purple sea urchins (Alaska to California and circumtropical), erizos (Chile, Peru, Mediterranean, west Atlantic and Caribbean), kina (New Zealand, China), and purple crowned urchin (Australia). Howel Williams, *Sea Urchin Fisheries of the World: A Review of Their Status, Management Strategies and Biology of the Principle Species* (Draft Background Paper, Marine Resources, Department of Primary Industries, Water, and Environment, Tasmania, 2002), p. 4.
4. Aristotle, *The History of Animals*, trans. D'Arcy Wentworth Thompson, (The Internet Classics Archive, http://classics.mit.edu/Aristotle/history_anim.4.iv.html) Book IV, part 5.
5. W.N.P. Barbellion, *The Complete Works of W.N.P. Barbellion (1889–1919)*, November 3, 1908 (www.pseudopodium.org/barbellionblog/index.php?p=72, 1/1).
6. Andrew Dalby, *Food in the Ancient World A–Z*, (Routledge, 2003).
7. One researcher has noted that the Californian male red sea urchin yields only orange roe, while yellow is usually produced by this species' females. Uni-eaters in Japan may incline to one color or the other depending on the locality, but only the orange roe is used in the bottled salted version of uni). S. Kato and S.C. Schroeter, 'Biology of the red sea urchin, *Strongylocentrotus franciscanus*, and its fishery in California', *Marine Fisheries Review*, 47(3):1:20.
8. Euell Gibbons, *Stalking the Blue-Eyed Scallop*, Chambersburg, PA: Allan C. Hood & Company, Inc., 1964), pp. 133–34.
9. Sea Urchin, 1998. (http://diver.net/seahunt/d_rurchn.htm).
10. Personal communication, June 2006.
11. University of California Cooperative Extension, *Sea Urchins*, Sea Grant Extension Program Publication, 1995, http://seaurchin.org/Sea-Grant-Urchins.html., p. 7/15.
12. Ibid., p. 10/15.
13. Elizabeth Reichert, 'Aphrodisiac Afternoon', *France Magazine*, 56 (Jan-Feb 2003), pp. 20–25.
14. Thomas A. Ebert and John R. Southon, 'Red Sea Urchins can live over 100 years: confirmation with A-bomb 14carbon, *U.S. Fishery Bulletin*, 101(4), (2003), pp. 915–922.

Eggs in the Talmud

Susan Weingarten

The Mishnah and the Babylonian Talmud [BT] have a whole tractate called ביצה *Beitzah*, Egg. It is called 'Egg' after the first word in the first sentence: *An egg which is laid on a festival...* The Jerusalem Talmud [JT] rather more sensibly calls the tractate: 'Festival,' since in all these cases, after an initial disagreement about egg-laying, the rabbis of the Mishnah and Talmud[1] move on to discuss other laws relating to Jewish festivals, including cooking laws, when inevitably eggs come in again briefly.

However, there are some thousands of references to eggs all through the Talmudic literature. I have collected them and classified them, and in this paper I wish to discuss a few interesting aspects, mostly dealing with food, but also touching on other uses of eggs in the Talmudic period in the land of Israel, the Roman province of Syria/Palaestina.[2]

Hens

It is unclear when the hen was first domesticated in the ancient land of Israel.[3] The Hebrew word תרנגול *tarnegol* (from Akkadian *tarlugallu* cf. the Latin *gallus*) is not found in the Bible.[4] Hens were, however, clearly well established by Roman times. The Talmudic literature provides a vivid picture of them. Other domesticated birds included peacocks, pheasants, geese and especially pigeons or doves, but none of these seem to have been raised for their eggs.[5]

Raising hens for their eggs was something which could be done with little effort by the very poorest, with little expenditure needed on fodder. From the gendered Hebrew and Aramaic descriptions, this was typically a woman's occupation. When discussing what should be considered the minimal signs of habitation of a building, the Mishnah [M] notes the presence of a handmill – and chickens.[6] Hens clearly ran around the courtyard[7] and sometimes even the house:[8] the Mishnah also permits chasing an escaped hen home on the Sabbath or upturning a basket for chicks to climb into.[9] Hens were accepted legally as liable to cause damage, and sometimes were tied up in an attempt to prevent this.[10] It was clearly common in Talmudic Palestine for paid workers to have little businesses on the side, so the rabbis forbade people to buy wool or milk from a shepherd in case this was stolen from his master, but eggs and chickens, they said, could be bought anywhere: i.e. everyone had them.[11] There were, however, liable to be problems over ownership: you were not allowed to use someone else's hens to hatch your eggs without the owner's agreement.[12] On the eve of Passover, when only the most vital work was allowed to distract people from their

Eggs in the Talmud

festival preparations, it was permitted to put hens to brood, or replace a dead broody hen by a live one.[13]

Eggs and measurements

Hens' eggs, then, were common and much appreciated. Among the very poor, who presumably could not afford much in the way of crockery, the shells made a welcome addition to household vessels. They could be used to hold small quantities of precious oil for lighting – perhaps not as lamps themselves (they were presumably too delicate to stand up to the heat), but certainly as feeders for lamps. We know this because the use of such feeders was prohibited by the Sabbath laws.[14] Thus the basic measure of volume in the Talmudic literature, readily available to anyone, was half an egg. This would vary little from place to place, unlike the larger formal units of volume of the Graeco-Roman world, which were set to local standards.[15] People in the Roman world also used this informal measuring unit at times.[16]

From this handy eggshell the rabbis derived further measures: if an egg was the basic unit for volume, so fuel too could be measured in units of the amount needed to *cook* an egg.

> What sort of cooking? asks the Mishnah, and replies: The lightest of eggs beaten up and put in an אלפס *ilpas* pan [= the Greek λοπάς *lopas*].[17]

Similarly an oven was considered finished once it was hot enough to cook this lightest of eggs – or even the more primitive cooking arrangement of three stones roughly plastered together to balance a pot on top.[18] But an egg by itself may not have been considered very tasty: the rabbis reckoned that the basic measure of spice or seasoning was enough spice to flavour 'the lightest of eggs.'[19] In Talmudic Babylonia the rabbis defined 'the lightest of eggs' as a hen's egg, because this was seen as the easiest to cook,[20] but we do not know if this was also the case in Palestine.

There was a further extension of the use of eggs as a unit of measurement, and here it is a measurement of time rather than quantity. In Tosefta [T] Sotah the rabbis are discussing the minimum time needed to commit adultery.[21] There are differences of opinion. Is it the time needed to roast an egg or the time needed to swallow three eggs? The BT reports that they decided on swallowing three eggs.[22] (We note here that the Greeks considered eggs as aphrodisiac.[23]) The word used here for swallow also means to sip, so that it becomes clear that the eggs under discussion were in a liquid or semi-liquid state.

Another measurement using eggs was the strength of salt water. Cooking is forbidden on the Sabbath, and the rabbis were concerned to define exactly what was meant by cooking. Just dissolving salt in water was not defined as cooking, but the making of הילמי *hilme*, a salt solution used for pickling vegetables which demanded expert knowledge was seen as cooking. And here the rabbis of the JT define *hilme* just like

271

Eggs in the Talmud

the Greek *Geoponica* – a salt solution strong enough to float an egg (about 10%).[24]

Salted, spiced and sweet eggs

Whether eggs were actually eaten with salt water, as is traditional among many Jews today at the Passover *seder* meal, is unclear from the source above.[25] They were certainly eaten sprinkled with salt, as there is a discussion of whether eggs or radishes may be salted on the Sabbath. Radishes may not be salted, as presumably this might change their taste by reducing their sharpness and so be considered cooking, but eggs are allowed. Seasoning with salt, indeed, was seen as pretty well essential when eating the eggs described as מגולגלת *megulgelet*. When a fast day fell on the Sabbath eve, people would begin to celebrate the Sabbath hungry, and this was not considered desirable: the Sabbath should be enjoyed. So the rabbis allowed people to assuage their hunger with minimal food towards the end of the fast, but without enjoying it, as was proper on a day of fasting and mourning. Thus it is reported that Rabbi Aqiva sipped a *megulgelet* egg without salt – eating to assuage his hunger but without being able to enjoy his egg.[26]

Guests at a feast on a festival were allowed to take home a small amount of food: a piece of meat, a loaf of bread and a spiced egg. Unfortunately we have no further details of the spices or seasoning used.[27]

Eggs were also eaten sweet. A minimal quantity of honey is defined in the JT[28] as 'enough to cook a light egg.' Was this egg then beaten up and fried in honey? The Apicius collection does have a recipe for dates fried in cooked honey.[29] Or were the eggs and honey cooked slowly together? The Apicius collection[30] has a recipe for a *tyropatina* made of eggs beaten with milk and honey cooked very slowly as a sort of custard, which may be what the JT means. There is also a sort of egg pancake which has honey poured over it, but this seems to happen after the eggs were cooked: the honey is not used as the cooking medium.

Cooking methods

There are a number of terms used for cooked eggs. I shall try to distinguish between them, so we can get some idea of how eggs were cooked and eaten. Some of these terms have parallels in Greek, and I shall also be looking at what the medical writer Galen had to say about eggs.

shliqta: boiled eggs שליקתא and *Mevushal* מבושל

In the Talmudic literature eggs are sometimes described as being מבושל *mevushal,* (from the root בשל *b-sh-l*) which is the general Talmudic word for cooking, usually denoting cooking in liquid. However, in other places eggs are described as being שליקתא *shliqta*, (from the root שלק *sh-l-q*) which also seems to mean cooking in water. It is difficult to know what the difference was here – if any. Were eggs which were *mevushal* soft-boiled, and *shliqta* hard-boiled? Or does *mevushal* refer to eggs cooked with food in liquid other than water? Certainly an egg which was *mevushal* is mentioned as being considered to absorb the tastes of spices: even its yolk was considered to absorb flavours.[31] It might be cooked with meat and absorb flavour from that.[32] Egg shells are indeed porous, and eggs *can* absorb smells and tastes. Claudia Roden, writing of present day Sephardi *haminados* eggs, cooked for a long time with onion skins, notes that these skins impart a faint taste and a brown colour, which are considered desirable additions.[33] A Talmudic egg which was *shliqta,* on the other hand, is only mentioned as absorbing by mistake, as it were. If it is boiled by mistake with impure eggs (i.e. eggs from an impure bird) or eggs which subsequently prove to have had an embryonic chick inside, it is considered to have been infected with their impurity, if the impure egg could have conveyed its taste to it, presumably after long cooking or if the shell was cracked. (We might remember here that in the Roman author Petronius' satirical account of Trimalchio's feast one of the guests is afraid to eat an egg lest he find a chick in it.[34])

There is further evidence in TUqtsin, which implies that the contents of the *megulgelet* egg are liquid, and might drip out when the shell is chipped, but the contents of the *shliqta* egg are assumed to be solid – or at least surrounded by a solid white.[35] A mediaeval rabbinical commentator, the Rashba, suggests that a *shliqta* egg is a scalded egg, i.e. one which has had hot water poured over it to cook it partly.[36] However, when I experimented with this, scalding did not cook the white sufficiently to remove the shell safely and leave a solid white.[37]

There is a text in MNedarim which perhaps casts some further light on this. It refers to someone who has taken an oath to abstain from certain kinds of foods. The Mishnah is defining the terms:

If a man vowed to abstain from מבושל *mevushal*, he is permitted what is צלי *tzli* (roasted) or שלוק *shluq* (=*shliqta*).[38]

Here *mevushal* and *shluq/shliqta* are seen as quite distinct cooking methods, as distinct as roasting and boiling.

Thus a *mevushal* egg may be an egg cooked with food and liquid, rather like *haminados* eggs cooked in the Sabbath pot today, while *shliqta* refers to an egg hard-boiled in water. However, it is also possible that the different terms refer to cooking *methods* rather than *results: eggs gently boiled as opposed to those boiled hard.*

Tzli: roasted egg צלי

It is clearer what is meant by צלי *tzli*, roasted eggs. Eggs were indeed roasted, sometimes together with onions and meat. On the Sabbath, cooking was forbidden, so that we are told that eggs should not be put to roast before the Sabbath unless it is clear that the roasting can be completed before the Sabbath begins.[39] Eggs, meat and onions tend to shrink if kept warm for a long time. If they are improved by shrinking, they cannot be eaten, as this is seen as a prolongation of the cooking process and hence forbidden. However, if when they shrink they are less good, they can be eaten on the Sabbath, as this is seen as an unintended and indeed unwanted effect.[40]

Eggs may not be put in hot sand or hot dust to part-roast on the Sabbath (in the heat of the Holy Land I can confirm this would be sufficient to cook them!) just in case people then start roasting them properly in hot lime or hot ashes. Rashi, a French mediaeval commentator suggests that eggs were also roasted on a גרדיל *gradil*, a grill put over the coals.[41]

Megulgelet: 'rolled' egg מגוגלת

A מגולגלת *megulgelet* egg (from the root גלגל *g-l-g-l*, to roll) was made by rolling it near a heat source, but not a very strong one: MShabbat talks of rolling near a water heater or in hot sand or the dust of the road (which is forbidden on the Sabbath).[42] We saw the source from TUqtsin refers to an egg which is *megulgelet*, rolled, and that this meant a liquid or semi-liquid egg. JTNedarim notes of a *megulgelet* egg 'that sick people eat their bread with it.'[43]

These sources relate to an egg which is liquid, or partly liquid. This is confirmed by the fact that the verb used for consuming *megulgelet* eggs is גמע *g-m-'a*, to sip or drink. These eggs were only minimally cooked, so perhaps consuming them was more like drinking a raw eggnog.[44] Thus in the episode we noted above, when Rabbi Aqiva takes a *megulgelet* egg without salt on a fast day, he is said to 'sip' his egg. He may have chosen a *megulgelet* egg in particular because of associations of eggs with mourning. The mediaeval Midrash Pesiqta Zuta writes:

> As an egg is *megulgelet* (= rolled), so is the cycle of the world: a generation goes, a generation comes….
> In earlier days they comforted mourners with lentils and other pulses, as peas, beans etc are all round.

The Midrash then tells us that the patriarch Jacob was preparing the lentils (what the AV calls a pottage of lentiles'[45]) for which Esau sold him his birthright, because that was the day his grandfather Abraham had died, and he was cooking the lentils for his father Isaac, the chief mourner, to comfort him. The Midrash then adds that one should give mourners

> both eggs and lentils – both are round and have no mouth, and the mourner does not speak his grief. [46]

We noted above that JTNedarim writes that sick people eat their bread with *megulgelet* eggs, mentioning them with other invalid foods. Thus these very lightly cooked and still liquid eggs were seen especially good for the sick.

Eggs in the Talmud

Eggs and milk were also sometimes given to young children if their mother got pregnant again while breast-feeding and her milk supply failed. We don't know how they were prepared: were the eggs rolled in hot sand to cook them a little, as here, or were they beaten and heated gently in a pan with the milk, as we shall see later? If the baby was very young they were presumably minimally cooked, if at all. [47]

rofiton eggs רופיטון *Termita* and טרמיטא

Mishnah Nedarim, that we saw above, continues thus:

> If a man vowed to abstain from מבושל *mevushal*, he is permitted what is roasted or שלוק *shluq* (=*shliqta*) .... and he is allowed טרמיטא *termita* eggs or gourds cooked in hot ashes.

The man who has vowed to abstain from מבושל *mevushal* food is still allowed טרמיטא *termita* eggs, and gourds cooked in ashes, i.e. not cooked with liquid in a pot. We have also seen that JTNedarim clarifies this Mishnah: the abstainer is not allowed מגולגלת *megulgelet* eggs, because sick people often eat their bread with these. However, the JT continues, the Mishnah says he *is* allowed a *termita* egg, and asks: 'What is טרמיטא *termita*?' It replies to its own question: This means רופיטון *rofiton*.[48]

Both these terms come from the Greek. The second century Greek doctor Galen also discussed these two sorts of eggs, explaining τρομητά *trometa*[49] as boiled eggs which 'tremble' – Andrew Dalby has explained this as an egg with a more or less solid white but a liquid yolk, which 'trembles' when shelled.[50] A ῥοφιτόν *rhophiton* egg, on the other hand, is a very liquid egg which can be sipped, *sorbilia* in Latin. However, the JT does *not* make a distinction between these terms and indeed uses *rofiton* as a definition of *termita* – either the terms were used indistinguishably in late antique Palestine or they were so close as to be able to stand in one for the other. It would not take very much heat or time to convert *rofiton* to *termita*, and we may suppose in practice in ordinary homes this is what often happened, as opposed, perhaps, to richer houses with more professional cooks.[51] Celsus, writing in Latin in the first century CE,[52] also uses these two almost interchangeably: when avoiding any food which has to be chewed, he recommends *ouis sorbilibus aut hapalis*. *Sorbilis* is literally 'sippable' and *hapala* translates as 'soft-boiled' or *trometa*. We saw that Talmudic *termita* eggs were used as invalid food. It is clear from Galen that Graeco-Roman doctors prescribed 'drinkable' or 'sucking' eggs – ῥοφιτά *ropheta* in Greek, *sorbilia* in Kühn's Latin translation, especially for invalids.[53]

The Mishnah and the Jerusalem Talmud were compiled in Palestine when the country was part of the Roman empire, both administratively and culturally. The Babylonian Talmud, however, was written in Babylonia where the local culture, including the food, was that of the Sassanian Persian world. It is not unusual for the BT to misunderstand Greek words as used in the Mishnah.[54] When it comes to *tormita* eggs (mentioned only once in the BT) the definition is quite different from the Palestinian sources.[55] Here Shemuel, who was both rabbi and physician in third century Babylonia, says that *tormita* is the word used for an egg which is shrunk by alternately cooking and cooling until small enough to be swallowed whole. Then, if the patient has a sore in his or her intestines, some of this will adhere to the egg, and when it is excreted the doctor can examine it for traces from the intestines and thus know what drug to prescribe. Apart from this fascinating window into ancient medicine, it is clear that here, too, the BT has a very different view of the *tormita/termita* egg of the Mishnah, and has substituted what may or may not be a local Babylonian medical use of eggs, but is certainly a different understanding of the Mishnah. That it has legendary accretions is clear from the text: the egg is put into hot water a thousand times, and a thousand times into cold – and the slave who knows how to do this is worth a thousand dinars! In the twelfth century the famous rabbi Moses Maimonides, who was also physician to the court of Saladin,[56] disagreed with the Babylonian Talmud. Maimonides in his commentary on the Mishnah writes that a *termita* egg was a very soft egg, not a very hard one. This upset the later rabbinical commentators: how could the great rabbi disagree with the authority of the Talmud? Some of them decided that he must be referring to the medical practices of his own day, which were different from those of the BT. Others saw that the JT, as we saw above, also mentions a *megulgelet* egg in discussing this Mishnah, and decided that this was what Maimonides must be referring to. Maimonides, however, who also wrote medical text books in Arabic, was familiar with Galen. He also gives the Arabic word for this way of preparing eggs, *nimbreshet*.[57]

Shrunken eggs

We have seen differences of opinion about eggs which 'shrink' during cooking – were they improved or spoilt? If they were improved this counts as cooking and is forbidden on the Sabbath. (Presumably this depends on how long they have been cooked for and how much they have shrunk – I roasted my Passover egg for longer than usual this year and found the white turned brown and was totally inedible but the yolk was delicious.)[58] The BT tells a story of some Palestinian rabbis and shrunken eggs:

> R Yose went to Sepphoris and found … shrunken eggs left on the stove [on the Sabbath] and forbade them to them. … Now does this imply that shrunken eggs go on shrinking and are thereby improved? Yes. For R Hama b Hanina said: Rabbi and I were once guests somewhere and eggs shrunk to the size of crab-apples were brought before us and we ate a lot of them.[59]

The JT notes that shrunken eggs taste like פנקריסין *pankrisin*.[60]

Eggs in the Talmud

Eggs beaten in an אלפס *ilpas* / λοπάς *lopas*

We saw earlier that one of the rabbinical measures of quantity was enough fuel to heat or enough spice to flavour 'the lightest of eggs beaten up and put in an אלפס *ilpas*.' This was clearly a very common way of cooking eggs in Talmudic Palestine – if we can judge from the number of times it is mentioned in the literature – and it is the way recommended by Galen too as the most nourishing. Galen recommends eggs of a moderate consistency cooked in a λοπάς *lopas* and removed from the fire while still runny.[61] Even the saucepan here is the same!

Egg and fish

We can learn a little more about methods of cooking eggs in the Talmudic literature from a discussion about cooking food on festivals, when the rabbis lay down that in certain circumstances two distinct and different kinds of foodstuffs are needed. They then discuss what can be considered two separate foods. In the JT there is a disagreement about fish with egg on it. One school of rabbis says this is to be seen as a single food, while others say it is two foods. However, everyone agrees that if you crumble [פירפר *pirper*] egg on salt fish or cut up leeks under fish or cook two things together in a pot, these are two different foods.[62]

It is clear from this debate that egg *on* fish must be different from egg *crumbled over* fish. The latter would seem to refer to pre-cooked egg (roast, hard-boiled or scrambled) crumbled over fish,[63] especially given the parallel with the leeks cut up under the fish. The egg *on* the fish, if sliced or balanced on top could certainly not be taken to mean a single foodstuff. Thus 'egg on fish' must be taken to refer to raw beaten-up egg the fish had been dipped into, or which had been spread on the fish – a sort of batter, which could be seen either as a single food when cooked with the fish in it, or as coating which could be removed after cooking, and hence two foods. (This may even be the earliest reference to the Sephardi fish cooked in batter which Claudia Roden has identified as the Jewish source of the English fish eaten with chips![64])

So far the discussion is in the Palestinian sources. The Babylonian Talmud discusses the same problem.[65] It too has fish with egg *on* it as the problematic case, but has different preparations of food as comparisons. What is the decision, it asks, if you crumbled an egg and put it *inside* the fish or puréed leeks and put them inside the fish? Everyone agrees here too that these are two foods, not one. But it is interesting to note the different methods of using the same food proposed by the BT. In the JT the eggs and leeks were placed on or underneath the fish. Here the crumbled egg is used to stuff the fish, and the leeks are puréed rather than chopped, and then used for stuffing too. Of course, like many Talmudic discussions, perhaps the use of these foods for stuffing is just theoretical – in order to provide a case for discussion – and not evidence of what was really done, but it is clear that the rabbis in Talmudic Babylonia, the land between the two fish-rich rivers, could conceive of cooking fish with a stuffing. If our fish with egg on it is the earliest example of the Jewish fish in batter identified by Claudia Roden as Sephardi, could we have here the earliest example of Ashkenazi gefilte fish?!⁶⁶

The 'bunch' and 'string' of eggs שלל *shellal* and אשכול *eshkol*
The *kosher* laws divide foods into three categories: meat and meat products, milk and milk products and *pareve* or neutral foods. It is forbidden to eat meat together with milk foods, but the *pareve*, neutral foods, can be eaten with anything. They consisted mostly of bread, vegetables and wine. But eggs were also considered neutral and could be eaten with anything, which made them particularly convenient for Jews who observed the *kosher* laws.⁶⁷ However, eggs are formed inside chickens, which are considered meat. The rabbis thus had to decide exactly when an egg changed from the category of a meat food to a *pareve* food, which could be eaten with anything. They decided that this was dependent on the development of the shell – if the unlaid egg had a shell, it was no longer 'meat' and could be eaten with anything.

In their discussions they note the various stages of development of eggs: first came a bunch of tiny eggs in the hen's ovary, for which they used the same word as is used for a bunch of grapes, אשכול *eshkol*. Next came the string of eggs, for which they used the word for a chain, שלל *shellal*. This referred to the string of yolks enclosed in a membrane and strung together. In my childhood, when butchers still sold tough old hens as 'boiling fowls' for the chicken soup, as opposed to younger and juicier 'roasting fowls,' you would sometimes find a string of eggs inside. They went into the soup too, and were accounted a great delicacy. Nowadays such old hens are rarely sold to eat, and it is many years since I have seen strings of eggs.⁶⁸ The rabbis of the JT indeed note that the taste of eating an egg found in the chicken is different from the taste of eating an egg that has actually been laid.⁶⁹ Following the string of eggs, came a whole egg inside a membrane, and finally a fully formed egg complete with shell which had not been laid. Only the last was considered to belong to the neutral, rather than the meat category.

Blood of animals is forbidden by Jewish law, so a blood spot in a fertilized egg means the egg cannot be eaten. However, if the egg could not possibly have been fertilized, it is allowed. So today there are no problems (or at least no problems of this kind) with the eggs of battery chickens. Until recently, however, this was a real problem for observant Jews. The BT thus has a discussion on when we must presume that an egg could have been fertilized. Clearly, it points out, it could have been fertilized if the hen had been near a cock. But how near is near?

> Rav Gamda said: Near enough for the hen to hear him crowing in the daytime. Rav Mari said: It should be presumed near when they were sixty houses away from each other. If they are separated by a river, then they are only considered near if there is a bridge. If there is only a plank of wood, they are not considered near … But there was a case when a hen even crossed a river on a plank … ⁷⁰

Eggs in the Talmud

Egg hats

There are further discussions of eggs which include a little more information of how eggs were cooked. MEduyot discusses the case of an egg beaten up and spread over vegetables.[71] It is then considered as connecting them (under ritual law), since once it was cooked it would create a solid mass of egg and vegetables. If, however, it is 'in the form of a hat,' it does not connect them. Here the beaten egg 'in the form of a hat' refers to an egg which has been lifted during cooking (presumably by the steam) into a sort of dome, so that there is air between it and the vegetables, and it does not connect between them. This sort of omelette over vegetables is particularly interesting because of the description of the 'hat.' The Latin author Petronius' account of Trimalchio's feast mentions *ova pilleata*, behatted eggs, and Dalby has suggested this might mean 'a way of presenting soft-boiled eggs wearing a *pilleus* or cap of liberty.'[72] The Mishnah, of course, is really talking about behatted vegetables, but it is tempting to think there may be some link here.

The compilers of the Talmudic literature were not ascetics, like some of their Christian contemporaries. They regarded food as something to be enjoyed, and hence something desirable. Thus it will be appropriate to end this discussion of eggs in the Talmud with the following Midrash. Some rabbis are talking of the time before the destruction of the Temple, which they conceptualise as a sort of Golden Age. They express their nostalgia for this time in terms of longings for the wonderful food that must have been available then, including the incredible sophistication of having hundreds of ways of cooking a simple egg:

> Rabbi Elazar b R Yossi said in the name of R Hinena b R Abbahu: Once upon a time a certain woman took her son to a chef[73] in the city of Caesarea to teach him a trade. He said to her: If he stays with me for five years I will teach him a hundred ways to cook an egg. At the end of five years she came to take him back, and he said to her: If he stays with me for another five years I will teach him another hundred ways of cooking an egg. Rabbi Judah the Prince heard this and said: We have not seen such good things in this world.[74]

Notes

1. For a brief explanation of the Talmudic literature, see my paper 'Nuts for the children: the evidence of the Talmudic literature,' in R. Hosking (ed.) *Nurture: Proceedings of the Oxford Symposium on Food and Cookery 2003*, (Bristol, 2004).
2. As ever, I am indebted to my friend and colleague Dr Yuval Shahar for his help with this paper. I am also grateful to the symposiasts for their useful comments on techniques, especially William Rubel.
3. M. Dor החי בימי המקרא, המשנה והתלמוד *HaHai biymei haMiqra, haMishnah vehaTalmud* (Tel Aviv, 1997,) 131–133: indications of a bird which lays eggs every day: c15th BCE; drawing of a

tarnegol: 1350 BCE.
4. The Karaites claimed that the word דוכיפת dukhifat (AV hoopoe) meant a hen, so that they were therefore unclean birds, but this was rejected by mainstream Judaism.
5. S. Krauss *Talmudische Archäologie* (Leipzig, 1910) vol i, 124.
6. Mishnah Ma'aserot iii 7.
7. MNedarim v 1.
8. MBava Batra iii 5.
9. MShabbat v 4; xviii 2.
10. MBava Qama ii 1.
11. MBava Qama x 9.
12. MBava Metziah v 4. This is only part of a complex legal discussion.
13. MPesahim iv 7.
14. MShabbat ii 4; Tosefta Shabbat ii 5.
15. Local measures: BTEruvin 83a tells us that a *modius* in Jerusalem was equal to 173 eggs, while in Sepphoris in Galilee it was 207 eggs.
16. Pliny *NH* 22.137.
17. MShabbat viii 5 ; ix 5 etc.
18. MKelim v 2; vi 3.
19. MShabbat ix,5 . This may well be referring to 'the lightest of eggs beaten up and put in an an אלפס ilpas' of MShabbat viii, 5.
20. BTShabbat 80b.
21. TSotah i, 2.
22. BTSotah 4a.
23. A Dalby *Food in the Ancient World from A to Z* (London, 2003) sv egg. The erotic associations of eggs in the Talmudic literature are various, and deserve a special study.
24. JTShabbat 14c; *Geoponica* 20, 46.
25. Contra : S. Krauss *Qadmoniot haTalmud* (Odessa, 1914) vol I, 275. (This is the Hebrew translation with expansions of Krauss op. cit. n. 4 above.)
26. BTEruvin 41a reports this of this Palestinian rabbi.
27. TBeitzah iv 10.
28. JTShabbat 11b.
29. *Dulcia domestica* : vii, 13,1.
30. *Tyropatina*: vii, 13, 7: *ova spongia et lacta* : vii, 13,8.
31. MTerumot x 12.
32. MNedarim vi 6; JTNedarim 39c.
33. Claudia Roden *The Book of Jewish Food* (London, 1997) 213.
34. Petronius *Satyricon* 33.
35. TUqtsin ii 16.
36. See the discussion of this by H.W. Guggenheimer in his commentary on the JTNedarim.
37. I removed the egg rather quickly – if left until the water cooled this might have cooked it sufficiently.
38. MNedarim vi, 1.
39. MShabbat i, 10.
40. JTShabbat 4b.
41. Rashi on BTEruvin 101a.
42. MShabbat iii 3.
43. JTNedarim 39cs.
44. See the paper in this volume by William Rubel for details of rere or rare eggs, minimally cooked by rolling them on coals in eighteenth-century France.
45. Genesis 25.29–34.

46. Pesiqta Zuta (Leqah Tov) Genesis 25.29.
47. See my paper: 'Children's foods in the Talmudic literature' in W. Mayer, S. Trzcionka (eds) *Feast, Fast or Famine: Food and Drink in Byzantium* (Brisbane, 2005) 150.
48. JTNedarim 39c.
49. Greek *trometa* became Palestinian Aramaic טרמיטא *termita*, Babylonian Aramaic טרומיטא *tormita*.
50. Galen vi 769, 706, (ed CG Kühn, Leipzig, 1823; repr. Hildesheim, 1965); A Dalby *Food in the ancient world from A to Z* (London, 2003) sv egg.
51. I am thinking here of the number of times my own attempts at soft-boiled eggs have turned out hard-boiled!.
52. Celsus *de medicina* 4.6.6. .
53. Galen loc.cit. (above n. 40).
54. See my 'Mouldy bread and rotten fish: delicacies in the ancient world,' *Food and History* 3 (2005) 61–72: Palestinian sources demonstrate use of Graeco-Roman garum-type fish sauces called מורייס *muries*, while the BT seems to misunderstand the meaning of the word *muries*.
55. BTNedarim 50b.
56. Legend has it that Saladin chivalrously sent him to treat the injured Richard the Lionheart.
57. Maimonides *Com on Mishnah Nedarim* ad loc. Charles Perry informs me this does indeed mean a soft egg.
58. William Rubel points out that this was because the egg was roasted on too high a heat.
59. BTShabbat 38a.
60. JTShabbat 5d; פנקריסין '*pankrisin*' are translated as apricots (all gold) by Jastrow, which seems unlikely from other contexts. Perhaps they are related to *panchrestarius*, a confectioner or panchreston, a remedy: cf Midrash Pesiqta deRav Kahana 12.
61. Galen loc.cit. (above n. 40).
62. JTBeitzah 61b.
63. Neusner's translation of the JT gives פירפר *pirper* as 'beat up,' not 'crumble,' but I have looked up all other uses in Talmudic literature, and פרפר *p-r-p-r* never refers to beating eggs.
64. Roden *Book of Jewish Food* (above n. 33) 100.
65. BTBeitzah 17b.
66. Roden, op. cit. 95. These suggestions are meant to be taken with a pinch of salt!
67. On Jews called 'egg-eaters' both by native Amerindians and in Baghdad: E Nissan 'On the treatment of some toponyms or ethnics in a sharh to the הגדה haggadah' מחקרי חג *Mehqere Hag* 12 (2001) 62.
68. These are apparently still available in China, however. Fuchsia Dunlop showed a photograph of them at the Symposium; see her paper in this volume.
69. JTBeitzah 60a.
70. BTBeitzah 7a.
71. MEduyot ii 4.
72. A Dalby *Food in the Ancient World from A to Z* (London, 2003) sv Egg.
73. The MSS have פ[ר]קרוס/פרקוניס *pa[r]qaros/parqonis* or פרכיטא *parkhita* here – possibly forms of *placentarius* or *panchrestarius*, a confectioner or pastry cook. The 10th-century Arukh seems to have had a different MS version: מגירוס *mag[e]iros*, a chef. See S Krauss *Griechische und Lateinische Lehnwörter im Talmud, Midrasch und Targum* (Berlin 1898) sv פרכיטא *parkhita*.
74. Midrash Lamentations Rabbah iii 6, 17. On this source see also my paper 'Magiros, nahtom and women at home: cooks in the Talmud,' *Journal of Jewish Studies* 56 (2005) 285–297.

The Egg and Ice

Caroline & Robin Weir

The egg has a ubiquitous place in the history of ice-creams and soda fountains.

In 1587, before ice-cream was known in Europe,[1] Francesco de Medici died. His death, it is rumoured, was due to an addiction to a partially frozen 'egg-nog'; an egg, alcohol and ice drink developed during his scientific experiments with ice. Unfortunately little is known of this incident.[A] Much beyond this, history does not relate.

The early versions of European ices were either sorbets or *sorbetti* (water ices without any dairy products added) or 'Iced Cream' quite literally, frozen cream, with added sugar and flavouring. There are very few references to adding eggs to ices in this period.

The reason for adding eggs to ices is partly as an emulsifier, partly as a thickener and in addition, to give it a richer flavour. It also was found to reduce the amount of cream needed and in so doing reduced the cost.

The egg yolk is approximately one third of the total weight of an egg and it contains about 33 per cent fat. The protein is in the yolk (about 3g/0.11 oz), and when heated with other liquids, combines with 18g to 20g of liquid, as in the case of milk, to make a custard. Temperature is critical as if over-heated or boiled, it either curdles or goes into lumps.

In a small recipe book, *c.* 1695,[B] almost all the recipes are for *sorbetti*, but there is a single recipe that includes eggs which were added to increase the richness.

By the early eighteenth century, frozen desserts were established amongst the European monarchies and aristocracy and then later in the century, with the improved availability of ice, began to be available to the wealthy upper classes.

How to serve ice-cream has always presented a problem. Initially it was served directly into small silver, porcelain or glass cups, or it was moulded in pewter or copper moulds into small fruits and other shapes, which gave the ice a presentational impact for the guests.

Ice-cream recipes

The earliest reference to adding eggs to ice-cream, as opposed to 'iced cream' (literally frozen cream) is in a small anonymous Neapolitan leaflet.[B] Probably produced to be sold or given away in conjunction with a sorbetière and/or ice-cream making equipment. Among the 23 recipes for ices in the Neapolitan leaflet is one for *Imperial Ammantecato* (Imperial Cream Ice) made with 2 carafes of milk and 10 egg yolks, with added candied pumpkin and cinnamon water (cinnamon essence). The egg yolks are however warmed but not cooked to a custard consistency and were there purely as a thickener.

It made 10 *giarre* of ice-cream. The *giarre* was the term to describe the small silver, porcelain or glass ice-cream cups used for serving ices in those days.

Imperial Ammantecato is an amazingly sophisticated ice-cream and delicious when made with real homemade candied pumpkin.

Menon

Menon's (1740–1795)[C] was the first cookery book to contain a large selection of recipes (over 45) for ices. His ices were, in many ways, more sophisticated than those of his contemporaries Gilliers (author of *Le Cannemaliste français*) or Emy (author of *L'Art de bien faire les glaces*). These are two of the most interesting recipes for ices containing eggs from Menon.

Glace du Beurre

Menon has a quite remarkable ice-cream referred to as a 'glace du beurre' which has 20 egg yolks to 32 fl oz (950g) of cream.[2] This gives approximately 32 per cent fat and 15 per cent sugar in an ice-cream with 54 per cent solids.[3] This glace was flavoured with orange-flower water and was frozen in *fromage* moulds (cheese-shaped moulds).

The egg yolks give about 25 per cent of the fat in this ice. It tastes like a cross between a super-rich custard and butter. He suggests that you eat it immediately it is made, with a spoon, 'de la meme façon que le beurre frais'.

Oeufs en glace

This ice is unlike anything currently available today.

> Take six eggs and hard boil them; you need to take the yolks and keep them whole as round balls; take six other fresh eggs which you break in two with great care so that they can be put together again whole, they should be marked. Put the whites of these eggs into a quarter litre of cream and beat together and put in a silver dish and heat on the fire as you would do for 'œufs au miroir' glazed eggs without letting them take colour on top. When they are done strain through a sieve like a 'marmalade' (fruit purée) ; let them cool and then add a little powdered sugar and put to freeze like other ices; when they have set, and you have worked them well, take the egg shells you put on one side and put a little in one half and the yolk in the middle, and contrive to fill them as if they were whole, fitting the shells one against the other. Wrap each egg in paper and put in a tin container (ice cave), with ice, as explained for iced peaches, and leave them until you need to serve them. These eggs are a kitchen dish, but can be served as dessert.

The Egg and Ice

The result of freezing hard-boiled egg yolks is a flavour like frozen egg-flavoured butter. The yolk can be eaten almost immediately from the freezer.

Emy
Emy[D] has approximately 25 recipes where eggs are included in the ice-cream among the 88 recipes in his book. This book was the standard text book for ices in France and a lot of Europe for at least 125 years, is possibly the reason why custard-based ices are often referred to as French ice-creams. Bear in mind that the ingredients for a custard were much cheaper and more readily available than cream and not so prone to souring.

Emy's ice-creams are basically made with a ratio of 4 egg yolks to 1 pint (32 oz) of cream and a quarter of a pound of sugar.

Mrs Marshall's custards for ice-creams
Mrs Marshall (1855–1905) produced two major books on ice-creams[E & F] which became standard manuals for the domestic ice-cream maker. They were sold extensively in England and in the English-speaking world.

Mrs Marshall, as she liked to be known, in *The Book of Ices* [E] has 5 basic recipes which she charmingly refers to as cheap, common, ordinary, ordinary improved and very rich. We are unsure about the difference between common and cheap!

Ice-cream	MILK	SUGAR	CORNFLOUR/ CORNSTARCH Or ARROWROOT	EGGS WHOLE	EGG YOLKS	GELATIN	CREAM
CHEAP	1 pt	¼ lb	½ oz	x	x	x	x
COMMON	1 pt	¼ lb	x	2	X	¼ oz	x
ORDINARY	1 pt	¼ lb	x	x	8	x	x
ORDINARY IMPROVED	½ pt	¼ lb	x	x	8	x	½ pt
VERY RICH	x	¼ lb	x	x	8	x	1 pt

Ice-cream	FAT	SUGAR	TOTAL SOLIDS
CHEAP	4 per cent	9 per cent	22 per cent
COMMON	5 per cent	14 per cent	27 per cent
ORDINARY	9 per cent	14 per cent	31 per cent
ORDINARY IMPROVED	21 per cent	14 per cent	43 per cent
VERY RICH	32 per cent	14 per cent	52 per cent

MRS. A. B. MARSHALL'S SCHOOL OF COOKERY.

SHOW ROOM for Moulds, Cooks' Knives, Cutlery, &c.

285

The Egg and Ice

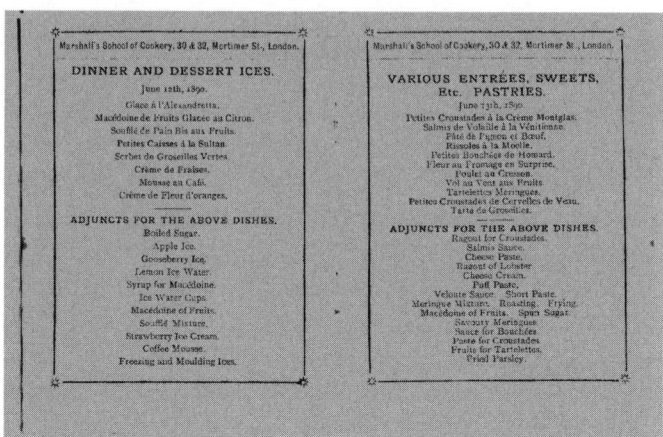

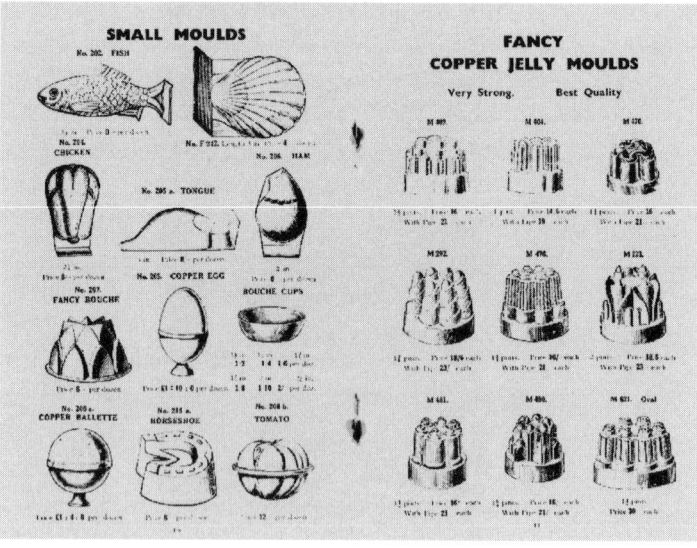

The Egg and Ice

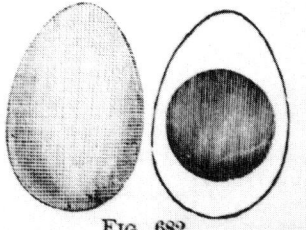

Moulded ice-cream

The mid to late nineteenth century saw the increasing availability of ice, then farmed on a commercial basis, and the increasing wealth of the upper and middle classes who wanted desserts that would rival the desserts eaten by the aristocracy. They fastened onto the impact of moulded ice-cream for desserts which pushed the production of ever more inventive mould shapes especially in the USA.

Few people realise the true size of the ice trade into New York City. In 1884 it was over 1,000,000 tons, that was equivalent to one ton for every man, woman and child who lived there.[H]

America excelled at ice-cream mould manufacturing although the very early moulds were imported mainly from England, Italy and France. American manufacturers such as Ernst 1849–1885, Eppelsheimer,1873–1971 and Krauss 1887–c. 1990, along with various other smaller companies, produced catalogues with the most exotic shapes and there was a mould for almost every conceivable shape and occasion. Even producing a four-foot-high (120cm) mould of the Statue of Liberty; a mould made of approximately 25 different pieces and contained 36 US pints (17 litres). Ten US pints (4.75 litres) were in the figure and 26 US pints (12.25 litres) in the base.

In England, Biertumpfel (1834–1917) and Harton (1836–1863) were major makers and both Biertumpfel and Benham (1817–c. 1937) were wholesalers and retailers of moulds. The moulds sold by Mrs Marshall were almost certainly made by Biertumpfel and Benham as well as by Cadot & Letang Fils in Paris.

The Egg and Ice

Egg-shaped moulds for ice-cream

In the eighteenth century Café Procope in Paris was famous for serving eggs made out of ice-cream and served in an egg cup.[G]

Ices in the shape of eggs, as well as nests and various types of birds, became popular among the newly wealthy middle class, in both England and the United States. In England the wealthy middle classes could now afford to have ice delivered and acquired ice-cream makers and ice caves. Unfortunately few collectors bother with egg-shaped moulds and they are relatively cheap to collect.[4]

The equipment and the know-how to make ices was produced and supplied by Mrs Marshall's two ice-cream books, her cookery shop and the Cookery School. The sheer number of ice-creams she demonstrated in a day (11 June 1890, below) we find amazing when you think they were made using ice and salt to freeze them.

Other notable recipes

Delmonico's in New York

Charles Ranhoffer was Delmonico's chef (1862–1896). It was without question the leading restaurant in New York for most of its existence. In his vast book, *The Epicurean*[J] is a notable recipe for Eggs à la Tremontaine in Red Wine Sauce.

This was a frozen egg, the 'yolk' is made of finely diced fruit frozen in whipped cream and the white of the egg is made of pistachio ice-cream. It was served with a thickened cold red wine, cinnamon and lemon sauce.

Mario Batali

Mario Batali, owner of Babbo in New York City, in his cookbook *Molto Italiano* has a gelato which contains 14 egg yolks. At Babbo and his restaurant Otto on 5th Avenue, he has reintroduced many interesting flavours. The gelato is 15 per cent fat[3] of which 6 per cent comes from the egg yolks and 13 per cent sugar[3]. Is this is a true gelato? A moot point.

Heston Blumenthal Ice-cream Egg

Heston Blumenthal, owner of The Fat Duck Restaurant at Bray, has featured in his tasting menu for the last few years a Mrs Marshall miniature Margaret cornet, beautifully made with piped decoration around the top and along the seam of the cone, in true Victorian style. When he was looking for a new idea for the new tasting menu we suggested he made the Procope Ice-cream Egg in an egg cup.

Heston being Heston thought our idea rather tame and although not yet available, he has now developed an ice-cream egg where the frozen egg has a liquid 'yolk' contained in an ice-cream 'white'. It has been covered in very thin chocolate to represent the egg shell. The shell can be easily broken with a spoon to eat the ice-cream egg and the liquid yolk.

His skill in developing a liquid yolk is the result of much research, to make a yolk that has sufficient alcohol and sugar to be solid when frozen in liquid nitrogen, (at more than -200°C). But after freezing the yolk is immediately encased in the ice-cream 'white' and put into a commercial freezer. The white freezes but the yolk becomes liquid at the commercial freezer temperature (approx -25°C).

The soda fountain and eggs

In American soda fountain lingo, 'Break it and shake it' was the ordering code for adding an egg to a milk shake.[R] 'Twist it, choke it and make it cackle' was the ordering code for a chocolate malted milk with an egg.[R]

There were a number of soda fountain books and weekly magazines that kept each soda fountain up to date with new ideas and recipes, they were mainly produced from correspondence with the magazine or the manufacturer of soda fountain equipment who produced the manual.

MacMahon[K] has an interesting description in his manual for making Egg Drinks.

> How to prepare Egg Drinks
> When serving egg drinks place the glass upon the counter, steadying the bottom of the glass with one hand and break a fresh egg by striking the rim of the glass, allowing the contents to fall into the glass on the first strike without breaking the yolk, raise the glass and add phosphate by placing the neck of the squirt bottle between the first two fingers, supporting the squirt top with the thumb; then draw syrup, put in a small quantity of cracked ice and shake well. Remove the glass from the shaker, allowing liquid to remain in shaker, fill with soda, use both streams at the same time, then throw from shaker to glass a few times. Serve with nutmeg on top. Ladies sometimes prefer straws served with the drink.

The drinks were flavoured with a range of syrups made from dried cumin or ginger as well as fresh orange or lemon peel all dissolved or 'macerated' in a weak solution of alcohol.

Egg lemonades and egg chocolates were made with an egg, a dash of cream and soda water and ice.

The Dispenser's Formulary

The most complete book for a soda fountain and the one that was recognised as the industry bible is *The Dispenser's Formulary*.[M] It included over 2,500 recipes and among these it had almost 40 cold egg drinks and almost 80 hot drinks of which 50 are hot egg drinks.

The Egg and Ice

Egg Shake
When an egg is added to a milk shake before shaking, it becomes an egg shake. Acid flavours should never be used in any of these as they curdle the milk.

Nogg
A Nogg is a type of milk shake served

> either hot or cold, [it] is a combination of egg, milk or cream, sugar, an aromatic flavour (not an acid), over which grated cinnamon or nutmeg is sprinkled before serving. It differs from a milk shake or milk and egg shake in that the egg, milk and sugar are beaten together into an almost emulsion, before the flavour, etc., is added, and before the final shaking.

Puff
A combination beverage containing one or more kinds of syrup, whipped cream or ice-cream, white of egg, shaken well together. Into this carbonated water, fine stream, is injected in quick dashes, and a maraschino cherry is added before serving. Serve with a spoon.
  Nothing will help you to build up a reputation as quickly as the proper dispensing of a select line of the popular egg drinks. ... Egg drinks are ten-cent drinks, and the syrups from which they are made should be of the fifteen-cent quality.

Egg Phosphates
These were drinks made with an egg, syrup of almost any flavour, a few dashes of 'Acid Phosphate' and carbonated water. Acid phosphate was a dilute solution made by adding sulphuric acid to bone ash.

Hot egg drinks
These were made to encourage business in the winter months when soda fountains found business difficult.
  The hot egg drink is delicious, if it be nicely prepared, but it certainly requires skill.

An egg may be served as a phosphate, as an egg chocolate or a coffee. Prepare same as for cold, after shaking, strain and draw off 1 glass of hot water to be sure that the water is very hot, then add the water slowly, stirring constantly so that the egg will not separate and lump up.

There were many flavours but malted milk, bouillon or wintergreen are a few of the more interesting.

The Egg and Ice

This is our favourite recipe:

Hot Egg Punch
Serve in a long thick soda glass. Take 2 ounces of cream, 2 ounces of hot milk, 1 ounce of plain syrup – or vanilla and one whole egg. Shake the egg with the above ingredients and then add a teaspoonful of Jamaica rum (or enough for the flavour required). Pour from shaker to glass four or five times. After putting glass in holder add hot water, stir; top with whipped cream and serve.

This makes a fine drink when a person is feeble or has been exposed to cold (Geo. A Zahn).

Mr George A. Zahn, it would appear, was the author of this recipe for the feeble!

Standard Manual and *The Soda Water Guide*
The Standard Manual [N] has almost 100 different recipes for egg drinks using a vast range of flavours including raspberry vinegar, cider, orgeat, tea, violet, and sarsaparilla.

The Spatula Soda Water Guide [S] includes well over 100 egg-based soda fountain drinks.

The egg is one of the most popular of all commodities dispensed at the fountain, and to-day hundreds of thousands of them are used annually in the preparation of carbonated beverages.

The Egg Cream
The ultimate marketing triumph around the start of the twentieth century in New York was the New York Egg Cream, which contained neither egg nor cream.

Andrew Coe in his article [Q] relates the history of this item which can still be found in a few cafés and luncheonettes in Manhattan and Brooklyn.

Developed as a cheap copy of an ice-cream soda or a milk shake, it could be produced at a fraction of the price. In the poverty-stricken lower East Side ghettos it was very popular and cheap.

They are well worth seeking out. A well-made New York Egg Cream is really delicious on a hot day. It also has far fewer calories than ice-cream sodas and milk shakes.

The Egg and Ice

Bibliography

A   David, Elizabeth, *Harvest of the Cold Months,* Michael Joseph, London 1994.
B   Anon, *Brieve e Nuovo Modo da Farfi Ogni Forte di Sorbette con Facilta,* Naples, c. 1695.
C   Menon, *La Science du Maître d'hotel Confiseur,* 1750.
D   Emy, *L'Art de Bien faire de Glaces d'office,* Paris 1768.
E   Marshall, Agnes B., *The Book of Ices,* Marshall School of Cookery, London 1885. (Weir, Robin et al. *Mrs Marshall, The Greatest Victorian Ice-cream Maker,* Smith Settle, 1998.)
F   Marshall, Agnes B., *Fancy Ices,* Marshall School of Cookery, London 1894.
G   Weir, Caroline and Robin, *Ice-cream, Gelato and Sorbetti,* Grub Street, London 2007.
H   *Harpers Weekly* (USA) August 30 1884, p. 565, 'Ice Farming'. Brewers were the largest users of ice, then meat packers and restaurants and cafés close behind.
J   Ranhoffer, Charles, *The Epicurian,* Charles Ranhoffer, Publisher, New York 1894.
K   MacMahon, Albert, *American Soda Water Dispenser's Guide,* Goodall & Loveless, Chicago, c. 1892.
L   Liddell, Caroline & Weir, Robin, *Ices, The Definitive Guide,* Grub Street, London 1995. (*Frozen Desserts,* St Martins Press, New York 1997.)
M   Staff of The Soda Fountain, *The Dispenser's Formulary or Soda Water Guide,* D. O. Haynes & Co., New York 1915. *The Soda Fountain* was a weekly magazine published in New York.
P   Hiss, Emil, *Standard Manual of Soda and other Beverages,* Englehardt, Chicago 1900.
Q   Coe, Andrew, 'The Egg Cream Racket', *Gastronomica,* Summer 2004, pp. 18–25.
R   Weir, Robin, *Disappearing Foods. Proceedings of Oxford Food Symposium 1994,* Prospect Books, Totnes, Devon 1995, pp. 215–220.
S   White, E.F., *Soda Water Guide and Book of Formulas for Soda Water Dispensers,* Spatula Publishing Co., Boston. Mass. 1925.

Acknowledgements

We would particularly like to acknowledge the help and advice from Ivan Day and would like to thank John Gauder for the loan of the huge pewter egg ice-cream mould. We would also like to thank Gillian Riley and Josephine Bacon for translating French and Italian, both old recipes and text.

Notes

1. The endothermic effect of salts on ice was unknown in Europe before the mid-seventeenth century.
2. In order to arrive at these figures we have calculated on the basis of cream being 35 per cent fat and used small eggs. This could vary considerably as the fat content in milk was usually higher in the spring than in the autumn.
3. Current ice-cream production for 'Super Premium' ice-creams contains 8–11 per cent fat and 16–18 per cent sugar.
4. I showed a collection of about 10 egg ice-cream moulds at the Symposium, ranging from sparrow to small dinosaur egg sizes.

Salvador Dali's Giant Egg

Carolin C. Young

The concept
According to American art dealer Julien Levy, in 1938 Salvador Dali intended to construct a ten-foot boiled egg:

This was to be made, the gigantic boiled egg, from the separated whites and yolks of more than a thousand real eggs, poured into aluminum molds for boiling. By invention of Dali's, the mold for the yolk could be collapsed and extracted through a tube in the egg-shaped white section. Standing in the gallery, it was to be tasted by visitors using spoons three feet long, so that they could dig in as far as the yolk and ascertain that the egg was REAL.[1]

Dali never realized the concept. The purpose of this paper is to figure out how to build it.

History and background
Briefly summarized, eggs were such an important symbol in Salvador Dali's œuvre that the Dali museum in Figueras, Spain, in which he is entombed, has giant eggs looming boldly skywards as its turrets. The egg, traditionally considered a symbol of fertility and femininity, became a personal metaphor for the artist's eroticism. He claimed this originated in his boyhood, when he snuck into the family kitchen and was transfixed by '[t]he beaten white of an egg, caught by a ray of sunlight cutting through a swirl of smoke and flies, [which] glistened exactly like froth foaming at the mouth of panting horses rolling in the dust and being bloodily whipped to bring them to their feet.'[2]

During the 1930s, however, Dali hit the apogee of his 'food phase' and, one could also argue, was at the height of his artistic powers. He had developed his mature style and lexicon of symbols – fried eggs without the plate, baguettes, soft watches 'like Camembert', etc. – but had not yet become the self-promoting caricature of himself that later caused the acerbic André Breton to nickname him 'Avida Dollars' (an anagram of Salvador Dali).[3]

The giant boiled egg, composed entirely of real eggs, exemplifies Dali at his best: playfully toying with notions of what is real versus surreal and blurring the borders between art and life. The concept is utterly simple and yet incredibly complex. An everyday foodstuff, merely by being blown up in scale, becomes transfixing, Yet it is composed of what it looks like it should be. Metaphorically layered, the sculpture evokes the artist's personal mythology as well as the egg's more universal symbolism; and is the central prop for an ephemeral performance during which viewers literally consume the piece, a teasing reference to the consumption of art and the 'cannibalistic' impulse.

The piece addresses the artist's concern with the 'new hunger' of modern consciousness, in which, 'we find suddenly that it does not seem enough to devour things with our eyes, and our anxiety to join actively and effectively in their existence makes us want to eat them.'[4] The egg encapsulates the contrast of hard and soft, the envelope and the hidden flesh; it is both the 'phantom' and the 'specter' that Dali discussed in his 1934 essay, 'New Colors of Spectral Sex-Appeal.'[5]

Dali's three-foot-long spoons hint at the complex games within games hidden beneath the surface of his seemingly simple concept. The elongated handle length corresponds to the ten-foot egg's monumental girth, however, no normal-sized human being could actually reach it into his or her own mouth.

The artist was not, however, the first to attempt an oversized egg. Harlan Walker pointed out that eighteenth-century English cookbook author Hannah Glasse published recipes for 'an Egg as big as Twenty' and 'A Grand Dish of Eggs.'[6] The latter calls for the yolks to be boiled in a bladder and the whites in a pair of egg-shaped half-molds. Richard Fitch of Hampton Court Palace Kitchens informed me that far earlier Thomas Dawson's *Good Housewife's Jewel* of 1596/1597 contains a recipe for 'A Made Dish of the Proportion of an Egg for Flesh Days'. This replaces the yolk with a meat stuffing, which is inserted into a large bladder, surrounded with egg whites, and then boiled in broth.

These earlier recipes, although far more modest than Dali's colossal vision, reveal that it, with Surrealist bravura, masterfully taps into an ancient, if esoteric, human longing for a massive egg.

Rules of the game

Conceived in 1938, and with recipes that anticipate it by many centuries, Dali's giant egg is clearly an idea whose time has come. *The Guinness Book of World Records* agrees and has allocated a brand new category for the 'Largest Boiled Egg', pending successful completion of the project (claim #168684).

In April 1996 the Rotary Club of Piet Retief, KwaZulu-Natal, South Africa, set the record for the world's largest Easter Egg, which was 25′1″ tall (7.65 m) and made out of chocolate and marshmallow. An artificial egg, claiming to be the world's largest egg, towers over Winlock, WA (figs. 1 & 2) but is not listed with Guinness. Never before, however, has anyone attempted the record for the world's largest boiled egg.[7] Therefore, the Guinness Book people have invited me to establish some rules for this category in case, at a future date, someone wishes to break the record. My suggestions are as follows:

GUIDING PRINCIPLE: The egg must look like an egg, taste like an egg, and be made of eggs.

Salvador Dali's Giant Egg

1. Because food authority Harold McGee places his discussion of the 'boiled egg' under the umbrella of an 'Egg Cooked in the Shell' (advising against this rather brutal and trouble-laden method); and the American Egg Council's EGGCYCLOPEDIA actually calls the term 'boiled egg' a misnomer – the Guinness World Record Category will henceforth be called the 'Largest Egg Cooked in the Shell.'[8]

    Eliminating the necessity of finding a swimming-pool sized body of boiling water opens the range of cooking methods to include steaming, or slow-cooking under embers, which are used to prepare Arabic *hamine* eggs or Middle Eastern *hamindas*.[9] As McGee briefly summarizes and molecular gastronomist Hervé This expands upon, the proteins in eggs coagulate well below water's boiling point, 100°C (212°F). In fact, This calculates that one of the proteins in the whites (ovotransferring) cooks at 62°C (144°F) and that perfect doneness on the yolks is achieved at 68°C (154°F).

2. As Dali proposed, the egg must be REAL and should be composed of the separated whites and yolks of actual eggs. According to McGee, the yolk comprises just over one-third of the weight of a shelled egg, while the whites constitute just under two-thirds.[10]

    Dehydrated egg yolks and whites, although technically egg products, may *not* be used. Not only does such a tactic evince poor sportsmanship, it also loses an important aesthetic nuance in Dali's concept: the cracking and separating of many thousands of eggs.

    Eggs include a few features that Dali did not mention: several layers of membrane and chalazae (twisted cord-like strands of egg-white proteins), which anchor the yolk into the correct place. Because This has shown these to have negligible impact upon either the cooking or taste of an egg these will be considered optional.[11]

3. Artificial supports or ingredients may *not* be used. Although the record-setting 25-ft. chocolate egg was lined with reinforced steel supports, these (in my humble opinion) are tantamount to cheating. The 'largest egg cooked in the shell' must be made *only* from eggs or substances contained in eggs.

4. Dali did not specify what the shell should be made of (or even if it should have one), however, the 'largest egg cooked in the shell', by definition, requires one. Given Dali's desire for the Surreal egg to be REAL, the previous rule is extended to include the shell itself.

    Having originally contemplated materials from biscuit porcelain to fiberglass that might effectively imitate eggshell, I am grateful to Hervé This for explaining that calcium carbonate ($CaCO_3$), the basic chemical compound of a real eggshell, can easily be made into a solution and then sprayed into a solid form.

    An eggshell is, in fact, roughly 94 per cent calcium carbonate, augmented by small amounts of magnesium carbonate, calcium phosphate and other organic

matter such as protein, whose presence and quantity depend upon the diet and age of the hen.[12] These latter components, therefore, they are considered discretionary components.
5. There are no limits on the use of molds, cooking devices, or other equipment. The egg may be built in pieces, as Hannah Glasse instructed; by two cooking processes (mold within a mold), as Thomas Dawson proposed; or by extruding an inner mold from a hole in the egg, as Dali suggested.
6. Observers must be able to taste that the egg is real. Future attempts to break this record will not be required to have three-foot spoons. However, Dali's proposal requires them.

The shape and volume of the egg

Total Length	10 ft.	= 3.05 m.
Total Surface Area	198.78 sq. ft.	= 18.47 m^2
Total Volume	253.90 cu. ft.	= 7.19 m^3
		= 7190 L

John Bennett, of Proun Space Studio, the architectural part of the team that created the 'Towers of Light' temporary memorial for 9/11, generously produced a rendering of a ten-foot egg [fig. 3]. The shape derives its harmonious proportion from the Golden Number (F = 1.6180339...) much touted by Vitruvius, Leonardo da Vinci, and most recently made famous in Dan Brown's unavoidable *Da Vinci Code*.[13]

Calculating from a length of ten feet as the starting point, Bennett estimated that the egg's total volume will be 254 cubic-feet; and, approximating five eggs per American one-cup measure, cheerfully reported that 'only' 151,993.6 eggs will be needed.

This initial analysis led to more questions. What kind of eggs had been used for this estimate? What would the giant egg weigh before and after cooking? And, if the shell was included in the ten-foot height then wouldn't its thickness reduce the number of eggs needed to fill the interior?

And what of an egg's clearly visible air space? Including large air pockets in a gigantic egg could endanger its structural soundness. Nevertheless, how much space might be needed to allow for expansion and/or contraction during cooking?

On a more basic level, inconsistencies between English and American measuring systems made it quickly apparent that although the end result will be a ten-foot egg, the project should be calculated with the metric system. Harlan Walker pointed out that not only is the United States gallon only 86 per cent of the British gallon, but also the 'standard one-cup' US measure, which on many examples is marked 250 ml, does not equate to this measure. To avoid further confusion, the ten-foot egg will henceforth be known as the 3.05-meter egg and all measurements will be metric.

Salvador Dali's Giant Egg

Behavior of eggs

An initial set of experiments demonstrated that, depending on the method used, eggs gain up to almost 2 per cent weight after boiling. These findings prove that the giant egg will need to allow room for the contents to expand during cooking. Moreover, since Hervé This has demonstrated that eggs cooked at temperatures well below the boil retain even more water, further experiments will have to be conducted to determine the degree of expected expansion.[14] However, the current experiment also shows that cooked eggs must be used to determine the maximum weight of the ten-foot version.

Shell to Interior Volumes, Weights, and Masses
   Density of Shell (Calcium carbonate): 2.83 g/cm^3
   Approx. Density of Egg White: 1.01 g/cm^3
   Approx. Density of Egg Yolk: .95 g/cm^3
   Approx. Total Egg Density: 1.16 g/cm^3

According to the EGGCYCLOPEDIA, an eggshell normally weighs approximately 9–12 per cent of an egg's total weight. Blowing the egg up exponentially in scale, we might expect the eggshell to become a smaller percentage of the total weight. However, wanting to insure that the shell will be strong enough to contain its contents (lest the expression 'egg in your face' take on new meaning), for simplicity's sake, and as a place to begin, I estimate a shell at 10 per cent of the total egg weight.

Solid calcium carbonate has a density of 2.83 g/cm^3.[15] Since density equals mass divided by volume, by figuring out the density of egg whites and yolks, and calculating the relative proportions of the interior mass, the volumes and weights of both shell and interior can be calculated.

To estimate the density of egg whites and yolks, I weighed 100 ml samples of cooked whites and yolks, and took the averages, which are 1.01 and .95 g/cm^3 respectively. A shelled egg contains approximately ⅓ yolk and ⅔ white. Therefore, to calculate the total egg density:

$$X = .10 \text{ shell wt.} + .9 [(.33 \times \text{yolk wt}) + (.66 \times \text{white wt})] / \text{volume}$$

If, for example, I wanted to build a 100 ml egg, then:

$$X = (.10 \times 2.83g) + .9 \times [(.33 \times 95g) + (.66 \times 101g)] / 100ml = 1.16$$

Then, imagining that I want to build an egg with a total volume of 7.19 m^3 (which I do), the weight (in kilograms) of my egg is:

$$1.16 = x / 7190 \text{ L} = 8340.4 \text{ kg}$$

Total Weight: 8340.4 kg
Shell Weight: 834.04 kg
Interior Weight: 7506.36 kg

Working backwards, the shell will be 10 per cent of the total, which is 834.04 kg, and the interior will weigh 7506.36 kg.

Thickness of the Shell
The thickness of the shell can now be estimated using density, mass, and surface area to determine what the third dimension should be. However, since we will be calculating the kg / m³ instead of kg / L, the formula is:

2.83 g /cm³ = 834.04 kg / (18.47 m² x thickness) = 1.59 cm

Numbers of Eggs

154,962 English 'medium' or American 'large' eggs.

The interior weight of 7506.36 kg can also be used to calculate the approximate number of eggs necessary to fill the remaining volume. However, this depends, of course, upon the type of eggs. Not entirely joking, Harlan Walker suggested that using ostrich eggs would save a lot of time, although it might be difficult to find enough of them.

Prior to cooking, standard class A French eggs weighed an average of 55.8 g. These are roughly compare to English 'medium' eggs, which the British Egg Information Service defines as 53–63 g (replacing old sizes 3–5) and American 'large' eggs, which are 24 oz per dozen. Since these are the most widely available eggs, and certainly the cheapest, similar eggs will likely be chosen for the project.

The shelled, cooked French eggs weighed an average of 48.44 g, or .04844 kg, which means that approximately 154,962 eggs will be required to completely fill the egg.

Of course, we do not intend to completely fill the egg, however, since breakage can be expected, this number provides a useful basis for other calculations.

Basic 'Recipe'
How then does one successfully turn more than 150,000 real eggs into one ten-feet tall? How might quantity affect the cooking process? What is the proper cooking method? How could the problems of an overcooked, rubbery egg white or an undercooked egg yolk not grow exponentially with the size of the egg? I posed these questions to molecular gastronomy expert Hervé This, who, after generously discussing the project with me, kindly contributed the following recipe:

Salvador Dali's Giant Egg

Dear Carolin Young

About the Dali egg, here is my proposal :
1. make a mold from concrete from two parts
2. spray some carbonated solution (many successive layers) in order to make a shell
3. inside the shell, put a smaller mold, and, in between, pour some egg white
4. heat the entire object to solidify the egg white
5. inside the white, pour some yolk
6. Heat again, from the inside (to reach 60°C, so that the yolk is at the verge of coagulation), then heat from the outside to reach a temperature higher than 63°C, and get the coagulation of the yolk.

And finally, do not forget to add a poster on the spoons, with the German proverb: 'if you have to dine with the devil, use a long spoon'.

cheers

Vive la connaissance!

Hervé THIS
_____

Groupe INRA de Gastronomie Moléculaire[16]

Execution

Easier said than done! The logistics of successfully orchestrating the giant egg – from separating the 154,962nd egg before the others become a mammoth breeding ground for salmonella, to flipping one giant half onto the other without burying the 'egg team' under a gelatinous mound of oozing egg – require expert planning and creative thinking. Dali, who loved nothing better than a soft, putrefying gooey mass (except perhaps eggs) would have considered such accidents resoundingly beautiful, however, my own head began to spin with the possibilities for disaster. I realized that I needed serious technical and artistic assistance, from someone with the peculiar bent of mind necessary to seriously contemplate making a ten-foot boiled egg.

With magical Surrealist synchronicity, only days after I received This's recipe, my friend Charles Foster-Hall appeared, unsummoned, at my door. An English artist, Foster-Hall for several years worked for the New York contemporary artist Jeff Koons, not only famous for Lucite-encased vacuum cleaners, basketballs floating in fish tanks, and his marriage to the Italian porn-star/senator Cicciolina, but also for creating the world's largest porcelain sculpture (depicting Michael Jackson and his pet-chimpanzee) as well as a 13-meter topiary sculpture of a puppy. More recently, Foster-Hall created a mural in Sussex with a team of 500 volunteers. Clearly, the man for the job, he has come on board to develop and manage the egg's execution.

Working from Bennett's egg rendering, Foster-Hall designed a ten-foot mock egg, which we presented at the Symposium (see Addendum).

However, before we actually attempt the REAL ten-foot egg, we will first experiment with building two-foot versions, 'to work the kinks out,' as Foster-Hall said. Simultaneously, plans for the full-scale version are underway.

Possible strategies

The most challenging aspect of executing This's instructions will be reuniting the two halves of the egg. Foster-Hall realized that instead of creating two lengthwise halves (like a deviled egg), we should halve the egg horizontally, top and bottom (figure 4) so that gravity will pull the two pieces together when it is displayed upright (and, who wants a ten-foot egg that's lying pathetically on its side). The difficulty of reuniting the two halves, nevertheless, remains. Ted Selker, director of the MIT Media Lab's Counter-Intelligence/Kitchen of the Future group, suggests borrowing a merry-go-round, and getting it to spin fast enough to pull these massive pieces together using centrifugal force. I can't help but think that Dali would have enjoyed seeing his giant egg born on a carnival ride, nevertheless, after contemplating the challenge of locking two several ton quivering masses correctly into place, Foster-Hall developed an alternate scheme by which the egg could be built up as a single whole (figure 5). Still dissatisfied, we together elaborated yet a third proposal (figure 6), quite similar to Dali's original idea, from which we had started.

Although the molds and shell can be finished in advance, regardless of the method used, a successful egg will require efficient movement through the process once the first egg has been cracked, which can be made easier by having a custom workplace, sufficient numbers of volunteers and the correct equipment.

The workspace should have three distinct areas: a clean, spacious egg cracking center; a cold room, where opened whites and yolks can chill until cooking begins; and a furnace room capable of containing the mold(s) and of being heated to high temperatures.

J. Marc Meltonville and Richard Fitch developed a high-speed egg-separating technique while preparing a historic recipe that required several thousand eggs. Fitch cracked eggs into a bucket while Meltonville, wearing rubber gloves, fished the yolks out, apparently achieving a rate of 120 eggs per hour. Although inexperienced volunteers might be slower, the strategy would be efficient. Other volunteers could periodically empty the buckets and bring the contents to the chilling room, where they could be kept just above the freezing point until cooking.

The project will obviously require hundreds of volunteers to execute. Dali's giant egg is a community project as much as it is a concept, a sculpture and a performance.

As the eggs are being separated, the mold(s) will be lined with a layer of natural membrane, such as sausage casings that will keep the shell from getting too soggy and provide, when the egg is opened, the Dalinian aesthetic frisson of peeling away the membrane on a real boiled egg. Structurally, we hope this will also help counterbalance the gravitational pull of the contents.

To cook the egg, we first thought that the positive mold, holding the space for the yolk, could be constructed to conduct heat, and, when removed, that a second heating cover could replace it. So too, the mold itself could be heated. Win Burleson, of the MIT Media Lab, suggested also inserting a number of heating rods into the deepest parts of the interior, staggered so as not to undermine the egg's structural stability. Sensors could indicate when it reaches the correct temperatures. Selker refined this idea with the possibility of, perhaps using egg proteins themselves, creating a fabric of electrical conductors distributed through the interior like the veins in a leaf.

However, the most efficient scenario would be to put the molds into a furnace room, heated to the correct temperature, and to quickly pump the whites (then yolks) through tubes that would almost fully cook them to the correct temperature by the time they reach the interior. Plenty of steam should circulate through the room, to allow the egg to absorb water, and, to encourage the circulation of air, the molds should be hollow and have holes in their sides.

Exhibiting the egg

Architect John Bennett has agreed to design a low and unobtrusive egg cup, that will focus attention on the soaring egg.

The cup should fit into the mold(s), which will continue to encase the egg while it travels, so that when fork-lifted into place, it would be standing in its cup. The mold pieces could then be removed from around it.

At this point, a small layer of calcium carbonate can be sprayed around the seam, sanded smooth, and, if desired, a coat of mineral oil brushed over the entire shell to give it the 'bloom' of commercial eggs.

For the egg's opening (in all senses), a Guinness World Record authenticator will be present, together with a crowd gathered to watch (and taste). The egg can be 'cracked' with a chisel and, in order to let people really reach into the yolk, a portion of the white can be shoveled onto a tarp. Alicia Rios has volunteered to be the egg's 'Dalinian muse' by creating a suitably outlandish and memorable ceremony for its unveiling.

Three-foot long spoons will be given or sold to each viewer to keep; or, large sudsy containers will be accessible so that the spoons may be cleaned and reused. Designer Constantin Boym, famous for his collectible Missing Buildings and Buildings of Disasters series, has agreed to apply his style and ironic wit to creating them. Armed with these frustrating objects – long enough to reach into the center of the yolk, but too long to place in one's own mouth – visitors will have to feed one another if they are to taste the egg.

After this initial 'eating' of the art, an exhibition of the shell, cleaned of its contents, with video and photographic documentation of the entire process, could sustain and extend the life of the project.

What, however, does one do with several tons of rotting egg that might remain? The contents could perhaps be donated to farming cooperatives for use as a soil fertilizer. The 'egg team' intends to dispose of its biodegradable art responsibly.

Whither the giant egg?

Although the idea of constructing Dali's giant egg has generally met with enthusiasm and excitement, a few curmudgeonly souls have questioned it. One friend begged me not to do it because he found it disgusting. This, I consider an early success since that which elicits disgust was considered the pinnacle of Surrealist beauty.

Another told me that the project was offensive, given starvation and world hunger. To this, I respond that although the quantity of necessary eggs is large, it is not sufficient to solve such problems. The British Egg Information Service estimates that in Great Britain alone 28 million eggs are consumed on a daily basis.[17]

Dali's giant egg will be a joyous, happy, and staggering aesthetic marvel, as well as a technological tour-de-force that builds community spirit to boot.

Why build a giant egg? Why not build a giant egg! It is perhaps best to allow Dali to justify himself in his own words. Frustrated by not realizing his dream of the giant boiled egg (among other zany concepts, such as a taxicab raining from the inside), he turned his attention to designing the 'Dream of Venus' pavilion for the 1939 World's Fair; thwarted again when the committee for the amusement area told him: 'A woman with the tail of a fish is possible; a woman with the head of a fish [which the artist intended to erect] is not possible,' the artist wrote a 'Declaration of the Independence of the Imagination and the Rights of Man to his own Madness,' and had hundreds of copies dropped from a plane over New York City (he noted that it was a very good thing that no such committee had existed in ancient Greece).[18] Moreover, in his 1933 essay 'Concerning the Terrifying and Edible Beauty of Art Nouveau,' Dali declared, 'The new Surrealist age of 'cannibalism of objects' ... justifies the following conclusion: Beauty will be edible or it will cease to be.'[19]

Addendum: the big egg at the Oxford Symposium

During the week prior to the symposium, Foster-Hall and I, with Hayley Matthews, John Matthews and the indefatigable Justin Roebuck, built a life-sized model of the giant egg in north London at an artist's warehouse called The Chocolate Factory. The accident of having Charlie AT the Chocolate Factory seemed an auspicious incidence of Surrealist magic. And, although the schedule was tight, on Thursday, 1 September

Salvador Dali's Giant Egg

2006, we had successfully transformed wood, wire mesh, garden tie, staples, newspaper, and plaster of Paris into a very eggy, if unpainted, sculpture, standing proudly ten feet tall (figure 7).

Unfortunately, the truck, which we had rented to transport the egg, was just an insy-bit TOO SMALL. *Quel horreur!* As we steadied ourselves for the possibility of total failure, Roebuck suggested slicing our sculpture into pieces. Indeed, throughout a long night, he and Foster-Hall sawed through damp plaster, wire and wood and added supports so that the fragile pieces might survive the bumpy journey (figure 8). Finally, at 5:30 a.m., Foster-Hall and I set off for Oxford.

St. Catherine's College kindly let us reassemble our egg in their Lecture Hall. However, we could only begin after another group finished an event. At 10:30 p.m. Foster-Hall and I, with the help of Jane Levi, Doug Duda, and first-time symposiast Christine Deussen, unloaded our Humpty Dumpty egg, hoping, but not quite sure, that we could fare better than all the king's horses and all the king's men (figure 9).

At 1:30 a.m. we had only succeeded in reuniting the egg's bottom half. In a flash of Surrealist inspiration, I realized that it was silly to keep going that night. The prototype could not only be completed but would also better reflect the collaborative nature of the larger project if we asked other symposiasts to assist us after the Saturday banquet.

For the entire first day of the symposium, the giant, unpainted egg, propped in pieces in the Lecture Hall, looked as if an enormous alien had just hatched out of it.

But, after dinner, numerous symposiasts generously joined in to repair it (figure 10). Jake Tilson, Doug Duda and Andy Smith helped Foster-Hall rejoin the three slices of the top half. Another team applied a new layer of *papier mâché* over the seams of the bottom half. The College loaned us several hair dryers, which yet another group used to speed-dry the wet surface, which a third group then painted pristine white. Cherry Ripe and Christine Deussen organized wine, refreshments and music to keep everyone going while others watched and cheered us on. Alicia Rios, a vision in yolk-yellow satin, unveiled her ingenious egg costumes, which featured Dali-inspired, fried-egg hats and rehearsed her performance with Raymond Sokolov. Robin Weir took photographs. Everyone recorded their participation in the 'official egg team book,' which lists those who help the project along (all will eventually be eligible to receive the Guinness Book certificate).

At 3:30 a.m. the egg was finished – except for the seam where the two, wet halves had been joined. New symposiast Lissa Streeter heroically painted it early the next morning, before the first session (figure 11).

On Sunday afternoon, Rios, Sokolov and Foster-Hall helped me present the finished egg to the assembled symposium (figure 12). While I outlined the project and read relevant quotes from Dali's essays of the 1930s, Foster-Hall 'cracked' the egg so that Rios and Sokolov could demonstrate the three-foot-long spoons. (They also, with an improvised flapping of legs under the speakers' table, irreverently clarified the psycho-sexual allure of the intrauterine chamber that Dali had proposed at the same time as his egg.) However, the most thrilling moment was when everyone who had helped the night before joined us in front of the egg for photos and a round of applause (figure 13).

The *papier-mâché* prototype not only augmented the paper's presentation but also began to teach 'the egg team' what it will be like to build the REAL version. Obviously, one of the biggest lessons we learned is that a ten-foot egg has a diameter of seven feet, one inch. We knew this on paper but had not taken this measurement sufficiently into consideration. More importantly, we learned from those who pitched in to help finish the egg that the project's greatest magic lies not so much in the result but in the process of collaboration necessary to make it.

My thanks to those who contributed to the egg at Oxford. Those who signed the 'egg book' are: Caroline Conran, Andrea Curry, Christine Deussen, Doug Duda, Tara Elwin, Rien Fertel, Len Fisher, Johanna Hecht, Cathy Kaufman, Benjamin Keene, Jane Levi, Jeffrey Lizotte, Máirtín Mac Con Iomaire, Nancy McArthur, Alicia Rios, Cherry Ripe, Claudia Roden, Andy Smith, Raymond Sokolov, Lissa Streeter, Dan Strehl, Hervé This, Jake Tilson, Harlan Walker, Robin Weir, Barbara Ketcham Wheaton, Vikki York-Edwards.

Select Bibliography

Dali, Salvador, *The Collected Writings of Salvador Dali*, ed. and trans. by Haim Finkelstein (Cambridge: Cambridge University Press, 1998).

EGGCYCLOPEDIA (http://www.aeb.org/LearnMore/EggFacts.htm).

Glasse, Hannah, *The Art of Cookery Made Plain and Easy; Which far exceeds any Thing of the Kind yet published... To which are added... One hundred and fifty New and Useful Receipts*, new ed. (London: Printed for W. Strahan, etc., 1770).

Levy, Julien, *Memoir of An Art Gallery* (NY: G.P. Putnam's Sons, 1977).

McGee, Harold, *On Food and Cooking: The Science and Lore of the Kitchen*, rev. ed. (NY: Scribner, 2004).

Rojas, Carlos Cavimontes, 'Geometry of the Parabola According to the Golden Number: From the Harmony of Nature to that of Architecture,' http://members.tripod.com/vismath7/rojas/.

This, Hervé, *Molecular Gastronomy: Exploring the Science of Flavor*, trans. M. B. DeBevoise (NY: Columbia University Press, 2006).

Young, Carolin C., *Apples of Gold in Settings of Silver: Stories of Dinner as a Work of Art* (NY: Simon & Schuster, 2002).

With contributions by: Charles Foster-Hall, Hervé This and the 'Egg Team' (in alphabetical order): John Bennett, Constantin Boym, Winslow Burleson, Jane Levi, Ted Selker and Harlan Walker. I am also grateful for suggestions from J. Marc Meltonville and Richard Fitch.

Notes

1. Levy, p. 205.
2. Dali quoted in Young, pp. 287–8.
3. Breton quoted in Young, p. 276.

4. Dali, 'The Object Revealed in Surrealist Experiment', *This Quarter,* vol. 5, no. 1, (Sept. 1932), pp. 197–207, in Dali p. 242.
5. Dali, 'Les nouvelles couleurs du sex appeal spectral', *Minotaure* vol. 5 (Feb. 1934), pp. 20–2, in Dali pp. 201–7.
6. Glasse pp. 201–2.
7. http://www.guinnessworldrecords.com/content_pages/record.asp?recordid=49151.
8. McGee, pp. 87–8; EGGCYCLOPEDIA 'B' (http://www.aeb.org/LearnMore/Eggcyclopedia/B.htm).
9. McGee, pp. 85, 89; This, pp. 30–1.
10. McGee, p. 75–7.
11. This, p. 30.
12. EGGCYCLOPEDIA 'Shell'.
13. Rojas.
14. This, pp. 30–1.
15. 'Calcium Carbonate' in *Wikipedia:* http://en.wikipedia.org/wiki/Calcium_carbonate.
16. e-mail from Hervé This to the author, 31 May 2006.
17. http://www.britegg.co.uk/ukeggs05/ukeggs4.html.
18. Levy, p. 220.
19. Dali, p. 3, originally published as 'De la beauté terrifiante et comestible de l'architecture modern style,' in *Minotaure* (Paris) 3–4 (12 Dec., 1933).

Salvador Dali's Giant Egg

Figures 1 & 2 (above). Giant egg at Winlock, WA.
Figure 3 (below). John Bennett's rendering of a ten-foot egg.

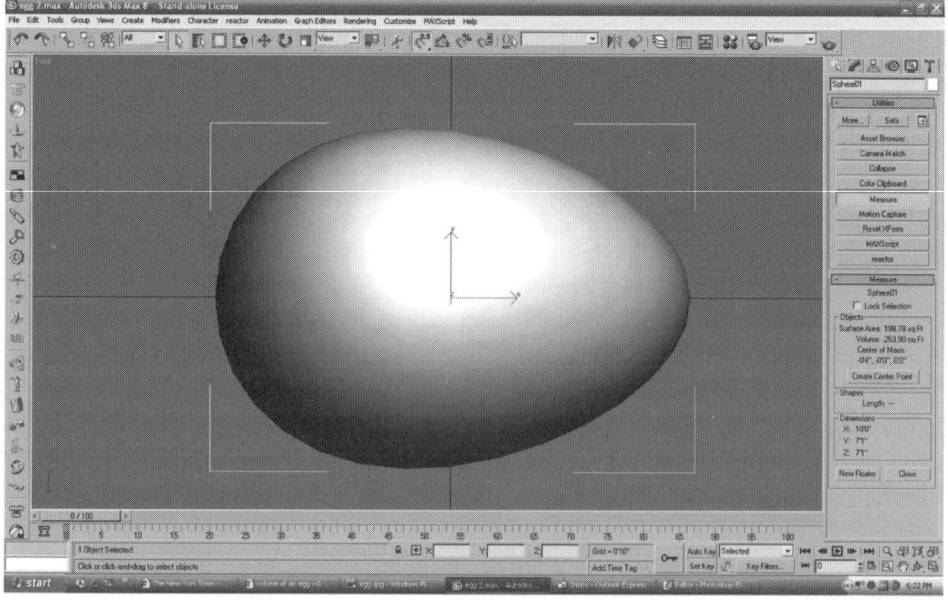

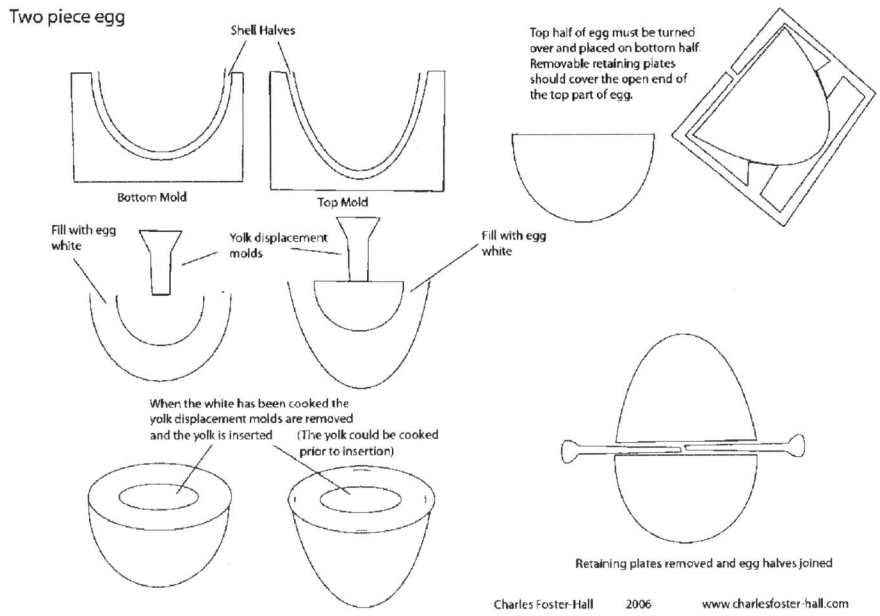

Figure 4 (above). Charles Foster-Hall's design.
Figure 5 (below). The design for a one-piece egg.

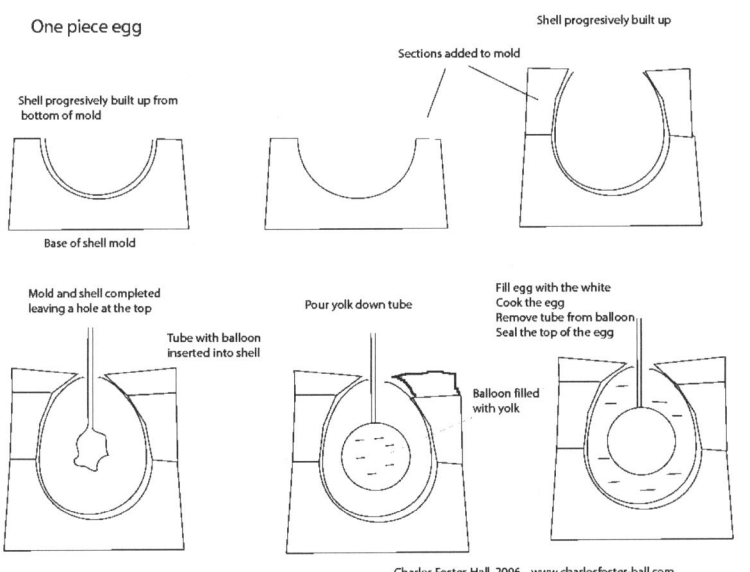

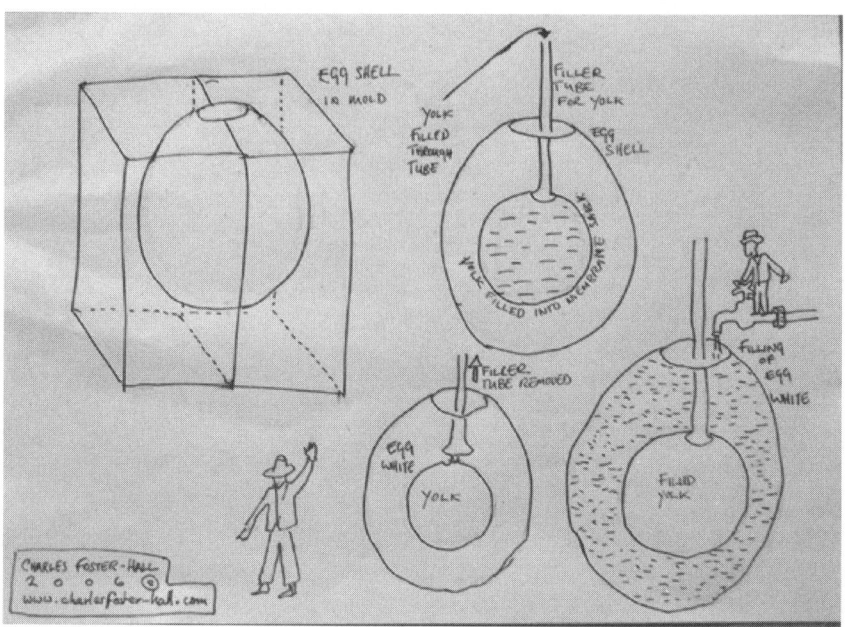

Figure 6 (above). Charles Foster-Hall's third proposal.
Figure 7 (below). The egg at The Chocolate Factory.

Salvador Dali's Giant Egg

Figure 8 (above). The egg ready for transport.
Figure 9 (below). The egg in pieces at St Catherine's.

Figure 10 (above). The egg in reconstruction.
Figure 11 (below). The egg in one piece and painted.

Salvador Dali's Giant Egg

Figure 12 (above). The egg presented.
Figure 13 (below). The egg applauded.

311

The Importance of Eggs in Rural Communities in Istria (Croatia) between the Wars

Tanja Kocković Zaborski

The egg is a symbol of the renewal and rebirth for many nations throughout the world. The belief that the world was created from an egg is common to Celts, Greeks, Egyptians, Phoenicians, Canaanites, Tibetans, the people of Siberia and others. In Christianity, the egg is a symbol of new and eternal life. Even outside of Easter practice, eggs were an important part of everyday life.

The question 'What was the value of eggs in rural households in Istria between the two World Wars?' struck me during my field-studies in the area of north-western Istria. This article is a set of 'answers' to that question which have so far been collected or, in other words, the beginning of a broader investigation on the subject.

Rural cuisine

In the majority of peasant households in Croatia in the period between the end of the nineteenth and the middle of the twentieth century, diet and cookery were very simple. This can be seen both through the food choices and the way food was prepared. None the less, this simplicity did not act as an obstacle to the acceptance of various influences and cultural trends that might filter in from neighbouring regions, or even distant continents. Thus New World crops such as corn, potatoes and beans were all incorporated into the Croatian way of life by the nineteenth century (where natural conditions favoured their growth) and they had become dietary staples.

Rural nutrition was based largely on domestic agricultural output – that produced by peasants themselves. Very few foods were imported from elsewhere. The complex geography of the Croatian littoral gave rise to a very varied agricultural production and, therefore, considerable regional differences in nutrition.

Coastal region

Cooking in the Istrian region of Croatia used to be done in the kitchen, the central room of the house, over the open hearth. As was the case everywhere, cooking was done by women and culinary knowledge was passed from mothers to daughters.

Food was mostly cooked in earthenware or metal pots hung from pot-hangers, while stewing was done in shallow pots placed on tripod stands. In this region, frying and grilling were done on a metal grating called *gradele*, which was placed above the fire.

Meals were served in the kitchen on a high kitchen table. However, food was not served on separate plates, but everyone helped themselves from one common dish. Children sat at a separate lower table, around the hearth or on the floor.

Traditional food in Istria

The main characteristics of Istrian cuisine are that the meals are mainly cooked, not salads or raw food; spices and home-grown herbs are common; plenty of fish; wine vinegar; olive oil; and wine as an important cooking ingredient. There were three main meals: morning, midday and evening. Coffee was made out of roasted and ground barley. The everyday rural menu contained *maneštra* – thick soup that was eaten as the main course. Its main ingredients are beans (*fažol*), potato and smoked ham bone. There were other common meals, such as *fritaja, fritada* – scrambled eggs combined with chicory leaves, wild asparagus or in some rare cases bacon or smoked ham. Polenta was also one of usual meals in homes of the poor. It was made of corn meal and cooked over the open hearth.

After World War I polenta was slowly replaced by pasta. Even today *fuži* are the favourite side dish, and they are prepared for festive occasions such as weddings. They are served with chicken or mutton sauce, called *šugo*. As a side dish as well as a main dish, potato is invariably popular. *Njoki* were also a customary part of festive menus. *Njoki* are dumplings made of potato dough. They were served with different kinds of sauces (*šugo*). Salads were often composed of radicchio, both chicory and dandelion, combined with beans or potato.

Meat was eaten only on special occasions – at weddings and during holidays. Pork was one of the commonest meats. Otherwise, they ate chicken (chicken soup, chicken sauce), as well as turkey, lamb and goat. Meals based on seafood and clams were characteristic of coastal cities. Today, in catering establishments, truffles are being served as a traditional Istrian food, but this is an anachronism. Hunting for truffles has been present in Istria since the late 1920s.

Easter eggs

In all parts of Croatia Easter eggs have had at least three purposes: they have been given away as presents, they have served as vehicles for decoration (in economically developed areas) or they have been played with (especially on Easter Monday). The prohibition of egg consumption during Lent goes back to the seventh and eighth centuries, which was probably why eggs began to be considered primarily Easter-food. It is still not clear why eggs were coloured and where that tradition comes from. It is probably of considerable antiquity, which is supported by finds in Germanic, Scandinavian and Slavic tombs. Also, decorated eggs of some Slavic nations such as Croatians, Ukrainians and Poles show several common forms and techniques of ornament which may indicate a common, ancient origin.

Depending on the economic situation in a given area, the number of eggs available at Eastertide for decoration varied. In north-western and central parts of Croatia the

The Importance of Eggs in Rural Communities in Istria

importance of eggs as a means of payment was greater than elsewhere, and in consequence there were fewer decorated eggs at Easter, and their adornment was simpler.

The colours most often used for colouring Easter eggs were different shades of yellow, red, brown and black. At the end of the nineteenth century chemical dyes colours slowly started taking the place of natural colours (made from bark, flowers, grass, onion) which had been used up until that time.

Different techniques of egg decoration (such as adorning with melted wax or the colouring of whole eggs) bring with them different local terminology.

The most frequently used technique in Croatia is decorating with wax, followed by the scraping of colour from eggs. With regard to the typology of ornaments, it is rather difficult to determine which ornaments are characteristic for which part of Croatia. However, we can outline an abundance of plant motives, stylised crosses, and geometric shapes. Apart from ornaments, inscriptions on eggs are also important. Inscriptions are not a rule, but when they are used they can contain different dates, names of places and authors, as well as greetings or love messages.

It is peculiar to Istria that eggs were marked according to the day when hens laid them. On St Joseph's Day, 19 March, they were marked with horizontal lines, and on St Benedict's Day, the 21st of March, with vertical lines. Or they were simply marked with names of saints. Other eggs were coloured by cooking in onion skins or coffee grounds. After blessing the food, every household member would eat one of the specially decorated eggs for Easter breakfast, and if there were not enough eggs, everyone would get half an egg. The remains of the Easter breakfast (especially egg shells and crumbs) had protective qualities, and therefore had to be thrown into the garden and onto the soil in order to accelerate plant growth, and to chase away pests (especially snakes). It was also put inside shoes in order to prevent snake bites.

The most active egg-decorators were invariably women. If they were skilful and adept at the task, they might undertake it for third parties for a small compensation. Such 'adorned' eggs would be exchanged for two 'regular' ones, or would be sold for money (a custom which is still current).

As I have already mentioned, it was also possible to play with eggs. These games could be seen as a way of establishing fellowship among players.

There are a couple of different games: the oldest known information about the so-called 'egg crushing' dates from the year 1380 in Zagreb. It was played on Easter Monday among adults and children, and it has survived the centuries. We know that in mid-twentieth century it was recorded in almost every part of Croatia. It was played in a way that children would take an egg into their hand and knock with it onto the egg of their opponent. The winner is the one whose egg remains whole, and as a prize he gets his opponent's egg.

There are two games especially characteristic of Istria: hitting the egg *(hitat u jaje)* and bowling with eggs. Hitting the egg with a coin, or *hitat u jaje* was played on Easter or Easter Monday and most often with an older person who would have some small change. A child would put an egg in a corner, and others would throw coins at it. The winner of this game is the one who hits the egg, which becomes his prize. If nobody hits the egg, a child gets the coins.

Bowling with eggs is a very similar game in which everyone denotes their eggs with special marks so they can recognise them. The players agree on which coins they will use to hit the eggs, and the winner is the person who manages to hit the designated egg, which he gets as prize. If a player misses an egg, the coins go to the egg's owner.

Eggs as presents
Eggs as presents often feature in seasonal celebrations in many villages in different regions of Croatia.

Koledari (Christmas carolers) – a group of single young men and older boys who sing occasional songs around the houses of a village during the time after Christmas or on St Stephen's Day (26 December) – are given eggs as presents from members of those households. At the end of their procession they have a feast of those items they have received as gifts, either at the village inn or at somebody's house.

Apart from Christmastide, eggs also feature as gifts during Shrovetide processions that were another common seasonal rite. In the villages of north-western Istria, on Ćićarija, during the 1950s, people would sell a proportion of the gifts they had received (eggs and sausages) to meet the cost of wine they bought for a feast of the remaining free comestibles at the end of every procession.

The chief objects of presentation and exchange during Easter are eggs and bread. That kind of present-giving is not without commitment; there is an unwritten rule of reciprocity or mutuality.

In the custom of presenting eggs during Easter we can recognise social connections and relations among members of the same or different communities. Eggs are exchanged among the closest, as well as the most distant members of family; among godparents; among different age and gender groups; also among a community and its distinguished members (priests, teachers). This latter custom some researchers see as relict of an earlier tax obligation to ecclesiastical and secular authorities (customarily paid at Easter), a tax that was most commonly paid in eggs and Easter rolls.

During the Easter holidays in almost all parts of Croatia it was common to present priests with eggs, Easter rolls and meat. In Slavonija and Podravina at the beginning of the twentieth century each act of present-giving was registered and recorded: in return parishioners would get confessional confirmations.

The exchange of Easter eggs among relatives is very common. In the region of Kastavština and central Istria a woman would bring Easter sweet bread or *pinca* and eggs into her parents' home. But that was not the case everywhere. Variations in the direction of gifts (from woman to her parents or a wife's parents to their son-in-law) are probably connected to the particularities of any given social system, the relation between sexes and the overall position of women in different regions.

The exchange of presents between those of the same or opposite gender, but proximate in age, had a special meaning. Girls and boys would show their affection for each other, or reject an unwanted partner, by using different inscriptions on eggs. Smitten couples exchanged Easter eggs or some other object as a sign of affection. In some districts, however, such as Međimurje where the public display of attraction or affection was avoided, this sort of exchange was performed in secret.

Giving away coloured eggs among people of the same sex and approximately of the same age is called *matkanje* or *sestrenje* (recorded until the World War II in north-western Croatia). The exchange of decorated Easter eggs took place on the first Sunday following Easter. Each girl taking part in the exchange had to make a contribution with food and money for an organised supper. Inability to take part in the ritual would mark a girl as being of lower economic status, condemned to exclusion from a central rite of passage during adolescence.

Every village or hamlet of that region had its local version of the custom. Friendships were made between younger people of the same or different gender, principally by the exchange of decorated eggs, but sometimes by exchanging other gifts such as sweet bread. This rite took place in different locations, depending on the age of the participants. Older people made the exchange in their homes, and the younger ones on the street, in front of a church or at crossroads.

Probably the most important thing during Easter time was giving presents to children. It is difficult to imagine today's kids satisfied with eggs as presents, even the decorated and coloured ones, or braided bread rolls with eggs on top (*jajarica/sotorić*), but these were one of the rare gifts that children received during Easter time.

Sometime in the second half of the eighteenth century in Central Europe there are records of a bunny that leaves hidden eggs for children in different secret places on Easter morning. During the nineteenth century the Easter bunny tradition was popularised, and during the twentieth century it became an inevitable mark of Easter and of giving presents during Easter (Capo-Zmegac 1997, p. 175).[1]

Eggs as means of payment

What was the historical situation like in Istria between the two World Wars? In 1813, the Austrians (after Napoleon's defeat) had authority over the entire province. They retained it until the end of World War I. In 1920, Istria was joined with Italy and the era of fascism began. Unfavourable economic circumstances as a result of the events of the war, as well as the political situation, forced a major part of the population to emigrate, mostly to the Kingdom of Yugoslavia, but also to South and North America.

Considerable poverty, famine, and the inadequate agricultural exploitation of the mountainous area of north-western Istria – Ćićarija – forced the population to rely on trade and commerce to remain integrated in the money-economy. Sales of vinegar, coal, wooden pots, flour and grain bins, milk, cheese and eggs to neighbouring

The Importance of Eggs in Rural Communities in Istria

regions in Croatia, Italy and Austria made it possible for the inhabitants to get the money they needed, in the first place to pay taxes to the state. The sale of food in larger cities – Rijeka (Fiume) and Trieste – was exclusively undertaken by women. After 4–6 hours of walking and carrying eggs, wool, curds and cheese in backpacks, women sold the merchandise themselves or already had families to whom they had promised the merchandise in advance. With the money gained they would mostly buy fabric, thread, cotton for knitting socks, buttons, knitting needles, tobacco, and carob for children. The remaining money contributed to their families' survival.

Deep and abiding poverty obliged many to turn to smuggling (an important element of the region's commercial profile from as early as the Middle Ages). In Rijeka there was a duty-free zone where products could be obtained 5–7 times more cheaply. Therefore women would walk up to 4 hours from Istria in order to buy flour, salt, sugar, coffee, oil, pasta, and paraffin for their families or for resale. Outside the months of winter, they made the journey in groups of mostly unmarried girls. In only the poorest families did older women engage in the trade. If they were caught by the Italian authorities, the women could end up in jail for 5–6 days. Their merchandise was confiscated, but they were allowed to choose themselves when they would serve their sentence.[2] Often, girls would marry Italian policemen. Such alliances were endorsed by village people because the brides would be going to wealthier areas such as Rijeka or to Italy itself. This changed, however, once the whole of Istria was annexed to Italy.

Females who among other things collected eggs in northern Istria were most often called Šavrinkas, after Šavrinija in the Slovene part of Istria where most of them came from. That is why the name Šavrinka most often designates a woman who traded in eggs even though she herself did not come from the region of Šavrinija. By collecting eggs over many years Šavrinkas made friends with families they bought eggs from. In the early morning hours of the summer months, every 8–15 days, younger women, but also married ones, would bring figs, grapes, cherries, thread, and cotton cloth to northern Istria. Women barely starting that kind of trade would carry their merchandise in baskets on their heads; the more experienced would have a donkey. Eggs were stored away wrapped in hay and put into linen saddlebags *(bisage)* which would be hung on the donkey's saddle. In that way the eggs were protected and kept from breaking, but there were of course situations when donkeys would get scared, run away or fall down. Baskets for human porterage would carry some 300–400 eggs; the saddlebags up to 1200.

The trade was regulated by a so-called two-weeks delay-payment. If the Šavrinkas had sold goods from the big towns to the village egg-suppliers on an earlier visit, they would take eggs as payment on their return a fortnight later. In rare cases Šavrinkas would pay for eggs in liras.

On their arrival in the village, the Šavrinkas would exchange the merchandise they had brought with them for eggs, milk and beans. These they would then sell in

Trieste. They would leave their donkeys in stables and, laying the saddlebags on the ground before them, they would sell the eggs to passers-by in the street. Should they not dispose of all their stock, they would offer it to local shops.

In the year 1936, 4 eggs could be exchanged for 10 'Popolari' cigarettes, the price of which was one lira. These women began their life in commerce as young as 14 years-old, and many continued the trade until well past middle age. The exchange did not decline until the 1970s. It is clear from other sources that this form of barter was not unique to Istria but found throughout Croatia.[3] In the village of Krašić near Zagreb eggs were exchanged in shops for a couple of sugar cubes or a glass of oil. In Zagorje during the 1930s eggs could be exchanged for salt, paraffin and matches. Most often eggs would be sold to women who then sold them in Karlovac and Slovenia.

Eggs as food

As I have already described, the *fritaja* or *fritada* (scrambled eggs combined with chicory leaves, wild asparagus or in some rare cases bacon or smoked ham) was a common item of consumption in the mid-twentieth century. The situation was somewhat different between the two World Wars. Precisely because eggs were in constant demand as an item of barter or payment, they were less important as an item of diet. However, there were exceptions. Because of their nutritive value, eggs were given to those who were seriously ill, to pregnant women or to women who had recently given birth.

For strength people ate batter-fried bread, as well as *žavajon* – beaten eggs with sugar, which would occasionally be enriched with three ounces of wine.

A few days after giving birth, women from the village would bring a basket (*paner/panir*) with sweet bread, honey and eggs for the midwife. In most cases, women from Ćićarija, according to fieldworkers, preferred to exchange those eggs for baby's baptismal robes.

Conclusion

In all parts of Croatia eggs served as a blank canvas for decoration; or they were used in games (especially on Easter or Easter Monday); or they were exchanged as presents between people of differing social status, between relatives, or between people of the same or different gender.

Poverty and a difficult economic situation as a result of war and conflict obliged a large part of the population (especially in north-western Istria) to turn to legal or illegal trade and barter. One of the most valued food products was eggs which during that period served as means of payment. Women from Ćićarija went to Rijeka and Trieste to sell eggs or they exchanged them with Šavrinkas who came to them bringing different foods and other products. Only later, as the economic situation improved in the mid-twentieth century, did eggs become an invariable part of everyday rural cuisine in Istria.

Bibliography

Capo Zmegac, Jasna, Hrvatski uskršnji običaji (Zagreb: Golden marketing, 1997).

Ivetac, Just, 'Goniči i Šavrinke', in *Jurina i Franina 1990*, ed. Aldo Kliman, (Pula: Otokar Kersovani, 1990), pp. 101–103.

Tomšić Marijan, 'Šavrinke', in *Jurina i Franina 1991*, ed. Aldo Kliman (Pula: Europlanning – Verona, 1991), pp. 128–132.

Notes

1. In this text I do not want to get into explaining the origin of the Easter bunny tradition.
2. Women most often chose winter time when there was no agricultural work.
3. I assume, based on the information from literature, that such trade was more characteristic of less developed parts of Croatia.

The Importance of Eggs in Rural Communities in Istria

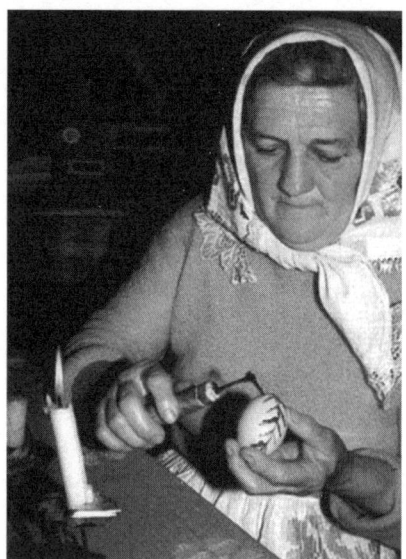

Figure 1. Decorating with wax.

Figure 2. Easter breakfast.

Figure 3. Fritaje.

The Importance of Eggs in Rural Communities in Istria

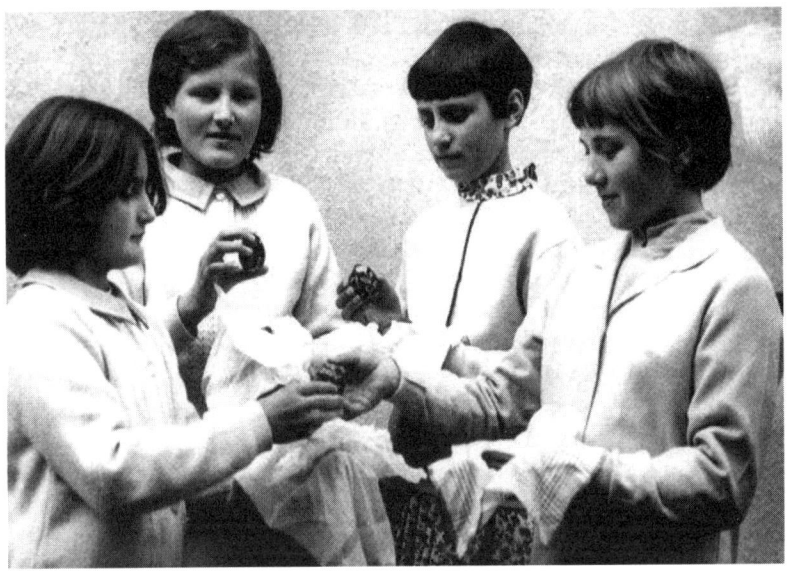

Figure 4. Matkanje.

Figure 5. Šavrinkas.

About Eggs, Two Countries and a Cake, or, How the Lack of an Ingredient Can Tell us about Social Changes

Marcia Zoladz

> Who is Silvia? What is she,
> That all our swains commend her?
> Holy, fair and wise is she;
> The heaven such grace did lend her,
> That she might admired be.
> …
> Then to Silvia let us sing,
> That Silvia is excelling;
> She excels each mortal thing
> Upon the dull earth dwelling:
> To her let us garlands bring.[1]

A matter of taste

There are moments when the loveliness of some person evokes beautiful and loving verses such as Silvia's poem, in William Shakespeare's *Two Gentlemen of Verona*. To render her homage, we are invited to praise her and adorn her with garlands. Nothing to be given to the lovely Silvia, if she had been real, could be compared to the greatest of all gifts – to have her qualities immortalized in a sonnet. But how do we establish the relation between a poem and a cake?

In Brazil, at the end of the nineteenth century, there were similarities in the way that poetry and recipes were part of everyday life. Noting down poems in personal notebooks was common. They were studied in school and recited by aunts during family reunions. Some verses were taken out of their context to serve as a moral lesson and short rhymes were frequently presented in parties, baptisms and first communions. Another common practice in those days was that of honoring friends with an acrostic – each letter of the person's name became the first word of a verse, sometimes, depending on the author's talent, the verses were rhymed. Children, duly combed and dressed up, were called upon to recite to the guests. Poems, good or bad, just like recipes for sweet and savory dishes, were part of the life of the *cariocas* (the inhabitants of Rio de Janeiro). Due to this proximity with the daily routine, many times we find them all noted down in the same old notebook.

Rio de Janeiro, then Brazil's capital, was one of the most beautiful cities in the world.

About Eggs, Two Countries and a Cake

Its scenery and its geographical location on a gorgeous bay occupied an exotic and sensual place in the world's imagination. As in all capitals south of the Equator, adequate sanitary measures were not taken and yellow fever was rampant. As the capital of an Empire with blood ties to the European aristocracy, the city's inhabitants aspired to a more cosmopolitan life – its elite wanted to live as their European counterparts. This meant copying cultural habits adopted in France, since the Brazilian royal family was related to the French one. The old notebooks tell us about family travels and about recipes given by a restaurant's 'maître' or by the cook of the ship taking them to Europe.

Some years ago I began collecting copies of old recipe notebooks. They interested me, but what really attracted me was the possibility of glimpsing into a Brazilian lifestyle that no longer exists. These notebooks were very personal and therefore they bring more than just recipes to our present day. They point out the moments when Brazilian cooking started being influenced by different cultures. At first, the list of cooking ingredients was of Portuguese origin, with some African and Native influence. The notebooks consulted are from the first moments of the Brazilian Republic, between 1890 and the second decade of the twentieth century and their lady writers are from the country's capital city, Rio de Janeiro, as well as from Minas Gerais, a more central region and great provider of gold during the eighteenth century.

By the end of the nineteenth century these notebooks and cookbooks already contained a repertoire very similar to our modern Brazilian trivial cookery. French influence is more strongly felt in the books, with recipes for soufflés and other dishes, such as Lobster Bisque, served in European hotels. This group of recipes reflects the changes slowly occurring in larger Brazilian cities, with the end of the Empire and slavery. None of these recipes are unexpected in a changing society, as a middle class emerges, substituting slave labor with new professions, the meaning of eating and cooking developed from very sensible habits into a more elaborate urbane and bourgeois understanding.

But what made a large group of Brazilian ladies, housewives, mothers, with a very down-to-earth life in a tropical country at the end of the nineteenth century, immortalize, by a gesture similar to Shakespeare's three hundred years earlier, the existence of another Silvia?

The truth is that this Silvia, as opposed to the other one, was perpetuated in a cake recipe, not any recipe of a simple cake, but a cake with one of the finest ingredients in the history of sweets – almonds. Silvia was important enough to appear in innumerable recipe notebooks from the end of the nineteenth century and in some cookbooks published in the first half of the twentieth century. What makes her stand out from amongst other cake recipes in this same period? As well as showing up in notebooks and cookbooks from very different origins, the cake's name is in English. This is why the recipe of Silvia's Cake is an opportunity – even if very slim – to try to discover the reasons which made a large number of people like a specific cake or sweet at a specific moment.

About Eggs, Two Countries and a Cake

What makes a cake liked and accepted?

What is needed to make a cake's recipe accepted by a large group of people? The taste helps, of course. Even though some cakes have no extraordinary feature, they still become well known and are baked and appreciated until today.

From a personal point of view, first we are attracted by the cake's format and this in itself may be an important fact to consider. Some prefer layer cakes; others prefer round and tall cakes, while still others may prefer very small cakes. We also examine the cake's dimensions, we observe the plate or stand where it is exposed and we praise the dishes and cutlery with which it will be served. We hope the taste lingers for a long time in our mouths and in our memories. Before eating, especially sweets and cakes, we study them, we honor them and pay reverence to their cook. Then, we help ourselves and maybe add a little jam, a sauce or ice cream. Finally, before the first bite, we feel a certain anxiety about the flavors and textures we are about to taste. Then, as in a poem, we are inebriated by the way its text – or better, its flavors – enchant us.

The preference for some specific ingredients helps put a cake in the list of favorites for a decade. But for a cake to become listed as a favorite sweet in a determined geographical, political or linguistic region, as in the case of some German, Austrian and Hungarian pastries, a great number of people are needed to prepare and serve it at many occasions. Moreover, a consensus must be created – a large group comments on the recipe, others eat the sweet or cake and spread the word about it to an even larger group, until the recipe is finally written down in notebooks.

Repetition of one or more recipes with the same ingredient may point to the period when said ingredient was introduced into the market. It can also be the result of a better production process or the prolonged harvest of a certain food, such as, for example, more oranges and tangerines for sale for a longer period of time. This increased offer generates a sales increase and, consequently, new recipes appear. The introduction of new electrical kitchen gadgets also helps spread recipes, as was the case of a chocolate-covered carrot cake recipe introduced into homes together with a new blender. To stimulate the blender's use, it was accompanied by an instruction folder and some recipes of cakes, ice creams and pies.

The fact that several recipes have similar methods of preparation may indicate an enthusiasm, even if a short-lived one, with the introduction or expansion of new forms of food preservation, such as the refrigerator, which helped selling ice-creams and stimulated the creation of many mousses.

Differently from the books, the notebooks not only present recipes, but also mirror the interests of domestic life. Many notebooks started as a present to a new bride. Her mother or an aunt, or even the bride-to-be herself, motivated by the closeness of a new life, began collecting favorite family recipes and adding on those simple recipes which made up the weekly culinary repertoire. These are not the ladies' private diaries, but they do have a personal touch and the more notebooks consulted, the more their similarities, in the way recipes are classified, generally separated by savory and sweet dishes, meats divided by type, accompaniments, cakes and sweets. Well-organized, frequently wrapped in paper or fabric – they were a demonstration of housewifely qualities. The notebook's message is clear: displaying her tidiness, she will be well regarded in that which is the woman's main role in life: her family's well-being.

The similarities between the notebooks help understand what people within specific groups had in common. Besides the taste for prepared foods, soufflés, for instance, are present in all of the notebooks and the books. Many also contain recipes for home-made medicine, such as cough syrups. Considering that tuberculosis was a constant worry, that fear was not unfounded: a child with a cold and a fragile constitution could be contaminated by a sick adult.

Another interesting aspect in the notebooks is that they rarely make notes on the preparation of the main Brazilian dishes: rice, beans, *farofa*,[2] rice pudding, sago. Probably because these recipes and their preparation were part of a household's daily routine. Those dishes duly noted down, like an instant photo, reflect the moment when a group agreed in accepting, in absorbing, a novelty. Based on a recipe, one can try and understand how a part of these people's lives were and even come to some conclusions about a specific period.

The influence of the English language

One recipe called my attention by appearing in several notebooks and in some books. The Silvia's Cake stands out by being one of the few recipes with an English name, when normally recipes in this period had a strong French bourgeois influence. Recipes of soufflés, consommés, charlottes, bavaroises, are noted down side by side with those of guava paste, stewed meat, cookies and *brevidades*, petit-fours that use cornstarch instead of wheat flour.

Where did this cake come from? The recipe's name gives the impression that its origin is either English or North-American. At the same time, I wonder how this recipe arrived in Brazil and became, if not a popular cake, at least one sufficiently known to be included in the recipe notebooks and cookbooks at the turn of the century.

English and North-American companies arrived in Brazil around the second half of the nineteenth century. Many were involved in building power plants, telephone, telegraph and railway infrastructure, others were interested in mineral exploration. They brought professionals from their own countries to occupy the higher or the more specialized positions and, in many cases, they brought their families.

Because of the location of their activities in Brazil, in the other Latin American countries, in Africa, in India, in Hong Kong, these companies had to offer enough benefits to motivate their professionals to bring their families. Many of these companies were specialized in development of infrastructure in cities with serious sanitation problems, periodic epidemics, not to mention the enormous distance from their original culture. The employees and their families needed to arrive and adapt themselves quickly. Thus, the companies created a structure and a way of life to help them, building clubs, schools and hospitals as part of the integration effort.

As a direct inheritance of the East India Company experience, these works and constructions not only installed or modernized the infrastructure of some regions, but were also showrooms for the company's capacity to develop and execute projects. With this they increased their business in other countries. In some cities they built whole blocks, starting with the urbanization to the construction of houses and buildings, in the beginning only for their employees but later, for the local elites. If the company was established in a city with a bad climate compared to their own original home, it would quickly build up a club, with English-style gardens, sports fields and games room. Soccer, for instance, was introduced in Brazil in 1895 by Charles Miller and is a direct inheritance of this influence. Charles Miller was a son of English parents and member of the São Paulo Athletic Club, founded in 1888 by the British in Brazil.

In those days, French culture exerted a strong influence over the local upper classes, much stronger than the English culture. Familiarity with the French culture and the language was present in the daily routine of the children of wealthier families. This relation was visible as the children learned French, the young ladies read romantic French literature, in the influence of the dishes in menus prepared for the more formal occasions, imported party dresses, cultural trips to Paris, as well as in the numerous French words spoken daily, such as thanking with a gentle 'merci'. France represented a step above the peevish and parochial life. One must note that, as in any tropical colony, there was an enormous distance between life in Europe, especially that of the much-admired France, and that of Brazil at the end of the nineteenth century, one of the last countries to abolish slavery and to open their kitchens to paid labor.

In the old notebooks the foreign origin of the recipes are written down – Walnut Cake 'that Lolô brought from Germany' – is an example in Mrs. Marieta Marinho de Azevedo's notebook, dated 1906. While recipes from aunts, cousins and friends are part of the Brazilian reality, only their origin is mentioned – Fried Biscuits (Dudu, in same notebook). Possibly the closeness with Brazilian culture, or a process of cultural identity with France, made unnecessary a larger amount of explanations for those recipes with French names. Sometimes we see Mille-feuilles mentioned and, except for mentioning a dried fruit cake as an English cake and another as an American cake, there is no further noticeable reference to the Anglo-Saxon culture within the consulted notebooks. On the other hand, just one recipe uses an English name – Silvia's Cake. It would even be alright if the cake included ingredients typical of an English or North-American recipe, but the most intriguing aspect is why a recipe for an almond cake, of Mediterranean origin, receives an English name.

Home-baked cakes at the turn of the century – observations about eggs
When one speaks about an ancient recipe, the frequent commentary is 'I know, 15 dozens eggs, a kilo butter…', but the notebooks show differently. The large amount

of eggs is part of the Brazilian culinary tradition inherited directly from Portuguese sweet dishes, yellow, creamy and filled with flavor. Normally a large amount of eggs in a recipe is proportionate with the rest of the ingredients and result in enormous cakes, typical in houses with many members.

It is interesting to notice that the list of recipes neither grew nor changed much, and it is still possible to recognize by the same name cakes baked to this day or which were normally prepared until recently in the country. In the notebooks we find *Bolo Sem Nome* (cake with no name), *Cuca de Banana* (upside down banana cake), *Mães Bentas* (cupcakes), *Pão de Ló* (Sponge cake). One of the notebooks consulted is a recipe list compiled by Francisca Escobar, from 1917. As she states in the first page, her intention was to assemble a collection of recipes and publish a book. The money from its sales would go to the Red Cross chapter in Poços de Caldas, in the state of Minas Gerais. Publishing a compilation of recipes with very few copies was common practice then and still is today, in both Brazil and Portugal. They are known as charity books and usually include exceptional family secrets.

In the notebooks the ingredients' quantities are quite reasonable and are made for families or homes with a large number of people, not exaggerated, but probably around eight – after all, no one bakes a cake for fewer people than those in the household. The normal calculation is that a cake should go around for all the guests and the household members. Seen from this point of view, even those recipes chosen by Gilberto Freyre for his book *Assucar* – and there his intention was to document the disappearance of cakes baked in the large manor houses and sugar plantations by the north-eastern families – is understandable. After all, when three cups of sugar, three cups of manioc dough, one cup of butter and twelve eggs, as in the *Bolo Cavalcanti*[3] (Cavalcanti's Cake), are turned into a cake, it can feed a small crowd. To the large amount of eggs we must add large quantities of sugar, but this is an acquired taste, typical of a plantation culture.

The egg yolk and its strong flavor is always present in traditional Portuguese and Brazilian recipes. Its use goes back to the Middle Ages, at the time wars were waged by the Spanish Catholic kings to reconquer the Iberian Peninsula. As the Arabs drew back, the new regional lords established their local power and used the church's liturgy to reinforce it. The Reconquista, the war to drive the Moors out of Spain and Portugal by the Christian Kings, was a fight against the infidel enemy, and still part of the crusades.

One of the many explanations – and we must watch out here – for the existence of so many types of sweets with great quantities of eggs is that at that time a great number of church members – priests, bishops, cardinals and helpers – needed a great amount of liturgical and clerical vestments, and they had to be very neat and rich-looking, to contrast with the local population's hygienic habits – the clergy must present itself clean, starched and shiny. The churchgoing local baron or poor peasant or their families would not be able to compete with the Church's show of power.

Thus, a system was created in which convent nuns furnished the vestments ready to be worn at masses and parties. The starch used to keep the garments stiff was, for a long time, prepared with egg whites, later slowly replaced by gum arabic or cornstarch. The monasteries also furnished the holy wafers, thin biscuits made of egg white, for mass. A use had to be found for the remaining egg yolks. Convents started using these in larger quantities and more frequently in sweets. At this time, monasteries and nunneries needed to find self-sustaining ventures and thereby performed a series of services for the communities around them – from sweetmeats to medical services. And so, the excess of egg yolk sweets arrived in Brazil as part of an opulent culinary culture.

The heritage left by the Arab dominion over the Iberian Peninsula (eighth to thirteenth centuries) shows up in the taste for sweets. During the centuries they dominated the region they introduced sugar cane, later to become one of the main features of Portuguese economic expansion together with the commerce of spices from the Orient. Arab cuisine during the Caliphate was very refined and, although very much denied, influenced innumerable dishes in Portuguese cookery and, through it, Brazilian cookery.

What was found in the notebooks

The recipes reflect the routine of a kitchen and tell us which ingredients were available in Brazilian cities. Through them we can assess labor relations within a house – the shorter and simpler the meals, the higher the probability of that house having few servants, for example, or the more elaborate the dishes, one imagines that the members of that family enjoyed more formal daily luncheons and dinners. Also, there certainly exists a distance from the menus prepared for lunch and dinner. A typical lunch included, for example, rice, beans, a cut of meat and a *chuchu* (chayote) stew. At dinner the same *chuchu* would be served as a soufflé. The distinction was observed with desserts where, fresh fruit, fruit preserve or rice pudding were served at lunch and, at dinner, puddings, *papos de anjo* (small cakes, made with many eggs and bathed in sugar syrup) and more elaborate pies.

The difference in formality between lunch and dinner was also reflected, inasmuch as possible, in the etiquette and ceremonial; some houses had separate lunch and dining rooms. The tableware and the menus for these meals were different, as were those who sat at the table. Children were not usually present at dinners, neither were less-considered family or household members, such as godmothers and maiden aunts; they usually cohabited the children's universe.

How a recipe was measured and a cake baked

In the so-called culinary arts two items have been lost in the memory of time – first, the ingredients' flavors have changed beyond repair. When looking back to ingredients used in kitchens during the nineteenth century and in the first half of the twentieth, we see they were planted, the animals were raised and slaughtered, packed and transported in very different conditions, lasting for much shorter periods than today. Each harvest was consumed within that season. The list of vegetables was not long. Naturally, in a tropical country, some vegetables and fruits would have longer seasons and native ingredients, even one hundred years ago, were more varied. But the fruits were smaller and much tarter then than those in today's market, and less varied within the same kind. Pears, for instance were either the soft, watery ones, rare to find, or the hard, very hard ones, only used for cooking in sugar for preserve. The small, whitish guava worms were considered normal and the apples, very small and seasonal, always had little holes. Peaches, very tart, served for compote, jam was made from green figs and the purple sweet potato was used to make a sweet pulp paste with taste similar to that of the European chestnut. The purple sweet potatoes had and still have a very short season – from June to August.

The second item is the utensils – especially the stove. For the cake batter one needed a large bowl, a wooden spoon and a strong arm, otherwise the cake would droop – the battered dough would stay partially raw after being baked. For a cake to be beautiful, and here we return to Shakespeare's description of Silvia, it must be light, gentle and please many. How could this be accomplished with eternally rancid butter, different-sized eggs, whose quality and color depended on what the rustic chicken fed on, with dark wheat flour that went bad fast and was full of little pebbles from the flour mill and with no yeast (baking powder) to guarantee its growth? To make their color lighter, their appearance and flavor more delicate, alternative flours were added to the recipes of the finer cakes, those which would then, and still now, be served to guests on special occasions. Almond flour, cornflour, cornstarch, crushed or as powder, provided some camouflage to the wheat flour's dark color and provided a more seemly result.

Until the second half of the twentieth century, Brazil produced very small quantities of wheat and, therefore, since the colonial period it was substituted by other flours, namely corn or manioc flour.

The majority of the recipes still are the same to this day, some have gone out of fashion but there's nothing to stop them from being prepared. Some notebooks used the pound (445 grams) as measure, others used the saucer. The saucer is a very peculiar measure as its size varied according to the set of dishes each family retired from table use and sent to the kitchen. The saucer can be almost flat, which is the normal equivalent of a cup, or it can be full, with a lot of flour or sugar, around 250 grams.

In the nineteenth century the cakes were baked in the oven of a wood-fueled stove. The perfect time to bake the cake was right after lunch to serve it at teatime. A cake does not require a very hot oven, so its timing is determined by the oven's heat and, after lunch, firewood is no longer fed into the stove and therefore the heat simmers down. While the lunch dishes are being washed, the cake is being baked and this takes no more than 50 minutes.

About Eggs, Two Countries and a Cake

A cake is a cake is a cake

The big surprise is how this cake became the Silvia's Cake, with its name written in English in Brazilian recipe notebooks. If we analyze the following recipe, we find a flat cake with grated almonds in the dough and an orange icing. The quantity of sugar, in relation to the other ingredients, is not different from that recommended for cakes baked in the old homes, used to our sweet tooth, to a culture of plenty and to cheap sugar available at the local sugar mills. The end result though, is a cake different to those produced in the old farm kitchens. Smaller, with a more urbane appearance, spoken of as elegant, it does not use ingredients of markedly colonial origin – fewer eggs, no manioc or manioc paste (*puba*) and no cornflour. Even more, it has a sugar and orange juice frosting that plain cakes usually do not have. The cake reflects the change which Brazilian life was undergoing. Its name probably did not have to be written in English in the notebooks, but then, it would not have the same cultural importance.

The recipe may vary a little, but always uses the same measure of flour, sugar and butter. The number of eggs may differ, either five or four units, the text lists the ingredients and assumes the reader knows how to make a cake. The language is almost encrypted, the sentences quite incomplete, and only the frosting has a longer description. It was not written for beginners.

Sylvia's Cake[4] – as set down in the cookbook *Noções de Artes Culinárias* (Notions of Culinary Arts):

> 250 grams butter, 250 grams sugar, 250 grams flour, four whole eggs, two yolks, one saucer whole almonds, and then ground. Cream the butter, add the sugar and beat well, then the eggs, the flour and, lastly, the ground almonds. Bake in baking sheet lined with parchment paper. Regular heat. Frosting: 200 grams sugar, juice from two oranges, and the 'sap' of one more (obtained by grating the peel of an orange, mixing it with its juice and then straining the result). Cover the cake with this frosting as soon as it comes out of the oven. Let it cool, cut in small diagonal pieces.

The reason why the Silvia's Cake was so widely accepted was that it was more than a simple almond sponge cake. Its name in English represented modern times to a rural country with slavery still a living memory. A 'cake' (in English) brings to mind a very different vision of the future than an afternoon corn cake or a manioc pudding – even if it has a delicate taste and is soft when you bite it. The fascination is entirely in the name and very little in the recipe of an almond cake in a culture filled with almond cake recipes. But in Brazil we made a concession: to the cream of eggs, known in Portugal as *ovos moles* (floppy eggs), we added coconut milk – *baba de moça* ('maiden's dribble'), and this is a sauce served until today with the almond cake.

Why have we stopped baking Silvia's Cake and all other almond cakes? What changes were introduced in the life of Brazilians at the time to make all so-called refined cakes, with almonds or walnuts, no longer a synonym of refinement?

Little by little a new cake took over the position of best cake in the world – the chocolate cake. In Brazil, at the beginning of the twentieth century, these recipes still appear without baking powder, brownie-style or French chocolate cakes.[5] But in Brazil the chocolate cake only becomes synonymous with a good cake after the Second World War.

Tea and refreshments served with small cakes at a social gathering, Rio de Janeiro, c. 1913. (Augusto Malta/Instituto Moreira Salles)

Notes

1. Shakespeare, William, *Two gentlemen of Verona*, p.32
2. *Farofa*, it is a fluffy manioc flour side dish, with a very similar taste to the stuffing of turkeys at Christmas time in North-America.
3. Bolo Cavalcanti, *Assucar, p. 83*. One of the most delicate traditional cakes from the north-east of Brazil. The recipe: 'Beat very well 6 yolks, 6 whole eggs, 3 cups sugar. Add 3 cups of manioc gum ('puba') sieved, mix well. Add one cup butter, a little cinnamon, grated nutmeg, some grains of kümmel.'
4. *Noções de arte culinária*, p. 183. The recipe can be easily prepared: 250 grams butter, 1⅓ cup sugar, 1 cup flour, 4 whole eggs + 2 yolks, 250 g ground almonds. Cream the butter, add the sugar and beat well, add the yolks, the flour and, lastly, the ground almonds and the beaten egg whites. Bake in a rectangular baking sheet lined with buttered parchment paper. Bake at 200° C for about 50

minutes. Cover the cake with an orange icing as soon as it comes out of the oven. Let it cool, cut in small, diagonal pieces. For the icing: mix 1 cup sugar, juice of two oranges, and the 'sap' of one more (obtained by grating the peel of an orange, mixing it with its juice and then straining the result).
5. Caramel, 'Exquis au chocolat', p. 279.

Bibliography
Recipe notebooks
Mrs. Marieta Marinho de Azevedo, 1906.
Mrs. Francisca de Escobar, 1917.
The notebook from a family from Rio de Janeiro, c.1890 – s.d.

Alencastro, Luiz Felipe, org., *História da vida privada no Brasil*, vol.2 (São Paulo: Companhia das Letras, 1997).
Artusi, Pellegrino, *The Art of Eating Well*, translated from the Italian by Kyle M. Phillips III (New York: Random House, 1996).
Burton, David, *The Raj at Table, a Culinary History of British India* (London: Faber and Faber, 1994).
Camargo-Moro, Fernanda, *Arqueologias culinárias da Índia* (Rio de Janeiro: Record, 2000).
Caramel, Blanche, *Le nouveau livre de cuisine* (Paris: Editions Gautier-Languereaux, 1927).
Cascudo, Luis da Câmara, *História da Alimentação no Brasil* (Belo Horizonte: Itatiaia, 1983).
Costa, Maria Thereza A., *Noções de arte culinária* (São Paulo: Augusto Siqueira e Comp, 1921).
Darnton, Robert, *The Great Cat Massacre* (London: Penguin Books, 1985).
Edmundo, Luiz, *O Rio de Janeiro do meu tempo* (Rio de Janeiro: Conquista, 1957).
Elias, Norbert, *The Civilizing Process* (Oxford: Blackwell Publishers, 1996).
Farmer, Fannie Merrit, *The Boston cooking-school cook book* (New York: Little Brown & Co, 1923).
Flandrin, Jeand Louis and Montanarini, Massimo (English ed. Albert Sonnenfeld), *A culinary history of food* (New York: Penguin Books, 2000).
Freyre, Gilberto, *Assucar* (Rio de Janeiro: José Olympio, 1939).
Gay, Peter, *The Education of the Senses. The Bourgeois Experience: Victoria to Freud* (W.W.Norton: New York, 1984).
Horta, Nina, *Não é sopa, crônicas e receitas de comida* (São Paulo: Companhia das Letras, 1995).
R.C.M, *O cozinheiro imperial*, facsimile of the 2nd edition of 1843 (São Paulo: Editora Nova Cultural, 1996).
Mardam-Bey, Farouk, *La cuisine de Ziryiâb* (Actes Sud, 1998).
Maria, Rosa, *A arte de comer bem* (Rio de Janeiro: Livraria São José, 1961).
Mintz, Sidney W., *Sweetness and Power, the Place of Sugar in Modern History* (London: Penguin Books Books, 1986).
Modesto, Maria de Lourdes, *Cozinha tradicional portuguesa* (Lisboa: Verbo, 1983).
Queiroz Mattoso, Kátia, *Ser escravo no Brasil* (São Paulo: Editora Brasiliense, 1982).
Rozin, Elisabeth, *Blue Corn and Chocolate* (New York: Alfred A. Knopf, 1994).
Schoonover, David E. ed., *The khwan niamut or Nawab's Domestic Cookery* (Iowa City: The University of Iowa Press, 1992).
Toussaint-Samat, Maguelonne, trans. Anthea Bell, *History of Food* (Oxford: Blackwell, 1993).
Visser, Margaret, *The Rituals of Dinner* (New York: Grove Weidenfeld, 1991).
——, *Much Depends on Dinner* (New York:Collier Books, 1986).
Waines, David, *La cuisine des califes* (Actes Sud, 1998).
Zoladz, Marcia, *Portugiesisch Kochen, Gerichte und ihre Geschichte* (St.Gallen/Köln: Edition Diá, 1987).

Eggs: the Sauces and the Sauced

Sami Zubaida

The peculiarly unctuous nature of the egg and its physical properties have made it ubiquitous in sauce preparations in different food cultures. At the same time as a food item featuring as the principal ingredient in certain dishes, it has merited its own sauces. The paper ranges over different forms and eggs and sauces used for them in various contexts, cultural and culinary, such as hard-boiled and poached eggs. It then considers eggs as sauces in their contexts: raw eggs, poached, emulsion sauces and broths.

The hard-boiled egg must be one of the most versatile culinary inventions of mankind. So simple, portable, adaptable to myriad preparations. Street food in many parts of the world features the egg. In Baghdad of the mid-twentieth century, a snack, or meal called *abyad wa-bayd* (white and egg, playing on the word for egg which derives from white) was one of the most ubiquitous and cheapest of street foods. It became symbolic of popular and cheap consumption: one literary lawyer, in his memoirs, recalls how young penniless lawyers waiting for customers in a café, undercut the standard fee for petitioning the court. One sank so low that he agreed to do it for no money, just a lunch of *abyad wa-bayd*. So what was this folkloric snack? Sliced hard-boiled eggs in a wrap of *khubz*, naan-like tannour bread, with sundry salad elements, and crucially for Baghdadis of that period: *'anba*, mango pickle (from the Indian word for mango). But not the mango pickle we are used to now: a liquid yellow vinegary preparation redolent with turmeric and chilli, and, allegedly, suspicious ingredients like gum to add body. *'Anba* was one of the vices to which children and youths were addicted, and ate in cheap sandwiches (by itself!) when their parents were not looking, some in preference to chocolate or ice cream.

Eggs and *'anba*, at a more classy level, also featured as an element of the Jewish Saturday menu. Eggs were placed on the ledge of the covered pot containing the rice-stuffed chicken for the lunch, put together on Friday before sunset and placed on a wood/charcoal fire, covered with old blankets and cushions to keep the heat after the fire dies out overnight. The eggs cooked in the steam, almost 'caramelized' into a mahogany colour for the whites and a special texture for the yolk. They are known as *bayd 'ala-tebit*, *tebit* meaning 'overnight', the name of the Saturday chicken. This, by the way, is the Baghdadi version of a more widespread eastern Jewish genre of long-cooked Saturday eggs, now known as a street food in Israel called *hamin*, or the Sephardic Judaeo-Spanish *Huevos Haminados*. These eggs were served for a late breakfast, after the return of the men from the morning service, accompanied by a tomato salad, sometimes fried aubergine slices, and, yes, *'anba*, often of a superior quality than the street version, but still typically Baghdadi (it came in jars from India, known as the 'Ship-Brand', with a picture of a ship on the label, made especially for Middle Eastern taste, and still sold in Middle Eastern groceries in London and New York). I ate a version of these eggs at a Jewish home in Marrakech one Saturday: it was also cooked over the Saturday *dafina* (the Moroccan Jewish Sabbath lunch typically of beef, but sometimes with a calf's foot, and chick-peas or haricot), served dry with garnish of ground cumin and black pepper.

During World War II Iraqis were introduced, by the British army, to a new form of egg service: egg and chips. An elderly businessman reminisced that he and a fellow entrepreneur opened a café-restaurant to cater for British soldiers in Basra. They soon had to send couriers to scour the countryside for eggs and potatoes.

Back to the hard-boiled egg: it has elicited, in different cultures, many sauces to rival the *'anba*. I recall the egg curry of the university canteens of my student days (not bad if it weren't for the soggy rice). And I have come across old English recipes for egg in mustard and vinegar sauce. The ultimate, however, is the egg mayonnaise of our time (more below on egg sauces).

Poached eggs, though mostly a 'sauce' for other foods (more below) are also themselves objects of saucing. Many of the 'modern' sauces (mostly from the eighteenth century) are themselves egg based emulsions, as is the Hollandaise which forms the sauce for Eggs Benedict, of American brunch fame. Vinegar and roux based sauces of old had previously covered poached eggs, such as Sauce Robert (mostly used for meat and poultry). That is reminiscent of the *'anba* and curry genre for hard eggs.

Let me mention just two distinguished and not very common sauces for poached eggs, one the French (Burgundian) *Oeuf Meurette*, the second the Turkish *Cilbir*. The principle of *meurette* is a red wine sauce over poached eggs, with some variation in other ingredients: slivers of ham or bacon, mushroom, always butter, sometimes thickened with flour. The aesthetic effect (the mouth feel) is the unctuous convergence of the soft egg yolk with the red wine sauce. The Turkish *Cilbir* consists of poached eggs served in a hot yoghurt and garlic sauce (sometimes scented with sage), achieving a more typically Turkish taste in the intermingling of the soft egg and the garlicky yoghurt. In my experience both these dishes are now rare, and only found in eccentric establishments maintaining or reviving 'tradition' in their respective countries.

Eggs as sauce

The raw egg, especially the yolk, sometimes features as a sauce in itself. Most familiar in European cookery is, perhaps, the Steak Tartar, of raw ground beef mixed with seasoning and finished with a raw egg yolk on top, presenting a pretty picture, to be mixed in by the diner. Another is the common *Pasta alla Carbonara*, known by some as the 'egg and bacon' spaghetti, in which the cooked pasta is tossed with cubes of cooked ham (typically pancetta), sometimes with shallots and cream (bad idea) and finished on the plate with a raw egg yolk, to be 'cooked' in the hot pasta. A similar

Eggs: the Sauces and the Sauced

principle is seen in the Persian *Chelo Kebab*, kebab served on rice, when the hot rice is garnished with pats of butter, sometimes topped by a raw egg yolk, served in the half shell, to be mixed in by the diner.

Many people are now nervous about raw eggs, and tend to omit the yolk from above preparations or to cook it first, which ruins the effect.

The poached or soft fried egg also provide a sauce effect in so many dishes, notably the egg and bacon, the poached egg on toast, the egg and chips and a long list of others. Perhaps one of the most memorable such tastes is the classic poached smoked haddock with poached egg and butter: an inspired combination, and one of the high points of the much maligned British cookery.

The egg emulsion sauces: the mayonnaise, the hollandaise and the béarnaise, and derivatives from them. They all rest on the principle of emulsifying egg yolks with oil or butter, with various flavourings. By near consensus food historians seem to date these sauces to eighteenth and nineteenth centuries, maybe traces in the seventeenth (someone is bound to find earlier references!). The sauces of the Middle Ages and early modern Europe, in parallel with the Middle East, seem to have been based on sour materials like vinegar, verjuice and lemon, often sweetened with honey (or date/grape syrups in the Middle East). Spices were also common. Thickening agents included ground almonds. Flandrin remarked somewhere that, in Europe, these sauces survived to the present time mainly in England, such as in the domestic mint sauce, or the industrial bottled sauces (HP brown, ketchup, and Worcester sauce). The tomato, of course, made its contribution to the development of sauces everywhere. The egg emulsion sauces would appear to have been part of the food 'revolution' of the eighteenth and nineteenth centuries, which included a caution in the use of spices and greater emphasis on the natural ingredient. They certainly constituted one of the bases of saucing of European haute cuisine, starting in France. The other pillar was the roux, with its derivatives of béchamel, velouté and many others. Of the egg emulsion sauces the Mayonnaise became the most widespread and industrialised. Both Mayonnaise and Hollandaise came to be sauces for cooked eggs in popular dishes of egg mayonnaise and eggs Benedict respectively.

Egg emulsion sauces of a different kind, however, may have a much longer history. One, in particular, is what the Greeks call *Avgolemono*, and the Turks *Terbiyeli*. It is made by beating raw egg yolks into hot broth (meat or poultry), adding lemon juice then pouring it over the meats or stuffed vegetables, and for the Greeks as a chicken soup. I knew it as a soup in Greek restaurants, and even cooked it. Then, on a visit to a Turkish Aegean resort, I asked the cook what he was beating in a bowl, and he said *Terbiyeli*, which means 'well behaved'. He served it as a sauce over stewed mixed offal of tripe, head and feet meat, and it was delicious. Subsequently, my friend Rena Salaman enlightened me that the same sauce was widely used in Greece over meats, meat-balls and stuffed vine leaves, which I subsequently sampled with pleasure.

This sauce would appear to be of ancient lineage. Stéphane Yerasimos, *A la table*

Eggs: the Sauces and the Sauced

du Grand Turc researched palace menus from the earliest days of Ottoman conquest of Constantinople in the fifteenth century. Included in the menus served to Mehmet II (*Fatih*, or Conqueror) were descriptions of a sauce resembling the *terbiyali*, of eggs beaten into broth. Given that there were many continuities between Byzantine and Ottoman rule in the city, it may indicate a Byzantine ancestry for the sauce, or it could have been brought in from earlier conquests or invented. In any case, it does seem that this particular egg sauce has survived in that common cultural area over the centuries. Perhaps it can be more widely revived for general enjoyment.